State-Society Relations in Yugoslavia, 1945–1992

Edited by
Melissa K. Bokovoy, Jill A. Irvine,
and Carol S. Lilly

St. Martin's Press
New York

STATE-SOCIETY RELATIONS IN YUGOSLAVIA, 1945-1992
Copyright © 1997 by Melissa K. Bokovoy, Jill A. Irvine, and Carol S. Lilly.

All rights reserved. Printed in the United States of America. No part of this book may be used or reproduced in any manner whatsoever without written permission except in the case of brief quotations embodied in critical articles or reviews. For information, address St. Martin's Press, 175 Fifth Avenue, New York, N.Y. 10010.
ISBN 0-312-12690-5

Library of Congress Cataloging-in-Publication Data

State-society relations in Yugoslavia, 1945-1992 / edited by Melissa Bokovoy, Jill Irvine, and Carol Lilly.
    p. cm.
    Includes bibliographical references and index.
    ISBN 0-312-12690-5 (alk. paper)
    1. Yugoslavia--Politics and government--1945-1992. 2. Yugoslavia--Social policy--1945-1992. I. Bokovoy, Melissa K. (Melissa Katherine), 1961- . II. Irvine, Jill A. III. Lilly, Carol, 1959-

DR1302.S75 1995
949.702--dc20   95-12886
                                                                                     CIP

Book design by Milton Heiberg Studios

Printed in the United States of America by
Haddon Craftsmen
Scranton, PA

First edition: February, 1997
10 9 8 7 6 5 4 3 2 1

Contents

Preface v

Introduction: State-Society Relations in Yugoslavia, 1945–1992 1
Jill A. Irvine

Part I. Regime Consolidation and Strategies of Legitimation
Introduction 27
Carol S. Lilly

1. The People's Prince—Tito and Tito's Yugoslavia: Legitimation, Legend, and Linchpin 35
James Gow

2. State Cohesion and the Military 61
Robin Alison Remington

3. History Education and Yugoslav (Dis-)Integration 79
Wolfgang Höpken

Part II. Social Forces, Social Movements, and the State
Introduction 107
Melissa K. Bokovoy

4. Peasants and Partisans: Politics of the Yugoslav Countryside, 1945–1953 115
Melissa K. Bokovoy

5. Propaganda to Pornography: Party, Society, and Culture in Postwar Yugoslavia 139
Carol S. Lilly

6. Socializing the State: Civil Society and Democratization from Below in Slovenia 163
Jozef Figa

7. Feminist Movements in Yugoslavia, 1978–1992 183
Jill Benderly

8. The Role of Religious Communities in the Development of Civil Society in Yugoslavia, 1945–1992 211
Paul Mojzes

Part III. Nation and State
Introduction 235
Jill A. Irvine

9. Yugoslav Macedonia, 1943–1953: Building the Party, the State, and the Nation 243
Stefan Troebst

10. The Bosnian Muslims: The Making of a Yugoslav Nation 267
Francine Friedman

11. Reconstituting Serbia, 1945–1991 291
Nicholas J. Miller

12. "Serpent in the Bosom": Slobodan Milošević and Serbian Nationalism 315
Lenard J. Cohen

Conclusion: The Yugoslav Experience in Comparative Perspective 345
Valerie Bunce

Contributors 367

Index 368

Preface

In late May 1994, 22 scholars in the fields of history, political science, sociology, and religious studies from institutions in the United States, Canada, Great Britain, Germany, and Croatia gathered at the University of New Mexico in Albuquerque to begin the scholarly assessment of the communist period in Yugoslavia at a conference entitled "Partisans to Patriots: State-Society Relations in Yugoslavia, 1945-1992." Organized by the editors of this volume, the conference was intended to provide a forum for investigating key issues in Yugoslav history and politics that deserve a reexamination both in the interests of keeping up with the latest archival research and in light of recent events in southeastern Europe. Many of the chapters in this volume are a result of this forum.

The seeds of the conference and hence of this volume were planted on a warm day in Colorado in April 1992. Recently hired at western universities and weaned from the intense atmosphere of graduate programs in the East European field, we found a conference, the Annual Meeting of the Western Social Sciences Association in Denver, where we could present our current research, but also simply catch up on the events in Yugoslavia. Playing hooky one afternoon, we wandered about the foothills of Boulder, Colorado, bemoaning the increasingly desperate situation in the country of our specialization and the equally depressing state of literature on it. It seemed, at that point in 1992, that the only new literature consisted of journalistic accounts of the war and essays with a clear political agenda. Yet so much more was possible: a discrete historical era, the one on which we had focused our academic attentions, was ending. What struck us as we continued to ponder this newly defined historical period is how starved we were for a conversation about our specialty and, given the current situation, how necessary it was.

It was this realization about the importance of lively intellectual exchange that began to push us in the direction of initiating a scholarly evaluation of the era, one relying on recent research that would seek to inform current debates about Yugoslavia's fate while avoiding the pitfalls of presentism. We believed that the only way to begin the conversation was to do it across disciplines and generational lines. We, as young scholars, had done archival research in the 1980s that provided us material for our first monographs and articles. Yet this research would not necessarily inform the whole period. A longer view was needed and this could be provided by more senior scholars informed by their own research and experiences, as well as that of others. Thus we envisioned a scholarly evaluation that would engage junior and senior scholars in various disciplines in a conversation about the nature of the Yugoslav party-state and the society over which it had ruled.

Just over two years later, our collaborative efforts resulted in the conference in Albuquerque. These efforts could not have been successful without the generous support of the Joint Committee on Eastern Europe of the American Council of Learned Societies, the International Research and Exchanges Board, the University of New Mexico's Department of History, European Studies Committee, Russian Studies Committee, College of Arts and Sciences, and Office of the President, as well as the University of Oklahoma and the University of Nebraska-Kearney. We are grateful to all these institutions as well as to Larry Durwood Ball and Jane Slaughter for their advice and assistance in the nuances of publishing and editing a volume such as this. The final preparation of this volume could not have been done without the assistance of University of Washington doctoral student Teresa Balkenende and Ruth Mannes of St. Martin's Press.

Looking back at the conference from a distance of a year, we, as well as our participants, concur that the conference was a success, not only in terms of logistics, thanks to the invisible but tireless efforts of Melissa Bokovoy and her assistant Abbe Karmen, but also and especially for its collegiality and high level of scholarly content. Of the 22 scholars in attendance, 14 presented papers while 8 served as discussants. All of those presenting at the conference had finished their papers early enough that they could be distributed and read in advance. Consequently, the presentations were kept relatively brief, leaving plenty of time for discussion. The discussions were by far the best part of the conference—lively, yet respectful, diverse, yet well-integrated. The panel moderators—Dennison Rusinow, John Lampe,

Gale Stokes, Jim Seroka, Paul Shoup, and Jill Irvine—did an excellent job of maintaining a degree of unity in the progression of the discussions through their commentary and gracious moderating. We were particularly pleased with the complete absence of animosity at this conference despite the highly charged political atmosphere surrounding Yugoslavia's successor states. The concluding remarks made by Valerie Bunce and Ellen Comisso placed the evaluation of the Yugoslav communist period into a broader comparative discussion of state socialist systems in general. All in all, the conference succeeded in providing both rigorous and vigorous intellectual discussion and gave our volume contributors food for thought as they went back and revised their papers. We are particularly grateful to our colleagues Paula Lytle, Melissa Bokovoy, Carol Lilly, Robin Remington, Dijana Pleština, Wolfgang Höpken, James Gow, Jill Benderly, Jozef Figa, Andrea Feldman, Paul Mojzes, Ivan Grdešić, Francine Friedman, and Lenard Cohen, who provided papers to stimulate discussion, and to all participants whose mental acuity, grace, and humor made it a success. They have reaffirmed our faith in the future of South Slavic Studies, proving that professional activity and scholarly cooperation are possible and are especially precious under adverse political conditions.

Introduction
State-Society Relations in Yugoslavia, 1945–1992[*]

Jill A. Irvine

The collapse of Yugoslavia and its disintegration into brutal warfare have provided the endpoint to the historical era of socialist Yugoslavia. The purpose of this work is to gain a better understanding of this era and its relationship to the period that has followed it. It is based upon the premise that no complete understanding of current events in the Balkans is possible without a thorough analysis of developments preceding them. By examining the character of state-society relations throughout the period from 1945 to 1992, this volume aims to provide a better understanding of the successes and failures of the Yugoslav socialist state, as well as the reasons for its violent demise.

Yugoslavia has generally been omitted from the theoretical literature on the crisis and collapse of state socialism in Eastern Europe and the former Soviet Union. Instead, studies of the former Yugoslavia have focused on the various situational factors that led to the outbreak of the Yugoslav wars of succession. This study proceeds from the assumption that the Yugoslav case cannot be excluded from comparative investigation of regime transition in Eastern Europe, both because it provides valuable empirical material and because no complete study of the current conflict in the former Yugoslavia is possible without placing it in this larger analytical framework.

Indeed, the violent outcome of the collapse of state socialism in the former Yugoslavia makes its inclusion essential for understanding the dynamics of regime change in state socialist systems. Therefore, while the chapters here provide detailed case studies of Yugoslav actors and processes, and are rich in contextual detail, they may also suggest analyses applicable to state socialist regimes in general.

In attempting to illuminate the causes and consequences of the collapse of state socialism in Yugoslavia, this work joins others that have reexamined the dynamics of state socialism in the past several years. While some scholars have emphasized the fundamental flaws of the command economy as the sources of the crisis,[1] others have pointed to the primacy of exogenous factors[2] or the legitimation crisis faced by party elites.[3] In particular, the relative strength of the state and society under state socialism has been the source of much debate and discussion as scholars seek to explain the process and timing of this system's collapse. While some argue that its rapid disintegration was due to the internal weaknesses of the state,[4] others emphasize the legacy of the socialist "hyper-state," and the dangers it posed for liberalizing reforms.[5] Similarly, while many scholars attribute the collapse of state socialism in large part to the pressures exerted by an increasingly confident civil society,[6] others point to the relative weakness of both state and society under state socialism and warn of the difficulties caused by the underdevelopment of civil society in relation to the West.[7]

Most studies agree, however, that, whatever the reasons, during the last two decades of its existence the power of the state, measured by the resources party elites had at their disposal, was diminishing at the same time that the power of society, measured by the autonomous activity of its members, was increasing.[8] This study examines these two developments in Yugoslavia, focusing on the interactive relationship between state actors and social forces. Since that relationship was not static, but frequently reconfigured, this work investigates its dynamic features throughout the entire socialist period.

There are two methodological issues that must be considered in a study of this kind. The first involves the temptation to recast the entire period in terms of its outcome. The final failure of socialist Yugoslavia offers us the advantage of hindsight, and it is both natural and worthwhile to review the preceding era in an attempt to understand better the causes of that failure and to seek out those elements that contributed to the regime's demise. This analysis presupposes that the breakup of the Yugoslav state and the failure of state socialism more generally were not inevitable. Therefore, in order to avoid the danger of confusing causality with inevitability, it is also important to examine those elements of socialist Yugoslavia that contributed to its cohesion and to some 40 years of relative stability. Indeed, the contributions to this volume suggest that the boundaries between those elements that created cohesion and those that destroyed it are not clearly delineated. Some elements that appeared to provide legitimacy and stability to the regime in its earlier period are precisely those that would later contribute to its disintegration. This discontinuity in the cohesive consequences of certain regime strategies reflects the changing nature of state-society relations throughout the socialist period. While this work cannot address every element that contributed to the successes and the ultimate failure of socialist Yugoslavia, it does provide a sampling of case studies that may illuminate the complex and shifting dynamics of state-society relations and their consequences for the current period.[9]

The second methodological consideration involves the variables to be employed in examining the relationship between state and society. Since the state and society are both abstractions, the best way to discuss the complex relationship between them is to look at real individuals and groups who interact. Literature on state-society relations often talks about the actions of both without specifying who, exactly, is doing the acting. Providing detailed case studies of concrete actors, groups, and institutions can mitigate this problem and provide the basis upon which hypotheses may be formed. Drawing upon original research, the following contributions provide a deeper understanding of the interaction between party elites and social forces as well as of the institutions mediating their relations. By examining developments in Yugoslavia within this framework, this volume aims to fill a critical gap in previous approaches to the Yugoslav socialist state.

THE THEORETICAL FRAMEWORK

Past studies attempting to characterize the features of the Yugoslav political system after 1945 have generally reflected the changing analytical approaches to the study of state socialist regimes elsewhere in Eastern Europe and the Soviet Union. Application of the totalitarian model to the study of Yugoslav politics was mitigated earlier in the Yugoslav case in recognition of Yugoslavia's break with the Stalinist mode of other "peoples' democracies."[10] Nevertheless, analysts of the period from 1945 to 1960 continued to view Yugoslavia in terms of its deviation from the totalitarian model and its occasional backsliding toward it. Since the main analytical categories of that model were ideology, coercion, and the activities of party leaders, studies focused on such questions as the revision of communist ideology,[11] the extent to which nationalism prompted the deviations in Yugoslavia,[12] and the rise of Tito.[13] More recent studies have considerably expanded our understanding of this period by illuminating internal faultlines within the Communist Party[14] and popular pressures exerted on the party leadership.[15]

The totalitarian approach to the study of state socialism in Yugoslavia declined with the rise of a new framework in the 1960s. Based on the application of the fundamental premises of modernization literature to the study of Eastern Europe, this framework postulated that the technological imperatives of the shift from extensive to intensive economies would result in political pluralization.[16] According to this model, this phase of the modernization process would be led by modernizing elites, both within and outside the party. In contrast to the earlier understanding of the Stalinist period, the modernization framework characterized politics as competition among these elites for resources and influence.

This new approach to the study of socialist systems resulted in a series of excellent studies on Yugoslavia that focused primarily on pluralist forces within party and state structures.[17] The focus on conflict and cooperation among elites illustrated how the federal structure of the party-state resulted in fierce competition among elites, particularly at the republic level. The character of elite political activity, however, was disputed among the authors of these studies. While Steven L. Burg emphasized the elements of elite negotiation and compromise by applying the consociational model to the Yugoslav context, Pedro Ramet argued that elite competition was characterized by coalition-building according to the balance of power theory in which each republic attempted to pursue its own interests while preventing the emergence of a single, most powerful republic (hegemon).

While these studies shed much light on the manner in which elite competition influenced institutional change, they did not focus on the impact of societal pressures on this process. The emphasis on social forces became the focus of various studies on Eastern Europe in the 1980s due to the failure of state socialism to develop in the way postulated by the modernization framework.[18] It also reflected an awareness of the new social and political reality in places such as Poland where Solidarity was exerting enormous pressure on the regime and causing the modification of state socialist institutions. The growth of civil society in Eastern Europe, reflected in the articulation of its ideology, its development of new organizational forms, and its adoption over time of a more explicitly political role, resulted in a greater scholarly focus on society in studies of Yugoslavia as well.[19] Yet the application of this framework was only in a preliminary phase at the time of the dissolution of the League of Communists of Yugoslavia (LCY) in 1990.[20]

The authors in this volume renew the effort to trace an emerging civil society in Yugoslavia, focusing particularly on the interaction between social forces and state structures and actors. Their contributions are divided into three parts that examine various aspects of state society relations in Yugoslavia. In Part I, "Regime Consolidation and Strategies of Legitimation," the authors focus on the strategies employed by the Yugoslav communists to legitimate their rule in the postwar period. The authors in Part II, "Social Forces, Social Movements, and the State," consider the ways in which various elements in society responded to, resisted, and in some cases forced modifications in the party's policies. In Part III, "Nation and State," the authors examine the role of national, republic, and regional interests in socialist Yugoslavia and question the extent to which republic elites manipulated and shaped national aspirations for their own political purposes.

REGIME LEGITIMACY AND CONSOLIDATION

The particular problems that state socialist regimes faced in attempting to legitimize their rule has been the subject of renewed examination by scholars who view the collapse of state socialism as the result of a profound crisis of legitimation.[21] The boundary between coerced and uncoerced submission to authority is often difficult to delineate, especially in state-socialist systems.[22] It is clear, however, that state socialist regimes expended considerable energy attempting to generate a measure of support for their rule. As the costs of relying upon coercion became too great after the initial phase of regime consolidation, state socialist regimes turned toward other methods of inducing acquiescence to their authority. The problems state socialist regimes faced in legitimizing their rule changed over time, as did their strategies for resolving them.

There are several advantages to approaching the study of legitimacy in state socialist regimes by examining the legitimizing strategies employed by ruling elites. First it focuses our attention on the important questions raised in this volume concerning the relationship between state and society. The particular way in which regime elites approached the problem of generating support fundamentally shaped the interaction between state actors and social forces. Moreover, the particular legitimizing formulas adopted by state socialist elites consisted of various, often competing strands. Looking at the problem in this way forces us to examine the adaptive nature of the regime's legitimizing strategies and the complex interaction among the various strands of their approach to the problem of generating popular support. While analysis of the legitimizing logic of state socialism, which seeks to pinpoint a fundamental, underlying principle of legitimation, has produced essential insights, this work offers a more dynamic approach that accounts for the shifting and multifaceted formulas of regime legitimation.[23] Finally, by examining the legitimizing strategies of state socialist elites, we avoid the problem of attempting to measure, or make assumptions about, the extent of consent or support for these regimes. Rather, the regime's legitimizing strategies are understood as providing the framework for state-society relations and shaping the form and content of social activity and movements in relation to the state.

State socialist regimes initially relied heavily on ideological and symbolic strategies of legitimation and this approach was effective in many ways. Marxist-Leninist ideology bestowed upon the party a right to rule that was unconnected to governmental or economic performance. As long as the regime ensured that public discourse remained within the correct ideological framework, the party's right to rule could not be challenged. This ideological strategy of legitimation, however, exacted a certain cost. A striking feature of the state socialist regimes, perhaps as Giuseppe Di Palma argues their defining feature, was the extraordinary lengths to which they were forced to go to maintain their monopoly on public discourse.[24] Control over the actual meaning of language became essential to these regimes' ideological and symbolic sources of legitimation.[25] The role of civil society in this fight over values, expressed in the struggle over the language of public discourse, was an essential component of the legitimation crisis faced by state socialist regimes and a main thrust of civil society activity.

Despite their importance, ideological forms of legitimation did not remain the sole sustenance of state authority throughout the period of state socialism. The loss of elite faith in the official ideology, the shift from extensive to intensive economies, and the challenge from civil society all necessitated other strategies for generating popular acquiescence to state socialist rule. Most regimes turned toward economic performance, in some cases pursuing a dual form of legitimation, ideological for elites and material for the populace.[26] While the regimes may have intended for these ancillary forms of legitimacy to reinforce their ideological and symbolic sources of legitimacy, they frequently had the effect of qualifying or undermining them. Relying on economic performance undermined the logic of the system of "rational redistribution" and allowed the public to evaluate the regime in terms other than its formula of the leading and directing role of the Communist Party.[27] Moreover, it was a profoundly weak form of legitimation, based upon instrumental criteria, and highly vulnerable should the regime fail to perform well economically.

As the disastrous consequences of relying so heavily on economic performance for legitimation became clear, state socialist elites increasingly turned to other approaches such as nationalism and pseudo-democratization. These too, however, created difficulties for the regimes. Democratization challenged the party's monopoly on power and created popular frustration when it failed to materialize, while nationalism, when directed against the Soviet Union, created dangerous tensions in bilateral relations. Though it was more effective when it targeted domestic minority groups, nationalism also threatened to undermine the ideological basis of the regime by identifying a different basis of collective identity and interests.[28] Thus, even as the legitimizing strategies of state socialist regimes became more diversified, they became less effective and more mutually contradictory.

In contrast to other state socialist regimes in Eastern Europe, the Yugoslav party-state initially appeared to have an exceptionally strong (and diversified) basis of legitimation, which provided it considerable cohesion and stability. First, as has been frequently pointed out, the Communist Party of Yugoslavia (CPY) came to power through an indigenous revolution and so did not face the difficult task of attempting to legitimize a regime imposed by a foreign power. The Partisan revolution further provided legitimacy to the two new institutions associated with the cohesion of the party-state, the federal system and the army. Second, while the regime relied on ideology, it was an ideology of its own making. The development of self-management as a critique of Soviet bureaucratic socialism permitted the regime to use the promise of democratization more effectively and to respond more flexibly to changing domestic circumstances. Third, the break with the Soviet Union allowed the regime to use anti-Soviet nationalism to its benefit and enhanced Tito's already considerable popularity. Finally, in part because of Yugoslavia's privileged position vis-à-vis the West and Third World countries, the LCY's strategy of relying on economic performance appeared successful for a relatively long period of time. Since it was not the central element of the regime's legitimizing strategy, as it was, for example, in Edward Gierek's Poland, the regime was initially less vulnerable to the economic difficulties that appeared with the recession of the 1970s. This changed, however, in the decade after Tito's death, as rapidly declining standards of living, largely blamed upon poor decisions made by the LCY leadership, increasingly eroded the legitimacy of the regime.

The relative success of the Yugoslav Socialists in legitimizing their rule raises the question of why their legitimacy evaporated so thoroughly, and in a way that called into question the very existence of the state. The contributions to this volume offer some tentative answers to this crucial question. First, they suggest that, the legitimacy of the regime was linked to the very existence of the state, calling the latter into question as the former eroded. For example, while Tito's charismatic leadership provided a measure of legitimacy to the regime during his lifetime, his direct and personal association with the well-being and even survival of the regime undermined it after his death. As James Gow illustrates in chapter 1, the Yugoslav leader failed utterly in preparing the country for his successor, focusing instead through purges and institutional tinkering on preventing the emergence of a challenger during his lifetime. Moreover, according to Wolfgang Höpken, in its efforts to legitimize the party-state through socialization and education, the regime identified the entire political system with Tito personally, thus creating doubts about its survival after his death.

The military, which had initially bolstered state cohesion, also contributed to its disintegration in its final years. As Robin Remington argues in chapter 2, it was precisely because of its cohesive force that Tito endowed the Yugoslav People's Army with great political weight and presence in the institutional machinery of the state. However, despite efforts to ensure national proportionality among the officer corps, this body never lost its predominantly Serb and Montenegrin character. Thus, although the army remained firmly committed to a

Yugoslav state, it appeared to endorse the more unitary constitutional order advocated by Serbs and rejected by Croats and Slovenes. The increasingly partisan character of the military's political role was starkly revealed when it began openly to support Serb forces fighting in Croatia in the summer of 1991, and Remington documents its transition from a Yugoslav to a Serb-Montenegrin force.

The biggest challenge the regime faced in legitimizing its rule was that this rule was founded upon the multinational Yugoslav state. The CPY had come to power during a civil war in which the continued existence of the Yugoslav state had been challenged by large portions of the population. As the only all-Yugoslav political force, the CPY's success became associated with the survival of the state. Therefore, the Partisan myth—that the CPY had led a popular revolution for national liberation—legitimized both the new regime and the new federal state. By claiming to be the only force capable of achieving a just solution to the national question through the implementation of federalism, the CPY made this the key to its own legitimacy and the state's cohesion. Later, the growing perception among especially Serbs, Croats, and Slovenes that the LCY had failed to achieve this goal undermined simultaneously the LCY's legitimacy and the viability of the state.

As these examples illustrate, institutions that initially provided the state a large measure of popular support and cohesion became increasingly ineffective and divisive in the last decade of its existence. As the founding myth of the state and Tito's leadership role became subject to greater scrutiny, bickering over the federal system enervated and paralyzed the decision-making apparatus. Moreover, self-management no longer appeared to provide measurable economic or ideological benefits, seriously eroding the legitimacy of the regime. What had once been elements of cohesion, now became elements of disintegration. This is not to suggest that the regime or even the state was doomed to failure at this point. But the weakening legitimacy of both the regime and state were interconnected and so jointly vulnerable to collapse.

SOCIAL FORCES, SOCIAL MOVEMENTS, AND THE STATE

Parallel with the growing problem of legitimacy, which progressively weakened the party-state, was the growing power of society. As the chapters by Carol Lilly and Melissa Bokovoy illustrate, the Yugoslav regime was always forced to live with autonomous social forces even during the initial period when it was most committed to eradicating them in the name of revolutionary redefinition. This inability to squelch social activity outside the purview of the party increased after the introduction of self-management (in 1952) and the reform of the federal system (in the late 1960s). As power was decentralized along functional and republic lines, more public space opened up for the expression of pluralist forces. Consequently, the Yugoslav system appeared to offer relatively favorable circumstances for the growth of civil society in the 1970s and 1980s.

In order to investigate the growth of civil society in Yugoslavia during the State Socialist period, it is necessary to define more clearly the different usages of this term. Civil society has been a central analytical category to the study of state society relations in Eastern Europe. At the same time, however, it has experienced a "conceptual stretching" that has prompted scholars to distinguish among various of its possible components.[29] Discussion of civil society must make an essential distinction between the two usages of the term. The first usage refers to civil society as a form of oppositional activity based on the "antipolitics" articulated so eloquently by Vaclav Havel in *The Power of the Powerless*.[30] The second usage of the term refers to the myriad autonomous associations and organizations between the household and the state in liberal democratic societies. While the first may have contributed to the second, it did not always do so. Indeed, the explicitly antipolitical philosophy of civil society "movements" in Eastern Europe often hampered them from creating such organizational forms.[31] Moreover, the collective conceptions inherent in their notions of democracy may have made them particularly vulnerable to takeover by other antiliberal ideologies.

It has frequently been asserted in the literature on civil society, whose framework was based largely on the Polish experience, that class and issue-based groups had the most significant impact on the weakening party-state. However, as the chapters by Jozef Figa and Jill Benderly indicate, in Yugoslavia these interests were subsumed by national ones with the growth of civil society in the early 1980s. In Yugoslavia, the nation-minded state-builders not the civic-minded democrats succeeded in molding the language of public discourse. Opposition elites articulated national grievances over other concerns and frequently forged alliances with party elites in order to achieve national goals. Given the propitious circumstances for the growth of civil society in Yugoslavia, the question arises of why it was directed primarily toward the achievement of national aims. Why, in other words, did nationalism instead of pluralism emerge in Yugoslavia?

There are at least two answers to this question, one applicable to all state socialist regimes and one more particular to the Yugoslav case. The first is that nationalism offered a useful framework within which to organize civil society. The emergence of civil society in Eastern Europe resulted in two analytically distinct processes.[32] The first was the creation of organizational forms: parallel universities, cultural and environmental groups, and others that were based upon and strengthened the "submerged networks" so essential to the more explicitly political role that many citizens in Eastern Europe came to play in 1989. These networks took different forms in different countries. For example, in Hungary they were centered on the second economy, in Poland on the Solidarity Trade Union. A second process in the emergence of civil society was the formation of collective identities that provided the alternative vision necessary for "living within the truth."[33] Nationalism frequently played an essential role in both these processes. By providing the organizational basis on which to organize civil society, its submerged networks, and the "referent" of an alternative collective identity, it became a significant factor in shaping emerging pluralist forces.

The second reason civil society was infused by nationalism involves the particular institutional features of the Yugoslav federal system. The federal system, redefined in the 1974 constitution, decentralized power and authority to the republics to such an extent that republic interests assumed primacy over all others. Significant interactions between state and society similarly occurred primarily at the republic level. Civil society, therefore, tended to be organized along republic lines and to articulate the interests of particular ethnic groups within the republic. This made these groups both organizationally and ideologically more vulnerable to takeover by nationalist groups who viewed political autonomy exclusively in national terms. Moreover, as Jozef Figa indicates in chapter 7 on civil society in Slovenia, the organization of pluralist forces within republics also made them more vulnerable to cooptation by republic party elites. In order to examine further the momentous consequences for socialist Yugoslavia of the way in which the federal system shaped state-society relations, we turn to Part III, which discusses the relationship between nation and state.

NATION AND STATE

The significance of the federal system in shaping the relations between state and society is one of the most intriguing insights to come out of the reexamination of state socialism since its collapse. Federalism had previously been dismissed by most scholars as an essential factor in explaining the interaction between state and society. This neglect of the structural importance of federalism reflected a bias in the state-building literature, which saw centralization as an inexorable factor of modern political life.[34] It was reinforced by scholars of federalism who argued that the federal principles of shared power and sovereignty were violated in one-party systems and that federalism was merely a propaganda device with no institutional effect.[35] It has become clear, however, that while one-party federalism did operate differently from federalism in a multiparty system, it nevertheless structured the relations between state and society in important and enduring ways.

First, the institutionalization of national identity in federal, state socialist systems reinforced individuals' personal sense of their membership in a particular national group. By treating national identity as a legal category, these regimes codified nation and nationality as a fundamental social classification and increased the potential for citizens to view their political identity in ethnic terms. Although one-party federal regimes attempted sporadically to impose a supranational identity, their efforts were ineffective and, in any case, were never meant to replace entirely the national identities of substate ethnic groups. Moreover, by dividing the state into a set of national jurisdictions, one-party federalist systems instituted nationality on a substate, territorial basis. Struggles among institutionally constituted (and regime-cultivated) national elites for scarce resources became an enduring feature of these systems, especially during periods of decentralization and reform. Finally, state socialist federal regimes pursued a deliberate policy of nation-building aimed at consolidating particular national groups in an effort to counterbalance within the new federation the previous political hegemony of the dominant nation.

These features of one-party federalism had several important consequences for the crisis and collapse of state socialism and post-socialist dynamics. First, fears of the centrifugal forces that would be released by decentralization stymied desperately needed economic and political reforms. Regional leaders were quick to take advantage of periods of economic reform to increase their institutional autonomy and mobilize popular support along national lines. These regional party leaders were often natural allies of reformers at the center, though they were frequently less interested in the economic aspects of reform than in decentralizing political power. Reform coalitions thus faced a serious dilemma. If they decentralized economic and political decision making, they risked releasing pressures for national autonomy they could not control; if they refused to decentralize, the reforms would fail. This dilemma hindered reform efforts in one-party federalist systems and provided justification for resistance to this process by anti-reform forces.

The federal system also rendered these systems particularly vulnerable to disintegration and sometimes violent struggle among competing national groups after the collapse of state socialism. As Valerie Bunce argues in the conclusion, the ethnoterritorial basis of one-party federalism created proto-nations and proto-states. Not only did these systems establish regions with the juridical status upon which to establish independence, but they provided republic elites with the resources to challenge the center. When the party collapsed, the dual models of territorial-political and ethnocultural nationhood employed in one-party federalist systems could not be easily reconciled.[36] The simultaneous reinforcement of numerous nations and a more limited number of territorial units associated with a titular nation rendered extremely difficult the task of establishing borders between newly independent political units. Moreover, these regimes' previous nation-building efforts reinforced the claims of a greater number of national groups to sovereignty over a particular territory.

The third consequence of one party federalism for post-socialist political developments was that it permitted communist leaders to cross over to the nationalist camp and to compete successfully against leaders with more genuine nationalist (and democratic) credentials.[37] Regional leaders were well placed to capture institutional resources with which to bolster their activities as ethnic entrepreneurs. By redistributing state-controlled resources and building political machines, they were able to play the ethnic card more effectively than their rivals and thereby maintained their power.

These dynamics of one-party federalism also apply to the Yugoslav case, but they developed further there. As Bunce points out, the fact that national mobilization occurred in Yugoslavia before the collapse of the LCY helps explain why the breakup of the Yugoslav state was more violent than the Czechoslovak or Soviet cases. Several chapters in this volume document this process. For example, in chapter 10 on the development of the Muslim nation, Francine Friedman illustrates how the designation of Muslims as a separate national group in Yugoslavia in the late 1960s resulted in the mobilization of Muslims' national sentiments in Bosnia-Hercegovina in the 1980s. What we must account for in the Yugoslav case, then, are differences in the earlier timing and greater extent of ethnic mobilization. In what ways were they a function of the Yugoslav federal system? To what degree were they a result of manipulation from above or were leaders also pushed from below?

The evolution of federal institutions in the Yugoslav socialist state goes a long way toward explaining the greater extent of national mobilization there. As Stefan Troebst illustrates in chapter 9 on Macedonia, federalism had been a central preoccupation of party leaders since their bid for power during the World War II and was inextricably linked to the legitimacy of the regime. While the central party leadership was prepared to tolerate regional autonomy during the war in order to gain popular support, it rejected such measures after consolidating its power. By 1945 it had imposed a Bolshevik model of federalism, which featured unitary party control over a nominally federal state. Nevertheless, elements of the earlier confederal model were introduced with the political reforms of the late 1960s and enshrined in the constitution of 1974. Although it is not entirely clear why Tito relented under Edvard Kardelj's pressure to redefine the federal system, it appears to have been at least in part an ad hoc response to the situational imperatives of reform. Tito certainly never intended that this attempt to strengthen the loyalty of certain national elites would ultimately weaken the state itself.

The main consequence of the new federal system was that it shifted the locus of power and legitimacy to the republics. By significantly augmenting the power of republic party organizations, it vastly increased institutional incentives for regional elites to sponsor ethnic mobilization within the republics. Not all regional leaders were in a position to capitalize equally on these opportunities. For example, while Croatian leaders pursued such a strategy during the "Croatian Spring" in 1971, they were hindered from doing so thereafter, due in large part to the more repressive atmosphere there concerning the national question. During the 1980s, the party leadership in Croatia was split between a hard-line group gathered around Stipe Šuvar, who fought to stamp out expressions of "national chauvinism," and a moderate but cautious group of reformers committed to "staying the course" forged by the 1974 constitution. By the late 1980s, Croatian leaders, inside as well as outside the party, began to express national sentiments more openly. Nevertheless, when the Croatian Democratic Union (CDU) formed in 1989, and announced its program for achieving Croatian national aims, it was dismissed as an irrelevant, marginal element. The strong popular and elite agreement about the post-socialist political agenda characteristic of Serbian politics was not yet present in Croatia.

By contrast, in Serbia there was a steady growth in political participation that focused primarily on national issues from the mid-1980s. Slobodan Milošević became an indisputably popular leader by using populist tactics to articulate Serbian national grievances. Charging that Serbia had been weakened immeasurably by the socialist regime (and possibly by its association with the Yugoslav state), Milošević called for a reassertion of Serbian strength and control, above all over its two autonomous provinces—Kosovo and Vojvodina—but by implication also over Serbs living in the republics of Croatia and Bosnia-Hercegovina. In addition to mobilizing popular support along national lines, Milošević united the opposition and party elites around him on a program of achieving Serbian national aims. When state socialism collapsed in Yugoslavia in 1990 (largely as a result of forces exerted in other republics and abroad) there was strong elite and popular agreement about the overriding goals of reuniting and strengthening the Serbian nation and state. These contrasting patterns of mobilization in Croatia and Serbia had momentous consequences for party leaders themselves and for the futures of their republics.

While the introduction of the confederal system provided greater incentives and opportunities to regional elites to sponsor ethnic mobilization, it is a mistake to focus solely on elites in explaining the greater extent and earlier timing of ethnic mobilization in socialist Yugoslavia. The contributions in this work cast doubt on the frequent assertion that ethnic mobilization and national animosities were due wholly to the activities of unscrupulous leaders, manipulating the populace for their own political purposes. Rather, as Lenard Cohen argues in chapter 12 on Slobodan Milošević, nationalism worked because it was supported by a cultural underpinning and resonated well with the public. According to Cohen, Milošević—the consummate political opportunist—*responded* to popular pressures (in this case Serb anger over the situation in the Kosovo), in deciding to take up the nationalist cause. In chapter 11 Nicholas Miller completes this picture by providing a clear examination of the extent to which Serb intellectuals had adopted a nationalist state-building agenda before Milošević's bid for power and independently of his influence. Milošević's achievement was in uniting the various forces that had adopted a state-building agenda and harnessing them to the resources of the state. Although detailed evidence concerning Croatia is unfortunately not presented in this volume, a similar dynamic was evident during the Croatian Spring, when party leaders were pushed from below into championing the cause of Croatian autonomy to a greater extent than they would have otherwise.

To lay exclusive blame on particular leaders or elites offers a simplistic rendition of a complex interaction between state and society. Strong institutional pressures undoubtedly caused regional leaders to sponsor ethnic mobilization, which played a crucial role in the dissolution of the Yugoslav state. But these leaders were successful because intellectuals outside the party and other forces in civil society had become preoccupied with achieving particular national aims. Bitter struggles over the distribution of power within the state resulted in unyielding and mutually incompatible ideas among different national groups about the future organization of the state and ensured that electoral politics would revolve around this issue in the post-socialist period.

STATE-SOCIETY RELATIONS IN POST-SOCIALIST YUGOSLAVIA

This book is about the socialist period in Yugoslavia but it also is intended to shed light on developments in the post-socialist successor states and suggest directions for future research. The outbreak of war has naturally focused attention on the violent breakup of the Yugoslav state. It is important to keep in mind, however, that the process of building new states and political systems is proceeding even in the midst of the current conflict and will have a significant impact on its outcome. Thus an examination of state-society relations in Yugoslavia from 1945 to 1992 can tell us a great deal about the reconstruction of the Yugoslav successor states and their prospects for establishing democratic polities.

In examining the current efforts to create new institutional structures and practices in the former Yugoslavia, it is useful to draw upon analyses of regime transformation that have applied to the rest of Eastern Europe. Including the former Yugoslavia in this wider discussion can enhance current research on the Yugoslav case and enrich analysis of the process of regime transition. The first insight suggested by the chapters in this volume regards the interactive relationship between elites and mass publics in the process of regime transformation. There has been much discussion and debate about whether this process should be characterized as shaped primarily by elite or mass actions. While previous literature on regime transitions placed great weight on political elites, others have argued for the necessity of "bringing society back in" to regime transition theory.[38] Drawing upon research about political transitions in Latin America and southern Europe, the former emphasize the centrality of pact-making and negotiation among oppositional and regime elites; the latter point to the central role of civil society in toppling the state socialist regimes and shaping their successors. This work suggests that the process of regime transition can best be understood as a complex mixture of societal and elite activity and negotiation. Thus it points to the importance of understanding the interactive role of both in the current process of change.

A further conclusion that can be drawn from this study is the need for an analytical bridge between the expanding literature on nationalism and studies of regime transition. While there has been little cross-fertilization between the study of nationalism and regime change (the former being concerned primarily with developing general theories of nationalism), they have grappled with many similar questions, among them the relative roles and causal weight of elite and mass action. Some scholars have emphasized the manipulation of the public by political entrepreneurs who employ nationalism as a tool for realizing their own political ambitions.[39] They focus on the institutional resources provided to regional elites under state socialism and the facility and effectiveness with which many communists have taken up the nationalist cause. Others point to the mass appeal of its "ideology for hard times" and stress the critical danger of support for the extreme right by the public.[40] These latter portray a civil society decimated by state socialism and buffeted by the economic and political dislocation of the collapse. This volume suggests that analyses of nationalism and of regime transition must draw upon one another in order to provide a framework for addressing these questions. The salience of nationalism to regime change makes Yugoslavia a crucial area for such study.

An examination of the effect of ethnic mobilization on regime transition in the Yugoslav case suggests several interesting points about the process of building new political and state institutions. The first methodological point suggests the necessity of disaggregating the study of the transition in one-party federal systems to a comparative analysis of its dynamics in the various republics. In the Yugoslav example there is not one revolution at the center but several different revolutions occurring in the republics. Indeed, it is extremely difficult to distinguish between regime and opposition elites when looking solely at the center. The dynamics of civil protest and bargaining among regime and opposition elites in the various Yugoslav republics have had a significant impact on the outcome of the transition and on the character of the polities that have emerged in the successor states.

A second point raised by examining the impact of ethnic mobilization on the process of regime transitions relates to the electoral success of regime elites after the collapse of state socialism. Critics have argued that regime transition literature cannot assist in explaining the different fortunes of former communist elites in electoral competition.[41] The evidence provided in this volume suggests that examining the ways in which these elites employed nationalism provides a key to answering this question. For example, judging from the different political fortunes of party elites in Serbia and Croatia, it appears that those party elites who sponsored ethnic mobilization were in a better position to weather the change to electoral competition. Thus while the Communist Party of Serbia (renamed the Socialist Party of Serbia [SPS]) retained its political position in Serbia and Slobodan Milošević his title as defender of the Serbian nation, in Croatia Ivica Račan and the newly named Party of Democratic Change, which failed to promote the national cause, were pushed aside in favor of a new center-right party, the CDU, headed by former socialist turned dissident Franjo Tudjman.

Bringing ethnic mobilization into the picture can also shed light on the process of elite negotiation and pacting in Yugoslavia and in other cases. Regime transition studies alert us to the fundamental importance of the decisions and interactions of regime and oppositional elites during the "conditions of uncertainty" characteristic of the collapse of the old authoritarian regime.[42] They posit decision-making models, often using rational choice theory, to illumine the process of pact-making between regime and opposition elites. This approach has provided useful analytical categories for understanding the coalitions that emerge during a regime crisis and their impact upon its outcome; however, it has overlooked questions about how ethnic mobilization may affect the character of the opposition forces, the coalitions they form, and the agenda of the pacts they produce. For example, in the Serbian case, opposition and regime elites formed a pact in which state-building aims (Great Serbian state) were to be the main priority of the regime. This pact accounts for the astonishingly high level of substantive agreement on national goals characteristic of post-1990 Serbian politics.

CONCLUSION

This work has attempted to illuminate the elements of cohesion and disintegration characteristic of state-society relations in Yugoslavia from 1945 to 1992. In presenting a number of detailed case studies on aspects of this theme, it has provided a rich and complex picture of the successes and failures of the Yugoslav socialist state, one that does not permit simple explanations for its subsequent demise. The Yugoslav state was not, it indicates, flawed from the outset. Nor did it disintegrate simply as a result of the decisions and actions of a few bad leaders. Rather, a complex and initially successful legitimizing formula became increasingly dysfunctional, as a result of both exogenous and endogenous factors, at the same time that social mobilization was exerting greater pressures on the party-state. The particular institutional features of the Yugoslav federal system ensured that these growing tensions in state-society relations would become conflicts over the relationship between nation and state and over the distribution of power among republics. These conflicts ultimately resulted not only in the dissolution of the Communist Party, but of the entire state as well. Nevertheless, while the Yugoslav state has been eradicated, important features of state society relations in the socialist period remain. They continue to play an important role in the reconstruction of the successor states.

Notes

*This introduction has benefitted from the comments of conference participants and, in particular, the contributions of Melissa Bokovoy and Carol Lilly.

1. Janos Kornai, *The Socialist System* (Princeton, NJ: Princeton University Press, 1992).

2. Katherine Verdery, "What was Socialism and Why did it Fall?" *Contention*, 1 (fall 1993), 1-23.

3. Ivan Szelenyi and Balazs Szelenyi, "Why Socialism Failed: Toward a Theory of System Breakdown—Causes of Disintegration of East European Socialism," *Theory and Society*, 23 (April 1994): 221-30.

4. For example, see Giuseppe di Palma, "Democratic Transitions: Puzzles and Surprises from West to East," Program on Central and Eastern Europe Working Paper Series, Harvard University Minda de Gunzburg Center for European Studies, Working Paper Series #8.

5. George Schopflin, "Obstacles to Liberalism in Post-Communist Polities," *East European Politics and Societies*, 5 (winter 1991): 189-94.

6. For example, Ekiert postulates that the strength of what he calls "political society" was crucial to the process leading to political liberalization in Eastern Europe. Grzegorz Ekiert, "Democratization Processes in East Central Europe: A Theoretical Reconsideration," *British Journal of Political Science*, 21 (July 1991): 285-313. See also, Vladimir Tismaneanu, *Reinventing Politics—Eastern Europe from Stalin to Havel* (New York: The Free Press, 1992).

7. David Ost, "Shaping a New Politics in Poland: Interests and Politics in Post-Communist East Europe," Program on Central and Eastern Europe Working Paper Series, Harvard University Minda de Gunzburg Center for European Studies, Working Paper Series #8. For an elaboration and partial critique of this view, see Laszlo Bruszt and David Stark, "Remaking the Political Field in Hungary; From the Politics of Confrontation to the Politics of Competition," in Ivo Banac, ed., *Eastern Europe in Revolution* (Ithaca, NY; London: Cornell University Press, 1992), 13-55.

8. Valerie Bunce, "Two Tiered Stalinism," in Kaximierz Z. Poznanski, ed., *Constructing Capitalism: The Reemergence of Civil Society and Liberal Economy in the Post-Communist World* (Boulder, CO: Westview Press, 1992), 25-45.

9. Portions of this paragraph were taken from a conference report written by Carol Lilly.

10. The weaknesses of the totalitarian model have been well analyzed. For an early insightful critique of this model, see F. Fleron, "Toward a Reconceptualization of Political Change in the Soviet Union," in Frederic J. Fleron Jr., ed., *Communist Studies and the Social Sciences, Essays on Methodology and Empirical Theory* (Chicago, IL: Rand McNally, 1969), 222-43. For a more recent critique, see David Stark and Victor Nee, *Remaking the Economic Institutions of Socialism, China and Eastern Europe* (Stanford, CA: Stanford University Press, 1989).

11. A. Ross Johnson, *The Transformation of Communist Ideology: The Yugoslav Case* (Cambridge, MA: MIT Press, 1972).

12. Zbigniew Brzezinski, *The Soviet Bloc, Unity and Conflict* (Cambridge, MA: Harvard University Press, 1960).

13. Phyllis Auty, *Tito: A Biography* (New York: McGraw-Hill, 1970).

14. Ivo Banac, *With Stalin Against Tito, Cominformist Splits in Yugoslav Communism* (Ithaca, NY; London: Cornell University Press, 1988).

15. Jill A. Irvine, *The Croat Question, Partisan Politics in the Formation of the Yugoslav Socialist State* (Boulder, CO; San Francisco, CA; Oxford: Westview Press, 1993).

16. The main work that articulated this new framework was Chalmers Johnson, ed., *Change in Communist Systems* (Stanford, CA: Stanford University Press, 1970). For a recent discussion of this approach see Ekiert, "Democratization Processes in East Central Europe: A Theoretical Reconsideration," *British Journal of Political Science*, 21 (July 1991):285-313.

17. Steven L. Burg, *Conflict and Cohesion in Socialist Yugoslavia; Political Decision Making Since 1966* (Princeton, NJ: Princeton University Press, 1983); April Carter, *Democratic Reform in Yugoslavia: The Changing Role of the Party* (Princeton, NJ: Princeton University Press, 1982); Pedro Ramet, *Nationalism and Federalism in Yugoslavia 1963-1983* (Bloomington, IN: Indiana University Press, 1984).

18. For example, see David Ost, *Solidarity and the Politics of Anti-Politics, Opposition and Reform in Poland since 1968* (Philadelphia, PA: Temple University Press, 1990); H. Gordon Skilling, *Samizdat and Independent*

Society in Central and Eastern Europe (Columbus, OH: Ohio State University Press, 1989).

19. For example, see Pedro Ramet, ed., *Yugoslavia in the 1980s* (Boulder, CO; London: Westview Press, 1985).

20. Yugoslav scholars were also examining the character and evolution of their state, but under the watchful eye of the Titoist regime, which wished to emphasize the inevitability of a unitary South Slav state. When Croat historians tried to introduce the notion of separate national identities in 1970-71, central party authorities reasserted their control and purged Croat academic circles. It was only when centralized state control began to disintegrate in the 1980s that many historical works, especially in Serbia, portrayed the Yugoslav nations as separate in their interests, ambitions, and goals. Much of their work assumed a clearly polemical tone, however, and was of dubious academic quality. For a full discussion of postwar Yugoslav historiography, see Ivo Banac, "Historiography of the Countries of Eastern Europe: Yugoslavia," *American Historical Review*, 97 (October 1992): 1084-104. See also Steven K. Pavlowitch, *The Improbably Survivor, Yugoslavia and Its Problems 1918-1988* (Columbus, OH: Ohio State University Press, 1988), 129-42.

21. This perspective argues that a main weakness of state socialist regimes was their inability to reproduce elites, and it attributes the collapse of these systems to the loss of elite will to rule. For example, see Giuseppe Di Palma, "Legitimation from the Top to Civil Society: Politico-Cultural Change in Eastern Europe," in Nancy Bermeo, ed., *Liberalization and Democratization, Change in the Soviet Union and Eastern Europe* (Baltimore, MD: The Johns Hopkins University Press, 1992), 49-80; Ivan Szelenyi and Balazs Szelenyi, "Why Socialism Failed: Toward a Theory of System Breakdown—Causes of Disintegration of East European Socialism," *Theory and Society*, 23 (April 1994): 221-30; and Jerry Hough, "The Logic of Collective Action and Pattern of Revolutionary Revolt," in Frederic J. Fleron, Jr. and Erik P. Hoffmann, eds., *Post-Communist Studies and Political Science, Methodology and Empirical Theory in Sovietology* (Boulder, CO; San Francisco, CA; Oxford: Westview Press, 1993), 347-70. For a critique of these "throw in the towel" explanations of the collapse of state socialism, see Laszlo Bruszt and David Stark, "Remaking the Political Field in Hungary; From the Politics of Confrontation to the Politics of Competition," in Ivo Banac, ed., *Eastern Europe in Revolution*, 13-55.

22. See Katherine Verdery's introduction to *National Ideology under Socialism: Identity and Cultural Politics in Ceausescu's Romania* (Berkeley, CA: University of California Press, 1991).

23. For an excellent example of this first approach see ibid.

24. Di Palma, "Legitimation from the Top to Civil Society: Politico-Cultural Change in Eastern Europe," 49-80.

25. Katherine Verdery, "Theorizing Socialism: A Prologue to the 'Transition,'" *American Ethnologist*, 18 (August 1991): 419-39.

26. Di Palma, "Legitimation from the Top to Civil Society: Politico-Cultural Change in Eastern Europe," 49-80.

27. Verdery uses this term in her article, "Theorizing Socialism."

28. See Verdery's introduction in, *National Ideology under Socialism*.

29. For examples see Ekiert, "Democratization Processes in East Central Europe: A Theoretical Reconsideration," 285-313.

30. Vaclav Havel, et al., *The Power of the Powerless*, (Boston, MA: Faber and Faber, 1987).

31. I am grateful to Ellen Comisso for making this point.

32. David Apter, "Democracy and Emancipatory Movements: Notes for a Theory of Inversionary Discourse," Discussion Paper, Geneva Switzerland: UN Research Institute for Social Development, 23 (1992). See also Craig Chaney, "Bringing the Actor Back In: Social Movements and Collective Identity in Regime Transitions," paper presented at the Annual Meeting of the American Political Science Association, New York, 1-4 September, 1994.

33. Havel, et al., *The Power of the Powerless*, 56-58.

34. For a more thorough critique of the failure of the literature on state-building to treat nationalism adequately, see my introduction to *The Croat Question*. For a recent effort to relate theories of nationalism to the state-building process, see Peter Rutland, "State Failure and State Building in Post-Socialist Europe: Implications for Theories of Nationalism," paper presented at the Annual Meeting of the American Political Science Association, New York, 1-4 September, 1994.

35. For example, see Daniel J. Elazar, *Exploring Federalism* (Tuscaloosa, AL: University of Alabama Press, 1987); and William J. Ricker, *Federalism*,

Origins, Operation and Significance (Boston, MA; Toronto: Little Brown and Co., 1965).

36. Rogers Brubaker, "Nationhood and the National Question in the Soviet Union and Post-Soviet Eurasia: An Institutionalist Account," *Theory and Society*, 23 (February 1994): 47-78.

37. Philip G. Roeder, "Post-Soviet Institutions and Ethnopolitics," paper presented at the Annual Meeting of the American Political Science Association, New York, 1-4 September, 1994.

38. Daniel V. Friedheim, "Bringing Society Back into Democratic Transition Theory after 1989: Pact Making and Regime Collapse," *East European Politics and Societies*, 7 (fall 1993): 482-512.

39. For example, see David D. Laitin, "The Nation Uprisings in the Soviet Union," in Bermeo, ed., *Liberalization and Democratization, Change in the Soviet Union and Eastern Europe*, 138-77; and Philip G. Roeder, "Post-Soviet Institutions and Ethnopolitics," paper presented at the Annual Meeting of the American Political Science Association, New York, 1-4 September, 1994.

40. For example, see Paul Hockenos, *Free to Hate, The Rise of the Right in Eastern Europe* (New York and London: Routledge, 1993); and George Schopflin, "Post-Communism: The Problems of Democratic Construction," *Daedalus* (summer 1994), 127-41.

41. Dean McSweeney and Clive Tempest, "The Political Science of Democratic Transition in Eastern Europe," *Political Studies*, XLI (September 1993): 408-19.

42. Craig Chaney, "Bringing the Actor Back In: Social Movements and Collective Identity in Regime Transitions," paper presented at the Annual Meeting of the American Political Science Association, New York, 1-4 September, 1994.

Part I

Regime Consolidation and Strategies of Legitimation

Introduction

Carol S. Lilly

The chapters in Part I, while clearly addressing this volume's overall theme of state-society relations, place their emphasis on the state—how it envisioned state-society relations, how it hoped to construct that relationship, and on what basis. Their purpose is to examine the means by which the League of Communists of Yugoslavia (LCY) established and maintained its control over the state and population. Assuming that the party relied on more than just coercion to attain its goals and maintain its position in power, we understand "strategies of legitimation" to mean both the ideological principles and practical policies by which the ruling party sought to establish the validity of its claim to and monopoly of power.[1]

The chapters included, by James Gow, Robin Remington, and Wolfgang Höpken, address the respective roles of Tito, the army, and education in establishing and maintaining the communist party-state's legitimacy. These topics do not, of course, exhaust the regime's repertoire of legitimating strategies, yet they were among the main forces that the LCY relied on to support its position and hold the country together. The question is: How well did each work, for how long, and why? The answers, though appropriately diverse, contribute to our understanding of both why communist Yugoslavia eventually collapsed and, what is just as important, how it managed to survive for so long.

Despite the variety of topics covered, certain common themes appear here. Most evident, perhaps, was what Valerie Bunce has described as, "the tension between the LCY's need for support and its desire to transform society."[2] That tension may also be described as a ceaseless and daily conflict between ideology and politics—between the party's ideological promise to create a new and better society and its need to stay in power long enough to do so. In terms of legitimation, it represents the conflict between the party's own ideologically based legitimacy from above and its simultaneous need to construct legitimacy from below.

Max Weber's description of the sources of legitimacy, based on tradition, legality, and charisma, though clearly relevant to this discussion, leaves no room for the communists' belief in their own legitimacy on the basis of Marxist ideology. Therefore, we propose a two-tiered understanding of the quest for legitimacy in communist Yugoslavia. The first tier consists of what Giuseppe Di Palma calls "self-legitimation" or "legitimacy from the top." This form of legitimacy, he explains, does not require popular approval but relies entirely on Marx's theory of history whose validity need not be proved by popular acclaim.[3] While communist leaders expected popular acclaim to accompany Marxism's final and inevitable victory, they did not propose to abandon this ideology until the working class had achieved "true consciousness." Rather, the elites sought to develop that consciousness using the resources available to them by their monopoly on power. This meant that the communist ideology had to be an ever-present part of the public discourse. In order to maintain their integrity and their own sense of legitimacy, party leaders had to keep restating their long-term program and its promise of a better future. One might question for how long individual party leaders believed in the ideology and its promises, but even if some lost faith, they could not let go of their program, at least not publicly. They needed the ideology to justify both to themselves and the broader public the continued hegemony of the communist regime; thus they had to consistently publicize and propagate their ideological agenda.

In order to realize that agenda, however, the Communists had to remain in power, and for that, they needed public acceptance of their regime; that is, they needed legitimacy from below. This second tier of legitimacy would be gained through more traditional Weberian methods, including most significantly the appropriation of traditional values and symbols and the construction and manipulation of charismatic authority. This need to consider political realities and cultural traditions meant that communist leaders often had to adopt policies and follow approaches that were seemingly incompatible with their own source of legitimacy—Marxist ideology. Indeed, a willingness to respond to societal pressures and adapt official policies to suit Yugoslavia's unique and evolving needs was a major component in the party's strategy for legitimacy from below. The question then is, how well did these two forms of legitimation work together? To what extent was the party able to achieve and maintain a workable balance between ideology and politics? Did the party's ideologically based and politically oriented policies complement each other or were they contradictory? And in either case, what effect did that have on the party's claim to legitimacy? The party's maneuvering between its ideological program and the political requirements of power appears in each of the chapters.

James Gow's chapter, "The People's Prince—Tito and Tito's Yugoslavia: Legitimation, Legend, and Linchpin," addresses the role of personality and the "great man" in postwar Yugoslavia. Gow considers both the extent to which Tito held the state together and his role in legitimating LCY rule. He begins by describing the identification of communist Yugoslavia with Tito and explains how that association helped legitimate communist rule. Gow continues by describing Tito's own particular skills and attributes—his political showmanship and instinct, as well as his effective personal combination of ambition and pragmatism. He then, however, points to Tito's main failing—a lack of vision—aptly describing him as the "director" but not the "author" of Titoism.

Ultimately, Gow concludes that although Tito's image helped support communist rule in Yugoslavia, the country's demise may also be traced to him. First, Tito's extraordinary success in making his control omnipresent was also his failure, for it prevented anyone else from acquiring legitimacy. As a result, when Tito died, no one else had any legitimate authority. Secondly, Gow blames Tito's lack of vision for his failure to provide for succession. Fearing that it might threaten his own position in power, Tito declined to transform the Yugoslav political system in the direction of democratization when he had the opportunity. Thus we see that the very attributes that contributed to the survival of communist Yugoslavia for the 35 years of Tito's rule—his tactical skills, charisma, and pragmatism—ensured the failure of the regime after his death.

Gow's depiction of Tito's charisma as a carefully designed and managed legitimating strategy aimed at maintaining the party's position in power points to the tension between ideology and politics. The party encouraged the identification of Yugoslavia with its leader, believing that it would enhance the popularity of the regime, even though the "great man" approach is clearly at odds with Marxist ideology. Indeed, as Gow's chapter clearly demonstrates, the approach did work as long as Tito was alive, but proved vulnerable to a changing environment after Tito's death, and his eventual demonization in many parts of the country. At that point, the regime's and Yugoslavia's identification with Tito ceased to be a source of legitimacy and served to diminish its stability and longevity.

Robin Alison Remington's chapter, "State Cohesion and the Military," investigates the evolving role of the military in state legitimation and cohesion. Remington questions the changing role of the military's reputation in legitimating the communist regime, and its responsibility for the dissolution of the state. This chapter traces the evolving role of the Yugoslav military through four distinct periods. The first was in the immediate postwar era when the military was nearly synonymous with the new regime. In this period, the military contributed to the regime's legitimacy through its near-mythical role in the wartime struggle against fascist occupiers and through its later potential in fending off a feared Soviet invasion. State cohesion thus developed first in reaction to a perceived external threat. The view of the military as defender of the state against outside enemies corresponds to a strategy described by Paula Lytle that allowed LCY leaders to demonize enemies with traditional labels such as "outsiders," rather than promote their own program and ideology.[4] In the 1960s, with the reduction of the perceived external threat, the military lost its status as a sacred cow and developed as an institutional interest group that now had to compete for resources. Its role as a force for legitimacy declined, as did its role in state cohesion when, after 1968, the military was decentralized and Territorial Defense Units (TDUs) were formed in each republic. The third phase of military development in Yugoslavia followed the internal crises of 1971-1973 when Tito, frightened by the force of nationalist sentiments, restrengthened the military and reopened the door to its political activity, giving it a primary role in maintaining state cohesion. Finally, the fourth phase witnessed the ill-conceived and bungling attempts of the military to secure that cohesion after Tito's death.

Remington concludes that in its clumsy and often brutal attempts to save the state, the military, in fact, ensured its destruction.

In chapter 2 we see again that a politically motivated strategy that had at one time helped to legitimate and maintain the regime, would, in the face of later political, social, and economic changes, destroy it. The military was originally effective in the struggle against the enemy as an outsider. But when the borders of Yugoslavia began to change in 1991, so too did definitions of "insiders" and "outsiders." No longer was residence within Yugoslavia's borders the essential criteria; rather, status as an insider or an outsider now increasingly depended on one's national origin and loyalties. The military gradually identified itself with a new set of insiders and became the enemy to those now on the outside. At that point, it ceased to function as a force for cohesion and became instead a weapon in the state's destruction.

Remington's chapter also raises the issue of decentralization and its role in legitimation and cohesion. Decentralization of the Yugoslav military after 1968 came at least partly in response to social pressures from below. It thus demonstrated the party's awareness of nationalist sensitivities and contributed to popular support for the regime. Yet that decentralization contradicted the military's ideological program and impeded its goal of creating loyal Yugoslavs. This dilemma calls to mind Istvan Deak's excellent study of the Habsburg officer corps, which described the surprising ability of the Habsburg military organization to nurture a sense of dynastic loyalty among officers of many different national origins. The contrast to the Yugoslav situation is striking and suggests that an analogous study of the training received by Yugoslav officers might be enlightening.[5]

In both chapter 1 and 2 we see how the party used nonideological methods and traditionally effective symbols to maintain its legitimacy from below. Yet party leaders could not afford to neglect Marxist ideology as the source of their own sense of legitimacy. The need to keep the ideological agenda in view may be seen in chapter 3, "History Education and the Yugoslav (Dis)-Integration." Wolfgang Höpken addresses the quest for legitimacy by investigating the role of education. He asks to what extent the party was able to use its monopoly over education to consolidate its own position, enhance state cohesion, integrate a complex society, and ultimately create a common identity for all Yugoslav citizens.

Chapter 3 focuses on the teaching of history and the attempt to create a common "historical memory" in Yugoslavia. According to

Höpken, Tito learned from failed prewar attempts not to insist on Yugoslavism and instead relied on a combination of two ideological slogans: "self-managed socialism" and "brotherhood and unity." The emphasis on "self-managed socialism" in historical education, Höpken asserts, meant placing primary focus on ideological identity, rather than civic values. More concretely, it resulted in a preoccupation with party history, leaving no room for alternative historical memories.

Education's second main focus, the slogan "brotherhood and unity," also represented an essentially ideological approach, as it adopted the Marxist view that under socialism the national question had been solved. Accordingly, the national question was almost never a topic in itself among history texts; it was presented not as a "normal conflict," but as a bourgeois issue that had been successfully resolved within the self-managed socialist system. History texts avoided discussing sensitive topics and sought instead to link national historic identities with a common Yugoslav consciousness through what Höpken calls superficial reciprocity or numeric Yugoslavism, meaning, "a little bit of Yugoslav history, a little bit of your history, a little bit more of my history."

Höpken concludes that the communist-dominated educational system failed to achieve its ideological goals or to teach in a way that combined diversity with unity. This conclusion links Höpken's chapter to many broader educational issues, provoking the questions: How should one teach diversity without sacrificing unity? And what exactly did the LCY do wrong? Here it seemed that the party's policies were too restricted by ideology. But what were the party's options and would any other approach have worked better?

Höpken's conclusions illuminate the essential conundrum of postwar Yugoslav politics. For LCY leaders now found themselves entangled in a web of their own design. The party's ideological dreams simply never transpired. Those policies driven by ideology failed to realize the party's promise of an egalitarian utopia. Consequently, the exaggerated role of the party and the ideological avoidance of the national question in history texts only papered over contentious issues, while it bred cynicism about LCY promises both among the population and party members. The failure of the party's ideological policies ultimately resulted in a loss of faith among many Communists, culminating in a failure to retain even legitimacy from above.

Those legitimating policies driven by political considerations and relying on traditional legitimating devices were more successful and may be credited with keeping the party in power for so long. Yet they proved vulnerable to changing conditions within the state. Tito's cult of personality unquestionably contributed to the stability of the regime, but also created a power vacuum after his death. Politicization of the military aided in LCY legitimation in the first years after the war, but by 1990 the army's attempts to interfere in politics only worsened the conflict. Finally, decentralization, though a key source of legitimacy, nonetheless undermined the party's ideological agenda and disarmed many previously successful legitimating strategies. Taken to its greatest extreme, it turned insiders into outsiders and transformed the old labeling game from a force for unity into weapon of destruction.

So, how might party leaders have avoided this conundrum? Would greater consistency with Marxist ideology have produced better results? Almost certainly not. Could the party have saved its position in power and its state by abandoning ideology? Di Palma would seem to say "no," claiming that though "a 'virtuous' regime can live without popular support; it can hardly live when it no longer believes in its own virtue."[6] Yet the qualifier "hardly" may be relevant in the case of the former Yugoslavia, for there, the communist regime—or rather certain parts of it—have maintained their hold on power by sacrificing both state cohesion and, for all intents and purposes, Marxist ideology. They have substituted for that ideology a nationalist one, while continuing to rely on the more traditional approaches to legitimation, simply replacing old enemy "outsiders," old charismatic leaders, and old military myths with new ones.

Notes

1. Any discussion of legitimacy in communist regimes must, of course, take into account the role of coercion which served as a constant backdrop to their non-coercive activities. Thus, Katherine Verdery has described legitimacy as the nonorganization of an effective counterimage of a regime. For if a regime is seen to have effective mechanisms of force, certain parts of society may choose not to organize against it. From this perspective, legitimacy is not coterminous with consent, nor is it the same as the Gramscian term *hegemony*, which implies that the majority of the population adopts the ruling strata's cultural values and belief system. It does assume that the regime is often able to present its policies and goals in ways that do not contradict preexisting cultural values and

belief systems. Katherine Verdery, *National Ideology Under Socialism: Identity and Cultural Policies in Ceaușescu's Romania* (Berkeley, CA: University of California Press, 1991), 10.

2. Valerie Bunce, wrap-up commentary at the conference, "Partisans to Patriots: State-Society Relations in Yugoslavia, 1945-1992," Albuquerque, NM, May 19-22, 1994.

3. Giuseppe Di Palma, "Legitimation From the Top to Civil Society: Politico-Cultural Change in Eastern Europe," in Nancy Burmeo, ed., *Liberalization and Democratization: Change in the Soviet Union and Eastern Europe* (Baltimore, MD: Johns Hopkins University Press, 1991, 1992), 49-80.

4. Paula Lytle, "Opposition and Resistance to Communist Consolidation," paper presented at the conference "Partisans to Patriots."

5. Istvan Deak, *Beyond Nationalism: A Social and Political History of the Habsburg Officer Corps, 1848-1918* (New York: Oxford University Press, 1992).

6. Di Palma, "Legitimation From the Top to Civil Society," 56.

1

The People's Prince—
Tito and Tito's Yugoslavia:
Legitimation, Legend, and Linchpin

James Gow

Tito's Yugoslavia has fallen apart in violence and ruin. It disintegrated at the end of a ten-year period during which Tito's position in Yugoslavia had come to be questioned and the system he created to keep Yugoslavs together became the vehicle for its dissolution. There is no understanding the end of Tito's Yugoslavia in 1991 without understanding Tito's place in it. Legitimation in communist Yugoslavia was a complex process in which Tito and his legend provided the linchpin. The president's personality and political acumen were decisive in determining the character and course of communist Yugoslavia from its creation, and the bases upon which it was founded, all the way through to its demise, which was predicated on the constitutional arrangements he bequeathed to the country.

Tito was not everything in the Yugoslav political system—World War II, the external environment, political doctrine (including the theme of self-managing socialism), a federal structure, and relative economic success were all key elements. But he was paramount and necessary. By passing his role as the linchpin in a legitimation crisis vicariously to the military, he placed both the army loyal to his memory and the country to which it was umbilically linked in a precarious position which, in the end, neither could bear. Both Tito's image and the army became the foci of delegitimating critiques in the 1980s in Yugoslavia.

While there will likely be some rehabilitation of Tito's reputation—his period of rule is already coming to be seen as a golden age, viewed through the prism of the Yugoslav war of dissolution—there can be no doubt that the creator of Tito's Yugoslavia was also responsible for the framework for its destruction: that framework, at a minimum, required another Tito, something Tito himself was not prepared to face. Rather, Tito avoided and blocked those developments that might have led Yugoslavia toward a different fate.

TITOISM AND TITO'S YUGOSLAVIA

Tito was just one element in the political composition of communist Yugoslavia, albeit the most important. This was partially a product of express efforts at personality cultivation within the country, as well as more random and opportunistic ones outside it.[1] Vladimir Dedijer's *Tito Speaks* is the exemplar of the way in which Yugoslavia officially fostered the image of the great, defiant man, both at home and abroad. Of course, Tito was a popular figure, both in Yugoslavia and outside it. As Stevan Pavlowitch has commented, Tito's standing with Britain, in particular, was enhanced by the "self-publicity of British friends of Tito's Yugoslavia."[2] Tito's greatness was confirmed by extensive publication of his writings, by his omnipresent image in Yugoslavia, and by celebration of him in poetry, music, novels, and film. This was exemplified in collections such as "Mi Smo Titovi—Tito Je Naš"—the title taken from a popular Partisan song that continued to be taught and sung into the 1980s.[3]

Although Tito was not the only factor in the legitimation of postwar Yugoslavia, most of the others may in some way be associated with the president for life, under the heading of "Titoism." There were six major features of Titoism:[4] World War II and the foundation of the second Yugoslavia, the federal structure of the state, the rupture with Stalin in 1948 and the doctrine of nonalignment, the specifically Yugoslav variant of socialism—self-management—and the relative economic well-being that stemmed from these conditions. Titoism might be taken variously to mean any one of these bases or a compound of them all, backed by an effective performance that resulted in popular support.

The importance of victory in World War II as a basis for legitimation in the second Yugoslavia was twofold: first as the rejection of interwar Yugoslavia, which had been regarded by large segments of its population as an unjust arrangement; secondly, as a symbol of successful resistance against an alien invader. The first version of Yugoslavia, poor and riven by nationalist tensions, had failed to persuade non-Serbs within the Yugoslav community, especially Croats, that the Kingdom of Yugoslavia really was their country. This weakness and the subsequent divisions meant that the country was overrun and easily split in 1941. The ensuing manysided and bloody war became both communist revolution and national liberation.

Tito's position as leader of the victorious liberation movement was critical. Having led a movement that had managed to embrace all Yugoslav communities and overcome the enemy occupier and its proxies, Tito was in a revered position, both inside and outside Yugoslavia. Another important part of Tito's success was the formation of a federal structure, which attempted to remove the perception of ethnic injustice found in the first Yugoslavia by offering a version of the country in which national aspirations would be accommodated by a federation.[5] In this way, the Communists were able to create a broad base of support because they identified their aims with those of most of the people and without their cause being the property of any particular ethnicity.

At the end of the war, this federal concept was given form in a constitution modeled on that of the Soviet Union, which though federal in form was highly centralist in its content. The fact that the Partisan Movement had been a federal, or even confederal, structure left underlying pressures and, after the Soviet-Yugoslav split in 1948, the Yugoslav system began to change in a way that would end with a real federation. In a country of such diverse composition as Yugoslavia, the existence of a formal component that was itself a nation-state within the federation was important.[6] To some extent, support for Yugoslavia was a function of identity expressed through the federal units. Yugoslavia could accommodate all its communities, giving each of them a stake in it.

The federation came to have more substance than the Communists expected as a result of the rift with the Soviet Union in 1948. A number of factors fed into that split, although they coalesced essentially around the autonomous character of the Yugoslav revolution and the related reluctance of Yugoslav Communists to follow Moscow's direction. Soviet efforts to subordinate the Yugoslavs went against the grain of Yugoslav achievements. Self-confident after the war and having popular support, Tito and the Yugoslavs defied Stalin, following the decision to expel them from the Soviet sphere.

Independence from Moscow but adherence to communism left Yugoslavia with a pivotal position between East and West in the Cold War. Both sides at different times came closer to Yugoslavia, but for both the main objective was to prevent Yugoslavia falling into the other's hands. Tito exploited this position, playing one off against the other with various benefits in terms of trade and financial and military assistance. Yugoslavia's independent character was also reinforced by Tito's role in promoting the Non-Aligned Movement in which Tito and his Yugoslavia sought to be the leading force for socialist development in the developing world. Although the Non-Aligned Movement had little of substance in it, it was important symbolically, especially for Tito. Leadership of a movement embracing more than 50 states gave Tito an international platform—allowing him diplomatic prominence and enhancing his reputation domestically. This last factor was notable in reinforcing the sense of an independent path and the country's and its leader's importance in global politics.

The other factor that really distinguished Tito's Yugoslavia was the doctrine of workers' self-management. An essential part of the survival of the Yugoslav leadership after the split with Stalin was the elaboration of a new ideological base for the system. This was intended as the explanation of the ways in which Yugoslavia was different from and, indeed, better than the Soviet Union. Drawn from a return to the Marxist classics and identification of the excessive state role in the Soviet perversion of communism, in the new Yugoslav version, the state would "wither away" and the workers would take control of production and their own fates. Although the primary reason for elaborating a new doctrine was to offer an ideological explanation and defense for Yugoslavia's independent stance, it also initiated a gradual process of partial reform. By the time the doctrine was finally elaborated in 1952, the crisis with the Soviet Union had passed and the new tenets were little more than words on paper. It proved impossible, however, to keep the issue as an abstract principle. Having accepted on paper that an analogy of independence from the centralizing tentacles of Moscow was decentralization within the political system, it was inevitable that some should begin to claim in practice what they were told existed in theory. Consequently, while the Communists maintained their grip in many areas, decision making was decentralizd both to self-managing enterprises (under the guidance of party cells) and to republican administrations. This enabled the Communists to garner support twice over—first by demonstrating their independence and then by giving people the semblance of a say through limited democratization. This became a key basis for legitimation in the Yugoslav system.

Decentralization and self-management became important factors in legitimation not only because they were defining marks of Yugoslav independence, but also because they were features in the creation of greater prosperity and freedom. The limited economic autonomy permitted by the self-management system allowed the generation of a restricted market. That made for improved production processes, growth in the labor market, and an opening up to the outside world, particularly in terms of tourism. All of this made Yugoslavia a country attractive not only to western institutions interested in propping it up against reintegration into the Soviet bloc, but to those able to exploit the economic advantages it provided. The combination of external loans and investments meant that many Yugoslavs found themselves in a country that gave them a comfortable life—relative prosperity and social protection.

All these key features of the post–World War II Yugoslav system were important bases for legitimation and there was broad support for the regime,[7] although there were also critical periods at which it was challenged. It was the effective negotiation of these moments that provide the crucial lubrication in the mechanics of legitimation. The essence of Titoism was the ability to adapt and adjust at critical junctures. In this way, principles such as federation and self-management that were originally not intended to have substance, came to have meaning when circumstances demanded adaptation. In all Yugoslavia's defining moments, the regime survived not only because it had support, but because it was able to boost support by proving itself able to negotiate crises. Through all of this, Tito was the indispensable medium of modification.

In the early 1960s, reform movements, particularly in Slovenia and Croatia,[8] objecting to Belgrade's domination and the preponderance of Serbs in federal bureaucracies, demanded reform. Although the second Yugoslavia's federal form had resulted in some devolution, it remained Serb-dominated in key respects. In the armed forces, the intelligence and security services there was a disproportionately large number of Serbs.[9] Similarly, although the "national key" system for ensuring proportionality in high positions promoted a good number of non-Serbs to prominent positions within the diplomatic service,[10] within the federation, there were also large numbers of Serbs in the structures of the League of Communists. In Bosnia, for example, during the 1960s when the Serbs constituted 42 percent of the republic's population, they composed 57 percent of the party, and, in the 1980s when the Serb share of the country's total had fallen to 32 percent (while the Muslims had risen from 26 percent to 41 percent), the proportion of Serbs in the party remained the largest, at 44 percent.[11] Decentralization, it was thought, would combat Serb influence and would mean greater realization of the principles of both self-management and federation—and therefore a deconcentration of central power and considerable liberalization. Throughout the 1960s, power passed increasingly from Belgrade to the republics, especially after 1966 when Tito's heir apparent, Aleksandar Ranković was sacked as interior minister and purged from the party along with his supporters.

Dissipation of power was so extensive that in 1971, Yugoslavia looked ready to fall apart. But Tito, backed by the army, asserted his personal authority and began a purge, in particular of the Croatian party, which had demonstrated the most prominent separatist tendencies. Party authority was reaffirmed through the use of democratic centralism. However, constitutional amendments, later confirmed by the new 1974 constitution, made clear that tighter party control was in fact to be exercised by republican parties.

The 1974 constitution created a federation of six republics and two autonomous provinces. The two provinces were carved out of Serbia partly to give a measure of self-rule to communities with significant non-Serb populations, but also to hamstring Serbia's domination of Yugoslavia. The creation of the provinces was a compromise. It gave tangible control over their own fates to the inhabitants of the provinces, yet bowed to Serbian sensibilities by allowing the republic to retain ultimate sovereignty and superficial integrity. Most of all, it meant that Serbia, formally at least, kept the birthplace of the Serbian Orthodox Church, Peć in Kosovo, within its republican limits. Yugoslavia remained a country under party control, but essentially at the republican and provincial level with Tito looming over it all, ready to knock heads if need be.

Although the Central Committee kept ultimate authority, away from it each party acted practically autonomously. Yugoslavia had become a nine-party system; in addition to the eight federal components, the army-party organization was given status equivalent to the provincial parties in the Central Committee of the League of Communists of Yugoslavia (LCY). The army, having backed Tito in 1971 and as the only truly pan-Yugoslav institution, was charged with the "constitutional role" of preserving the federation's territorial integrity.

Meanwhile at the federal level, "head of state" became a collegiate presidency composed of a representative from each of the eight federal entities and an ex officio general and president for life, Tito—who was "President of the Presidency," a job that would be rotated annually after his death. Also included in the federal structure were a governmental body called the Federal Executive Council headed by a prime minister (titled its president) and mainly concerned with economic management; a bicameral parliament with a Federal Chamber and a Chamber of Nations and Nationalities; and the League of Communists of Yugoslavia with its shadow, the Socialist Alliance, as the leading forces in the system, each with its own presidency and president. Each segment of the federation followed a similar pattern with the most important individual being the president of the collective presidency of the republican League of Communists.

At the center of this arrangement was Tito and his personal authority. A web of political offices had been designed to prevent the accretion of excessive power; neither communist nor nationalist demagogues would be given the chance to control the country. Without Tito, this diffuse system left nobody with enough power or authority to act decisively and nobody who could be held responsible for crisis, chaos, or the lack of an adequate political response. The mechanisms of the 1974 constitution appeared to work while Tito was alive to intervene and settle disputes. After Tito's death in 1980, however, no individual could assume his role and the collective presidency, composed of individuals representing republican and provincial interests, proved unable to offer swift, resolved, and authoritative leadership.

Yugoslavia did not fall apart immediately after Tito's death, as many had predicted, but it gradually slid into a polygenous crisis. The devolution of power had left no ultimate authority at the center without Tito. This was shown in the first post-Tito financial crisis in the country. The crises of the 1980s in may ways stem from the moment when Privredna Banka of Zagreb was unable to repay a

$500,000 loan to western banks. Although the central bank in Belgrade had more than enough hard currency reserves to cover this, it could not act without agreement from the republics to save the bank. Western banks, chastened by their recent exposure in Poland and the need to reschedule the Polish debt, thought Yugoslavia was bankrupt as well and lost confidence. Because devolved power meant the central authorities were unable to react swiftly enough, the West imposed harsh fiscal pressure on the country.

The 1970s in Yugoslavia had been relatively prosperous. But the boom created by the mix of limited market mechanisms and loans from the IMF and western banks was now curtailed by the imposition of financial constraints on Yugoslavia. As a result, the economy nose-dived, sharpening increasing internal chaos along the way. The growing economic, social, political, and national crises of the 1980s could not be resolved, indeed they were aggravated by the division of power in Yugoslavia. The republican and provincial leaderships had created fiefdoms. In these, nationalism increasingly supplanted communism as a base of legitimacy as regional leaders protected their own republic's (and thus their personal) interests. Even on occasions where it seemed possible to find a policy that would reconcile various republican interests, there was little real commitment to making it work, because that would have meant sacrificing republican interests deemed important by the republican elites.

It was the operation of the communist system within republican parameters that enabled the accretion of power. The party's role as the leading element and sole source of political decision, coupled with the prerogatives of democratic centralism and control of information media and employment, meant that republican leaderships were able to establish strong positions for themselves. It is doubtful that the center could have lost so much control to the republics without the presence of the monistic communist model, as it was that model that enabled republican leaders to invest themselves with remarkable leverage.

After a period of concerted action in the first six months of 1990, the republics returned to charting their own courses: Slovenia went one way in search of a (West) "European" economy with Croatia looking to head after it; Serbia and Montenegro took an opposite course, which is to say they advocated back-to-the-future central state control of the economy; Bosnia-Hercegovina and Macedonia went nowhere, their relative weakness leaving them needing to find a middle way that would protect their interests, but not alienate Serbia. It became clear that republican leaders held the upper hand in the last two years of the communist system in Yugoslavia. While the communist system retained force, the federal chiefs still had the possibility of using democratic centralism to impose some discipline in the republics. Republican leaders, therefore, while evermore assertive, still feared federal use of democratic centralism and other party mechanisms to bring them into line. With the end of the communist system, the last facade of central regulation was lost. So was Tito's Yugoslavia.

TITO AND TITOISM

If Titoism provided the major wheels of legitimation in Tito's Yugoslavia, then the axis upon which they all turned was Tito's personality. This is not because he was their architect, nor because he had full confidence in them. Neither was the case. It is rather that his impeccable political instinct allowed these things to the extent that they consolidated his own power. Tito's own power was his primary interest. This defined the limits of the liberalization that served to consolidate his position: those limits were at the point where Tito's power could begin to be threatened.

Not even Tito's conceits undermined his talent for power, yet he was impelled by vanity. It is hard to escape the conclusion that Tito's talent was given energy by his vanity and that it was this, rather than revolutionary idealism, which motivated him—although he was clearly attached to communism and the Soviet Union. The suggestion that had he emigrated to the United States as a young man (which he almost did), he would have become the managing director of General Motors is probably indicative of his ambition. The essential image is that of a typical Yugoslav from a poor background wanting to make good and seeking to make a mark—whether as a successful businessman, a soldier (he had a promising spell in the Austro-Hungarian army as a noncommissioned officer), or as a revolutionary leader. His introduction to revolution and communism came only after a spell in Russia, where he had been captured as a prisoner of war in World War I. The experience seems to have seized the then young Josip Broz's imagination.

Tito was a political showman who loved attention and relished travel. He enjoyed wearing uniforms. These were often in the tradition of Viennese operetta, or Hollywood kitsch, rather than a communist military leader.[12] Tito was criticized in the West in the first years after World War II for his proclivity to wear uniforms. Tito's personal biographer, Vladimir Dedijer, rebutted this by saying that Yugoslavia was "particularly threatened, that Yugoslavs like their army and are fond of uniforms, and that Tito . . . is also Minister of Defense."[13] Although the intention was to place emphasis on the threat to Yugoslavia at the time, the key part of this is surely the notion that Yugoslavs love uniforms. In general, appearance is very important to the Yugoslavs and its importance is not understated. Tito was always clothes-conscious, even in wartime,[14] and he knew that the Yugoslav people were too. The importance of this has been encapsulated by Dušan Makavajev: "His people, our people, our peoples, liked that—his kitsch was a useful glue."[15]

Yet Tito's vital characteristic was political instinct. His former comrade, critic, and biographer Milovan Djilas judged his only real talent to be political.[16] It was perhaps political judgment that enabled him to avoid hubris. He never allowed himself to get into a position where he could fall from delusions of grandeur, or power: "One of the most remarkable aspects of his personality was that he never became drunk with power, was not corrupted by it even though he enjoyed it . . . He accepted the trappings of his almost royal position and of greatness—but never to excess."[17]

Tito combined a sense for what Yugoslavs wanted with his own ambition and a vigorous pragmatism. This served him, his party, and his country well in critical times: in terms of the patterns of legitimation outlined earlier, whenever there was a defining crisis of legitimacy, Tito's instinct told him which way the wind was turning and which way to cut on the waves.

The military achievement of the Partisan Movement, the defense of the country against the Soviet threat in 1948, and the introduction of the system of socialist self-management owed much to Tito's ability to define vital moments and choose the right responses. It was his political rather than his military abilities that were decisive in the Partisan struggle—indeed, the former compensated for weaknesses in the latter.[18] In 1948, Tito had sensed the strength of Yugoslavia's position internationally in the context of the growing Cold War. He understood it as a question of the state and power. Yet he was persuaded of the critical importance of ideology when a number of deputies—Milovan Djilas, Edvard Kardelj, and Vladimir Bakarić—set out to reinforce resistance to Stalin in this domain.[19]

In the end, it was recognizing the significance of having a coherent principle around which to argue Yugoslavia's defense that enabled solid resistance to Stalin's pressures: defending Yugoslavia within the framework of communist ideology was easier if there was a "Yugoslav way." Finally, with reference to that which made the Yugoslav way different, Tito "understood that to make self-management absolute, to invest it with ideology, would strengthen national independence and underline the singularity of Yugoslavia."[20] But Tito was in no way prepared to allow the logic of self-management to impinge on, much less challenge, the system of government that enclosed his power.

Tito's political talent was in knowing how far not to go in his own terms. He realized, for instance, the value of self-management as a source of ideological strength, but recognized that if it was freely allowed to develop, it would jeopardize his regime.[21] The same was true of his international role. Tito never wholeheartedly abandoned his commitment to communism or the Soviet Union. Even at the time of the break with Stalin, the Yugoslav leader "could not imagine . . . that socialism could be built in any way that differed essentially from [his] understanding of the Soviet model," and the rupture with Stalin seemed initially to be a misunderstanding that was not "irremediable."[22]

Tito's ambivalence was most clearly demonstrated in the 1950s when, courted by Khrushchev, he was coming closer again to Moscow, but his hopes were dashed by events in Hungary. Tito, reluctantly, supported the Soviet invasion on a temporary basis because Hungary had been undergoing a counterrevolution—that is, the communist regime was being overthrown. However, he insisted that once the value of restoring socialist progress had been accomplished, Soviet troops should go. In this period, Tito allowed the reformist communist Hungarian Prime Minister Imre Nagy Yugoslav sanctuary. Tito could not countenance the end of a communist regime because that would have implications for his own, but he also could not fail to back Communists pursuing a separate road to socialism, because that, too, had implications for his position. When the Soviets reneged on promises about Nagy's safety if released into their custody and executed him, Tito turned away again from Moscow.[23]

He was to follow the same pattern in the 1960s, when a period of reconciliation was ended by the Soviet-led Warsaw Pact invasion of Czechoslovakia. Once again, Tito's longing for the respectful embrace of Moscow was disappointed. While Tito would never sacrifice his own brand of communism to the Soviets, it is hard to avoid the impression of an estranged lover who, in his heart, was always moved by the prospect of a reconciliation but, as soon as it seemed that one was in the air, was swiftly reminded of the reasons for parting ways in the first place.[24]

His leadership of the Non-Aligned Movement was not only a vehicle for Tito to appear as leader of an international movement, but was also a manifestation of an alternative socialist model to the developing nations of the world, one not necessarily based on servitude to the Soviets. It was, nonetheless, conceived as a "progressive" movement. In ideological terms, it was united only by the collective purpose of the majority of its members, recently decolonized, to oppose anything western and imperial, while not necessarily falling under Moscow's sway. The countries in the movement may be said to have been "non-aligned against the West."[25]

In spite of his orientation toward Moscow and because of the inherent problem in that relationship, Tito kept good relations with the West. This included personal friendships, such as that with Sir Fitzroy Maclean, the British Member of Parliament and soldier who had been Churchill's special envoy to the Partisans during the war and who became the only foreigner to be allowed to own property in Yugoslavia. It also included positive diplomatic relations with prominent western figures, such as U.S. presidents Eisenhower and Nixon, as well as the British monarch who returned Tito's official visits.[26] Tito knew just how to maximize his own position by playing off East and West.

Playing the superpower blocs against each other was another manifestation of Tito's cultivation of the half-measure. "Tito's way," both within and outside the country was defined by being neither one thing nor another. "Neither East nor West," the slogan of nonalignment, had layers of meaning, including being neither capitalist nor Stalinist, neither state-run economy nor open market, neither unitary nor pluralist. All of these were accommodations to suit tactical need and to give Tito and his country advantages from both worlds, if not always the best from them. Tito's real talent was the political judgment, in the words of Anouilh's Becket, to be able to do what was necessary, when it was necessary.[27]

This mixture of pragmatism and instinct was counterbalanced in Tito by a lack of vision. Tito was not so much the author of Titoism as the equivalent of a film director on a studio production: others provided the ideas and the materials, he decided which would go into the final product. The final product was always that which would preserve Tito's position and ensure that Yugoslavia was his. It is in this context that not only Tito's talent and achievements, but also his critical failure must be understood. For here we find the "contradictory and unpalatable facts" that Tito's Yugoslavia was better than that which emerged in the 1990s, but that Tito and his Yugoslavia carry a great liability for those developments[28]—although final responsibility can lie only with those who took charge of the country's violent destruction.

TITO'S LEGACY

The critical failing of Tito's Yugoslavia and its titular eminence was the failure to take the country beyond tactical ducking and diving in a direction where its cohesion was not dependent on either the mortal president for life or an external definition between two rival power blocs. Neither East nor West, neither one thing nor another, Tito's Yugoslavia was probably condemned by two limitations imposed by the "Great Dictator." The first of these was the failure—perhaps deliberate—to make adequate provision for succession within the limits of the Yugoslav model. The second, possibly related way in which Tito's Yugoslavia was left hamstrung without him was the squandering of advantages and of opportunities to place Yugoslavia on a firm and cohesive footing.

Although at various stages Milovan Djilas, Aleksandar Ranković, and Edvard Kardelj seemed to be possible inheritors of the Titoist crown, by the time Tito died there was no heir apparent. Tito had outlived the self-managing ideologue Kardelj, who died the year before his leader. He had also purged potential successors (or competitors) in Djilas and Ranković. His sudden separation from his fourth wife Jovanka in 1977 came to look as though it was an action in similar vein when in 1989 it was revealed that he had relied on a team of "helpers" and his wife for a number of years.[29] There had previously been suspicions that Jovanka had both been chosen and "delivered" by Ranković as head of the security services.[30] Jovanka's banishment was comfortable,[31] but it was a banishment and ensured that there was no possibility of the president for life's wife inheriting her husband's mantle: there would be no "don't cry for me Yugoslavias."

The following year, at the Eleventh Congress of the LCY, Tito made provision for his succession. Tito intended that he should be replaced with the institutional arrangement of a rotating collective presidency—which is to say, he intended to be irreplaceable. Tito ensured that there would be no individual to follow him, no figure to equal or diminish his greatness. Having taken note of what happened to Stalinism after the death of Stalin, he guaranteed that no one would succeed him and then denounce Tito and Titoism.[32] There "would be no Tito II."[33]

The collective leadership arrangement would both preserve his unique position and provide a mechanism to neutralize power struggles after his death. In this roundabout of cooperation and competition, aside from the inspiration his memory would give, Tito endowed the army with his cloak.[34] The army was devoted to Tito as the defining symbol of the revolution in which the YPA had been born and of the country to which it owed loyalty and on which it depended for a future. At secret meetings in 1971, military leaders and Tito had met to address Nationalist developments in Croatia. Impressed by the degree of concern expressed by veterans, Tito now relied on the army to take his role as federal arbiter of republican contests. In the new arrangement, the institutionalized representatives of republican interests would have to work with each other to make the country function. To do so they would have to use the unifying principle and guiding mantra of Tito's name. If they forgot to do so, the army, always loyal to "Tito's path," would be there to remind them.

Experience of the decline and collapse of the Yugoslav state has given rise to one critical question, to which there can be no definitive answer: Did Tito intend Yugoslavia to expire without him? If his vanity is considered then this would seem a likely proposal. It is certainly a view that the power-seeking portrait painted convincingly by his closest collaborator Djilas suggests.[35] A confirmation is Tito's reported remark to another wartime colleague, the devoted Svetozar Vukmanović Tempo, in 1978: "There is no Yugoslavia." However the tone and the supplementary comment that "There is no party anymore," convey a premonitory sense of mourning on Tito's part.[36] Nonetheless, it is not impossible to conjecture that Tito, given his understanding of the people and the system, must have known what would happen. And whether or not he meant or knew it, there can be no doubt that this was the situation into which he led Yugoslavia.

Tito was the life force of the Titoist system. Without him, the gray party bureaucrats needed to invoke his name. They depended on his spiritual presence. When Tito fell ill in the last hours of 1979, he was kept alive on life support machines in the Ljubljana Medical Centre for four months. Keeping the old man alive in these months was imperative for his inheritors in the collective: the supreme leader's authority, if not his life, had to be breathed into his composite beneficiary. Once Tito finally left them, on 4 May, 1980, the message was "after Tito—Tito!" The state remained quite unquestionably "Tito's Yugoslavia." The importance of keeping Tito's Yugoslavia afloat was also apparent to an array of outsiders, the "Friends of Yugoslavia" dismissed by Nora Beloff,[37] who organized multibillion dollar assistance and debt-rescheduling programs based on governments, international financial institutions, and private business, to keep the country on its own life-support system. For a time, Tito's name could create the illusion that the ramshackle, disparate compression functioned as a single entity, even as the 1980s proved the opposite to be reality.

It was important for the conglomerate regime to draw on Tito's essence because Tito was genuinely popular with ordinary people. He was loved by those, like Djilas,[38] who were close to him in the elite even after their ways had parted, and he was loved by the anonymous masses.[39] While the Day of Youth, *štafeta*, in which Tito's birthday was celebrated by the relay of a torch around the country to finish in a great ceremony in Belgrade, was clearly part of a "cult of personality," it was also something to stir people, at least while Tito was alive. (After his death, in the mid-1980s, the ritual would become one of the points of protest for critics in the Slovene Youth Movement.) Tito's popularity remained beyond the end in some parts of Yugoslavia. Even now his image can still be found in parts of former Yugoslavia—in Macedonia, Sandžak, and Montenegro. Moreover, when tens of thousands of *Sarajlije* protested for peace on the eve of Bosnia's descent into perdition, Tito's picture was carried prominently.[40] In 1992 as catastrophe cast its shadow over Bosnia, in a major poll involving more than 100,000 respondents, 14 out of every 15 Yugoslavs regarded Tito as an historically positive figure,[41] and even as a "new Yugoslavia" was being created by Serbia and Montenegro, a committee was formed to celebrate the centenary of Tito's birth, in which the first subcommittee was tasked with "piety."[42]

By the tenth anniversary of his death, Tito, rather than the mystical link between the Yugoslavs, had become the scapegoat for many of Yugoslavia's ills. His successors in the rotating federal presidency began dropping references to his name, his real successors—the party barons in the republics—began to challenge Tito's Yugoslavia. In the second half of the 1980s, "the original Yugoslav peoples of state repudiated Tito personally and/or rejected the system and constitutional disorder he bequeathed."[43] Yet there was a high price for spurning Tito's title. For all the easy pickings of shifting responsibility onto the past (especially in the case of Serbia, where Tito's Yugoslavia, because Tito had been a Croat, became an anti-Serbian conspiracy), the gnomes of no hope allowed "their and his regime's claims to legitimacy to be questioned."[44]

By the end of Tito's Yugoslavia, there was little nostalgia evident for Titoist days. The only carrier of Titoist messages was the army that Tito had entrusted as Praetorian guard of his heritage. Ten years after his death, only the army retained Tito as an icon. The weekly *Narodna Armija* persistently wrote about Tito and Tito's way, perhaps to excess, as the consequence was a quest for the past rather than an accommodation with the future. In the end, the army, built of the same multiethnic fabric as the country as a whole, could not withstand the disintegrative processes that were enveloping Tito's realm. Titoist dinosaurs in the supreme command tried to hold onto their and Tito's land, while others among their number worked with Belgrade for the creation of a new Yugoslavia rid of "unreliable" inhabitants, with new borders carved out of Croatia and Bosnia.[45] Tito's army was riddled with the same faultlines as Tito's Yugoslavia. It was not fortuitous that it carried the burden of keeping the state unified.

The chances to give Yugoslavia a different direction, which could perhaps have kept it together, had been frittered away. There are three senses in which this is the case. The first concerns the location of the federal capital in Belgrade, the second, the acceptance of pluralism, and the third, the transformation of the system. As the second Yugoslavia was being formed, there was discussion among communist leaders about placing the capital of the new country in Bosnia. This could have been an important way of avoiding perceptions of Serbian domination in the federation—it might, for example, have made it harder for other Yugoslavs to be unable to tell the difference between the Serbian, federal, and federal military leaderships in Belgrade.[46] Had the capital of the federation been placed in Sarajevo, the federal balance and Bosnia's place would clearly have been different. However, Tito personally rejected the idea of situating the federal capital in Bosnia, arguing variously that it was unacceptable to do this because Ustaša leader Ante Pavelić had wanted to make Banja Luka the capital of his Independent State of Croatia, because in July 1941 the Yugoslav Communists had vowed to liberate Belgrade, and because Belgrade had already begun to operate as the federal capital after its liberation in October 1944.[47]

At one level, the principle of plurality in political life was accepted. But it was applied to the Communist Party structure. Pluralism in Yugoslavia, although it had other interesting and democratic manifestations,[48] more than anything meant a plurality of communist parties. The construction of a second Yugoslav state based on the principles and forms of ethnic plurality and federation offered a great deal in terms of reconstructing the country, as well as improving on and reaffirming the country's common goals. However, this turned out to be the limit of pluralism for Tito, who could only accept power structures he could control. Anything else would have required his power to be subject to critical appraisal—something no autocrat could sanction. Instead, Tito and his regime treated this form of pluralism as a substitute for democratic pluralism.[49] The result was to incubate a set of party-states in which republican and national interests became the determining features, rather than pan-Yugoslav political and economic questions. Instead of full-blown political pluralism, Tito adopted a halfway measure.

As for transformation of the system, there were two moments when Yugoslavia could have been placed on a firm and cohesive platform. To discuss them at all is to extemporize on a theme of speculative imagination, orchestrated by the methodological shadows of epistemology and ontology: Tito acted in certain ways, therefore there is, in one sense, no point in lamenting "what might have been."[50] There is no escaping the reality of Tito's choices and the fatalistic possibility that, within the constraints of his nature and character, he could never have acted in any other way than that which he did. Nonetheless, it is possible to suppose that there were moments when, at least in theory, the possibility of real choice existed. The following speculation is therefore invented on the existential assumption that there were at least two times when Tito might have acted differently.

One of these periods was at the end of the 1960s when, following the demise of the arch-conservative Ranković, liberal, technocratic, and nationalist reform movements in various parts of Yugoslavia were vibrant, creating democratic pressures and seeking a new economic approach. Holding hands with the army, because of fears created by the nationalist movement in Croatia, Tito squashed reform proposals, in particular from the young liberals dominating Belgrade and Ljubljana. This was a time when the various constituencies in the country might have agreed on a unified Yugoslav program of democratic and economic reform. Instead the leaders were purged. Given the nationalist pressures within Croatia at the time, it is arguable that to have given reformist movements their heads would only have led to dissolution 20 years before it actually occurred. Equally, it was unlikely, given Tito's twin needs to accommodate the generals and to play equitable parent with all the nationally sensitive children in his family of republics, that he could only have removed leaders in Croatia. To have dealt only with Croatia would have been to further antagonize the Croats and confirm their perceptions of Serb-domination. Therefore, so as not to alienate the Croats further, Tito had to purge reformist leaders in other republics. In spite of these reservations, it remains possible to imagine an outcome in which nationalist impulses in Croatia were tempered by Tito's intervening to impose limits without initiating a purge. Ultimately one considerable consequence of that purge was the rise of an ambitious party bureaucrat with a taste for power—Slobodan Milošević, who was more than anyone else responsible for engineering the circumstances through which Yugoslavia collapsed.

If there are doubts about Tito's room to maneuver in the early 1970s, then the real moment at which there might have been a different Yugoslavia was 1952. Whereas in the early 1970s, strong nationalist pressures meant that greater openness held the real prospect of division, the circumstances of 1952 were far more conducive. The key factor was that the combined agencies of Tito's personal authority and the preceding years of threat from the Soviet Union added to a still strongly centralized political system which created perhaps the best conditions in the short and troubled history of the Yugoslav state for both democratization and consolidation of a united Southern Slav country. At no other time did Yugoslavia have such a marked degree of unity, such a pronounced and disciplining external threat, the prospect of democratization, and a leader generally popular and unambiguously accepted. These were the conditions for the success of a democratic Yugoslavia.

Tito missed this exceptional opportunity—perhaps because for him at heart it was not an opportunity but a threat—and retreated from reform. Had the introduction of market elements indicated by the newly elaborated theory of self-management been introduced in practice at that stage, rather than in a piecemeal fashion in the next decade, Yugoslavia might have known a happier fate. Had Tito accepted the logic of democratization that went with this, then the Yugoslav republics and peoples might well have become securely and harmoniously bound together by the integrative forces of a truly common market.[51] Instead they got limited democratization, limited pluralism, and a restricted market that labored under the drag of the self-management system.

The result, four decades later, was a war of dissolution that emerged, among other things, from the assertion of sovereignty by a number of party-controlled autarkies and quasi-autarkies. While elements of the market were useful in creating consumer support for the regime, Tito would not sanction the relaxation of his party's control for the well-being of the country as a whole. Only he could unify the Yugoslavs. Other forces could not be allowed to do so for fear they would undermine his place in history.

In the end, Tito's Yugoslavia could, perhaps, muddle through without Tito, so long as the Cold War compress in which the Yugoslav alternative had been evolved was there. With the collapse of communism in Europe in 1989, the discipline of the straitjacket withered away completely. It was an ironic addition to Tito's legacy. But without "Tito's path" in Tito's Yugoslavia, European history might have been different, particularly with regard to the place of communism. Tito's half-in, half-out regime sowed the seed of polycentrism in the previously monolithic communist movement.

Had Tito's intuition made him take advice to go all the way over to the western camp and the western model, Moscow's monopoly of truth and power in the communist world might have been unchallenged—Yugoslavia would simply have joined the opposing camp. Moscow's stopping halfway and declaring that there were different roads to socialism was its undoing however. Thereafter, it would be possible to challenge its hegemony by pointing to the alternative communist model provided by Yugoslavia. The point was not the model itself, but that it was possible to be different—as Hungarians, Czechoslovaks, and others sought to show. This critically weakened the Soviet monolith in Europe and when it crashed, Yugoslavia, which had propped itself up against it, crumbled as well.

CONCLUSION

Tito was a monster for some, a smart operator for others. There can be little doubt that, as a supreme pragmatist, were he to come back for five minutes, he would in short measure dispose of the warlords, gang leaders, and mendacious thugs who have overrun the country that he made and that made him. The "gentle tyrant" died in 1980 as the "people's king."[52] His legacy was the idea of a more liberal and laissez faire socialism on the way to social democracy and private initiative with a thousand boutiques blooming. This was a brand of socialism which had a human face and body in some respects. At the same time it was a system that was neither fish nor fowl, one in which things were done by halves. Tito was the obstacle to being all one thing or another. He restricted moves in the interest of preserving his own power and prestige. The critical moments in the evolution of Tito's Yugoslavia occurred at the beginning of the 1950s and the 1970s. At both points, Tito capped pressures for change by strengthening party control at the expense of democratic and market development, yet made concessions to those demanding devolution of power by installing party control at the republican level. At that time a tactical success, this became the time bomb that would lead the country into a constitutional impasse by the end of the decade following Tito's death.

It is worth noting that, in many respects, the most prominent leaders of, and in, some of the mini-states that have succeeded Tito's Yugoslavia are mini-Titos.[53] Serbian President Slobodan Milošević shares a string of Titoist characteristics: impeccable short-term political intuition, a common touch, and a primary interest in safeguarding power, supplemented by absolute preparedness to remove potential rivals before they can even begin to become a threat. The leader of the Bosnian Serbs, Radovan Karadžić, also shows signs of endowment with the instincts of self-preservation and shrewdness characteristic of both Tito and Milošević. In addition, these attributes have led him in many senses to play (presumably without intention) Tito to Milošević's Stalin, as from May 1993 onward, Karadžić became Frankenstein's monster, increasingly resisting his creator's control.[54]

Finally, whereas Milošević may have been the inheritor of Tito's down-to-earth and "ordinary" self, Croatian President Franjo Tudjman is clearly Tito's successor as the stereotypical Yugoslav fascinated by finery and status.[55] This is expressed both through his love for fine clothes, uniform, and pomp—he appears, at times, quite openly to present himself in Tito-like clothes—and his aping of the former autocrat, for example using Tito's private residences and island at Brioni, as well as through his obvious desire to be taken seriously as a political leader on the international stage. While all these post-Yugoslav leaders share traits with Tito, there is a crucial contrast. Whereas each of them has some aspect of Tito, it was Tito who embraced all those features in one personality: in a quasipoetic sense, as Tito's Yugoslavia exploded, fragments of his personality, which had been so important in binding it, landed in different corners of his erstwhile realm.

In the end, his personality, which took him so far in terms of his life, probably undermined his achievement. There can be little doubt that had Tito not been guided primarily by his own pragmatism, ambition, and vanity, things could have been different. In memoriam, Tito was left with half what he sought from posterity—as befits his record. He is remembered as the leader who could marshal all the Yugoslavs into one state and keep the lid on nationalist pressures through a series of tactical and intuitive responses to situations.

For a few years after his death, Tito was essential to the state and his reputation was golden. However, ten years later Tito became a scapegoat for the ills of Yugoslavia. Now, many ordinary people are already beginning to look (through unreliable lenses) to halcyon days—perhaps Tito will get the place in history for which he appears to have wished. He was "a child of the twentieth century";[56] he will always have a place in the history of that century. This will be by virtue of being better than anything that followed on the territories of the South Slavs. However, his name must be squarely and conspicuously placed on the register of those responsible for the fate of Tito's Yugoslavia, for it was his achievement that he would have no more than an impersonal, mechanical, collective succession and it was he who imposed crucial limits on Yugoslavia's opportunities to become something organically more stable and qualitatively superior to Tito's version of the country. In the final analysis, the great Partisan leader, like the Grand Old Duke of York, led his men up the hill and led them down again—and was duly feted for his accomplishment—but, when he died, he deliberately left them halfway up, so they were neither up nor down.

Notes

1. Vladimir Dedijer, *Tito Speaks* (New York: Simon and Schuster, 1953).

2. Stevan K. Pavlowitch, *Tito: A Reassessment* (London: Hurst and Co., 1993), 106.

3. *Mi Smo Titovi—Tito Je Naš* (Zagreb: Spektar, 1975).

4. The following is abstracted from James Gow, *Legitimacy and the Military: The Yugoslav Crisis*, (London and New York: Pinter/St. Martin's, 1992) 21-25.

5. Jill Irvine, *The Croat Question: Partisan Politics in the Formation of the Yugoslav State* (Boulder, CO: Westview, 1993), 250, see generally pp. 89-184. See also Aleksa Djilas, *The Contested Country: Yugoslav Unity and Communist Revolution* (Cambridge, MA: Harvard University Press, 1991).

6. In the various Yugoslav constitutions, the federating republics were understood as "sovereign" and "nation-state" formations that exercised their sovereign rights through the federation. See, for example, Articles 3 and 5 of the 1974 Constitution of the Socialist Federative Republic of Yugoslavia, *Službeni List*, Belgrade. For a discussion of the significance of this in the breakup of the state, see James Gow, "Serbian Nationalism and the Hissing Snake," *Slavonic and East European Review*, 72 (July 1994): 456-77.

7. See Bogdan D. Denitch, *The Legitimation of a Revolution: The Yugoslav Case* (New Haven: Yale University Press, 1976).

8. See Irvine, *The Croat Question*, 258-72.

9. See Gow, *Legitimacy and the Military*, 142.

10. The difference between the military and security services, on the one hand, and the diplomatic service, on the other, was that the top posts in the military rarely went to non-Serbs, whereas this was far more commonly the case in the latter. Nonetheless, even though the head of a

mission, such as that in London, might have been Macedonian, as many as 16 out of a staff of 20 might be Serbs—albeit from Croatia or Bosnia. (This is based on discussions with diplomatic officials from the former Yugoslavia.)

11. The proportion of Serbs in the Bosnian party was a function of the Partisan legacy—Serbs had been most threatened by the Ustaša terror and had, as a consequence, joined the party in the greatest numbers. It is also of note that the proportion of Serbs in the party appeared to be a greater concern for Croats than for Muslims. See Sabrina P. Ramet, *Nationalism and Federalism in Yugoslavia, 1962-1991*, 2nd. ed., (Bloomington, IN: Indiana University Press, 1992); Foreign Affairs Committee, *Central and Eastern Europe: Problems of the Post-Communist Era*, Session 1991-92, Vol. 1 and Vol. 2 (London: HMSO, 1993); and for Croatia, see Irvine, *The Croat Question*, 259 n. 11.

12. According to filmmaker Dušan Makavajev, the first uniform Tito ever wore, while still a young worker, was as an extra in an operetta at Osijek. Dušan Makavajev, "Opinions: Bloody Bosnia," Channel 4 TV, August 8, 1993.

13. Dedijer, *Tito Speaks*, 416.

14. See Phyllis Auty, *Tito: a Biography* (Harmondsworth: Penguin, 1974), 280. She notes British Prime Minister Churchill's reference to Tito's "gold-lace straightjacket" after their meeting in 1944.

15. Makavajev, "Opinions."

16. Milovan Djilas, *Tito: The Story From Inside* (New York: Harcourt, Brace Jovanovic, 1980), 7.

17. Auty, *Tito*, 338.

18. Djilas, *Tito*, 11-15.

19. This process was the substance of the paramount study by A. Ross Johnson, *The Transformation of Communist Ideology* (Cambridge, MA: MIT Press, 1972).

20. Djilas, *Tito*, 76.

21. Ibid.

22. Dennison Rusinow, *The Yugoslav Experiment, 1948-1974*, (London: Hurst, 1977), 32.

23. See Pierre Maurer, *La reconciliation soviéto-yougoslave, 1954-1958* (Cousset: DelVal, 1991), 161 ff.

24. See, for example, Pierre Maurer's account of the moves toward and then away from a Soviet-Yugoslav reconciliation in the mid-1950s. Maurer, *La reconciliation.*

25. Nora Beloff, *Tito's Flawed Legacy: Yugoslavia and the West 1939-84* (London: Gollancz, 1985), 159.

26. Phyllis Auty writes of the way in which Tito won the "admiration and liking" of numerous international personalities. Auty, *Tito*, 340-41.

27. Jean Anouilh, *Becket, ou l'honneur de Dieu* (Paris: Collection Folio, 1959), 66.

28. Mark Wheeler, "Tito and His Legacy," Paper presented to the Institute of Contemporary History, University of London, 2 December, 1993.

29. Pavlowitch, *Tito*, 80.

30. Djilas, *Tito*, 144 and 149.

31. It was a mark of Tito's rule that, although he was ruthless in preserving his hold on power, Yugoslavia was undoubtedly a less pernicious place for its enemies than other dictatorships. For example, the capital punishment rate in Tito's Yugoslavia was one of the lowest in the world (although there was extensive elimination of forces opposed to the Communists immediately after World War II). The infamous Goli Otok, likewise, took its toll on guilty and innocent "enemies" of the regime, but the system remained one in which there was "freedom by degrees" so long as the regime itself was not threatened. Moreover, while some, such as Djilas, spent time in jail, many of those who had fallen from grace, such as Ranković, simply faded into anonymity.

32. Djilas, *Tito*, 169-70; Pavlowitch, *Tito*, 84.

33. Pavlowitch, *Tito*, 84.

34. See Gow, *Legitimacy and the Military*, 57-58.

35. Djilas, *Tito*, 169.

36. Quoted in Jasper Ridley, *Tito: A Biography* (London: Constable, 1994), 409.

37. Beloff, *Tito's Flawed Legacy*, 15.

38. Djilas, *Tito*, 153.

39. This was warmly evoked in Goran Marković's 1992 film *Tito i Ja* where, even though a child's eye-view of the absurdities of Tito's Yugoslavia comically ridicules the country, there is still affection for Tito.

40. In a new biography, which is less biography of Tito and more personal account of Yugoslavia (heavily spiced with negative comments on the Croats and Roman Catholicism), Richard West reports that the situation was similar in Mostar, where he had been detained by a broken ankle. Richard West, *Tito and the Rise and Fall of Yugoslavia* (London: Sinclair-Stevenson, 1994), 392.

41. Pero Simić, *U Krvavom Krugu: Tito i Raspad Jugoslavije* (Belgrade: Filip Višnjić, 1993), 181.

42. Ibid.

43. Wheeler, "Tito and His Legacy."

44. Pavlowitch, *Tito*, 90.

45. See James Gow, "One Year of War in Bosnia and Hercegovina," *RFE/RL Research Report*, 2 (4 June 1993), and "The Role of the Military in the Yugoslav War of Dissolution," *Storia delle Relazioni Internazionale*, Anno IX, 1993/1.

46. Gow, *Legitimacy and the Military*.

47. Dedijer, *Novi Prilozi*, 207-8.

48. See, for example, April Carter, *Democratic Reform in Yugoslavia: The Changing Role of the Party* (London: Frances Pinter, 1982).

49. Pavlowitch, *Tito*, 107.

50. In attempting to cast this interpretive light on Tito's life and legacy through myriad "unknowables," I am especially grateful for the challenges and nuances offered by Carol Lilly, Jill Irvine, Melissa Bokovoy, John Lampe, Mark Wheeler, and Denny Rusinow, all of which strengthened the present interpretation, as well as my original conviction that Tito could have turned Yugoslavia in different directions at certain moments but chose not to.

51. A unified system at this stage could well have obviated those later developments that saw the politics of economic disparity blurred with nationalist agendas and, then, translated into divorce. That divorce, in the form it came, was eventually a derivative of the system devised as a result of the

communist compromise of the early 1950s. Without this, the nature of the federation would have been different. Had the propitious conditions of this period been exploited, it is not inconceivable that economic, regional, and communal differences would have been no more pernicious in Yugoslavia than in the United Kingdom, or the United States

52. Makavajev, "Opinions."
53. It might be noted that Tito and his successors were attuned to and betrayed by many of the characteristics of the homo balkanicus identified in the majestic and unparalleled work of Dinko Tomašić—essential reading for all who would understand the subtexts of Yugoslav society. Dinko Tomašić, *Personality and Culture in Eastern European Politics* (New York: George W. Stewart, 1948).
54. See James Gow, "Serbia and Montenegro: Small 'FRY,' Big Trouble," *RFE/RL Research Report*, 3 (7 January 1994), 133-34.
55. See Mark Thompson, *A Paper House: The Ending of Yugoslavia* (London: Vintage, 1992), 281-82.
56. Sir Fitzroy Maclean, *Tito: A Pictorial Biography* (London: Macmillan, 1980).

2

State Cohesion and the Military

Robin Alison Remington

ARMY, STATE, AND SOCIETY

This chapter focuses on the role of the military in supporting the state cohesion of the former Yugoslavia. From Hegel's concept of the state as the "march of God in history" to the Marxist conviction that human freedom requires the "withering away" of the state, there has been a fascination with the state as both liberator and repressor. Whether one glorifies or vilifies the state, understanding the role that states play in the modern international system is essential to analyzing the relationship of the military to state cohesion in the former Yugoslavia.

The state is a juridical unit that has become the primary player within an evolving international system. In the mid-1990s, that international system still has limited, frequently contradictory rules governing the behavior of states toward one another and lacks effective enforcement mechanisms. Consequently, armies are often crucial as the first line of defense from external threats to the state, as instruments of internal security, and as elements of power in the achievement of national goals. Militaries that play an active role in consolidating and stabilizing the state contribute to state cohesion and legitimacy. If the political culture identifies the army with the people, the military not only defends the state from outside attack, but also serves as an instrument of popularly accepted goals. Thus state cohesion and legitimacy are rather like Siamese twins. Without legitimacy, state cohesion erodes from within; without state cohesion, politicians cannot provide the public policies or economic performance essential to legitimacy.[1]

Among modern political and military elites alike, it is generally accepted that the military is a profession in which the civilian state is both client and boss.[2] This always poses certain dilemmas. Democratic governments have tried to solve the problem by depoliticizing the officer corps in the liberal-democratic model of civilian control. Conversely, communist regimes have relied on controlled politicization, typically described as the "totalitarian" or "penetration model,"[3] relying on a united, hegemonic party to keep soldiers in the barracks. Although Yugoslav reality never fit the penetration model,[4] its underlying premise of civilian control via a deliberate politicization of the officer corps followed this model.

Because professional armies are expensive operations, military establishments in both democratic and communist societies operate as corporate interest groups on matters of budget, manpower, functional rivals, and perceived arenas of professional autonomy. This relationship is not a one-way street. Modern states need professional armies and modern militaries cannot survive without a state to serve. In short, whereas state cohesion is an element of power for politicians in or out of uniform, state cohesion is the lifeblood of the military as a corporate political actor.

The relationship of the military to state cohesion in the second Yugoslavia reflects a range of political, economic, and strategic variables. The salience of those variables seesawed dramatically over time depending on the external security environment and the domestic and foreign policy objectives of civilian leaders, most importantly Tito's objectives. This analysis focuses on four stages in the development of the Yugoslav People's Army (YPA) from World War II to the dissolution of the Yugoslav state in 1992.

STAGE I: THE PARTISAN VANGUARD

In 1941 the Communist Party of Yugoslavia (CPY, after 1952, LCY) organized a partisan resistance movement that was to become the armed forces of Yugoslavia. The army, in turn, was the training ground of the postwar party as the predominantly peasant soldiers became the rank and file of the party. Whatever the merits of their ten-month ideological indoctrination on the run, these soldier-communists supported the party leadership as much or more for its military credentials than for its commitment to revolutionary goals. In this sense we can say that the army legitimized the party that created postwar Yugoslavia, while as James Gow has maintained, its ties to that party subsequently legitimized the army as a political actor.[5]

By 1945, Yugoslav Partisan forces had grown into an 800,000 member force,[6] which had served as both the womb of the party and the midwife of the second Yugoslav state. Officially, Partisan solidarity provided an integrating myth for a "revitalized belief system" in support of a common Yugoslav cause.[7] The party promised a socialist Yugoslavia based on "brotherhood and unity" in which some nations would not be "more equal" than others. The assumption was that Yugoslavs whose solidarity was forged in battle could build a brave new Yugoslavia under the direction of the "Club of '41"—those party leaders who had joined at the beginning of the war and whose revolutionary credentials had been built in the army. From this flows the belief that the military was the foundation of state cohesion and legitimacy alike up through the 1950s. That perception was further strengthened by Yugoslavia's split with Moscow in 1948, which then presented the military as the main defender of an independent Yugoslav state.

The problem with state cohesion as a function of external threat is that it only papers over, but does not solve, internal tensions. The image of the army as midwife to a new and better future neglects the fact that many soldiers had become Partisans in order to fight against, not for each other. Although the numbers are hotly disputed,[8] there can be no doubt that Ustaša atrocities and Serbian reprisals intensified interwar hostilities and grievances between the two most populous nations, which had to come to terms with each other if the second Yugoslavia was to achieve a survival level of cohesion.

Although both Croats and Slovenes had fought in their own Partisan units during the war, their numbers in both the officers corps and ranks after the war were much lower than those of Serbs and Montenegrins. Even into the 1990s, although the army was multinational at the highest command level, Serbs and Montenegrins made up 63 percent of the officer corps.[9] Ustaša units and regular Croatian and Slovenian army soldiers turned over to Tito by the British did not survive to seek careers in the postwar Yugoslav military, and, in any case, Slovenes were inevitably a minority in the Partisan army. The antimilitary attitudes predominant in Croatia and Slovenia were further reinforced by the party's use of the army to consolidate its own power and eliminate any competitors, many of whom had an ethnonationalist perspective. In these circumstances, many Croats and Slovenes felt like second-class citizens in a state defended by a predominantly Serbian army.[10]

Conversely, for Serbs who believed that the Germans and their Croatian allies were intent on Serbian genocide, joining the Partisans was a matter of survival. Moreover, the political culture among Serbs and Montenegrins glorified the warrior and considered the sword far more honorable than the plowshare.[11] Ivo Andrić has captured the Serbian-Montenegrin belief in war as an instrument of state-building, claiming that it provided "a deep sense of our history and racial destiny. . . . It all moves *beautifully, logically* from the less to the great, from the regional and the tribal to the national and the formation of the State" (italics mine).[12]

By 1960, Khrushchev had abandoned Stalin's blanket hostility toward the West in favor of peaceful coexistence. With the removal of that external threat, frozen conflicts began to thaw and economic nationalism emerged in the growing debate over market socialism. Meanwhile, questions were increasingly raised as to just what the defense budget was buying and the defense minister faced demands for a peace dividend by other sectors of society. The assumption that what was good for the YPA was good for the party and the state now disappeared and the military became a corporate, institutional interest group needing to bargain for money, manpower, and professional autonomy. This fact added another significant variable in the role of the Yugoslav military as a factor of state cohesion.

STAGE II: THE YPA AND THE GENERAL PEOPLE'S DEFENSE

The 1968 "allied socialist" intervention into Czechoslovakia and the subsequent Brezhnev Doctrine of limited, class-based sovereignty in the socialist commonwealth revived the specter of a Soviet threat. In response, the YPA, whose manpower reserves had by now shrunk to 200,000, elaborated the mixed military doctrine of General (Total) People's Defense.[13] Making nonresistance against invading forces treasonous, the doctrine required that each republic form its own defense units. As a result of this radical decentralization of the armed forces, the professional miliary was now confronted with a constitutionally "co-equal" rival in the form of the Territorial Defense Units (TDUs).

The return to a dual military defense strategy based on massive civilian resistance organized by TDUs was based on a number of shaky assumptions. The doctrine assumed that Yugoslavs agreed on what they would be fighting for, not just whom they would fight against. It assumed that reorganization of the armed forces could escape the ethnonationalist tensions so evident in other sectors of Yugoslav society. Finally, it assumed that professional and nonprofessional defenders can "mix" well whether or not the country is under attack. All of these assumptions proved incorrect.

Creation of the TDUs seriously weakened the cohesion of the Yugoslav military and its ability to protect the cohesion of the state. Continued Serbian dominance of the middle-level officer corps meant that in some cases Slovene and Croat territorial units were commanded by Serbian reserve officers. Whether this occurred by design or demographic necessity, it was not popular. Conversely, in the context of rising ethnonationalism in 1970-71, military professionals increasingly suspected that supporters of the TDUs did so in order to establish the basis for "national armies."[14] As a corporate interest group, the professional military now faced a substantial blurring of its mission and an escalating internal security problem.

By 1971, rising ethnonationalism in Croatia was a matter of great concern to military professionals. In a NIN poll that June, 54 percent of the officers interview responded that the main danger to the country was "nationalism and chauvinism" not external aggression.[15] Indeed, General Rade Bulat went so far as to demand the "federalization" of Croatia to safeguard the rights of the Serbian minority.[16] His suggestion can be seen as a forerunner of the 1990 demands for "sovereignty" in Krajina.

It is difficult to pin down the role of the army in 1971 because there were multiple military as well as civilian players responding to the ethnonationalist drama sweeping Croatia. Officially, the YPA military establishment was under civilian control, ready to serve the state. However, individuals in the professional military and, even more, the veterans' organizations undeniably fostered the siege mentality that led to the purge of the Croatian party leadership. In addition, YPA leaders who reportedly personally attempted to convince Tito of the danger of nationalist excesses provided part of the information base that led to the subsequent crackdown.[17]

On December 23, 1971, Tito called upon the army to defend the revolution from internal enemies as well as those at its border and raised the specter of civil war.[18] He thereby reversed the trend toward party dominance in civil-military relations and signaled that when the chips were down, he counted on the army, not the party, as the primary defender of the state. In his campaign to extend the purge of autonomous regional party leaders to Serbia, Tito again relied heavily on military veterans whose "faith in the party [was] now again confirmed."[19]

The 1974 Tenth LCY Congress clearly reflected a renaissance of military influence and status.[20] Twenty-one generals and other high-ranking officers took over key party posts; for the first time since 1946, the Ministry of the Interior was again headed by a general. By the Eleventh Party Congress in 1978, the actual number of ranking officers in the Central Committee was somewhat higher than the 15 slots reserved for the armed forces because six generals were also sent forward by regional party organizations. Most important, the 1974 Constitution recentralized the armed forces, dropping the "co-equal" status of the territorial defense units and referring to the professional military and TDUs as an "integrated, unified whole."[21]

In short, well before Tito died in 1980, increased military access to the highest level of party-state decision making had substantially strengthened the political mission of the Yugoslav military. This military penetration of party and state political institutions was undoubtedly intended as a factor of state cohesion. In fact, however, it had the opposite effect.

STAGE III: THE POST-TITO
POLITICAL MISSION OF THE MILITARY[22]

The March 1981 rioting of an estimated 10,000 to 20,000 protestors demanding republic status for Kosovo was the first test case of post-Tito state cohesion. It was a test the military failed. Although army and security units restored order, their military successes created more problems than they solved in terms of the role of the military in post-Tito Yugoslavia and who would pay for it.

Not surprisingly, The YPA concept of defending the revolution in Kosovo was seen very differently by Kosovar Albanians who considered the military to be an occupier, repressing legitimate grievances. Albanian conscripts were increasingly isolated in the army, suspected of—and sometimes engaged in—subversive activity. Whether or not the 20-year-old Albanian who turned his gun on fellow soldiers in the Paracin barracks in southern Serbia in September 1987 was a part of such a conspiracy, the incident inflamed a backlash of Serbian nationalism and facilitated the rise of Slobodan Milošević.

Meanwhile, another effect of the Kosovo crisis had been to intensify Slovene objections to sharing the defense burden. During the increasingly heated debate over military budget hikes,[23] Defense Minister Branko Mamula bluntly criticized those who put ethnonationalist interests above common Yugoslav interests and he openly asserted the military's responsibility for "cohesion of the country."[24]

Ultimately, accusations of military plotting to remove the pluralistically minded Slovene leadership coupled with the badly bungled trial of Slovene youth journalist Janez Janša and others for betraying military secrets became catalysts for an increasingly strong Slovene nationalist movement.[25] Whatever the tangled and perceived facts in that case, the YPA's heavy-handed approach and its insensitive refusal to use the Slovene language during the trial undoubtedly escalated the conflict between the YPA and Slovenia. In these circumstances, it is not surprising that Slovenes experienced the federally imposed martial law to quell Albanian resistance to the March 1989 "reunification" of Serbia as a threat to Slovenia's constitutional autonomy as well. Now Albanians and Slovenes alike posed a threat to the internal cohesion of the state and the armed forces. Still, amid growing civilian paralysis, the military was more cohesive than the party and did function as its backbone, if not that of the state.

STAGE IV: ON THE ROAD TO CIVIL WAR[26]

Faced with widespread rejection of communist regimes in the neighborhood and undoubtedly aware of the popular fascination with the Romanian revolution in December 1989, the LCY gave up its monopoly on political power at the January 1990 14th Extraordinary Party Congress.[27] This acceptance of multiparty competition shifted the debate from pluralism within the political system to pluralism within the party itself. In that debate, Serbian and other more conservative delegates had enough votes to defeat the Slovene demand that the party become a confederation of independent, republic organizations, but not enough to keep the congress in session after the

Slovene delegates walked out. Although officially only postponed, the congress never resumed and the party never recovered from the blow. As the LCY died, so too did the hopes of Communists in the YPA that the party could somehow overcome its internal ideological and political disunity.[28]

The message of military delegates to the 14th Congress had been one of unambiguous support for a federal state in which the YPA would continue to have a political role in a Yugoslavia capable of making policy and paying for defense. While conceding that political pluralism was "now our reality," Dr. Dimitrije Baucal, chairman of the Committee of the LCY in the Federal Secretariat for National Defense, insisted that such pluralism must not "threaten the country's integrity."[29] Nonetheless, Petar Simić, then president of the LC-YPA, was considerably more flexible than many of the civilian delegates. In supporting postponement of the congress, he noted that "all the blame does not belong to Slovenia alone.... Ultimatums, blockades, pressure and faits accomplis have never resulted in the resolution of problems between peoples."[30]

TRAUMA AND TRANSITION

Notwithstanding attempts by the YPA to delay the process of civilian political decay, the outcome of the congress came as "no surprise."[31] Now as the party faded from the political scene, the army adopted a go-slow approach. When questioned about the continued existence of party cells in the army, YPA spokesman Col. Vuk Obradović replied that the status of the LC-YPA would be determined by the new constitution and implementing laws. Until such measures were enacted, the federal defense secretariat would "abide by the existing constitution under which LCY organizations are active in army units and headquarters."[32]

Nonetheless, the army began to delink itself from the LCY by eliminating ideological content in such documents as the Federal Secretariat of Defense's new plan for moral education of recruits that emphasized "defense of our common land, Yugoslav patriotism, and the combat traditions of our nations and nationalities."[33] The problem was finding a new political partner committed to "Yugoslav Patriotism." Even before the League of Communists let go of its monopoly on power, political parties, associations, and movements on all sides of the political spectrum had begun openly organizing, with or without permission. From the army's point of view, Slovene and Croatian center-right parties as well as some of the Serbian opposition parties, were unfit partners on two counts. First, they were not committed to Yugoslavia as a going concern. Secondly, their demands for subordination of the YPA to republic assemblies or for national armies were flatly unacceptable.

Officially, the YPA supported "democratization and reform short of subverting the constitutional order, redrawing the internal boundaries or breaking up the country."[34] Thus, despite Serb dominance in the officer corps, the military establishment's agenda was considerably closer to Prime Minister Ante Marković's Alliance of Reform Forces than to Slobodan Milošević's Socialist Party of Serbia (SPS). However, the weak showing of the Alliance for Reform Forces in republic elections in the fall and winter of 1990 did not bode well for the prime minister's government party.

In the meantime, the army attempted its own experiment in party-building. Along with the announcement that LCY cells within the military would be dissolved,[35] came the birth announcement of the League of Communists—Movement for Yugoslavia (LC-MY) in the form of a letter inviting LC members in the army to join the new party. Here there were certainly political links to Milošević whose wife, Mirjana Marković, had a prominent place at the top of the new party hierarchy. The retired generals leading the party also openly supported Milošević's SPS in the December 1990 Serbian elections.

Yet the LC-MY did not solve the army's problem of finding viable national parties with whom to establish a partnership. While civilian politicians argued over the legal basis of the emerging multiparty political system, the military leadership consistently positioned itself on the side of defending the existing constitution. Thus, the military leadership entered into the whirlwind of ethnic-territorial-bureaucratic conflicts centered around competing confederal-federal constitutional agendas. As tensions rose during multiparty republic elections, army spokesmen alternated between quiet consultations[36] and militant rhetoric. By midsummer, with Kosovo under what many Kosovar Albanians experienced as virtually perpetual martial law,[37] the army warned of "the unforeseeable consequences" of Yugoslav disintegration.[38] As Serbs in the predominantly Serbian city of Knin took up arms to conduct what Croatian authorities viewed as an illegal referendum on Serbian autonomy within the republic,[39] fears grew in and outside of Yugoslavia that there would be no time to develop political alternatives to civil war.

THE FAILURE OF INTERNAL DETERRENCE

By the spring of 1991, the Yugoslav military was sinking in the quicksand of civilian political decay. Attempts to demobilize the Croatian militia and arrest the Croatian defense minister on charges of organizing an armed rebellion were derailed. Army tanks rolled into Belgrade to protect governmental institutions and, coincidentally, Milošević's government from 100,000 student and opposition demonstrators protesting his stranglehold on the media, economic incompetence, and authoritarian style.

When the Collective presidency declined Milošević's request to give emergency powers to the Yugoslav army, the Serbian president rejected the authority of the federal presidency.[40] After ten days of what appeared to many observers as the prelude to a military takeover or the withdrawal of Serbia from Yugoslavia, the stormy confrontation of republic politicians posturing as ethnic gladiators subsided. During this lull, the High Command of the YPA issued a statement assuring the country and the world that the army would stay out of politics but would not tolerate armed interethnic conflict or civil war.[41]

The crisis resumed in mid-May with the Serbian-Montenegrin move to bloc the Croatian representative to the Collective State presidency, Stipe Mesić, from rotating into the job of the presidency on schedule. Notwithstanding the Serbian leadership's continued rhetoric in the name of Yugoslavia, rejection of Mesić appeared to confirm speculation that Milošević had given up on Yugoslavia and had embarked on a land grab in the name of "Greater Serbia."[42]

By the end of June 1991, Slovenia and Croatia declared "independence." The general feeling among knowledgeable Slovene observers during the preceding week was that this was only another step in the political maneuvering surrounding the confederal-federal constitutional debate. After the declaration, however, and reportedly in violation of a deal cut with the federal government for joint customs presence while negotiations continued,[43] the Slovenes forced out federal customs agents and attempted to move their border with the rest of Yugoslavia to the border with Croatia. The shooting started when the YPA went in to reestablish the federal customs presence on Slovene borders. When Janez Janša, now Slovenia's defense minister, announced that the army had declared war against Slovenia, control over the Slovene political scene fell entirely into the hands of those policy-makers for whom independence was equated with separation.

Who gave orders to whom and who was responsible for what in the Slovene war remains very fuzzy. Prime Minister Marković has accused the army of acting on its own,[44] while the army insists that it was acting in accordance with decisions of the government and that the presidency and other politicians were avoiding responsibility.[45] Their mutual recriminations only worsened relations between the government and the army, while further weakening Marković's credibility.

Although the European Community was able to broker a cease-fire in Slovenia, from the perspective of civil-military relations and expanding violence, of greater importance was the humiliation of the YPA in Slovenia. Even if one accepted the army's assertion that the Slovenes lied about their losses, the public figures of four members of the Slovene Territorial Defense, ten foreigners, and roughly a hundred members of the YPA killed speak volumes.[46] The stripping of young soldiers of clothes as well as weapons before sending them back to Belgrade in pajamas and the public gloating in Ljubljana accelerated Serbianization of the federal army.[47] In the wake of the Slovenian war, moderates in the YPA lost ground, while hard-liners more and more openly supported the activities of Serbian irregulars in Croatia. As one colleague warned while we watched a defensive YPA press conference on Belgrade television, "This is our most dangerous time. The army is unpredictable—a wounded animal."

As civil war came to Croatia, the military command structure had changed. Now the army's pride and reputation were on the line, virtually assuring that the Croatian blockade of YPA garrisons in Croatia would bring a very different response than the aborted show of force in Slovenia. For the military establishment, this was no longer a war to defend the Yugoslav state. With 25,000 soldiers and their families held hostage, the conflict became a war of Croatia against the army. Amid the escalating conflict, the federal government essentially vanished. Prime Minister Marković was not reported as a party to the perpetual cease-fire agreements and his demands that Defense Minister Veljko Kadijević and other high-ranking military leaders resign fell on deaf ears.

By October half of the state presidency—led by Montenegrin Vice-President Branko Kostić in an alliance with representatives from Serbia and the no-longer autonomous provinces of Vojvodina and Kosovo—assumed the powers of the federal parliament. In response, President Mesić, Croatia's representative, supported by the representatives of Slovenia, Macedonia, and Bosnia-Hercegovina condemned the takeover as a coup.[48] Despite the virtual lack of international reaction, Mesić was right.

With parliament gone and the presidency split, there is no doubt that the YPA was operating in a vacuum as a corporate entity in a race for its own survival. The armed forces that had perceived its post-Tito mission to act as a buffer among warring ethnic groups,[49] had step by step become the engine of the civil war. Now the YPA was an army in search not of a party but of a country. In that search, its fate, as well as that of the civilian coup-makers clinging to power, was sealed by the decision of the European Community to yield to German pressure and recognize Croatia as well as Slovenia by January 15, 1992. Meanwhile, the army itself was hemorrhaging with desertions, under attack in Montenegro,[50] accused of treason within Serbia proper,[51] and unable to control the proliferating armed and undisciplined irregular militias.

TENTATIVE CONCLUSIONS

State cohesion involves the successful consolidation of power and transformation of that power into recognized legitimate authority. In examining the role of the military in achieving state cohesion in the former Yugoslavia, this analysis has identified four stages of civil-military relations within which military influence functioned very differently.

Stage I
Under conditions of revolutionary euphoria and external threat, the military was a key factor in a state cohesion that rested on its role in the creation of the state, the repression of opposition to the Yugoslav communist revolution, and the perception of the YPA as the first line of defense against a potential Soviet attack. For those who identified with the Yugoslav state-building agenda or with a level of national integration that could become the focus of Yugoslav nation-building, the military was seen as legitimate and this, in turn, legitimized the state.

Stage II
In the early 1960s, the campaign for market socialism legitimized economic nationalism. This led to tensions over who paid the bills for defense and tarnished the perception of the military as the core element of state cohesion. Meanwhile, the 1968 creation of the Terri-

torial Defense Units (TDUs) as a potential functional rival to the professional military weakened the cohesion of the YPA and ultimately of the state.

Stage III

Tito's reliance on the army during the Croatian crisis of 1970-71 and the increased political role of the military after 1974 produced a short-term gain in the appearance of state cohesion but created elements that ultimately undermined the state. First, it intensified the military's perception of its political mission. Second, it tied that mission to the party's leading role. Perhaps most important, Tito himself gave the military primary responsibility for holding the state together. In this regard, I agree with Gow's analysis that the godfather of Yugoslav communism saw not the party, but the army, as the carrier of Titoist messages.[52]

Stage IV

In post-Tito Yugoslavia, the Titoist political solution increased expectations for a reordering of ethnonational relations and brought demands for republic status for Kosovo. The military contained the Kosovar Albanian separatist aspirations, but at the expense of direct conflict with Slovenia. The willingness of the federal government and YPA alike to disregard constitutionally protected rights in Kosovo became an important factor in the eventual Slovene declaration of independence. Subsequent military mishandling of the attempt to return federal customs officials to Slovene borders by force only strengthened those in Slovenia who equated "sovereignty and independence" with destruction of the existing Yugoslav state.

On one level, Ante Marković was prophetic in his judgment that when the federal army started bombing, it meant the end of Yugoslavia.[53] Yet in terms of state cohesion, Yugoslavia had already been fundamentally weakened by the 1974 Constitution that replaced Tito's charismatic authority with an elaborate consociational political system lacking shared legitimate authority. Long before the shooting started, the military, whose mission was to defend the state, had no legitimacy in Slovenia and Croatia. Moreover, in Ljubljana and Zagreb, the legitimacy of that state itself depended on its radical reorganization in ways absolutely unacceptable to Serbia and about which military leaders had serious reservations. In these circumstances, the state was a juridical shell. It had eroded from within.

Any military has only four instruments for achieving state cohesion: long-term political socialization of recruits, repression in the name of an at least marginally acceptable civilian government, assumption of a guardian role behind a viable civilian leadership, and coup d'état. The first did not survive the creation of the TDUs. More importantly, however, in post-Tito Yugoslavia there was no acceptable civilian government or viable civilian leadership. Although by 1991, all conditions for a coup existed—lack of civilian legitimacy, economic crisis, and social unrest—the military was divided and fearful of precipitating civil war. In the end, the dissolution of state cohesion in the former Yugoslavia, while caused by many diverse factors, may also be traced to Tito's politicization of the army and the military's own inept attempts to save itself and the state. Only the republic civilian politicians could have brokered a compromise short of war. There was no political will or international priority to force them to do so.

Notes

1. For an excellent in-depth study, see James Gow, *Legitimacy and the Military: The Yugoslav Crisis* (New York: St. Martin's Press, 1992).

2. See Samuel P. Huntington's classic study *The Soldier and the State: The Theory and Practice of Civil Military Relations* (Cambridge, MA: Harvard University Press, 1957).

3. See Amos Perlmutter and William M. LeoGrande, "The Party in Uniform: Towards a Theory of Civil Military Relations in Communist Political Systems," *American Political Science Review* 76, 4 (December 1982): 778-89.

4. Robin Alison Remington, "Civil-Military Relations in Yugoslavia: The Partisan Vanguard," *Studies in Comparative Communism*, XI, 3 (autumn 1978): 250-64.

5. Gow, *Legitimacy and the Military*, 29.

6. See Gow, *Legitimacy and the Military*, 37. Also, A. Ross Johnson "The Role of the Military in Yugoslavia: An Historical Sketch," in Roman Kolkowicz and Andrzej Korbonski, eds., *Peasants, Soldiers, and Bureaucrats: Civil-Military Relations in Communist and Modernizing Societies* (London: George Allen & Unwin, 1982), 181-98.

7. M. George Zaninovich, *The Development of Socialist Yugoslavia* (Baltimore, MD: The John Hopkins Press, 1968), 44.

8. Serbian author Dr. Lazo M. Kostich cites German sources to substantiate his estimate of 750,000 Serbian victims in *Holocaust in the Independent State of Croatia* (Chicago, IL: Liberty Press, 1981), 4. Western estimates have tended to use 300,000 to 350,000. See British historian Fred Singleton, *Twentieth-Century Yugoslavia* (New York: Columbia University Press, 1976), 88. There are claims that as many as a million Croats died in Serbian atrocities, see Ivo Omrčanin, *Diplomatic and Political History of Croatia* (Philadelphia, PA: Dorrance and Co., 1972), 181.

9. *Vreme*, 4, no. 139 (23 June 1993): 35.

10. Postwar centralization of the YPA exacerbated ethnonationalist dissatisfaction. See Drago C. Sporer, "Politics and Nationalism within the Yugoslavian People's Army," *Journal of Croatian Studies*, XX (1979): 118-21.

11. Milovan Djilas, *Land Without Justice* (New York: Harcourt, Brace, 1958), 39.

12. Ivo Andrić, *The Bridge on the Drina* (New York: Signet, 1967), 250-51.

13. See Dennison I. Rusinow, "The Yugoslav Concept of 'All National Defense,'" *American University Field Staff (AUFS) Reports*, November 1971.

14. Lt. General Viktor Bubanj, *Politika*, 20 December 1970.

15. *NIN* (Belgrade), 20 June 1971.

16. *NIN* (Belgrade), 19 September 1971.

17. *The New York Times*, 25 May 1972.

18. *Borba*, 23 December 1971.

19. *Politika*, 16 March 1973.

20. See Slobodan Stanković, "The Yugoslav Party Congress and the Army," *RFE Research* (13 June 1974).

21. *The Constitution of the Socialist Federal Republic of Yugoslavia* (Belgrade: 1974), 70 and 200.

22. Revised from Robin Alison Remington, "Political-Military Relations in Post-Tito Yugoslavia," in Pedro Ramet, ed. *Yugoslavia in the 1980s* (Boulder, CO; and London: Westview Press, 1985), 56-75. See also Marko Milivojević, "The Political Role of the Yugoslav People's Army in Contemporary Yugoslavia," in Marko Milivojević, John B. Allcock, and Pierre Maurer, eds., *Yugoslavia's Security Dilemmas* (Oxford: Berg, 1988), 15-59.

23. Slobodan Stanković, "Yugoslavia's Army Budget Comes Under Fire," *RFE/RL Background Report* (30 December 1982),1-5.

24. *Narodna Armija*, 14 April 1983; quoted by Slobodan Stanković, "Yugoslav Defense Minister Calls the Army 'Backbone of the System,'" *RFE/RL Background Report* (28 April 1983),1-6.

25. Gow, *Legitimacy and the Military*, 78.

26. Revised from Robin Alison Remington, "Yugoslav Soldiers in Politics: On the Road to Civil War," Occasional Paper, No. 9109, October 1991, University of Missouri-St. Louis Center for International Studies. Sponsored by a grant from the University of Missouri Weldon Springs Fund. See also, Robin Alison Remington, "The Yugoslav Army: Trauma and Transition," in Constantine P. Danopoulos and Daniel Zirker eds., Civil-Military Relations in the Soviet and Yugoslav Sucessor States. (Boulder, CO: Westview Press, 1996): 153-73.

27. *Politika*, 24 January 1990.

28. Aleksandar Tijanić, "March Step: The Army is Against Federalization of the LCY," *NIN*, 3 December 1989 in Foreign Broadcast Information Service, 20 Feb. 1990.

29. *Narodna Armija*, 18 January 1990; Joint Publications Research Service—Eastern Europe, 9 May 1990.

30. *Danas*, 6 February 1990 in FBIS, 30 April 1990. Reportedly at the press conference after the Slovene delegates walked out of the LCY 14th Party Congress, the army also agreed that the work of the congress was illegitimate without Slovenia, Radio Ljubljana, 23 January 1990 in FBIS 24 January 1990.

31. Simić reported to the LCY committee in the Army that: "[O]ver the last 15 years or so [the federal party] allowed the republics and provinces to develop and consolidate their narrow national interests. . . . In circumstances of economic crisis these penetrated the LCY with negative economic, political, and ideological effects." Tanjug, 14 February 1990 in FBIS 16 February 1990.

32. Tanjug, 28 March 1990 in FBIS-EEU, 29 March 1990.

33. Tanjug, 18 May 1990 in FBIS-EEU, 21 May 1990.

34. Weekly press conference of Colonel Obradović, Tanjug, 9 May 1990 in FBIS-EEU, 10 May 1990.

35. Statement by the Federal Secretariat of National Defense that all political organizing should be banned from the armed forces, Belgrade Tanjug domestic service, 13 December 1990 in FBIS-EEU, 14 December 1990.

36. Note reports of a meeting between the Slovene leadership and Defense Secretary Kadijević just prior to the spring elections *Borba,* 19 April 1990 in FBIS-EEU, 23 April 1990, and with the new President of Croatia Franjo Tudjman during the crisis surrounding the Serbian minority in Knin. When Tudjman briefed the Croatian presidency on his talks with the SFRY presidency, the Croatian presidency specifically welcomed the statement that the "JNA neither has nor will participate in actions directed against the democratic government." The Army was also taking measures to call to account certain members of the armed forces who arbitrarily took part in the unrest. Tanjug, 22 August 1990 in FBIS-EEU, 23 August 1990.

37. Milan Andrejevich, "The Yugoslav Army in Kosovo: Unrest Spread to Macedonia," *RFE Report* (23 February 1990), 38-41.

38. *Narodna Armija* (Belgrade) 5 July 1990; quoted from Milan Andrejevich, "Serbia Cracks Down on Kosovo," *RFE Report* (27 July 1990), 48-53.

39. *The New York Times,* 20 August 1990.

40. English-language text of Borisav Jović's March 15 resignation and Milošević's March 16 speech, *Politika: The International Weekly* (Belgrade) 23-29 March 1991.

41. Statement by the Armed Forces Supreme Command Headquarters. Belgrade Domestic Service, 19 March 1991 in FBIS-EEU 91-053, 19 March 1991.

42. See Stephen Engelberg, "Carving out a Greater Serbia," *The New York Times Magazine,* 1 September 1991, 18-38.

43. Author's interview with then U.S. ambassador to Yugoslavia, Warren Zimmerman, in Belgrade, June 1991.

44. *Vreme* (23 September 1991): 5-12. In July the Prime Minister had gone on television and insisted to no avail that he had been left out of the decision-making loop by army commanders. Indeed, in Belgrade the popular reaction was that Marković was trying to save himself by abandoning the military establishment.

45. *Narodna Armija,* 6 July 1991; for an expanded account, see the army weekly English-language monograph, "The Truth About the Armed Conflict in Slovenia" (Belgrade: Narodna Armija Publishing House, 1991). Subsequently then Defense Minister Kadijević published his own personal account, *Moje vidjene raspada: Vojska bez država* (My Perspective on the Collapse: Army Without State.) (Belgrade: Politika, 1993).

46. Radio Belgrade, 6 July 1991.

47. Within Yugoslavia Serbianization of the YPA is sometimes dated from 1988-90, when conscripts were given the right to serve in their home republics. Evidence to the contrary can be seen in Defense Minister Kadijević's assurance to Croatian President Tudjman that members of the armed forces who took part in the August 1990 unrest in Knin would be "called to account," and in the army's later pledge to stay out of politics when the Serbian- sponsored state-of-emergency failed to gain acceptance by the state presidency in March 1991. There is no doubt, however, that Serbian dominance in the YPA increased when Slovene and Croatian officers were removed from responsible positions during the summer of 1991. *Vreme* (21 June 1993): 34.

48. *The New York Times,* 5 October 1991, and *Politika: The International Weekly,* 12-18 October 1991.

49. Repeated by Defense Minister Kadijević in the Hague, *The New York Times,* 11 October 1991.

50. On November 16, families of 40 Montenegrin soldiers told to report for duty held a sit-in in President Bulatović's office. *The New York Times* 22 November 1991.

51. Serbian reservists who left combat positions accused the army of "incompetence, meaningless casualties, and treason." *Politika: The International Weekly,* 5-11 October 1991.

52. Gow, *Legitimacy and the Military,* 25.

53. *Vreme* (23 September 1991): 12.

3

History Education and Yugoslav (Dis-)Integration

Wolfgang Höpken

INTRODUCTION

"Are complex societies able to develop a reasonable identity?" The German philosopher, Jürgen Habermas, asked this question in the mid-1970s in an article discussing the chances of modern societies developing a common identity capable of integrating different social classes, religious, and ethnic groups.[1] The Yugoslav society, complex as it was, can certainly serve as the most striking example for a negative answer to that question. Regardless of who bears responsibility for the country's split, Yugoslavia's failure resulted mainly from the lack of such a common identity among its nationalities and peoples.

What is called a society's common identity depends among other things on two variables: First, a set of "common values," which are not just imposed "general interests" or even ideological stereotypes,[2] but represent the cognition of rules and regulations or—in the words of Clifford Geertz—"common sense as a cultural system."[3] Second, a common identity usually is based on what has been called "historical memory," which determines "what should not be forgotten" in a certain community. This historical memory helps to differentiate one group from another; it bases group identity on the consciousness of a common tradition, and in so doing stimulates solidarity and loyalty among its members.

Collective memory and group identity, as cultural theory has stressed, are closely linked together.[4] Ethnic groups and nations, therefore, have been defined as "communities of memories"— "*Erinnerungsgemeinschaften*" as Max Weber called it.[5] While a common value system is rooted in normative rights, institutions, and common perceptions of the present and prospected future, a common historical memory is a construction of the past, it is an "invented tradition."[6] It exists as a "set of codes," both narrative and symbolic, transmitted by communication and rites and forms of "ceremonic communications." (The famous "Gazimestan" manifestation, celebrating the 600th anniversary of the battle of Kosovo Polje in 1989, which played a prominent role in the mobilization of Serbian politics under Slobodan Milošević, probably can be seen as a paradigm for this kind of "ceremonic communication.") Last but not least, professional historiography and historical education are among the institutions that create this common memory.

Multiethnic societies usually find it harder to develop a common identity. Their attempts to develop a value system and common historical memory, going beyond ethnic boundaries, are always in tension with the individual ethnic group's need to stress its own separate historical memory, to affirm its own identity and group solidarity. Certainly, for a country like Yugoslavia, it was even more difficult to create such a common memory capable of integrating its different ethnic groups.

After all, a historical identity is usually more stable and its integrative capacity higher if it can be based on the memory of a "long common past." (This is exactly why all ethnic groups tend to draw a picture of their own past that claims a longtime ethnic continuity.) The Yugoslav state, "young" as it was, could hardly refer to a long common tradition among its peoples; it simply had only a short story to tell. Socialist Yugoslavia was in an even worse position because part of the common Yugoslav past, namely the interwar experience, due to its biased character and national antagonisms could hardly contribute to a common memory favoring a Yugoslav identity.

Already then, pre-socialist attempts to develop a Yugoslav identity by creating a common memory through education had failed. Historical education before the Yugoslav unification, as Charles Jelavich has shown in his research on pre-1918 South Slav textbooks, did not succeed in promoting a common identity. While nineteenth and early twentieth-century Croatian textbooks were written more in the spirit of "Yugoslavism," Serbian textbooks in particular up to the eve of World War I favored a historical memory based predominantly on Serbian national traditions. None of the books, Serbian, Croatian, or Slovenian, transmitted a substantial knowledge of each other among the South Slav peoples. "The educational system of Serbia and Croatia," as Charles Jelavich has concluded, "did not adequately prepare students for South Slav Union in 1918."[7]

Interwar Yugoslavia's historical education was no more successful. During the first decade after the establishment of the new Yugoslav state in 1918, textbooks more or less followed their pre-1918 patterns. It was only after the Yugoslav king had abolished the constitution in 1929 in order to shape the process of nation-building, that the educational system was also reformed in the spirit of Yugoslavism. Refraining mostly from openly hostile stereotypes and images and, indeed, reflecting even more the other South Slav nations' histories than in the pre-1918 decades, the new textbooks were nevertheless not better prepared for bringing the Yugoslav peoples together. Now stressing an idealized picture of the so-called three-named-nation of Serbs, Croats, and Slovenes, their common links and constant desire for a common state in history, this attempt to build a collective historical identity around the idea of a monarchistic Yugoslavism failed for at least two reasons. First of all, it obviously contradicted the political reality of an unsolved national question; the presented picture did not coincide with recent political experiences and therefore lacked persuasive content. Secondly, even the new textbooks, written in the "spirit of Yugoslavism," were, in their underlying assumptions, promoting a Serbian-based historical consciousness. It would be too simple to call it just a greater-Serbian view of the past, but by making the tradition of a state and the "dynasty" the didactical fix points and key issues in their presentation of the past, most interwar textbooks gave Serbian history a strong advantage and left the objectives of historical education highly biased.[8]

Titoist Yugoslavia apparently tried to learn from its predecessor's inability to develop a common identity among its citizens. Yugoslav identity was not to be built by marginalizing individual identities in favor of one ethnic group, but on "nonethnic grounds." Instead of basing such a collective identity on alleged and suspicious common ethnic and language ties, Yugoslavia's Communists founded their paradigm for solidarity among Yugoslav ethnic groups and nations on two "supra-ethnic" elements. First, they emphasized the "all-Yugoslav" (and not just South Slav) historical experience of a joint struggle for freedom, independence, and a common state during the "National Liberation War," symbolized in the famous slogan of *"bratstvo i jedinstvo"* (brotherhood and unity). Second, they relied on a common sense of ideological values, coded in the term *self-managed socialism*. Both elements were intended to offer a specific and apparently unique Yugoslav political identity to all its peoples. Anticipating that highly fragmented societies need a kind of "universal ethics" to develop an integrative capacity, these two patterns were meant to replace the missing ethnic and cultural homogeneity by a consensus of values and common historical memory. Of course, both of these patterns were primarily designed to fulfill the party's need for political support. They had first of all to legitimize the party's rise to and claim for power; in addition, they were intended to homogenize the society under the imperative of an undisputable system of ideological norms for behavior.[9] But at a first glance, both terms indeed seemed as favorable for integrating the multiethnic community as for stabilizing the societal and ideological status quo of socialist rule. The appeal to the National Liberation War was not only an attempt to gain a *self*-legitimacy for the ruling party (in contrast to the other East European communist parties with their mostly imposed legitimacy). It also proclaimed a short but important common historical tradition going beyond individual ethnic experiences and histories. By referring to self-management, they expected to establish a *value*-based legitimacy that would count for more than the usual communist rhetoric.

TEXTBOOKS AND HISTORICAL EDUCATION DURING THE TITO ERA

The Yugoslav system, no less than other socialist systems, has tried to implement its identity concept by means of political socialization; education has played a prominent role in that attempt. "Self-managed socialism" and "bratstvo i jedinstvo" as the key issues of the identity concept were the most desired values among the educational objectives and therefore lay at the very center of all textbooks during the entire Tito era. While both core paradigms were rather simply constructed during the first two years of socialist Yugoslavism up to the mid-1940s and were modeled on traditional patterns of political mobilization and "agitprop" style,[10] later on, they had to become more sophisticated. The ideological ambitions of self-management proved difficult to put into practice, and reality showed more conflicts and contradictions than had been predicted, hindering attempts to present this objective convincingly in education. Moreover, ethnic self-consciousness among Yugoslavia's nations and nationalities became more apparent after the mid-1960s, a process that the party not only had to answer with a more sophisticated federalism and more respect for ethnic identities,[11] but that they also had to reflect in textbooks and in the teaching of history. The task of balancing the individual ethnic identities; that is, balancing the appeal to one's own separate historical memory with the overall Yugoslav values and historical consciousness on which the party's legitimacy was based, now became even more challenging.

Already from a first and superficial didactical view, however, Yugoslav textbooks were not very original in trying to respond to this challenge. Textbooks were usually written in boring language, overloaded with text on gray paper, reflecting the little respect that the rulers actually had for school and education. In their content, history textbooks constantly lagged behind the more sophisticated results that Yugoslav academic historiography had gained. As Croat historian Mirjana Gross has recently put it, academic historiography had to work "in the shadow of stereotypes" of party policy, but "without direct political pressure from the Central Committee."[12] History and social science textbooks, in contrast, were not permitted any such maneuvering room. Their contents had to be in strict accordance with party policy and the necessities of party legitimacy were always at the core of their objectives. It was the "para-historiography" of those historians close to politics from whom textbook authors drew their references.[13] Written with the obvious intention *not* to stimulate the students' individuality and independent thinking, they presented simple explanations and undisputed evaluations of the past, leaving no room for any multi-perspective views. While during the late Tito era there were some halfhearted attempts to improve the didactical quality of the textbooks, historical education in general remained poor.[14]

Self-management, as mentioned earlier, was one of the core objectives for history and social science textbooks. And, as a comprehensive content analysis of Yugoslav textbooks by a Belgrade group of educational specialists and psychologists in the early 1980s revealed, creating loyalty and identification through the idea of self-managed socialism was still the dominant educational objective in all textbooks from elementary language books up to high-school history texts. In its content, this objective hardly differed from the official rhetoric about self-management, reflecting not even the level of discussion and Marxist theory that had developed over the years.[15] Universal civic values based on individual rights such as "the realization of the rights of men" or "standing in for democracy," on the other hand, ranked far behind in the catalog of the desired values of education. Even a strong army was a much more visible objective transmitted by textbooks than such civic society values. Students were to develop mainly an ideological not a civic society identity.[16] In this aspect, Yugoslav textbooks did not differ essentially from textbooks and educational objectives in other socialist countries, basing their main educational goal not on the didactical principle of individuality as in western civic education, but favoring a collective identity. Such an education—not just in Yugoslavia, but in all socialist countries—simply produced a set of codes necessary for behaving in conformity with the existing political system, but nothing like an identification with the system.

Especially in textbooks and educational material for the lower grades, the ideological values were often closely linked with Tito himself, identifying the system strongly with the leader.[17] In identifying the system with the ruler, however, education became a victim of its own objectives; for a system so closely bound to its leader could hardly be transformed in the post-Tito era. Just as the "system-values" simply broke away when the system was shaken in the late 1980s, so too did its identification with its former leader lose all credibility. It might, of course, be highly questionable whether the system, due to its lack of democracy and economic efficiency, could have developed something like a stable, value-based Yugoslav identity that could have been transformed in the post-Tito era; certainly, the chosen bases of education did not prepare students well for post-Tito conditions.

Within the general purpose of legitimizing the system, history textbooks in particular had the task of affirming the ideological objective of system loyalty by enhancing the existing system to a historic necessity. They did so by presenting a picture that restructured the past almost exclusively around the party and its ideology. The exaggerated share of the so-called History of the Worker's Movement in textbooks (regardless of the fact that the Yugoslav lands are even

TABLE 3.1
THE DISTRIBUTION OF SUBJECTS IN SOUTH SLAV TEXTBOOKS
IN THE NINETEENTH CENTURY AND UP TO 1918

Number/Percentage of pages that appear in text on:

	Publication Year/Pages*	Europe/ World	Other Balkan/ Neighbor	Other Yugoslav/ All Yugoslav	National
Serbian Textbooks:	1993/75(1)	18 (24 %)	9 (12 %)	10 (13 %)	35 (46.6 %)
	1992/118(2)	61 (51.6 %)	7 (5.9 %)	23 (19.5 %)	4 (20.3 %)
	1976/216(15)	47 (21.8 %)	8 (3.7 %)	89 (41.2 %)	5 (30.1 %)
Croatian Textbooks:	1988/126(6)	59 (46.8 %)	—	42 (33.3 %)	15 (11.9 %)
Slovenian Textbooks:	1992/53(2)	40 (75.5 %)	1 (1.9 %)	3 (5.7 %)	7 (13.2 %)
	1992/165(3)	140 (66 %)	21 (9.9 %)	13 (6.1 %)	37 (17.4 %)
	1991/155(4)	57 (36.7 %)	2 (1.3 %)	53 (34.8 %)	27 (17.4 %)
	1973/150(8)	54 (36 %)	—	51 (34 %)	36 (24 %)
Macedonian Textbooks:	1992/129(2)	42 (32.6 %)	9 (7 %)	17 (13.2 %)	59 (45.7 %)
	1992/165(3)	43 (26.1 %)	14 (8.5 %)	21 (12.7 %)	82 (49.7 %)
	1992/94(5)	13 (13.7 %)	11 (11.7 %)	18 (19.1 %)	46 (48.9 %)
	1972/230(7)	55 (23.9 %)	10 (4.3 %)	86 (37.4 %)	78 (33.9 %)
	1972/316(10)	145 (45.9 %)	14 (4.4 %)	67 (21.2 %)	83 (26.3 %)

*Numbers in parentheses refer to specific texts listed in annex.

TABLE 3.2
CENTRAL SUBJECTS OF POST-1918 HISTORY AND THEIR REFLECTION
IN YUGOSLAV AND POST-YUGOSLAV TEXTBOOKS (IN NUMBERS OF PAGES)*

Subject	Serbia (1)1993	Serbia (11)1981	Croatia (6)1988	Croatia (1)1993	Slovenia (6)1991	Slovenia (7)1976	Macedonia (1)1992	Macedonia (6)1982
October Revolution	2	10	6	2.5	6	7	3	—[1]
Unification of 1918	3.5	6.5	6	5	3.5	2	4	2
Interwar Yugoslavia								
Politics	8.5	4	6	5	3.25	3.25	2.5	1.5
National Question	1	2	3.5	7[2]	5.5[2]	6[2]	16[2]	7.5
Social Issues	—	1	3	—	.5	.25	—	1.5
Communist Party	.25	10	12	—	7	3.5	4	8.5
World War II								
General and Occupation	8	8.5	30	37	22	24.5	21	26
Partisans	26	44	39	27	40	43	33	68
Ustaša/Independent State of Croatia	3.25	.25	.75	—	.25	.5	—	.5
Četniks/Other "Traitors"	2	.75	.5	2	1.5	1	—	.5

Socialist Yugoslavia

Socialist Transformation	3.5	8.5	—	9	3.5	8	4.5	3.5
Self-management	1.5	14	—	16[3]	5	2.5	9	6.5
National Question	6[4]	1	—	17[5]	4[2]	—	11[4]	—
LCY	—	2	—	4	—	—	—	—
Foreign Policy	3.5	1.5	—	8	4.5	4.5	3	5.5

* Numbers in parentheses refer to specific texts listed in annex.

[1] The book starts with 1918.

[2] 1976—only on Slovenes in Austria; 1991—four pages on Slovenes in Austria; 1993—three pages on Slovenes in Austria.

[3] Three pages on the Yugoslav crisis during the 1980s and three pages on the disintegration of Yugoslavia since 1990.

[4] On the disintegration process of Yugoslavia during the 1990s.

[5] Twelve pages on the disintegration process of Yugoslavia.

[6] Two and a half pages on the autocephalous Macedonian church, eight and a half pages on Macedonians in Bulgaria, Greece, Albania, and abroad.

now predominantly agrarian), the equally exaggerated treatment of the Communist Party in chapters dealing with interwar Yugoslavia, usually occupying nine to ten pages or more (which was in striking discrepancy to the party's real political significance before 1941), and the even more prevalent share of party and Partisan politics and military events in the chapter on World War II, covering usually more than half of the entire second World War period in the textbooks and almost four fifths of the description of the war on Yugoslav soil (see table 3.2), are just some examples of how the young generation's historical consciousness was preoccupied with party history, leaving almost no room for alternative historical memories. It was not so much the biased and one-sided interpretations of crucial issues that made textbooks so problematic during the Tito era, as their unbalanced and selective historical memory. Historical education of this type ultimately produced exactly the vacuum that would be filled with historical myths and prejudices later on when, during the years of increasing national antagonism in the late 1980s and 1990s, the official views on history more and more faded away with the party's decreasing legitimacy and control. Yet while critics often lamented the little real effect that this kind of education obviously had within the process of socialization, bemoaning the little and superficial knowledge students had about the foundations of Yugoslav socalism,[18] their remarks had no significant consequences for educational practice.

An even more important element in the party's obvious inability to develop a common Yugoslav identity through education could be seen in its approach to the second fundamental educational objective, "bratstvo i jedinstvo." While an education for "bratstvo i jedinstvo" during the 1950s and early 1960s was clearly based on a unitarian Yugoslavism,[19] expressed in the predominance of the Yugoslav component, education and textbooks since the late 1960s and 1970s reflected the process of federalization under way. With the increasing shift in competences toward the republics, educational policy now passed almost exclusively into the hands of the republics. As a result, textbooks now had to transmit the general system values and concept of Yugoslav identity within a concept of separate national historical identity.[20]

Educational policy since the 1970s constitutional amendments and the 1974 Constitution certainly led to a remarkable respect for ethnic individuality in education (something worth remembering given today's circumstances), guaranteeing even smaller ethnic groups an educational system in their own language and culture.[21] These concessions, however, could hardly be considered sufficient to prepare students for peaceful cohabitation in a multiethnic and multicultural society. As had occurred with self-management, "bratstvo i jedinstvo" became more and more a noneducational objective whose real effect on the students' socialization was very limited. Despite, or more likely because of its prominent place in textbooks and its incessant repetition, the slogan degenerated into an empty cliché.[22] What's more, by reducing "bratstvo i jedinstvo" to an empty stereotype, the textbooks did not provide the students with any competences for behavior.

Even a cursory view of the structure of textbooks indicates why the educational system had so little effect in making "bratstvo i jedinstvo" a value that could have an impact on behavior. First of all, the texts provided only a kind of a "numeric Yugoslavism," based on proportional consideration of both Yugoslav and separate national histories. The party simply applied to education the same kind of superficial quotas that it had implemented since 1971-74 in composing state and party organs. The League of Communists, itself, being caught in its own authoritarian limits, failed to develop a kind of "conflict-culture" to deal with ethnic distinctiveness, but rather escaped into a system of "guided ethnic management." While this system could at best provide a solution for coping with multiethnicity in institutions and in resource distribution, in education it could not substitute for didactical concepts on interethnic learning and the spread of competence in dealing with others. To put it a bit simplistically: history textbooks usually presented "a little bit of Yugoslav history, a little bit of your history, a little bit more of my history." A Vojvodina textbook from the late 1970s provides a clear example: in dealing with nineteenth-century history it offered two and a half pages of history on Serbia, two pages on Bosnia-Hercegovina, two on Montenegro and Macedonia, two on Croatia and Vojvodina, one and a half on Slovenia and, because a lot of Romanians live in Vojvodina, one page for the Romanian "national movement." Table 3.1 illustrates this reciprocity in more detail: most of the textbooks show an almost identical share of "Yugoslav history," while descriptions of the other Yugoslav nations' and nationalities' history differing only between a total share of 34 percent and 41 percent among the individual republics. The space dedicated to one's own "national history" was usually the largest relative to the other individual nations. As a rule, however, it ranked behind the entire Yugoslav history in the curricula. Two deviations from this pattern are striking: while the share of "national" history was remarkably low in Croatian textbooks of the 1980s (just 12 percent in the 1988 textbook!), it was remarkably high in Macedonian ones (37 percent). Both undoubtedly reflected the political situation during the late Tito era in those republics. The figure for Croatia clearly mirrored the antinationalist climate in Croatia following the events of 1970-1971, which contributed to the famous educational policy of Stipe Šuvar seeking to reduce national history in favor of not only Yugoslav history but Marxist social education. Šuvar's policy obviously produced a strong reduction in the amount of Croatian history taught in class. Meanwhile, the constant attempt to strengthen a Macedonian national identity, gave education there the advantage of a remarkably more extended emphasis on national history than in the other republics. (Unfortunately I did not have access to Albanian textbooks from Kosovo, which might have shown a similar pattern during the years of increased provincial autonomy between 1971 and 1981.)

From the very beginning, however, this kind of numeric Yugoslavism in the teaching of history gave room for frustration on all sides. The relatively little space it allowed for national history sometimes created the feeling of a national identity losing its historical basis, a fear that was especially articulated in Croatia during the late 1970s and 1980s.[23] On the other hand, the system led to almost constant complaints about the students' little knowledge of the history of the individual Yugoslav nations.[24] While some simply demanded more "teaching for Yugoslavism,"[25] which hardly had any chance under conditions of late Titoist federalism, others more realistically recognized the fundamental didactical problem of how to teach a separate national and common Yugoslav historical identity at once. A joint research group of Belgrade and Zagreb-based historians in the early 1980s revealed how little the historical knowledge transmitted by various Yugoslav history textbooks had in common, but they had no alternative to offer—*"recepte nemamo."*[26] As in academic historiography, which since the early 1960s had increasingly abandoned the task of writing a common "Yugoslav history" and that, since the 1970s had become more and more fragmented, Yugoslav textbook authors and educational specialists were increasingly unable to develop a didactical concept linking a respect for individual historical identity with some kind of common Yugoslav identity.

What had even a greater impact on the deficit of education is the fact that the *national question* was never really made an objective for education. The party's educational goal was to make the students believe that the issue was in good hands, not to prepare them for national diversity and conflict. Given the significance of the national question in the history of the Yugoslav peoples, it is more than striking how little room this topic occupied in the teaching of history and the social sciences. Neither on the national question in interwar Yugoslavia nor on national conflicts in postwar Yugoslavia did Yugoslav students learn anything substantial in school. Surprisingly enough, even Croatian and Serbian textbooks presented very little information on this topic and were obviously reluctant to bring up the history of the Serbian-Croatian conflict too frankly in class. Only about two to three pages in Serbian and Croatian textbooks were dedicated to this crucial issue in interwar history, while the history of the Communist Party took up almost five times as much. Only Slovenian and Macedonian textbooks gave more room to the national question, dedicating most of that space, however—for obvious foreign policy reasons—to the fate of "co-nationals" abroad in Austria, Bulgaria, and Greece.

While the scant attention paid to the national question is significant, another didactical dilemma in this context is even more obvious: The national question was never presented in textbooks from the perspective of a "normal" conflict, deriving from ethnic, cultural, and social distinctiveness, and from conceivably well-founded differing interests. Inasmuch as textbooks during Titoist Yugoslavia dealt with national antagonisms, they presented them either in terms of "bourgeois class conflicts" or, as concerned postwar Yugoslavia, as more or less settled by party politics, making conflicts the result of "nationalistic deviations." In dealing with the interwar national question all textbooks (including Serbian ones!) simply followed the crude lines of the official party historiography, presenting national conflicts in interwar Yugoslavia as a consequence of the Serbian bourgeoisie's desire for hegemony and as a result of quarrels, but also bargaining and foul arrangements among all three South Slav bourgeoisies.[27] This picture, incidentally, lagged far behind the much more sophisticated interpretations arrived at by Yugoslav academic historians since the 1970s. The only conclusion students could draw from such a presentation was that as long as there was no bourgeoisie there could no longer be a national question.

The party's attempt to reduce national antagonisms to "class-conflicts" was most obvious in textbooks dealing with the bloodiest national conflict in Yugoslavia's history—World War II. The "Ustaša," the "Četniks," the question of terror and ethnic violence, World War II as a civil war, in short, all the hot topics that should have become a major subject for propaganda and nationalist manipulation in the dawn of the second Yugoslav state were never really made a subject for teaching. While the Partisans' strategy and victory occupied most of the space, only a few lines or at best one or two pages of general rhetorical condemnation addressed these substantial problems. In the 40 or 50 pages on Partisan war actions, usually little more than one or two pages dealt with the immediate Serb-Croat relations and conflicts during the war. And where textbooks did refer to these topics they did so once again by means of a superficially balanced view of reciprocity: all nations had their traitors, they all committed cruelties, no nation had more or less guilt. Only the "supra-ethnic" Partisans were on the right side, while quislings and traitors of all nationalities, together with the foreign occupiers were on the opposing side. Following this paradigm, Serbian textbooks of course mentioned that the "Ustaša had committed mass cruelties against Serbs, Jews, Gypsies, and dissident Croats" without, however, laying too much emphasis on that fact and generally avoiding the sensitive question of the number of victims. The texts were not eager to make explicit the differences between the Ustaša and Croats but, following the paradigm of reciprocity, they did add to their tales of Ustaša terror the fact that Četniks had committed crimes as well. The approach of Croatian textbooks to these topics was not substantially different, only stressing a bit more the fact that Croats should not be identified with the Ustaša and giving some more emphasis to Četnik behavior.[28] By presenting World War II in this way Yugoslav textbooks were avoiding conflicts that had emerged among those historians who had opened the historiographic Pandora's box, initiating discussions about each individual nation's "responsibility" for the fall of Yugoslavia in 1941 and collaboration with the Nazis. In Tito's time, these discussions were usually stopped by the party before they could become a source of national conflict.[29] History education's reluctance to make controversial issues a matter for textbooks or for in-class discussion found its bitter revenge in the late 1980s when historians and the historiography of this period would play a substantial role in heating up national emotions. The so-called Jasenovac controversy of the late 1980s and early 1990s, in which the question of the number of victims in the Jasenovac concentration camp was cynically instrumentalized for politics by both Serbs and Croats, probably would not have contributed to the climate of hatred so strongly had the topic been dealt with in a reasonable manner in schools during the Tito era.

A look at how the Partisan war was described in textbooks also reveals their extensively militaristic character. Reading Yugoslav textbooks on this topic, one is reminded of what the German poet, Gottfried Benn, wrote in the 1920s after an encounter with a Weimar Republic textbook: "I opened a textbook, any page, it deals with the year 1805: one victory in a battle at sea, two armistices, one military alliance, one restructures his troops, the others draws back (etc., etc.)— all on one page: it is the medical bulletin of a lunatic." It is not necessary to go into the details of how the Partisan war was idealized and how extensively wars in general were presented in Yugoslav textbooks. With their almost endless descriptions of battles, as well as by means of illustrations and by adding literature and poems, textbooks were reconciling students to the phenomenon of war.[30] Even without being too mechanical, one might well conclude that such textbooks were intentionally promoting an understanding that war might be not only something "normal" but legitimate, for which one must always be ready. Building political legitimacy and collective memory on an idealized picture of warfare, Titoist textbooks contributed to what Norbert Elias has called the "habitus of sanctionalized and ritualized violence."[31] The recent violent confrontation suggests the impact that such an education might have had on students.

Ultimately, it seems that the party's didactic approach was not to present the distinctiveness of peoples and make diversity the basic objective of learning. While education in postwar Yugoslavia allowed individual ethnic groups to be educated in their own languages and be informed about others on a superficial level, it did not develop the skills needed to "deal with others." The problem with textbooks in Titoist Yugoslavia, therefore, was not that they promoted nationalism (they did not), but that they did so little to contribute to a political culture prepared for the dangers of ethnocentrism. Their weaknesses in terms of concepts and content paved the way for alternative historical memories that apparently did offer a more convincing historical identity once the system came under nationalist pressure. To be fair, textbooks and the teaching of history shared this deficit not only with academic historiography—which, despite its internal variety along ethnic lines, did no more to contribute to a real pluralistic discourse, especially on "hot topics"—but also with an overall fragile political culture that was never really able to rest upon a value-based support.

HISTORICAL EDUCATION IN THE YUGOSLAV CRISIS (1990–92)

That history and historiography have played a prominent part among the driving forces that have turned national antagonisms into violent conflict in Yugoslavia has been often recognized and described in writings on the "Yugoslav crisis." Historical topics have been employed by all sides to legitimize the new political elites and their politics.[32] Naturally, historical education has also felt the repercussions of the breakup of Yugoslavia. All the post-Yugoslav states hurried to change their educational system, while, in the meantime, a first generation of history and civic studies textbooks appeared as a reflection of these political changes. All these educational reforms took place under the pretext of freeing history textbooks from their former ideological burdens and dogmatism and have indeed eliminated many formerly biased interpretations. Yet their impact has been extraordinarily unfavorable in many other respects. Surprisingly or not, the most recent developments in textbooks and historical education reveal not only some remarkable parallels, especially between Serbian and Croatian textbooks, despite their fundamentally differing contents, but also a good deal of continuity in their didactical principles.

To start with the parallels: strengthening national identity is now the unquestioned leading goal of education in all post-Yugoslav republics. All recent textbooks in all of the former Yugoslav republics under consideration here strongly reduced the "Yugoslav" aspect of history, from 30 to 40 percent in Titoist times down to 13 to 20 percent of the entire volume in the Serbian, Croatian, and Macedonian cases, and down to just 6 percent in the Slovenian case (see table 3.1). While previously, a common past of the Yugoslav people was stressed and often exaggerated in order to legitimize a common presence, the new textbooks obviously intend to demonstrate an entirely separate past in order to legitimize a separate future.[33]

On the other hand, the history of each successor state's own "co-nationals," that is, Serbs in Bosnia and Croatia and Croats in Serbia and Bosnia, have now gained particular attention in textbooks. For example, in preparing "a new unified textbook of the national history of the Serbian people," the ministry for education and textbook authors thereby responded to widespread criticism that, since the late 1980s, had complained about the "artificial division" of Serbian history in the old textbooks and the absence in them of the history of Serbs outside Serbia, which had left "generations of children deprived of the knowledge of whole parts of their own national history."[34] This renationalization of historical education is also characteristic of the most recent Croat textbooks and of the 1992 Macedonian textbooks, although in a somewhat less rigid dimension.

A second common feature of all post-Yugoslav textbooks, closely connected with the one just mentioned, can be described as *"de-Yugoslavisization,"* that is, a reevaluation and certain amount of self-distancing from the idea of Yugoslavism and the experiences of the two Yugoslav states. This concept is most drastically expressed in the latest Croatian textbooks, which focus on the Croatian "national state" as the guiding idea and fulfillment of Croatian history. The historical significance of phenomena like "Illyrianism" and "Yugoslavism" have been greatly reduced and are, at best, presented in the suspicious light of "illusionism." Both Yugoslav states, the "bourgeois" and the socialist one, are, in this picture, presented in the light of a continuous suppression of the national rights of the Croatian people.[35]

The attitude toward Yugoslavism and the Yugoslav state is not as pejorative in Serbian textbooks but is clearly ambivalent. Historical memory no longer sees the establishment of the Yugoslav state in 1918 and 1943 as *the* crucial issue, but focuses on the continuity of *Serbian* history.

The immediate consequences of current politics are, of course, most obvious in dealing with socialist Yugoslavia. All textbooks are siding with the politics of their current political leadership in their treatment of this issue. Tito's experiment has earned strong condemnation from all sides, again with the exception of Macedonia, and again with a striking similarity in their arguments, especially in Serbian and Croatian textbooks. Indeed, a third common feature in these textbooks is a clear trend toward "de-Titoization." This is not surprising and was, of course, necessary, bearing in mind the old textbooks with their repulsive personality cult. De-Titoization in the new textbooks, however, often means nothing but an exchange of heroes. While Tito's historical significance had been excessively inflated in former textbooks, now he is treated simply as a traitor to both Croatian and Serbian national interests.[36] In both Serbian and Croatian textbooks, history also serves as an immediate form of legitimation for the current political elite. While the most recent Serbian book simply declares the Seventh Session of the League of Communists of Serbia in 1987, which brought Milošević to power, to be the turning point toward the democratization of society and the defense of Serbian interests, Croatian textbooks present the presidency of Franjo Tudjman as the fulfillment of Croatian history.

What becomes obvious in comparing Serbian and Croatian textbooks is that both are following a very similar didactical concept in presenting their own history, despite their totally antagonistic contents. In each case, their own history is presented as a history of suffering, deprivation, and endangerment, caused always by the other nation.

An extreme example of this stereotyped view of history is presented in the textbooks' coverage of World War II. In contrast to Titoist times, the Ustaša terror now finds a great echo in Serbian textbooks, without any attempt to differentiate between Ustaša and Croats. In this way, history-teaching silently supports the view so widely aired in public during the Serbian-Croat confrontation since 1990, of Croats as a "genocidal people." Meanwhile, Croatian textbooks, being constructed entirely around the didactical fix point of Croatian statehood, have credited the Ustaša regime with having fulfilled the historical dream of a Croatian state, leaving more or less aside the question of its political character. While Partisans and Četniks are accused of a planned genocide against Croats and Muslims, the Ustaša terror has been downplayed to an "understandable reaction" to former injustices against Croats.

It may sound a bit stereotyped to posit the Slovenes as "the good" in comparison to "the bad" and "the ugly." But Slovene textbooks *are* trying in a much fairer way to cope with the past and with recent events. Of course, in dealing with the most recent developments, the latest Slovenian textbooks are in full accordance with Slovenian politics,[37] and are no less heavily "Sloveno-centristic." Nonetheless, they are clearly avoiding the heavily biased features of both the Croat and Serb texts. To be fair, one has to admit that in both Serbia and Croatia there has been some strong criticism against these textbooks. Yet the real impact of this reaction has so far been very limited.

Reading history textbooks in today's post-Yugoslavia is in many ways just as frustrating as it was during the Tito era. In both cases, history is not presented as open. The texts suggest no alternatives for the evaluations offered, and students have no options from which to choose. Historical identity is not based on discourse but on ready solutions. Education like this does not open the student's ability to develop a "historical *consciousness*," but simply distributes ready-made "historical *images*"[38] according to the nineteenth-century didactical standard on which textbooks from both sides are still based. Their main intention obviously is not to develop a "civic identity" based on an individual's critical examination of the past, but to supply political elites with legitimacy and to prepare students for the elites' current policies. Not only are contemporary Serbian and Croatian textbooks united in these crucial deficits,[39] they also show a striking degree of didactical continuity with Titoist Yugoslavia's historical education. While neither academic historiography nor history education in Tito's Yugoslavia prevented Partisans from turning into nationalists, it is also not likely that post-Yugoslav textbooks will help educate people in a spirit of a rapprochement on the basis of a civic society. Having finished his review of literature for the interwar German textbook mentioned earlier, Gottfried Benn came to the conclusion that, "words are sometimes more criminal than murder; and the thoughts will take revenge among the heroes and the masses." In this sense, just as the former textbooks did not build barriers against today's conflicts, today's textbooks could very well pave the way for future confrontations.

Annex: List of Textbooks Used in Tables

Serbian Textbooks

(1)*Istorija za VIII. razred osnovne škole* (Beograd: 1993).

(2)*Istorija za II. razred četvrtogodišnih stručnih škola* (Beograd; Novi Sad: 199).

(3)*Istorija za II. razred gimnazije prirodno-matematičkog smera* (Beograd: 1992).

(4)*Istorija za VII. razred osnovne škole* (Beograd; Novi Sad: 1992).

(5)*Istorija za I. razred trogodišnjih stručnih škola* (Beograd; Novi Sad: 1992).

(6) *Istorija za III. razred gimnazije prirodno-matematičnog smera i IV. razred gimnazije opšteg i društvenog-jezičkog smera* (Beograd; Novi Sad: 1992).

(7) *Istorija III. razred gimnazije opšteg i društveno-jezičkog smera i III. razred stručnih škola* (Beograd; Novi Sad: 1992).

(8) *Istorija za IV. razred srednje škole (kulturnološke-jezičke, pravno-biotehničke, prosvetne i dramske struke)* (Beograd; Novi Sad: 1992).

(9) *Istorija za VII. razred osnovne škole* (Beograd; Novi Sad: 1990).

(10) *Istorija za VIII. razred osnovne škole* (Beograd; Novi Sad: 1990).

(11) *Istorija za VIII. razred osnovne škole* (Beograd: 1981).

(12) *Istorija najnovijeg doba za IV. razred gimnazije* (Beograd: 1976).

(13) *Istorija najnovijeg doba za IV. razred gimnazije* (Beograd: 1973).

(14) *Istorija za VIII. razred osnovne škole* (Beograd: 1976).

(15) *Istorija za VII. razred osnovne škole* (Beograd: 1973).

Croatian Textbooks

(1) *Povijest za VIII. razred osnovne škole* (Zagreb: 1992).

(2) *Povijest za VII. razred osnovne škole* (Zagreb: 1992).

(3) *Povijesna čitanka 4* (Zagreb: 1992).

(4) *Čovek u svom svijetu* (Zagreb: 1992).

(5) *Moja domovina* (Zagreb: 1991).

(6) *Povijest 2. Udžbenik za usmjereno obrazovanje* (Zagreb: 1988).

Slovenian Textbooks

(1) *20. stoletje. Zgodovina za 8. razred osnovne šole* (Ljubljana: 1993).

(2) *Zgodovina 2 za tehniške in druge strokovne šole* (Ljubljana: 1992).

(3) *Zgodovina 3 Srednje izobrazevanje* (Ljubljana: 1992).

(4) *Zgodovina 7* (Ljubljana: 1991).

(5) *Zgodovina 2 Srednje izobrazevanje* (Ljubljana: 1991).

(6) *Zgodovina 8* (Ljubljana: 1991).

(7) *Zgodovina 8 za osmi razred* (Ljubljana: 1976).

(8)*Zgodovina 7 za sedmi razred* (Ljubljana: 1973).

(9)*Zgodovina 8 za osmi razred osnovnih šol* (Ljubljana: 1969).

Macedonian Textbooks

(1)*Istorija 7 za VII oddelenie* (Skopje: 1992).

(2)*Istorija 8 za VIII.oddelenie* (Skopje: 1992).

(3)*Istorija za III.klas gimnazija* (Skopje: 1992).

(4)*Istorija za IV.klas gimnazija* (Skopje: 1992).

(5)*Istorija za II.klas za site struki* (Skopje: 1992).

(6)*Istorija za VIII.oddelenie* (Skopje: 1982).

(7)*Istorija za VII.oddeleni* (Skopje: 1972).

(8)*Istorija za III.klas gimnazija prirodno-matematička nasoka* (Skopje: 1972).

(9)*Istorija za IV.klas opštestveno-jezična nasoka* (Skopje: 1972).

(10)*Istorija za III.klas gimnazija* (Skopje: 1972).

Montenegrin Textbooks

(1)*Istorija za VII. razred osnovne škole* (Titograd: 1983).

(2)*Istorija za VIII.razred osnovne škole* (Titograd: 1982).

Bosnian Textbooks

(1)*Istorija za 8.razred osnovne škole* (Sarajevo: 1985).

(2)*Istorija za 2.razred srednjeg usmjerenog obrazovanja* (Sarajevo: 1983).

(3)*Istorija—Povijest 8* (Sarajevo: 1979).

(4)*Istorija 7* (Sarajevo: 1973).

Vojvodinian textbooks

(1)*Istorija za 7.razred osnovnog vaspitanja i obrazovanja* (Novi Sad: 1983).

(2)*Istorija za VIII.razred osnovnog vaspitanja i obrazovanja* (Novi Sad) 1980.

(3)*Istorija za IV.godinu osnovnog obrazovanja odraslih* (Novi Sad: 1980).

Notes

1. Jürgen Habermas, "Können komplexe Gesellschaften eine vernunftige Identität ausbilden?" in *Zur Rekonstruktion des Historischen Materialismus*, 2nd ed. (Frankfurt/M: Edition suhrkamp, 1976), 92.

2. On the difference between "common identity" and "general interests," see Jean L. Cohen and Andrew Arato, *Civil Society and Political Theories* (Cambridge, MA: London: The MIT Press, 1992) 367-71. For a different perspective, see Ernest Gellner, *Conditions of Liberty* (London: Penguin, 1994). For the character of "value systems" under communism in Eastern Europe, see Ken Jowitt, "Organizational Approach to the Study of Political Culture in Marxist-Leninist Systems," *American Political Science Review*, 68 (1974): 3.

3. Clifford Geertz, *Local Knowledge: Further Essays in Interpretive Anthropology* (New York: Basic Books, 1983) 73-93.

4. The following is based on Jan Assmann, *Das kulturelle Gedächtnis: Schrift, Erinnerung und politische Identität in frühen Hochkulturen* (The Cultural Memory: Script, Memory and Political Identity in Early Civilizations) (Munich: Beck, 1992).

5. Max Weber, *Wirtschaft und Gesellschaft*, 5th ed. (Tübingen: J.C.B. Mohr, 1985) 238.

6. Eric Hobsbawm and T. Ranger, eds., *The Invention of Tradition* (New York: Cambridge University Press, 1983); Benedict Anderson, *Imagined Communities* (New York and London: Verso, 1983).

7. Charles Jelavich, *South Slav Nationalisms: Textbooks and Yugoslav Union before 1914* (Columbus, OH: Ohio State University Press, 1990); Charles Jelavich, "Nationalism as Reflected in the Textbooks of the South Slavs in the 19th Century," *Canadian Review of Nationalism*, 16, 1-2 (1989): 28 (quotation).

8. See Charles Jelavich, "Education, Textbooks and South Slav Nationalism in the Interwar Era," in Norbert Reiter and Holm Sundhaussen, eds., *Allgemeinbildung als Modernisierungsfaktor. Zur Geschichte der Elementarbildung in Sudosteuropa von der Aufklärung bis zum Zweiten Weltkrieg* (Berlin: Harrassowitz, 1994), 127-42, and the analysis of—mostly Serbian—interwar Yugoslav textbooks by Ljubodrag Dimić and Danko Alimpić, "Stereotypes in Textbooks in the Kingdom of Yugoslavia," in Wolfgang Höpken, ed., *Nationale Stereotypen und Feindbilder in*

Schulbuchern und Popularliteratur der Balkanländer (Braunschweig: Diesterweg, 1996).

9. On the role of ideological values and political culture in Yugoslavia, see Ivan Šiber, "Central and Eastern European Political Culture in Transition: From Communism's Decline to Nationalism's Triumph," in Russell F. Farnenm, ed., *Nationalism, Ethnicity and Identity: Cross-national and Comparative Perspectives* (New Brunswick, NH; London: Transaction Publishers, 1994), 371-99.

10. On the objectives of political socialization during the so-called etatist period of Yugoslav socialism up to the Tito-Stalin split, see Carol Lilly, "Problems of Persuasion: Communist Agitation and Propaganda in Postwar Yugoslavia, 1944-1948," *Slavic Review*, 53, 2 (1994): 395-413. Carol Lilly shows, however, that already during this early period of Yugoslav socialism, conflicts appeared between federal and republican institutions on one or several textbooks, indicating that already at this time of centralism and Stalinist party rule the tension between "common" and "individual" memory among the Yugoslav nations became obvious. For some principles of history textbooks and education during the 1950s and early 1960s, see John Georgeoff, "Nationalism in the History Textbooks of Yugoslavia and Bulgaria," *Comparative Education Review*, 10, 3 (1966): 442-50.

11. See Paul Shoup, *Communism and the Yugoslav National Question* (New York; London: Columbia University Press, 1968); Dennison Rusinow, *The Yugoslav Experiment 1948-1974* (Berkeley, CA; Los Angeles, CA: University of California Press, 1977); Sabrina P. Ramet, *Nationalism and Federalism in Yugoslavia 1962-1991*, 2nd ed., (Bloomington, IN: Indiana University Press, 1992).

12. Mirjana Gross, "Wie denkt man kroatische Geschichte? Geschichtsschreibung und Identitätsstiftung," *Österreichische Osthefte*, 35, 1 (1993): 73. On the development of postwar Yugoslav historiography, see also Ivo Banac, "Historiography in the Countries of Eastern Europe: Yugoslavia," *American Historical Review*, 97 (1992): 1084-104.

13. Andrej Mitrović, *Raspravljanja sa Klio* (Sarajevo: 1991), 132.

14. See as critics, Savo Birković, "Na marginama udžbenika. O nekim nedostacima udžbenika istorije za osnovne škole i škole usmjerenog obrazovanja," *Stvaranje*, 38, 12 (1983): 1483-514; Dijana Plut and Ana Pešikan, "Moć i nemoć: jednog našeg udžbenika," *Psihologija*, 14, 4 (1981): 114-27.

15. For the ideological basics in education in this field, see *Marksistička osnova udžbenika* (Novi Sad: 1976).

16. Dijana Plut, Natalija Daničić, and Boris Tadić, "Vrednosni sistem osnovnoškolskih udžbenika," *Psihološka istraživanja*, 4 (1990): 145.

17. For a "didactical" approach to this topic see, among many others, Žarko Masić, "Metodološki pristup u predstavljanju ličnosti i dela druga Tita u udžbenicima i priručnicima," *Škola i društvo*, 1-2 (1982): 5-10.

18. "Okrugli stol: Udžbenici i nastava marksizma u srednjoškolskom odgoju i obrazovanju," *Marksističko obrazovanje*, 11, 2-3 (1988): 67-117.

19. See as an example, Vasilije Damjanović, "Uloga nastava istorije u vaspitanju učenika nižih razreda osmogodišnje škole u duhu jugoslavenskog socijalističkog patriotizma," *Pedagoška stvarnost*, 3, 6 (1957): 455-61.

20. As an example of educational objectives under the conditions of the 1974 constitution, see *Ostvarivanje nacionalne ravnopravnosti u oblasti vaspitanja i obrazovanja* (Novi Sad, 1977).

21. As far as textbooks are concerned see, among others, the overview in Laszlo Girizd, "Informacija o zadovoljavanju potreba udžbenicima i problemi izdavanja udžbenika za škole na jezicima narodnosti," *Bilten Zavoda za izdavanje udžbenika*, 53 (1985): 69-74.

22. Plut, et al., "Vrednosni sistem," 147. See also Janez Stergar, "Narodnostna problematika v osnovnoškolskih učbenikov spoznavanja družbe in zemljepisa v SR Sloveniji," *Revija za narodnostna vprasanja*, no. 20 (1987): 247-60.

23. See especially the critiques of history curricula and history teaching policy in Croatia by Mirjana Gross, "Postoji li kriza istorije," *Politika*, 15 (October 1977): 14.

24. Sima Ćirković, "Kakva struktura programa istorije može pridoneti upoznavanja zbližavanju naše mlade generacije," *Nastava povijest*, no. 4 (1967-68): 1-14.

25. Miodrag Ignjatović, "Školuje li se današnja omladina za jugoslovenstvo?" *Borba*, 15 September, 1988.

26. Nikša Stančić, Djordje Stanković, Marijan Maticka, Drago Roksandić, and Ivan Obradović, "Jugoslavensko i nacionalno u ubženicima istorije," *Marksistička misao*,no. 2 (1983): 163-91.

27. See the following textbooks in Annex: Serbian 10: 44-47, 56; Serbian 11: 46, 53; Croatian 6: 154; Slovenian 7: 27; Slovenian 8: 27, 46; Macedonian 6: 19, 29, 33.

28. See textbooks in Annex: Serbian 10: 67, 75; Serbian 11: 71; Croatian 6: 218, 221.

29. One of the first of these controversies took place in 1964-65 following the publication of Velimir Terzić's *Jugoslavija u aprilskom ratu, 1941* (Titograd: Grafički zavod, 1963) and Franjo Tudjman's, *Velike ideje i mali narodi*, (Zagreb: Rasprave i ogledi Matica Hrvatska, 1969). Both soon came under attack, Terzić, for having ascribed responsibility for Yugoslavia's end in 1941 mainly to Croat "separatism," and Tudjman for allegedly "freeing the Croat bourgeoise from its treasonous role." When the party was losing its control over historiography during the 1980s, such controversies came up again, now playing a substantial role in the deteriorating relations between Serbs and Croats. See, for example, the heated discussions of the Croat historian Ljubo Boban with Terzić due to the 1986 edition of his 1963 book, and his debate with the Serbian historian Veselin Djuretić about Djuretić's book, *Saveznici i jugoslovenska ratna drama* (Beograd: 1985). Further details on the earlier conflicts may be found in Bogumil Hrabak, "Deviacije u savremenoj jugoslovenskoj historiografiji u tretiranju nacionalnog pitanja," *Istorijski glasnik*, no. 3-4 (1967): 123-80; for the later quarrels, see Banac, "Historiography in the Countries of Eastern Europe," 1084; Wolfgang Höpken, "Von der Mythologisierung zur Stigmatisierung: 'Krieg und Revolution' in Jugoslawien im Spiegel der von Geschichtswissenschaft und historischer Publizistik" (From Myth-Building to Stigma: "War and Revolution" in Yugoslavia in Historiogaphy and Journalism), in E. Schmidt-Hartmann, ed., *Kommunismus und Osteuropa. Konzepte, Perspektiven und Interpretationen im Wandel* (Munich: Oldenbourg, 1994), 165-202.

30. A representative example is a Serbian textbook from 1976. Out of six colored pictures on the first pages, four are called "Srpski ratnik" (Serbian Warrior) "27.mart" (The 27th of March), "Novi borac" (New Fighter), and "Prevoz ranjenika" (Transportation of the Wounded); out of 22 pictures in the text dealing with Yugoslav history from 1941 to 1975, 15 are illustrations of military actions. *Istorija za VIII. Razred osnovne škole* (Beograd: 1976), (Serbian 14). For a more detailed view on this problem, see also Vesna Pesić, Dubravka Stojanović, and Ružica Rosandić, *Patriarchalnost i ratništvo* (Beograd: 1994).

31. Norbert Elias, *Über die Deutschen. Studien zur Habitusentwicklung im 19. und 20.Jahrhundert* (Frankfurt/M: Editions suhrkamp, 1994), 45.

32. For the role of historiography in the last years' development see Banac, "Historiography in Eastern Europe," 1084-104; Gross, "Wie denkt man kroatische Geschichte?" 73-98; Stephen K. Pawlowitch, "From Legitimation to Demystification—Forty Years of Historiography" chapter 9 in his *The Improbable Survivor: Yugoslavia and its Problems 1918-1988* (Columbus, OH: Ohio State University Press, 1988); Wolfgang Höpken, "Geschichte und Gewalt: Geschichtsbewußtsein im jugoslawischen Konflikt" (History and Violence: Historical Consciousness in the Yugoslav Conflict), *Internationale Schulbuchforschung*, 15, no. 1 (1993): 55-73.

33. Pesić, Stojanović, and Rosandić, *Patriarchalnost i ratništvo*, 22; Dubravka Stojanović, "Stereotypes in Contemporary History Textbooks as a Mirror of the Time," in Höpken, ed., *Nationale Stereotypen* (forthcoming).

34. Quotation from the army newspaper, "Otkriće zatomljene nacionalne istorije," *Vojska*, June 10, 1993, 28; for former similar criticisms see, among others, Vasilije Krestić, *Istoričari* (Beograd: 1992), 149.

35. See especially the textbook by Ivo Perić, *Povijest* (Zagreb: 1992), (Croatian 1).

36. See Perić, *Povijest*, 134; *Istorija za VIII.razred* (Beograd: 1993), 153 (Serbian 1).

37. See Branimir Nešović and Janko Prunk, *20.stoletje. Zgodovina za 8.razred osnovne šole* (Ljubljana: 1993), (Slovenian 1). It is the only one among all of the post-Yugoslav textbooks that makes clear to a certain extent the interests and motives of the "opponent's" politics by, for example, presenting sources from the Serbian side to the student.

38. On the difference between "historical consciousness" and "historical image," see Karl-Ernst Jeismann, "'Identität' statt 'Emanzipation': Zum Geschichtsbewußtsein in der Bundesrepublik," ("Identity" instead of "Emancipation": Historical Consciousness in Germany), *Aus Politik und Zeitgeschichte*, 20-21 (1976): 14.

39. This, of course, should not have been understood as giving both sides an equal share of responsibility for the events since 1991; but it stresses the fact, well known from East European experiences in political transition in the meantime, that the institutional shift from communist rule to parliamentary politics has little to do with the establishment of the "civic society," of which a multiperspective education is an integral part.

Part II

Social Forces, Social Movements, and the State

Introduction

Melissa K. Bokovoy

It is perhaps this part that will illuminate most directly the strengths and weaknesses of the society underneath the system of Yugoslav state socialism. The chapters in this section discuss the history of communist Yugoslavia from the perspective of the ruled. Specifically they explore the social and political opposition to the party-state and its effect on the efforts of the communist elite to consolidate, legitimize, and continue their rule. What may come as a surprise to many people is the dynamic and nonstatic nature of the relationship of the Yugoslav communists to society throughout their rule, not just in the last decade.

Studying the breadth of the communist period in Yugoslavia requires a cooperative effort among scholars in many fields. Here, we have included new research done by scholars in the fields of history, sociology, and religious studies who have all examined the extent to which various social, religious, cultural, and intellectual groups induced the party-state to formulate and shape policies in ways that it had not originally intended. The actions or nonactions of these groups eventually laid the groundwork for more overt political movements.

Current historical research has focused on the period of the creation and consolidation of the Yugoslav communist state. Chapters 4 and 5 challenge the notion that in its early years the Communist Party of Yugoslavia (CPY) had an absolute concentration of power, leaving little room for individuals, classes, or society to maneuver. The other papers primarily focus on the last decade of state socialism in

Yugoslavia. Chapters 6, 7, and 8 explain the perspective of the ruled using the notion of civil society: How Yugoslavs in the 1980s began to form autonomous organizations and express ideas outside of and not dependent upon or even approved of by the party-state.

In the historiography of the creation and the consolidation of communist Yugoslavia, scholars have focused primarily on the subject of the party-state, its elites, its structures and institutions, its ideology, its state-building processes and strategies, and the place of the communist Yugoslav state in international politics. In the immediate postwar period, the Yugoslav Communists adopted and then adapted a state and party model bequeathed to them by the Soviet Union: a highly centralized, unitary party state, adhering to democratic centralism, that ensured no significant devolution of power from its center; a five-year economic plan that allocated resources to heavy industry; and educational and cultural policies that celebrated the victory of the Yugoslav Partisan army over reactionary, fascist forces, and extolled the virtues of the Soviet Union, Stalin, the communist partisans, and Tito.

These state structures and the elites that constructed them are portrayed in the literature as immutable, impermeable, and impervious to societal forces. It appears as if the communist elites had little connection to or were influenced very little by the society over which they ruled. Outside forces such as Stalin, the Red Army, the United Nations Relief and Rehabilitation Agency, the Communist Information Bureau, and the events of the Cold War, influenced and affected the policy debates and decisions of the CPY. Yet inside their state, the Yugoslav Communists appeared untouched by social forces. Workers, peasants, women, young people, and national elites were considered in terms of the state-building activities of the CPY. Policies, programs, plans, laws, ideological disputes between domestic and international communist elites and institutions became the benchmark of Yugoslav history of this period. What is lost in the history are the individuals and groups that were affected by the activities of the CPY, their attitudes, behavior, language, responses and resistance to the implementation of policy and the party-state's effort to dominate society and its individuals.

What becomes clear in the first two chapters of Part II is the reciprocal nature of the relationship between the Yugoslav communist party-state and society. These chapters examine two realms of conflict: first, the attempt to implement agrarian reforms in the countryside, and second, the CPY's attempt to dictate cultural norms and values to society as a whole. It is not the open political conflict of a civil society contesting open space free from state power and wishing to create autonomous groups and organizations outside of the state that one sees throughout Eastern Europe and Yugoslavia in the 1980s. The conflict described by Bokovoy and Lilly occupies a vast, hidden, and subjective realm existing between political debate and rebellion. It is a realm where its participants might very well describe their actions as being essentially nonpolitical or nonthreatening to the existence of the party-state. However, actions taken by individuals, whether artists, students, or peasants, in their cumulative and collective forms altered the way in which the CPY ruled over society.

Given the CPY's interpretation of its rise to power on the popular support of the peasantry, chapter 4 explores the nature of the CPY's relationship with the peasantry once the party-state began to implement its plan for the countryside. Policies included not only a popular land reform but the attempt by the CPY to limit the independence and autonomy of peasant production, consumption, and marketing. The party elites, through official channels, began to take note of reported actions undertaken by individual peasants or small groups of them that obstructed, contradicted, or blatantly defied their directives and decrees. While generally involving little coordination and planning, these acts attempted to thwart or prevent state and party usurpation of land, agricultural surplus, and consumption. Usually the peasantry's acts of resistance, such as black-marketing, withholding or underdelivery of agricultural produce for state collection, refusal to pay taxes, underreporting of land size, misreporting of crop yields, exaggerated claims about spoilage of grain, and theft or hoarding, targeted local representatives of state authority. In the eyes of the party-state, the actions and activities of the peasantry were criminal and were portrayed as socially or economically deviant behavior. In reality, within the realm of subjectivity, the peasants engaged in political conflict, signals to the party that they would not submit docilely to policies and directives contrary to their interests. Confronted with such acts, the party-state relented by 1953.

In chapter 5, Carol Lilly investigates how the CPY wished to create the new socialist Yugoslav man and women by direct social engineering, that is the party-state was to train the population to react in a common manner to the impulses sent by it, and why its efforts failed. The author states: "Among the tools by which the

CPY hoped to produce these changes was culture, including literature, theater, film, music, dance, and the fine arts." However, in these efforts by the party, neither the artists nor the public were passive and both were able to influence and force modifications in cultural production. Lilly brings to light the hidden realm of conflict between the party and society as she describes an artist's ruse to get a party official's acceptance for his work; the art students who engaged in debates about the new values in social and artistic life; the writer's recalcitrance to accept as poetry works that used words such as "bomb," Partisan," "freedom," and "hateful occupier"; the public's willingness to line up for a Hollywood musical; and hair and clothing styles copied from western fashion magazines. The Yugoslav artists and citizens rejected—not loudly or through formal channels but through small acts—the official fare as they sought out alternative or underground forms of culture. As a result, by 1950, the CPY adopted a new, more lenient stance toward alternative, western, and popular culture.

What these chapters reveal is how individuals, as well as the peasantry as a class, forced the Yugoslav Communists to reformulate their ideology and policies. Sometimes the adoption of a new ideological line or reversal on a policy simply tried to absorb a new trend or sentiment that had already developed and that the party was afraid would move beyond its control. However, in the constantly reconfigured ideology, state structures, and elite policies, each marginal activity that the party-state absorbed succeeded in continuously expanding the margins of what was permissible. By the 1980s, the margins were bursting; individuals and groups grew more confident in seeking out space free from state power. Individuals and their associations began to articulate a wide spectrum of beliefs, conceptions, and attitudes outside the state's purview. This phenomenon has been described by scholars as the reemergence of civil society in Eastern Europe.

The party-states of Eastern Europe and Yugoslavia tried to dissolve the characteristics of civil society, individualism, pluralism, and the free exchange of goods and services by the market. The consensus of its members for a society based on these values was replaced by a normative order created by the communist parties and enforced by its state. The state in state socialism was not an independent entity in public life, rather it owed its existence and substance to the party. As a creation of the party, the state took from it its most characteristic features: democratic centralism, its political, economic, and ideological ideas, and its cadres. The party and state essentially merged into one and the party gave to the state the tools—the army, the secret police, and the judiciary—to dissolve any institutions, behaviors, or attitudes not sanctioned by the party.[1]

The reemergence of civil society in Yugoslavia in the late 1970s and 1980s is the focus of the next chapters. The authors discuss how certain elements within Yugoslav society began to form autonomous organizations and how these organizations began to challenge the party-state. The movements of feminism, Slovenian pacifism, and ecology—coined New Social Movements (NSM)—planted the seeds for a new consensus within society on what rules of behavior and central values should be the basis of a state outside of the LCY's control. Whether or not a civil society emerged within the successor states of Yugoslavia and on what type of normative consensus it would be based is a central theme sounded throughout these chapters. Both sides are presented and it is up to the reader to ponder the answer.

In chapter 6, Jozef Figa argues that civil society emerged from a marginal cultural phenomenon, punk music and its movement, adopted by the youth of Slovenia. What is astounding is the complementary nature of chapter 6 with Lilly's chapter 5. Culture as demonstrated by Lilly operated at times outside the party's control and because of this, the CPY attempted to run ahead of a cultural trend and seek to absorb it for its own purposes. Yet with this absorption, the cultural phenomenon pushes the envelope of what is acceptable. Figa demonstrates how this continually expanding margin led to the creation of the New Social Movements in Slovenia and formed the seeds for a civil society.

Figa explores the process by which the absorption of the punk movement by the League of Socialist Youth of Slovenia (LSYS) led to toleration of other alternative forms of expression. Other individuals within Slovenian society who were interested in issues such as nonviolence, world peace, minority rights for those with alternative lifestyles, and ecology formed "circles of sympathizers and activists." Figa argues that these groups insisted on operating informally, without an organizational framework and by doing so made it difficult for party officials to accuse them of organizing anti-state plots. This type of strategy played to the Yugoslav party-state's pride and, more importantly, the Slovene establishment's pride concerning its progressive and democratic nature vis-à-vis the

USSR and Eastern Europe. By the mid-1980s the Slovenian establishment allowed for the existence and patronage of the NSMs by the LSYS.

The bulk of chapter 6, however, focuses on how one NSM, the peace movement, directly contributed to the confrontation between the Slovenian republican authorities and the federal state. The author discusses a series of events, mostly youth-generated, which brought the Slovenian party into conflict with one of the party-state's tools of order, the Yugoslav People's Army. Figa concludes that the impact of these events led the League of Communists of Slovenia (LCS) to support a view that was prevalent in Slovene society that "Yugoslavia in its Titoist, socialist, self-managerial version cannot contribute anything more to the cultural, political, economic, and social development of Slovenia." The LCS came down on the side of its increasingly emboldened, vocal citizens. By rushing to get ahead of Slovene society, the LCS directly challenged the legal, military, and political institutions of the Yugoslav state. The party-state, as we know, did not survive the challenge.

Figa leaves the reader with a triumphant view of the strength of civil society in Slovenia. In chapter 7, however, Jill Benderly seems to dissuade us of this conclusion as she focuses on the development, evolution, and bifurcation of the women's movement in socialist Yugoslavia between 1978 and 1992. Benderly argues that by the 1980s, a critique of self-managed socialism articulated by women in the academy and the media concerning women's place in the state had turned into a New Social Movement. This movement acted as an autonomous social force that simultaneously challenged the party-state and created its own alternative culture and network of initiatives. The discourse of the movement and its activism played a notable role in Yugoslav society in the late 1980s. Not only were issues such as marital rape and protection of reproductive rights brought to the forefront, but legislation was passed to address these concerns. Benderly portrays the movement in a favorable way because of the challenge that it issued to the party-state's claim to represent all social interests. However optimism fades into pessimism as the author explores how Yugoslav society stood on the threshold of pluralism—and the transformation of the party-state's attitudes, behavior, and values concerning women—and plunged into civil war.

Feminists in the Yugoslav successor states originally tried to organize across national lines to protest the war's impact on children, families, and women and to provide small-scale but significant opposition to the war and social services for its survivors. However, a rift developed within the multinational movement between those feminists who opposed nationalism and those who began to draw parallels between the victimization of women and the victimization of their nation. Benderly challenges the notion that some type of civil society developed in the successor states as the new nationalist regimes attempted to marginalize the nonnationalist feminists and attempted to coopt the patriotic ones. The nationalist regimes redefined women not only as enemies to be raped, but also as bearers of the nation.

Another view challenging the existence or beginnings of a civil society is presented in chapter 8 in an examination of the role of religious communities in the development of civil society in communist Yugoslavia. Paul Mojzes rejects the notion that religious communities played any significant role in the development of a civil society in Yugoslavia. However, his argument actually raises one of the problems in the study of the emergence, reemergence, and creation of civil society in Eastern Europe: Do these societies have traditions characteristic of what is defined as civil society? Mojzes discusses how the largest religious communities, namely, those of Eastern Orthodoxy, Roman Catholicism, and Islam were not likely to contribute to the creation of civil society in Yugoslavia because it was alien to their traditions as practiced in the Balkans. If anything, they were and are likely—even under conditions of greater opportunity for the free proliferation of autonomous organizations—to impede this process.

Mojzes concludes that the reason for this development is that the creation of civil society would tend to diminish rather than strengthen the social role of the religious communities as compared to the ethnoreligious constellations that asserted themselves in the late 1980s and early 1990s. The religious communities were and are not likely to promote autonomous social or political organizations since they cherish the opportunity to play a significant social and political role in the new nationalist successor states.

Chapters 6, 7, and 8 leave the reader with food for thought before Part III discusses the relationship of nation to the state. These chapters have shown the tenuous position of social movements in Yugoslavia in the face of emerging nationalist politics. The disappearance of these burgeoning social movements behind the wave of nationalism throws into doubt whether or not civil society actually had a chance to emerge in Yugoslavia.

Note

1. Zbigniew Rau, "Introduction," in Zbigniew Rau, ed., *The Reemergence of Civil Society in Eastern Europe and the Soviet Union* (Boulder, CO: Westview Press, 1991), 1-23.

4

Peasants and Partisans: The Politics of the Yugoslav Countryside, 1945–1953

Melissa K. Bokovoy

Communist Yugoslavia was one of more than a hundred new states that appeared on the global stage after 1939. In most cases, these new states rose from the ashes of World War II or threw off the shackles of imperialism, and sought transformation in revolution. In a process replicated by dozens of other new states, Yugoslav revolutionaries and politicians primarily targeted their revolutionary and state-building activity at the peasantry. In summer 1941, in order to defeat their ideological and nationalist rivals, the Yugoslav communists abandoned their natural allies and familiar terrain, the worker and the city, and fled to the hinterlands; they would not reenter a major urban center again until 1945. There, in rural terrain, they forged an alliance with a heretofore untenable ally, the peasant, who according to Engels, "possesses the most reactionary tendencies."

The Yugoslav Communists, as a revolutionary elite, tried to recruit peasants into their movement by promising social and economic reform, national self-respect, political representation, modernization, and social mobility. The experience of the Yugoslav Partisans points to the fundamental social and political contradictions inherent in this process of mobilization. On the one hand, the peasants were numerically, militarily, and economically essential to the revolutionary movement; on the other hand, they were often recalcitrant, obstinate, even rebellious, and thereby an obstacle to revolution and state-building. Ideological contradictions quickly emerged. Although the Yugoslav communist revolutionaries held up the peasant as the ideal national patriot, they soon discovered that neither traditional Marxist ideology nor the dominant Soviet model had a "place" for this peasant.

This chapter explores the Yugoslav Communists' relationship with its rural constituency between 1945 and 1953. It is not only an account of how an East European party-state sought to bring the countryside, its resources, and its inhabitants under state control. It is also a political tale about lower-class resistance among peasants and how their acts effectively mitigated and thwarted the claims made upon them by a state controlled by a dominant group, in this case, the Communists. In addition, it describes how the peasants were able to advance successfully their own demands for private property, production autonomy, and a lifestyle in opposition to the state's plans for them and in spite of the state's monopolization of violence. The peasantry defended its interests using methods James Scott calls "weapons of the weak."[1]

In Yugoslavia, conflict between the new communist elite, its party cadres, and the peasantry erupted soon after the Communists came to power in 1945. More than on any other topic, the top leadership bickered and quarreled over the type of policies necessary for the transformation of the Yugoslav countryside. One faction, which included Milovan Djilas, Moša Pijade, Boris Kidrič, and the economic council, supported the collectivization of agriculture and other coercive measures to bring the countryside under the control of the state. Another faction, which included Andrija Hebrang, Edward Kardelj, Vaso Čubrilović (the minister of agriculture), and the agrarian council, advised against rapid and complete collectivization on the grounds the peasants were not psychologically, politically, or economically prepared for such a dramatic step. This faction believed that some form of socialism was necessary in the villages but that the change must be gradual.

During these early years, political negotiation filled the plush and private interior of the Communist Party of Yugoslavia (CPY) leadership's offices, the public and paneled chambers of the federal parliament, and the serviceable offices and chambers of the various boards concerned with the countryside and its resources. Adding their voices to this policy cacophony were party cadres, parliamentarians, and regional and local officials who argued heatedly over the merits of the plans imposed from the top. Disagreement and dissension often broke out in the ranks when the CPY leadership's plans threatened the local and regional interests of its provincial cadres and when nationalist loyalties challenged the fragile unity and "brotherhood" of the Yugoslav socialist state. Nonviolent opposition among the rank and file often took the form of formal complaints, bureaucratic obstructionism, and direct refusal to implement policy when CPY policies ran contrary to a variety of provincial or nationalist interests.

When politics moved from policy formulation to policy application, resistance from all quarters became more pronounced. Two cases illustrate how the peasantry reacted to and resisted the CPY's policies in the countryside: The requisitioning and compulsory delivery of basic agricultural commodities (otkup or collections) beginning in 1945, and the CPY's decision to collectivize agriculture by forming peasant work cooperatives "with greater boldness and at a faster tempo" in January 1949. These two decisions demonstrate that when faced with resistance the Yugoslav Communists vacillated between their debt to the peasantry, and their conviction that socialist transformation of the rural world was necessary. "The permanent, continuous, daily strategies" and everyday acts[2] employed by the Yugoslav peasantry to protest collectivization and other policies induced the Communists to reformulate their ideology and policies in ways that they never intended.

POINT OF CONFLICT: COLLECTIONS *(OTKUP)*

During the war, the CPY had lured the peasantry into its revolutionary movement because they had much in common: similar enemies, economic aims, and the desire to redistribute land and property. Once the CPY gained power in 1945, it faced the task of political consolidation and economic reconstruction. In order to accomplish these tasks, the CPY, throughout 1945 and 1946, focused on the nationalization of industry, creation of a strong centralized state, formulation of a five-year economic plan, and the building of institutions that would bind the private individual landholder to both the state and cooperative sectors.

For the peasantry at this time, the momentous issues were the reforms promised to them by the CPY: land reform, liquidation of prewar debt, procurement of credits in order to purchase seed, livestock, machinery, and other agricultural inputs necessary for increased productivity and production, as well as individual and local autonomy. Common ground existed only in the fact that the CPY acknowledged the peasant's role in the National Liberation Struggle (NOB) and initially made good on its promise to redistribute land to liquidate peasant debt.[3]

Peasant disenchantment appeared when the CPY proved incapable or unwilling to provide agricultural credits, services, seed, livestock, and machinery to independent producers.[4] This discontent did not produce outright confrontation. However, conflict erupted when the CPY created and strengthened laws surrounding procurement, distribution, and consumption of agricultural products and capital. With the adoption of a policy on the collection and redistribution of specified agricultural products *(otkup)*, the CPY, in essence, was bringing the private, independent, and often recalcitrant peasant under state control. It was over these "voluntary" and compulsory deliveries that the peasants and Partisans first came into conflict over the role of the peasants in the new state.

Borba, as well as local communist officials, closely followed the activities and mood of the peasantry. As early as June 1945, there had already been complaints from various committees that the peasants were not bringing their produce to market because of depressed and inadequate prices for agricultural goods. The regional committee of the Communist Party of Croatia (CPC) for Dalmatia complained to the Central Committee of the Communist Party of Croatia:

> The party organizations as well as the Yugoslav National Front did almost nothing to explain to the people and to the peasants the aims of our government. [They need to explain] that by passing this order, the peasants are helping the entire nation by being both consumers and producers. Because of their confusion about the current inadequacies of the pricing policy, the peasants have stopped carrying their produce to market, except those products which are not for consumption."[5]

At the initial stages of this predicament, the economic council focused on the problems that pricing was causing and suggested that the government could encourage the peasants to bring their surplus to market by "eliminating the disproportion between the standard price of agricultural products and the price for production of those industrial products which the peasants buy."[6] In other words, they should create greater parity between the prices of agricultural products and industrial goods. In actuality, instead of "leveling the playing field," the government used pricing to discriminate against the individual, independent peasants who sold their surplus in the marketplace, and favored those peasants who sold their produce to state agencies.[7] The government did this either by setting higher prices at the state procurement centers, or heavily taxing the peasant who sold on the free market. Despite these economic ploys and pressures, the peasants continued to circumvent the state agencies. *Borba* reported a case in Novi Sad where local authorities rationed bread, but the peasants found a way to sell grain. Enabling, as the local officials complained, "private sellers to sell bread everywhere."[8]

In August 1945, Andrija Hebrang, chairman of the economic council, justified the introduction of this pricing system and the system of compulsory deliveries. He stated:

> Without a doubt, the most important problem facing us is at the present time. While we succeeded in planting 90% of the available land, a drought occurred and this will cut the return of the grain harvest in half. The drought partially or entirely wiped out the crops in Macedonia, Montenegro, Bosnia and Hercegovina, and Slovenia. We, therefore, must depend upon last year's reserves and the harvest from Serbia and Vojvodina.[9]

In order to tap into the harvest yields, Hebrang recommended a plan for the collection of corn, wheat, and grain. The state, acting through the state agricultural agency, Poljopromet, would direct the collection of grain, set the price of grain, and the quotas for each region,[10] a policy loathsome to the peasantry because of the way in which quotas and prices were set by inefficient, ignorant, and sometimes corrupt officials. In a September 2, 1945, *Borba* article, Hebrang noted the already existing hostility to the collection policy. Calling those who refused to recognize the validity of the law as enemies of the people and speculators, he admonished them for withholding their grain until higher prices were set and for not wishing to give up their surplus for those in the drought-stricken and war-torn regions.[11]

In response to peasant reaction and resistance to state agricultural policies, the state defined their activity as criminal. This is illustrated by the passage of a law on speculation, black-marketing, and sabotage.[12] While covering all aspects of economic life, this law singled out peasants' activity in the realm of damaging, destroying, and slaughtering animate and inanimate inventory as well as stating that any willful action against decrees or written instructions from the federal government would be punished. The state intended to punish offenders with a fine, forced labor from one month to ten years, confiscation of property and livestock, or, in extreme cases, with the death penalty.

In spite of such harsh sentences, the peasantry continued to fight against the state's interference in its agricultural production, marketing, and consumption. In January 1946, *Borba* reported that in Croatia, grain collection had fallen short by 58 percent for 1945.[13] This article noted that the failure was due to poor organization, planning, execution, and peasant resistance, and blamed the local people's committees for failure to propagandize the virtuous aims and goals of the collection.[14] Additionally, the CPY was particularly disturbed by the shortfalls in Vojvodina, supposedly the laboratory for cooperative and collectivist endeavors. *Borba* reported: "Even individual people's boards disrupted the carrying out of the collections . . . of the ones mentioned, they responded to local riots. For example, in Vojvodina, they [local boards] maintained that they did not deliver to Poljopromet because they held on [to the grain] for local consumption."[15] This article also chastised those boards that refused to clamp down on smuggling by the peasants and their selling of grain on the black market. Another report out of Vojvodina discussed the case of one peasant, Slavko Rakić, who was sentenced to five years of forced labor for stealing, pilfering from the common forest, and speculating.[16]

The CPY leadership could not help but hear the reports attesting to the resistance of peasantry, and to the problems of implementation on the local and regional levels. Responding to these difficulties, the CPY, in summer 1946, yielded to the peasant's reluctance and resistance to a procurement regimen with the adoption of the "Law concerning a General Amnesty to the Violators of the Orders concerning the Obligatory Collections of Agricultural Produce."[17] This law pardoned those peasants who had not yet completed or had not yet begun their sentences for violating the collection orders. A delegate from Serbia, Mustafa Hodža, stated that this law confirmed the generosity and the care of the national government for the "little guy, for those poor workers and peasants who willfully and consciously, or perhaps unconsciously, committed a mistake concerning their legal responsibilities."[18] Another delegate, Miloš Carević, argued that "this amnesty was a necessary and appropriate measure because it showed that the Federal Government took care of its people and had deep connections with the national masses."[19] With the passage of this federal law, the government acknowledged its dependency on the goodwill of the peasantry to carry out policies and reforms in the countryside.

By mid-1946, with a dwindling food supply and a growing urban population, the government could not afford to be overly magnanimous. The agrarian council proposed a series of measures aimed at procuring the peasants' surpluses without repeating the earlier mistakes. The council recommended the following: obligatory collection based on progressive rates; progressive taxation of the peasantry; contracting for crops; setting prices and tariffs that were not detrimental to the peasantry; easy access to credit; creating local and regional procurement boards and cooperatives that would place certain tasks and obligations upon the peasants and then make sure that the peasants fulfilled them; and securing positions on these committees for those sympathetic to the new communist government.[20]

Following the lead of the agrarian council and banking on the goodwill of the peasantry created by the general amnesty, the Skupština did not rescind the obligatory deliveries of certain agricultural products. Explaining its reason for passing the amnesty bill, and not rescinding the collection orders, the Skupština stressed that the amnesty was to bring to the attention of the peasantry those mistakes that had to be corrected, as well as admitting its own inadequacies. This bill not only stressed forgiveness, but it also emphasized the need to win the trust of individual peasants, and for them to learn to serve the greater good and not their individual interests.[21] By repealing the punishments, the CPY hoped to underscore the gravity of noncompliance to future directives and the importance of the concept, "the greater good." Tito addressed this issue in an article directed at Ladislav Bojnah, a peasant who had hidden him during the 1930s. Tito told his old protector: "Do not begin from an individual viewpoint, because that can divert a man; rather, begin from the universal/state viewpoint."[22] In Tito's opinion, the peasantry had to bear a large part of the burden for rebuilding the state. Yet, recognizing the resistance of the peasantry, the party tried to target for collection only specific crops and products that were deemed absolutely necessary for clothing and feeding the population. In 1946 and

1947, the Skupština passed a series of directives that called for the compulsory delivery of wool, cattle, tobacco, and grain in order to insure the supply of goods to the cities.[23]

Reports to the regional and federal agencies indicated that the reforms had little effect. The Ministry of Trade and Supply expressed dismay that only 20 percent of the projected collections had been realized in Vojvodina, Serbia, and Bosnia and Hercegovina. Local committees, such as the Regional Committee of Dalmatia, placed the blame for failure to reach collection goals on the "unfriendly elements in the village."[24] At a meeting of the economic council in late August 1946, Boris Kidrič, the new chairman of the council and minister of industry, complained that the mandatory collections had not produced the sought-after returns and he criticized local and regional committees for not being forceful enough with the peasantry.[25] Kidrič recommended using more aggressive measures to enforce the collection. In order to guarantee the supply of grain throughout the country, the government must control the market, and create a strong, informed collection service.[26]

Vaso Čubrilović, chair of the agrarian council, was more conciliatory. He attributed the problems not to willfulness on the part of the peasantry, but rather to the failure of the government to supply the villages with necessary production means, especially fodder, seed, and livestock.[27] He hoped to offset the additional burdens that would be placed upon the peasantry by supplying them with the goods necessary for increasing their agricultural output. Čubrilović and the council drew up their plan for 1946-48 on this assumption. Using bread grain as an example, the agrarian council projected that as efficiency increased, the peasant would keep more of his own produce even though the amount collected for the state would remain the same.[28] They strove to shrink the forced deliveries gradually, especially for the poor and middle peasants. If the peasants had any remaining surplus, they would be allowed to sell it on the open market.[29]

Additional sympathy came from the ministry of trade and supply, which reported that the peasantry alone could not be faulted for the delays. Instead, organizational problems and unrealistic projection targets plagued the collection process.[30] In December 1946, the regional committee of the CP Croatia for Dalmatia reported: "Not only did our corn crop fail, but the [otkup] targets were unrealistic, [otkup] procedures ill-defined, but the procedures were too little and too late to collect grain from the rich elements."[31] Finally, the drought in 1946 hampered the collection efforts as well. The Central Committee of the Communist Party of Serbia (CC CPS) complained of this problem to the Politburo in spring 1947.³² The appearance of such reports did not discourage the CPY from continuing the collection policy into 1947 and 1948 because it served more than economic needs. The Communists used the collection as a way of directly monitoring the individual peasant's production and activity. Peasant resistance informed the party leadership and members of the economic and agrarian councils that it would not stand passively by and allow the state to dictate to them how they would produce and dispose of their goods.

Peasant opposition also complicated the CPY's debates concerning industrialization and agriculture. For some members of the government and party, it was still not clear whether agriculture would bear the costs of industrialization or whether agriculture would benefit from industry. As reports continued to filter in from the countryside, the CPY decided to embark upon its five-year industrial schemes without a clear plan for the agrarian sector. They would spend the next two years, 1947 and 1948, in search of an agrarian policy.

THE SHOWDOWN: PEASANT WORK COOPERATIVES

At the Second Plenum meeting of the CPY in January 1949, Edward Kardelj, heretofore a peasant ally and staunch advocate for a gradualist line in the countryside, declared the CPY's intention to form the Yugoslav collective farm, the peasant work cooperatives "with greater boldness and at a faster tempo." This announcement of the CPY left little doubt now as to the long-term interests and motives of the Communists in the countryside; they wanted to create collective, centralized, and mechanized forms of agriculture. However, this policy directly violated the principle on which the peasants and partisans had based their relationship: "the land belongs to those who till it."

The Yugoslav Communists had known all along that they had to establish more work cooperatives and move toward collective forms of agriculture. This was part of the socialist experience, one that they accepted. But in their own minds, they had to take into account their own revolutionary experience and contribution to the socialist experiment, "the new revolutionary role of the peasantry."³³ They were not prepared in 1949 to dissolve what Moša Pijade had described in 1945 as "the indestructible union of peasants and workers, this is the condition for guarding [the gains] of the NOB."[34] Thus, a real dilemma loomed when the question of collectivization was raised at the Second Plenum—how was the CPY going to reconcile its wish to create collective forms of agriculture, meaning of course taking land away from the peasants, and simultaneously honor its promise of giving land to the same peasant who had fought and toiled next to the Communists and workers.

As it discussed the cooperatives, the CPY tried to remain true to its convictions as Communists, but were anxious that they not lose the peasantry in the process. Edward Kardelj reflected this attitude in his Plenum report, "Concerning the Policy of the CPY in the Village."[35] Kardelj's report on agriculture committed the CPY to construct more work cooperatives, but proposed gradually easing the peasantry into them. Kardelj emphasized that the call for quickening the tempo of change in the countryside did not mean an abandonment of moderate policies; a series of intermediary and evolutionary steps were still needed before drawing the majority of the working peasantry into the highest form of peasant work cooperatives.[36] The Plenum resolution adopted from his report stated that the CPY would pursue a policy of rapid creation of work cooperatives but "they had to be founded exclusively on the principle of voluntarism and conscious decision of the working peasantry and that any methods of direct or indirect pressure only weakens and does not strengthen the union of peasants and workers, which is the basis of our national state."[37] Kardelj recognized that not all peasants were prepared to walk directly into the work cooperatives. He explained: "If only we can simply say to the people, 'Here is your work cooperative, enter it.' But it is not easy for our peasant individualist, who has grown up with his land simply to hand over his seven or eight hectares to the work cooperative."[38]

Appreciating the attitude of the peasantry, the CPY proposed as the basis of its policy creating the simplest forms of the work cooperatives first. Its resolution stated: "There is still a need to create and develop not only work cooperatives of the highest type but rather the lowest type, because for the peasantry it is easier to move from a lower type of cooperative to a higher type, than it is to move from individual farming directly into a working cooperative."[39] With these words, the party showed itself unwilling to call for a Soviet-style collectivization drive.

Following the Second Plenum's recommendation of gradualism and voluntarism, in May 1949 the Skupština passed the "Basic Law concerning Agricultural Cooperatives," which defined the four types of peasant work cooperatives."[40] They varied in the degree to which the peasant surrendered his/her ownership rights. In the first type, the peasant retained ownership of the land and received fixed rent from the cooperative. In the second, the peasants retained ownership of the land and received, from the cooperative, interest on the value of the land. In the third, the peasant retained the ownership of the land but renounced any benefits from interest or rent. In all three, any member of the cooperative could leave and take his land back after three years. It was only the fourth and "highest type of cooperative" that could be equated to the Soviet kolkhoz, in which the peasant transferred his land, except his household, to cooperative ownership.[41]

The actions undertaken by the CPY in the early months of 1949 reveal a cautious and evolutionary policy, one that still relied on transitional institutions such as general agricultural cooperatives and peasant work cooperatives of lower types to induce change in the countryside. Of course, the CPY intended that eventually the entire peasantry would enter the highest form of peasant work cooperatives, but they were loathe to use coercive and violent measures. Nor would the Yugoslav Communists risk warfare in the countryside, which these measures would surely bring. Appealing to their patriotism while taking away their land would not draw the peasantry back into the Communists' fold.

CONFUSION AND CHAOS IN THE COUNTRYSIDE: THE PARTY CADRES

The Yugoslavs did not embark upon a Soviet-styled massive collectivization drive. The leadership knew that it would jeopardize the political and economic stability of the countryside with such a policy and it proceeded to develop a plan that would stress the gradual movement of the peasantry into more restrictive cooperation organizations. In addition, the CPY would not tie the creation of the peasant work cooperatives to a class warfare against the "kulaks."

Edward Kardelj reminded his listeners of the nature of Stalin's frontal assault on the countryside: "In the Soviet Union, they gathered and punished in their villages this and that kulak, they scattered the kulaks, took their lands and created kolkhozes. In the Soviet Union, the process of the creation of kolkhozes and the liquidation of the kulak were undertaken."[42] Kardelj pointed out that the Yugoslavs, unlike the Soviets, would not seek to create collective forms of agriculture simultaneously with a strike against the kulak. The Plenum resolution supported Kardelj's observations. It warned of adopting policies that relied solely on stereotypes of kulaks, as well as policies that did not take into account the conditions and circumstances of Yugoslavia and each of her individual regions.[43] Thus, the CPY did not use class as the criteria in its verbal, legal, and physical assault on the countryside; it targeted those who did not fulfill their obligations to the state and those who resisted, regardless of property and income.[44] And resist the peasantry did; poor, middle, and rich peasants had something to say to the CPY about peasant work cooperatives and the measures undertaken to ensure their entrance into them. But surprisingly, so did the peasant cadres.

Reports received from all the republics pointed to the ill-preparedness of the local cadres, how they did not understand their role in forming the work cooperatives. The party leadership assumed that its peasant members would be the first to join, and the next to join would be members of the peasant's family. As the commission for the village soon found out, this was not always the case. Some party members in Bosnia-Hercegovina refused to join the peasant work cooperatives while encouraging other peasants to join. As the report stated: "This has a very bad effect on non-party members and on party members who have joined the peasant work cooperatives (Seljačka radna zadruga or SRZ)."[45] Similar observations were made in Croatia several months later. Dimitrije Bajalica, an undersecretary of agriculture, noted evasive measures on the part of Communist Party members in Dalmatia. He wrote: "In Dalmatia, in the majority of srezes, a part of the CPY membership does not enter into the SRZ. In the Šibenik srez, there were 699 party members, only 372 enlisted in the cooperative."[46] Bajalica observed how younger members who were not landowners, richer peasant members, and some older members did not join the cooperative. Also, some party members excused their parents who refused to enter with them.[47]

In a report detailing the early campaign in southern Serbia, it was observed: "Although most party members enter, in some places many [members] still remain outside, there are even some examples of members openly arguing against the formation of peasant work cooperatives."⁴⁸ The CPY leadership had anticipated confusion among the peasant cadres, but it had not anticipated their enmity. This constituency was supposed to be the CPY's most solid core. But [their actions were] "definitely having a bad influence on the rest of the people," concluded an observer in southern Serbia.⁴⁹

Reflecting upon the data coming in from the countryside, Moma Marković began to raise the alarm among the top party leadership. In his report, "Work of the Party in the Village,"⁵⁰ he noted that some party organizations were distorting the focus of the policy. He observed that they were creating peasant work cooperatives while ignoring more moderate policies, including the general type of cooperatives and other methods for socialization of the countryside such as collections, communal sowing, advancement of agricultural in general, and contracting with individual peasants for industrial crops. He urged that the party quickly increase its work in organizing and strengthening the basic party organizations in the village. It was obvious that the local cadres had not understood or consciously ignored the subtleties of the Kardelj's report or the resolution.

The directives of the CPY and the actions of the local cadres had precipitated a severe crisis in the countryside. Collectivization, Yugoslav style, had not created political and economic stability in the countryside. The panacea for the Yugoslav troubles, the peasant work cooperative, had not become a model of efficiency, productivity, comradery, and socialist development. Instead, the peasant work cooperatives lacked sufficient land, leadership, and labor with no visible improvement on the horizon. The local cadres had made a mess of the implementation, either out of ignorance, willful misinterpretation, or downright subterfuge. But this was a body of peasants who, in the minds of the leadership, should support the CPY's policies in the countryside. However, the party seemed to forget that the local cadres had to answer not only to their bosses, but to their families, friends, and neighbors as well.

"YOUR MOTHER IS A COMMUNIST"

Throughout 1949, the Yugoslav peasantry showed remarkable tenacity and ingenuity in dealing with the peasant work cooperative campaign. As direct confrontation with the party was not advisable, given the strength of the Yugoslav army, the peasants pursued a wide variety of strategies to enforce their opinions and desires on the seemingly more powerful party. The commission for the village meticulously recorded dozens upon dozens of incidents directed against local officials and peasants who cooperated with the state. Taken as a whole, these reports show the endemic nature of peasant resistance and the fairly high level of silence and tacit cooperation among the poor, middle, and rich peasants.

The tactics employed by the peasants to defend their interests in light of the collectivization campaign varied in degrees of confrontation. What separates the actions of the peasantry in 1949 from their previous actions is the extent to which peasants used violence and physical assault to get their point across to the party. Within the first few weeks of the campaign, an eight-page commission report from Serbia remarked upon several instances of violence and public unruliness in the srez of Zemun. A local cooperative was conducting an informational and educational meeting when "a kulak" interrupted the meeting and shouted at the members of the SRZ: "Down with the work cooperatives, your mother is a Communist".[51] Much to the chagrin of the local SRZ officials, disorder erupted and the meeting ended, all in the presence of secretary of the Sreski committee. Not only had the meeting been broken up, but the tone of the communiqué expressed quite clearly the embarrassment experienced by the local officials whose failure was witnessed by the SK secretary. In the same region, a "kulak" had been murdered by some other peasants in order "to settle accounts" and when the police arrived to investigate, the police were stoned. As reported later, the murdered peasant had consented to join a peasant work cooperative and the other peasants intended to "persuade" him otherwise.[52] The author of this report added his own assessment of the situation in April 1949, "the kulaks, in some places, have openly begun to carry out violence and sabotage."[53]

Resorting to murder and mayhem is not so surprising given that the peasants had very few avenues of dialogue with the CPY. They struck out at local officials and even at some of their own who decided to cooperate and join the peasant work cooperatives. In 1949, a report from the village, Donji Mihaljac, described how "enemies" shot at the party secretary through her open window while she was dining. Luckily, she was only "lightly" wounded in the head.[54] Physical attacks or threat of bodily harm were also directed at those peasants who supported the regime through compliance to the otkup or membership in the work cooperatives. The peasants often warned their neighbors as to the consequences of their actions. Slogans heard in Croatia cautioned: "There will be war, and those who are found in the cooperative will be hung." [55] A similar statement was overheard by the commission for the village of Sutjeska in Serbia, "Soon there will be war."[56] The success of this type of intimidation is illustrated through the recounting of an episode from the srez of Kragujevac.

Milivoje Miličević, observing the otkup process, struck up a conversation with a local peasant and asked why he was reluctant to deliver his grain to the state collection agency. The peasant told him: "If I deliver all the grain [to the state collection agency], I don't dare return to the village, and if I don't deliver, you will punish me."[57] This peasant was all too aware of the retribution to be visited upon him by his fellow neighbors for meeting the requirements of the state. He saw little difference in village justice or state justice.

Intimidation by physical threat was not the only weapon at the disposal of the peasants. Some peasants, knowing their neighbors and families quite well, played upon fear. Dire consequences, other than physical abuse, were predicted for those peasants who cooperated with the state. One slogan warned those who entered the cooperative of the consequences in the afterlife, "He who enters into the cooperative, renounces Christ."[58] In one village in southern Serbia, the peasants appraised the economic repercussions of entrance into the cooperatives. The observer overheard this statement: "If you go into the cooperative, you will lose your property."

Threats of loss and deprivation sounded throughout Yugoslavia. A commissioner, reporting from the Croatia, noted how "some say land would be taken away, no work would be available for them in the SRZ, and they [the peasants] would have to go into industry."[59] In the same breath the commissioner explained that in other regions in Croatia, peasants warned of hunger and losing control over their families.[60] In Kosmet, some peasants threatened their Muslim neighbors that the work cooperative leadership "will take the veils off the women, you will eat from the cafeteria; they will order your children around; and you will no longer have a mosque or celebrate Ramadan."[61] The commission also described how in one mixed Serbian and Croatian village in southern Slavonia, the Serbs refused to enter into the peasant work cooperative unless the Croats also entered. The reason the Serbian residents gave for their demand was that they had suffered under the Croatian Ustaša in 1941 and they refused to suffer now, unless of course their Croatian neighbors joined them.[62]

Ostracism and isolation were other weapons used by peasants to discourage others from joining the work cooperatives. A report from Bosnia-Hercegovina described how one village treated those peasants who formed a work cooperative. First, this report noted that the more unsavory elements in the village had participated in its creation, obviously reflecting the bias of the local cadre. Not having the respect of the other peasants in the village, this peasant work cooperative could not attract others. In fact, these cooperative members found themselves isolated from the other peasants who lived outside the cooperative. The observer had his own assessment of why this happened. He depicted the cooperative members as "rude, crude and possessing too much bravado," and having attitudes that "negatively influenced the winning over of other peasants for the cooperative."[63] In his opinion, perhaps, the other peasants had good reasons to isolate these few.

In some documented cases, shunning or threat of expulsion from the family were used by peasants to prevent brothers, sons, daughters, and sisters from following the directives of the state. One account from Croatia told of the difficult decision a widow of a war veteran had to make. This widow had entered the peasant work cooperative, perhaps receiving a letter from a war veteran urging her to join the SRZ, but was forced to withdraw because her future daughter-in-law would not join.[64] Peasant cadres themselves had to face family pressure, some excused their parents from the peasant work cooperatives.[65]

Intimidation, physical and psychological, proved to be an effective device for conveying to the local authorities the dissatisfaction of the peasants to the party's policies. What is striking in all of these accounts is how the communiqués begin to describe the peasant's activities. In these confrontations, the local authorities and the members of the commission see these direct attacks on the party and the state as challenges to their authority, power, and legitimacy in the countryside. Many of the attacks were anonymous, but the party believed that these attacks had definite political or economic motivations behind them. This was not simple self-interest. The peasants were wrestling with the party for control over the countryside. Thus, the peasants who resisted were soon being defined as "enemies," and their actions as traitorous. They were acting against the state. They had not only made "unfriendly attacks on the cooperatives from the outside but attempted to break them up from the inside."⁶⁶

Reflecting on such reports, the communist leadership decided to retreat from its policy after 11 months. Local and regional committees had violated the directives calling for gradualism and voluntarism; the party had violated the principle that the land belongs to those who till it. No matter how gently the CPY had attempted to take the land away from the peasantry, the peasantry was not going to submit to such subterfuge. The party could continue its current policy of emphasizing the importance of the peasant work cooperative and risk continued violence and opposition in the countryside, or they could retreat. Retreat they did.

At the Third Plenum of the Central Committee of the CPY in December 1949, Boris Kidrič, examining the agricultural returns for 1949 and having been briefed by members of the commission for the village, announced the retreat of the CPY from its policy of forming peasant work cooperatives "with greater boldness and at a faster tempo." Citing the opposition of the peasantry and abysmal harvest returns, Kidrič told his colleagues and the party cadres that instead of focusing on the number of actual peasant work cooperatives established, they should "concentrate on internal organization and economic strengthening of the peasant work cooperatives."⁶⁷ By abandoning wholesale and rapid formation of the peasant work cooperatives, the CPY refused to pursue the establishment of work cooperatives through violence and coercion. This was no "Dizzy with Success" speech, to be followed by a hiatus of several months, and then a resumption of brutal collectivization. In the next three years, the CPY would try various measures to get the peasantry to join the peasant work cooperatives.

By the end of 1953, agricultural policy of the CPY had gone full circle. Agriculture was freed from direct state control; the importance of the peasant work cooperative decreased; and greater emphasis was put onto the general agricultural cooperative once again.⁶⁸ The peasantry had forced the CPY to respect the original principle on which their relationship was forged: "the land belongs to those who till it." Yet the CPY lost more than the political battle; it lost the moral one as well. As Jovan Veselinov observed in 1950, the Yugoslav Communists had lost their "most ardent supporters, now they hate us [the Yugoslav communists] the most."⁶⁹

CONCLUSION

The CPY's abandonment of collectivization and renunciation of state collection policies (otkup) demonstrate a heretofore unexamined dimension of the relationship between the party-state and society: the erosion or unhinging of the central authority by cumulative, long-term effects of "permanent, continuous, daily strategies of a subordinate rural class."[70] The Yugoslav peasantry communicated its dissatisfaction through everyday forms of resistance, subversive behavior duly noted and catalogued by the agencies of the new state. Scholars have tended to overlook this part of politics, because peasants lack representatives or voices in policy debates. They neither publish dissenting tracts nor openly declare their opposition. However, in very deliberate and subtle ways, the Yugoslav peasants communicated their discontent with the state.

In the face of strong opposition, the CPY acknowledged societal resistance and discontent, reversed policy, and adopted a new ideological line in order to placate the peasantry and re-exert control over rural society. The Yugoslav Communists feared that if the party-state failed to adapt its policies to rural realities, the peasantry would move beyond its social and political reach. Each acknowledgment or recognition of societal discontent, however big or small, whether rural or urban, expanded the margins of permissible behavior and possible action and forced the reconfiguration of ideology, state structures, and elite policies. This process began when the Yugoslav Communists entered the countryside in 1941, long before the urban centers and their inhabitants became actors in this drama, and long before the "disintegration" of state socialist regimes.

In the study of state socialism, the urban classes, intellectuals, students, and workers have ensured themselves a firm place in the historical record or a seat in the post-communist parliaments. However, the rural arena, far from the television cameras and the center of power, has been ignored in the current scholarship for it has produced few dissidents, playwrights, or nationalist politicians. This general quiet in the countryside does not mean that the cumulative acts of the peasantry throughout the entire communist period did not chip away at the party-state's power and legitimacy. On the contrary, the subversion and resistance of the peasants, not of their more spectacular urban cousins, posed the first serious challenges to the East European regimes, especially in Yugoslavia.

Notes

1. In this study, Scott develops the idea that the politics of peasants fall into the category of everyday forms of resistance. He postulates that most forms of everyday peasant resistance are deployed to thwart some appropriation by superior classes and/or the state. Scott argues that there is no requirement that resistance take the form of collective action. It may have affect in its cumulative form. He states: Lower class resistance among peasants is any act(s) by member(s) of the class that is (are) intended either to mitigate or to deny claims (rents, taxes, deference) made on that class by superordinate classes (e.g. landlords, the state, owners of machinery, moneylenders) or to advance its own claims (i.e. work, land, charity, respect) vis-à-vis these superordinate classes. Symbolic or ideological resistance (such as gossip, slander, the rejection of demeaning labels, the withdrawal of deference) are included in this definition. James Scott, *Weapons of the Weak: Everyday Forms of Peasant Resistance* (New Haven: Yale University Press, 1985), 290.

2. Ibid., 36-37.

3. On August 23, 1945, the provisional parliament (Skupština) passed the "Law on Agrarian Reform and Colonization". This law distributed land to peasants who did not have any land or had less than 1.2 hectares. "Zakon o agrarnoj reformi i kolonizaciji," *Službeni list DFJ*, no. 64 (23 August 1945), 621. For liquidation of peasant debt see "Zakon o konačnoj likvidaciji zemljoradničkih dugova," *Službeni list DFJ*, no. 73 (27 October 1945).

4. Throughout 1945, the provisional government passed laws and issued decrees which created communal agricultural organizations and regulated the agricultural sector. See legislation on Machine Tractor Stations: "Zakon o organizaciji državne poljoprivredne mašinske službe," *Službeni list DFJ*, no. 53 (27 July 1945), 466-467. Additional laws regulated the agricultural sector: "Rešenje o ustanovljenju Komisije za zadrugarstvo," *Službeni list DFJ*, no. 63, (24 August 1945), 611; "Rešenje o osnivanju Glavne poljoprivredne komisije za Vojvodinu," *Službeni list DFJ*, no. 53 (27 July 1945), 471-473; "Naredba o obrazovanju odbora za setvu," *Službeni list DFJ*, no. 19 (6 April 1945), 163; "Uredba o Agrarnom Savetu DFJ," *Službeni list DFJ*, no. 67 (4 September 1945), 657-658; "Rešenje o organizaciji poljoprivredne izveštajne službe," *Službeni list DFJ*, no. 19 (6 April 1945), 162; "Naredba o obaveznoj prijavi i gradjanksoj mobilizaciji poljoprivrednih stručnjaka," *Službeni list DFJ*, no. 32 (15 May 1945), 257;

"Uredba o plaćanju za ljudski rad i rad sa stokom u poljoprivredi," *Službeni list DFJ*, no. 43 (22 June 1945), 373.

5. Arhiv Instituta za historiju radničkog pokreta Hrvatske, Zagreb-Centralni komitet, Savez kommunista Hrvatske (Hereafter cited as AIHRPH), box 3, "Politička izveštaj drugskim CK KPH," Oblasni komitet KPH za Dalmaciju," 11 April 1945, 3.

6. AJ-Savet za poljoprivredu i šumarstvo, F4/K2/32. "Zaključci sekcije za agrarnu politiku," August 4, 1945.

7. Brashich, *Land Reform and Ownership, in Yugoslavia, 1919–1953*, (New York: Mid-European Studies Center, 1954), 56.

8. "Odluke Privrednog saveta o otkupa žita treba sprovesti brzo i odlaganja," *Borba*, 6 September 1945, 5.

9. "Izjava pretsednika Privrednog saveta Andrije Hebrang o planu za prehranu stanovništva u postradalim i pasivnim krajevima," *Borba*, 2 September 1945, 2.

10. Ibid.

11. Ibid.

12. "Zakon o suzbijanju nedopušten spekulacije i privredne sabotaže," *Službeni list DFJ*, no. 28 (23 April 1945), 213.

13. "Izjava pomoćnika pretsednika Privrednog saveta o nedostacima u organizaciji otkupa viskova žitarica," *Borba*, 9 September 1945, 1.

14. "Odluke Privrednog saveta o otkupa žita treba sprovesti brzo i odlaganja," *Borba*, 6 September 1945, 5.

15. "Iskustva i pouke iz kampanje otkupa žita," *Borba*, 2 January 1946.

16. "Agrarna rasprava u sremskom selu Dobanovicima," *Borba*, 26 January 1946, p. 3.

17. "Zakon o opštem pomilovanju krivica iz uredaba o otkupu poljoprivrednih proizvoda," *Prvo redovno zasedanje Saveznog veća i Veća naroda: Stenografske beleške 15 maj-20 jula 1946* (Belgrade: Narodna skupština, n.d), 342-43.

18. Ibid., 343.

19. Ibid., 344.

20. AJ-Agrarni savet F4/K37/F318, "Prinudni otkup, slobodna cena, i kontrakti (1946), and "Zakon o opštem pomilovanju krivica iz uredaba o otkupu poljoprivrednih proizvoda," 343.

21. "Zakon o opštem pomilovanju krivica iz uredaba o otkupu poljoprivrednih proizvoda," 342-343.

22. "Tito o situaciji na selu", in Dedijer, *Novi prilozi, za biografiju Josipa Broza Tita* (Belgrade: Rad, 1984) 3:243.

23. "Uredba o strizi i otkupu vune u ekonomskoj godini 1946-1947 od 5 Maja 1946," *Službeni list FNRJ*, no.38 (8 May 1946), 413-14; "Uredba o otkupu stoke za klanje od 20 Marta 1948," *Službeni list FNRJ*, no. 24 (29 March 1948), 265-67; "Rešenje o otkupnim cenama za duhan berbe 1947 od 3 Oktobra 1947," *Službeni list FNRJ*, no. 87 (10 October 1947), 1251-125.

24. AIRPH-CK SKH, Oblasni komitet KPH za Dalmaciju, Split, Broj 1631/46, Box 5, "Izveštaj: Oblasni komitet KPH za Dalmaciju, Split, Centralnom komitetu KPH," 24 November 1946.

25. AIRPH-CK SKH, Box 3, "Izveštaj od konferencije privrednog saveta, Beograd," 28-29 August 1946.

26. Ibid.

27. Ibid.

28. AJ-Agrarni savet F4/K37/F318, "Prinudni otkup, slobodna cena, i kontrakti (1946)."

29. Ibid.

30. AJ-Savezna planska komisija, F41/K264/F436, Ministarstvo trgovine i snabdevanja FNRJ, "Uprava za otkup poljoprivrednih proizvoda," 27 August 1946.

31. AIRPH-CK SKH, Oblasni komitet KPH za Dalmaciju, Split, Broj 1631/46, Box 5, "Izveštaj: Oblasni komitet KPH za Dalmaciju, Split," 24 December 1946, 4. Reports from all over Croatia flowed back to the Central Committee describing the failure of the 1946 collections. See a report from the district committee in Banija, AIRPH-CK SKH, Okružni komitet KPH Banije, Broj 383/46, Box 5 "Izveštaj: Okružni komitet KPH Banije," 9 December 1946.

32. Ibid.

33. Djilas, *Conversations with Stalin*, (New York: Harcourt Brace and World, 1962), 30.

34. Moša Pijade, "Pred agrarnom reformom," 228.

35. Edvard Kardelj, "O politici KPJ na selu," in Branko Petranović, Ranko Končar, and Radovan Radonjić, comps., *Sednice Centralnog komiteta KPJ (1948-1952)*, 6-48.

36. Tito argued that this was not a change in direction as had been the case in the Soviet Union. See Tito, "Pretres izveštaja o rezoluciji o osnovnim zadacima Partije," in *Sednice Centralnog komiteta KPJ (1948-1952)*, 69.

37. Ibid.

38. Ibid.

39. Ibid., 275. In response to Kardelj's ideas for the socialization of the countryside, Tito complimented Kardelj for "not theorizing and for proposing a concrete path for the development of socialism and how it is necessary for us to go through several types of cooperatives." See Tito's comments concerning Kardelj's report to the Second Plenum: "Pretres izveštaja o rezoluciji o osnovnim zadacima Partije, in Ibid., 69.

40. "Predlog zakona o zemljoradničkim zadrugama," *Sedmo redovno zasedanje Saveznog veća i Veća naroda: Stenografske beleške 25–28 maja 1949* (Belgrade: Narodna Skupština, n.d.) 249-277.

41. Ibid., 264.

42. Ibid., 70.

43. Rezolucija o osnovnim zadacima Partije, in *Sedmo redovno zasedanje Saveznog veća i Veća naroda*, 278.

44. Kardelj, "O politici KPJ na selu," in Ibid., 23.

45. Arhiv CK SKJ, V KVII/33, "Radne zadruge u Bosni i Hercegovini, February 19, 1949."

46. Arhiv CK SKJ, Komisija za selo, XV 1/46, Dimitrije Bajalica and Ante Bojanić, "Izveštaj o stanju i razvoju zemljoradničkog zadrugarstva u Hrvatskoj, May 28, 1949", 5-6.

47. Ibid., 8.

48. Arhiv CK SKJ, V-KIV/16, "Izveštaj o radu partiske organizacije na selu, February 28-March 19, 1949".

49. Ibid.

50. Moma Marković, "Rad partije na selu," *Komunist*, 3 (May 1949), 97-119.

51. Arhiv CK SKJ, Komisija za selo, XV 5 I/1, "Izveštaj po pitanju zadrugarstva, April 11, 1949", 1-8.
52. Ibid., 1.
53. Ibid.
54. Arhiv CK SKJ, Komisija za selo, XV 6 I/9, "Referat Druga Dragutina Saili-a na II Plenum KPH, 1949," 10.
55. Ibid., 9.
56. Arhiv CK SKJ, Komisija za selo, XV 5 I/1, "Izveštaj po pitanju zadrugarstva, April 11, 1949," 3.
57. Arhiv CK SKJ, XV 1/17, "Zapisnik, October 10, 1949," 2.
58. Arhiv CK SKJ, Komisija za selo, XV 6 I/9, "Referat Dragutin Saili-a na II Plenum KPH, 1949," 9.
59. Ibid.
60. Ibid.
61. Arhiv Jugoslavije, SSOJ F9, Milorad Pešić, "O nekim pitanjima ideološko-vaspitnog rada u organizacijama Narodne omladine," XIV Plenum, January 5-7, 1950.
62. Arhiv CK SKJ, Komisija za selo, XV 1/46, "Izveštaj ostanju i razvoju zemljoradničkog zadrugarstva u Hrvatskoj, May 5, 1949.
63. Arhiv CK SKJ, Komisija za selo, XV 7 I/2, "Izveštaj o sastanku Komisije za selo pri CK KPBiH održanog 6. April 1949", 3.
64. Once the CPY had embarked upon this collectivization campaign, it asked the war veterans to write letters to friends, family, and families of deceased veterans urging them to join the SRZ. See Arhiv CK SKJ, Komisija za selo, XV 5 I/1, "Izveštaj po pitanju zadrugarstva, April 11, 1949," 2. The recounting of the war widow's tale is found in Arhiv CK SKJ, Komisija za selo, XV 6 I/9, "Referat Druga Dragutina Saili-a na II Plenum CK KPH, 1949," 11.
65. See discussion in beginning of chapter.
66. Arhiv CK SKJ, Komisija za selo, XV 6 I/9, "Referat Dragutin Saili-a na II Plenum KPH, 1949," 9.
67. Boris Kidrič, "Tekući zadaci u borbi za izvršenje petogodišnjeg plana," in *Sednice Centralnog komiteta KPJ (1948-1952)*, 384.

68. "Zakon o poljoprivrednom zemljišnom fondu opštenarodne imovine i dodeljivanju zemlje poljoprivrednim organizacijama od 27 maja 1953," *Službeni list FNRJ,* no. 26 (1953).

69. Sava Dautović i Milorad Vučelić, "Svašta se dogadjalo," *Nin,* April 26, 1987, 51.

70. Ibid.

5

Propaganda to Pornography: Party, Society, and Culture in Postwar Yugoslavia

Carol S. Lilly

When the Communist Party of Yugoslavia (CPY) came to power after World War II it had a vision for what it claimed would be a new and better society. In order to realize that vision party leaders knew that they must change not only their country's political and economic system but its citizens, their values, morals, goals, aesthetics, and social behavior. Among the tools by which the CPY hoped to produce those changes was culture, including literature, theater, film, music, dance, and the fine arts. This chapter will examine state-society relations in early postwar Yugoslavia by evaluating CPY efforts to use culture as a means of bringing about change in the early years of its rule.[1]

The party's cultural policies after World War II may be divided into two distinct periods. In the years from 1945 to 1950, the CPY actively sought to use culture for political and ideological purposes, prescribing its appropriate form and content and severely restricting the production and distribution of any culture that did not serve those purposes. Party leaders believed, in this period, that by controlling the form and content of culture they could mold people's tastes and direct their interests. Already by late 1947, they could see that these policies were failing. The producers of culture either could not or would not conform to political dictates, while its consumers refused to modify their tastes and interests in accordance with party policy. At first, CPY leaders hoped to eliminate the shortcomings of their cultural policies through more rigorous implementation. By 1950, however, still dissatisfied with the results and more open to experimentation as a result of the Soviet-Yugoslav split, CPY leaders relaxed their cultural policies, allowing for more artistic freedom and greater variety in form and content. They had now come to believe first of all, that if culture were to change people's minds it must respond to their existing tastes and interests and second, that in an atmosphere of open ideological debate the socialist ideology and socialist culture would, in any case, inevitably prevail.[2] Ultimately, however, as socialist culture failed to take hold and western "decadent" and popular culture maintained its appeal, CPY leaders gradually lost faith in the utility of culture as a means of indoctrination. Culture, they increasingly seemed to believe, was simply too unpredictable a medium to be manipulated for political or ideological purposes. Consequently, despite the retention of certain restrictions and taboos, Yugoslavia's cultural scene after 1950 gradually freed itself from party dictates and reflected ever more the influence of nonsocialist, western, and popular culture.

The evolution of CPY cultural policies may serve as a case study in the overall utility of culture as a means of indoctrination. A belief in culture's educational and persuasive potential has animated a wide variety of political, religious, and commercial organizations since the beginning of time. The architects, sculptors, poets, and dramatists of Imperial Rome skillfully projected an image of the regime's all-encompassing power and glory through their creative productions; Catholic and Protestant churches used oral, visual, and print culture in the period of the Reformation and Counter-Reformation to win adherents and demonize their opponents; Jacobin idealists strove to alter French citizens' fundamental values and associations through the manipulation of culture, ceremony, and rituals; and American advertisers have used the power of popular culture to promote their products and consumerism in general.[3] Yet the ultimate value of such efforts remains uncertain. The effect of propaganda in general is nearly impossible to measure, to say nothing of culture's role in it.[4]

Nonetheless, this question of culture's value as a means of social indoctrination has spurred an ongoing debate among twentieth-century U.S. historians concerning the relationship between the producers and consumers of mass or popular culture. While some argue that the Hollywood entertainment industry is imposing its own warped values and cheap aesthetic tastes on a helpless public, others insist that it is only responding to preexisting popular tastes and demands.[5] This debate is clearly relevant to our discussion of state-society relations in Yugoslavia and in all communist-dominated countries where the state held a monopoly over the production and distribution of culture and manipulated it in a direct attempt to modify the values and aesthetic tastes of its citizenry. The rapidly changing social and political atmosphere in many formerly communist-dominated regimes today lends special relevance to these issues of cultural continuity and change. What role have cultural policies played in shaping today's social values and what role can they play in future attempts to remake society?

My research, while it does not and cannot quantify the long-term and perhaps unintended effects of the communist-dominated cultural milieu, suggests that culture is not easily employed as a direct means of indoctrination. In addition, it informs us about the nature of state-society relations in Yugoslavia—indicating that even in a communist-dominated regime neither the artists nor the public were passive, but were able to influence and force modifications in cultural production. After all, despite their position in power, CPY leaders ultimately had to rely for implementation of their cultural policies on individual artists, writers, and others who often consciously or unconsciously tailored the official message to suit their own personal interests and styles. Meanwhile, Yugoslavia's consumers of culture expressed *their* tastes and interests by boycotting much of the standard or state-sponsored fare and by seeking out alternative and perhaps underground or illegal forms of culture. In a market-driven society, such consumer activity would force the producers either to adapt their standard fare or to go out of business. Communist producers of culture, while not necessarily driven by the profit motive, also wanted consumers to use their products since otherwise they could not possibly influence and direct them. Consequently, they too found that they must respond, at least in part, to consumer demands. These pressures, combined with the new opportunities provided by the Soviet-Yugoslav split, ultimately prompted CPY leaders to reconsider culture's role in the transformation of society and to abandon their efforts to use it as a direct means of political and ideological indoctrination.

COMMUNISM AND CULTURE

Communists in Yugoslavia, as elsewhere, had a utilitarian rather than an aesthetic view of culture. From the perspective of the Communist Party, culture's primary function lay in its political and educational potential and not in its value as an expression of beauty or a source of entertainment.[6] CPY leaders expected writers, artists, and musicians to instill new and correct values in people and to develop their social consciousness, becoming, in Stalin's words, "engineers of the human soul." Cultural personnel were expected to fulfill this improbable mission by adhering to the Soviet cultural doctrine of "socialist realism," according to which culture must be realistic in form while providing the correct ideological bias. Culture, the Communists maintained, was always either a weapon of progress or of reaction; it affects people either positively or negatively and must be evaluated accordingly. Even ostensibly apolitical art, such as western light music or entertainment films, was said to divert people from the political and ideological struggle and serve foreign propaganda by "awakening an interest in superficial pleasures [and] drawing out lower instincts."[7] One article gave a particularly vivid description of how such "entertainment films" lured unsuspecting youths into a trap, comparing it to that first glass of wine that may ultimately lead to alcoholism.

> A man goes to the cinema—perhaps out of boredom: it's raining, it's cold, he's a young man alone and doesn't know what to do with his long afternoon, so he goes to the movies; or else he has a meeting with a girl or a friend and after they have talked a while they go to the closest cinema. The film is chosen without any criteria, the viewer just wants to have a good time and so, in as much as he looks for any particular film, he looks for a so-called "entertainment film." He thinks, and thinks, of course, incorrectly and naively: that for those few dinars that the ticket costs he will get a little thrill, have a little laugh, get a little scared, see some film "miracle," listen to some hit music—and that the entire entertainment is worth the price of admission and that for him, personally, the visit has no harmful effects. Such a young man or woman, leaving the cinema will eventually say that he "watched some nonsense," but that he "more or less had a pretty good time," and another time he will go again to "some such nonsense" in order once again to "more or less have a pretty good time." Regardless of the fact that such an-

swers and such a position toward bad film is reminiscent of the answer and position of a future alcoholic toward his first glasses of wine—such a stand does not correspond to reality. While that young man and woman, for their few dinars, thought that they were enjoying cheap entertainment—at the same time in the course of two hours a film was played out before their eyes which not only spoiled their artistic taste, but showed them human relations in a completely false light, it sold them a pig in a poke, a lie for the truth: all unnoticed it led their thoughts off onto the wrong path. Because it is necessary to confirm the fact: the so-called "entertainment film" as a particular type does not exist; there are only good, and therefore useful and entertaining films, and bad films.[8]

The party, therefore, had to ensure that culture used its influence in a strictly positive manner, spreading socialist values and perspectives among the masses. But since, according to communist ideology, the interests of the party and the people were identical, party propagandists confidently declared that the main function of culture was to serve the people. Party leaders had no tolerance for the theory of "art for art's sake," but demanded that cultural personnel speak in a language accessible to the people. After all, if the official culture did not reach the masses, it could not possibly transform them.

This insistence that all culture be accessible and appealing to the broad public represented an effort to abolish the distinction between popular and high culture.[9] In theory at least, CPY leaders did not wish to do so by lowering high culture's aesthetic quality. Rather, they hoped eventually to raise popular tastes to the level of high culture. Simultaneously, however, party leaders regularly and explicitly demanded that high culture—while retaining its artistic quality—be made accessible to the masses at their current level of education. In essence then, the CPY made three concurrent demands of culture—that it be ideologically correct, of high aesthetic quality, and popular.

The party sought to achieve these ends and exercise its control over the production and distribution of culture through party and state organizations, employing direct and indirect censorship as well as material and moral incentives. Yet despite the party-state's apparently pervasive apparati and seemingly broad opportunities to influence and direct cultural activities, party leaders were often frustrated in their efforts to use culture for ideological purposes. In the first place, the youth, low educational level, and inexperience typical of most CPY members in the first years after the war were reflected also in the party's departments for agitation and propaganda (agitprop). Thus although party leaders sought to staff their agitprop departments with "people who know how to write well, to speak well, who are ready-made Marxists and agitators," in fact, they had to admit, "there are no such people, or only a very few."[10] Consequently, those cadres charged with the direction and supervision of culture often lacked the ideological or artistic qualifications needed to fulfill their tasks.

Moreover, in the first postwar years, CPY leaders deliberately tolerated a limited degree of both political and cultural pluralism in order to prove their broad-mindedness and willingness to work with non-communists. Yet however cooperative such non-communist cultural personnel might be, they could not be relied on to create the kind of art and literature that would transform society in accordance with communist values. Of course, even communist cultural personnel did not always produce up to party expectations. Some exhibited individual tastes and preferences in art that did not always coincide with party dictates, while others, newly inducted in the party (and in some cases also newly literate), lacked both sufficient knowledge of Marxism-Leninism to ensure the ideological purity of their work and the necessary artistic skills to secure its aesthetic quality.

Finally, variety in the form, content, and quality of cultural works produced after the war reflected uncertainty, even among well-educated communists, as to exactly how socialist realist art should look. The theoretic and programmatic principles were clear, but when it came to putting those principles into practice even the most orthodox seemed to falter. In some cases their efforts were as crude and narrow as those of the novices they so often rebuked, while in others, they were more aesthetically pleasing but were then subject to criticism as insufficiently ideological, militant, relevant, or optimistic.[11]

This confusion greatly complicated the efforts of CPY leaders to direct culture, while it simultaneously offered greater creative opportunities to cultural personnel. According to painter Mica Popović, students at the art academy regularly engaged in widely varied arguments and polemics concerning the new values in social and artistic life, and they generally considered the dominant role of socialist realism more an irritant than a real hindrance to artistic creativity.[12] Thus, some artists devised clever methods by which they appeared to toe the orthodox line while in fact doing as they pleased. Vladimir Dedijer, for example, has recalled that the modernist painter, Vojo Dimitrijević, upon learning that a prominent party leader planned to attend his first postwar exhibit, quickly penned in appropriate titles for all of his clearly modernist paintings, including, for example, the title "Dream of a Wounded Partisan at the Battle of Sutjeska" under a picture of some Parisian hallucination. The party member in question was reported to have exclaimed after viewing the exhibit, "Today for the first time I understood the essence of modern painting."[13]

Cartoons published in the party's satirical journal, *Jež*, provide further evidence that various western and "decadent" art forms continued to prosper, though often under false pretenses. One article thus explained that, in the old days, cafe music had been performed in bars free of charge so that the customers would drink more, but that now all that had changed:

> In the first place, cafe singers no longer work under such names as 'Star' *[Danče]*, 'Lady' *[Kirče]*, 'Blondie' *[Beli]*, 'Blackie' *[Crni]*, and 'Beauty' *[Lepi]*, but advertise themselves as members of the Union Branch of Educational Workers; they don't sing in cafes, but in halls for cultural performances; they don't collect tips, but charge an entrance fee of 20-40 dinars; in short they behave like renowned artists.

The repertoire, it continued, had also changed only in name and was now called "artistic" folk music rather than "cafe" folk music:

> They pour out one "hit" after another—a man could easily get the impression that he has just made the rounds of every bar in what used to be called Aleksandar Street. Finally they reverberate songs from 'Sunny Spain' clicking their castanets and the audience can imagine just how Franco's troops are feasting today.[14]

Articles and reports from many other sources also recorded a lack of "quality" entertainment. A significant proportion of the movies advertised and shown in 1945 and even 1946 were not the highly praised monuments of Soviet socialist realism, but those dreaded Hollywood "entertainment" productions like *Andy Hardy*, *The Cisco Kid*, *Tarzan*, *That Girl From Paris*, *In the Wild West*, and *Hawaii Calls*. Moreover, while the party stressed that the working man should "spend his free time in a cultural manner," and that "in our life today, there is no place for entertainment without a purpose," several reports nonetheless complained that cultural performances were often followed by parties with alcohol and dancing. The dances themselves were often of the "warped western variety," and although jazz music theoretically did "not at all come into consideration for use," it was evidently quite common at parties and performances for youth. One report complained that even a song from the voluntary youth labor brigades had been put to jazz music.[15] The very thought makes one shudder.

Ultimately, it seemed that the party's combined demands on culture—that it be ideologically correct, highly aesthetic and popular—were impossible to achieve. Postwar cultural figures could create works of art, literature, or film that were popular, but which lacked aesthetic quality or correct ideological content or both. Or they could create works with high ideological content, but which were then utterly unappealing or unaesthetic or both. Or they could create works of high aesthetic quality, but which then lacked the correct ideological component or were unloved by the masses or both. Thus, the CPY found that it could neither induce its cultural personnel to produce quality socialist realist culture, nor persuade the Yugoslav population to use and appreciate the poor quality but politically correct materials they did provide.

In short, the party found that it had not been able to eliminate the gap between high and popular culture. Artists and writers of talent could not help but wish to create art and literature that corresponded to their own elevated tastes, while the Yugoslav public showed a clear preference for cafes, alcohol, light music, jazz, and dancing to concertos and operettas and for newspapers full of light news and sports to heavy-handed political journals. Youth still preferred comic strips and cowboy movies to socialist realist classics about resistance to "enemies of the people," and women preferred fashion journals with pictures of the latest Parisian evening gowns to those women's magazines that emphasized the role of new socialist females in the construction of socialism.

Clearly, the party's cultural policies were not creating new people with new values and aesthetic tastes. If anything, those policies countered party ends by forcing many producers and consumers of culture into a stance of opposition. For when Yugoslavia's artists and citizens rejected the official fare and sought out alternative or underground forms of culture, they were assumed to be rejecting also the party's vision of the future or at least its path toward that future. The alternative and underground culture thus acquired the mystique of a counterculture and a political relevance it might otherwise have lacked.

THE CULTURAL TRANSFORMATION

CPY leaders did not take long to discover this dilemma. Already by 1947 they worried over their failure to stimulate the production of new high-quality dramas showing correct theme and content.[16] And in 1949 Tito confessed his confusion and frustration with Yugoslavia's writers. "Frankly, our writers are not producing anything substantial.... I don't know what the matter is. In Old Yugoslavia scarcely anybody made a living writing.... Now poets, novelists, and journalists are well paid for everything they do; in fact, they receive huge honoraria for books they wrote before the war which are being reprinted; *but*—"[17]

The party's growing concern over the failure of its cultural policies also coincided with the beginnings of a new stage in its graduated strategy for the achievement of socialism. CPY leaders so far had focused primarily on securing political power and achieving economic stability. Thus their cultural policies had aimed mainly at the achievement of concrete political and economic goals. By late 1947 and early 1948, however, those primary conditions had been achieved, and CPY leaders could now advance to the third stage of transforming society, culture, and people themselves in accordance with communist values. As they did so and began to address the more complex tasks of ideological reeducation and indoctrination, their expectations for culture became more ambitious and their awareness of its failings more acute.

The question then was: how could these failings be eliminated? How could the party improve the efficacy of its cultural policies? Although no single document outlined these concerns, a variety of lesser statements combined with party responses to specific examples suggest that CPY leaders believed their failings in culture to derive first from the party's lack of attention to culture's ideological content and second from the inadequate ideological qualifications of most active cultural personnel. At this point, party leaders did not question the basic premises and goals of their cultural policies but sought only to improve their application. The party, they believed, must pay more attention to culture's ideological content and must do more to ensure the ideological purity and loyalty of its cultural personnel.

The June 1948 Soviet-Yugoslav split interrupted the party's attempts to change Yugoslavia's society and culture, forcing it to focus once again on the primary requirements of maintaining power and a stable economy. Yet the split's immediate impact on the party's cultural policies was barely perceptible and showed up only in an increased inclination toward more centralized party control over all aspects of Yugoslav life, culture included. Accordingly, party reports and articles throughout 1948 and 1949 called for increased party supervision over cultural work. Meanwhile, however, they continued to demand higher ideological content in art and, what's more important, higher ideological qualifications among cultural personnel. While the use of non-party cadres in culture had initially served CPY interests, it had now become clear that although cooperative and capable non-communists might satisfactorily repeat and promote party policies, they could not be trusted to imbue their cultural productions with the correct Marxist content and values. Consequently, agitprop reports beginning in late 1947 increasingly complained about the continued presence of non-communists in many crucial areas of Yugoslav public life, including culture.[18]

Party leaders hoped to rectify the situation partly by reeducating existing cultural personnel; yet they also and increasingly looked to the creation of new young cultural cadres, with a more correct social background and well-versed in the principles of Marxist-Leninist ideology. In a pair of lectures presented to the Higher Party School in Belgrade in the spring of 1949, agitprop leader Veljko Vlahović emphasized the need to replace old, professional, but ideologically dubious cultural and agitprop cadres with younger, perhaps less refined, but more reliable ones. Though conceding that some older intellectuals sincerely tried to grasp Marxism-Leninism and might succeed, many, he insisted, were hindered by their heritage and previous education. He thus urged that large numbers of the children of workers and poor peasants, "who are just as gifted as the sons of the petty bourgeoisie . . . be sent to art schools so that they may later become the pillars of culture in our country."[19]

CPY leaders had thus grasped the importance of cultural personnel in the transformation of society, but they still believed that such personnel could be trained and employed by the party-state for its own political and ideological purposes. By the end of 1949, however, another shift began to appear in the party's approach toward the role of culture in socialist construction. After all, the old policies still did not seem to be working, nor were the new young cadres living up to party expectations. Young writers, in particular, provoked much disappointment and frustration among party cultural leaders who complained that their work continued to reflect the influence of insufficient education, narrowness, and decadent and formalist literature.[20]

THE CULTURAL TRANSFORMATION TRANSFORMED

The gradual evolution of CPY cultural policies in late 1949 also reflected a more general shift in the party's approach toward socialist construction. Throughout 1948 and 1949, seeking theoretical justification for conflict within the socialist bloc, CPY leaders had begun to reevaluate the party's ideological principles by rereading and reinterpreting the classics of Marxism-Leninism. In the process, they had developed not only new political and economic ideas about how to achieve socialism, but also a more sophisticated and thoughtful understanding of cultural and social change. The most obvious indicator of the new approach was revealed in party leaders' increasingly critical attitude toward Soviet cultural theories, which were now labeled as "dogmatic," "chauvinistic," and "bureaucratic." Even more significant was the party's new emphasis on the importance of ideological debate and "the struggle of opinions" in bringing about the transformation of society.

The first step in this direction came from CPY leader Edvard Kardelj in his December 1949 speech to the Slovene Academy of Arts and Sciences. Kardelj openly opposed theories about the leading role of Soviet science, arguing that scientific workers must be free in their creation and that "without the struggle of opinions, scholarly discussion, criticism and the practical verification of theoretical statements, there can be no progress in science and no successful struggle against reactionary concepts and dogmatism in science."[21] Djilas made essentially the same points in his speech at the Third Plenum of the Central Committee of the CPY held also in December 1949. Calling for significant changes in the party's educational policies, Djilas now suggested that it was ideologically more effective to provide powerful and convincing arguments against incorrect views than to prevent their expression. He further argued that human consciousness could not be changed by administrative measures and that the administrative apparatus could not take for itself a monopoly on ideology "without simultaneously . . . curbing the initiative of the masses and inhibiting the growth of a healthy ideological struggle between the old . . . and the new."[22]

The following three years thus saw much open criticism of Soviet cultural models combined with greatly relaxed restrictions on cultural production and distribution. Under the new policies, CPY leaders became increasingly tolerant of alternative artistic trends in high culture and began to permit their publication and exhibition. Perhaps even more important was the party's new indulgence toward western and "petty bourgeois" popular culture as party leaders now seemed to accept that entertainment for its own sake was a legitimate form of culture, at least for youth.[23] Thus, beginning in early 1950, the party gradually relaxed its restrictions on imports of new western films and jazz music and on domestic production of light and popular culture. One report from the People's Youth organization even argued that the music schools should focus especially on creating good jazz orchestras so that they might appeal to youth.[24]

Apparently, party leaders had concluded that the gap between high and popular culture could not be eliminated by artificial and coercive methods and that since the two forms of culture must coexist, they might as well live up to their names—that is, high culture should be of high aesthetic quality and popular culture should be popular. It was better to permit artistic freedom, they had decided, than to destroy culture's aesthetic value or drive it underground into a position of political opposition. The most obvious indicator of the party's new approach came in the fall of 1950 when CPY leaders demanded that all newspapers and journals become financially independent and support themselves from their own sales.[25] With this decree, CPY leaders bowed to public pressure and accepted the predominance of consumer tastes, recognizing that as long as the official culture remained unpopular and ignored, it could never change anyone's mind.

The relaxation of CPY cultural policies engendered an immediate blossoming of new cultural production at all levels. Freed from the constraints of socialist realism, artists and writers again began experimenting with new and old approaches to culture. By the end of 1950 several new literary journals had emerged that openly supported a variety of modernist and clearly non-socialist realist artistic trends. Meanwhile the public, and especially youth, eagerly lapped up the new western delicacies now available in the entertainment world. One of the first new Hollywood films shown in Yugoslavia after the war—Esther Williams' *Bathing Beauties* translated as *Bal na vodi*—was outrageously popular; Yugoslav citizens lined up for blocks to see it over and over again. Likewise jazz music flourished and western fashions, now seen in western films and fashion magazines and on foreign visitors, suddenly appeared on urban youths throughout the country.

While the reforms had clearly opened up enormous new possibilities for the creation and distribution of much apolitical and, implicitly if not explicitly, non-socialist art and culture, they had not been intended to lessen the role of communist ideology in Yugoslav society. On the contrary, based on the premise that in a free struggle of opinions the communist ideology would inevitably prevail, they reflected the party's continued attachment to and extraordinary faith in Marxist-Leninist ideology. Nor had party leaders given up on culture as a means of indoctrination. Now, however, they argued for a less intrusive approach to cultural manipulation.

Cultural artistic trends, party leaders now admitted, could not be dictated, nor could the gap between high and low culture be eliminated by fiat. Rather, they now believed that given more educational agitprop and in the course of open ideological debate, "petty bourgeois," "reactionary," and "vulgar" cultural forms would gradually wither away on their own. Thus, several documents insisted that agitprop directed at culture, while no less important than in the past, must concentrate more on education and should not become a form of censorship. Banning "bad" films, one author insisted, although tempting, would only provoke a stubborn desire among children somehow to see the film. Therefore, he concluded, it would be better for parents, teachers, and others simply to discuss the film and in general to show more concern for the proper education of youth.[26]

Party cultural and agitprop leaders responded to the new cultural policies in a variety of ways. Some clearly welcomed the new opportunities for cultural freedom and became fervent promoters of the "struggle of opinions." Others, however, were plainly less comfortable with the modified policies. For many the new approach seemed confusing since it offered no concrete information as to how socialist culture should be achieved in daily practice. Party cadres had now been informed that they could not forbid alternative approaches to culture but that they must nonetheless prevent their harmful effects. How this was to be accomplished, no one knew. They further worried that reduced censorship would only encourage the spread of openly anti-socialist and "reactionary" culture. Thus, internal and public documents from the early 1950s speak alternately in voices of toleration and outrage, reflecting the party's uncertainty and concern about its new policies.

The publication of many new and unquestionably non-socialist realist works throughout 1951 and 1952 provoked a series of heated debates in literary journals as communist cultural personnel tried to work out the limits to and deal with the consequences of their new policies. These polemics clearly indicated the fears of many that cultural freedom had gone too far and might endanger the party's progress toward socialism. An internal report from 1952 neatly summarized these concerns. Arguing that while in 1950 and 1951 the party had struggled mainly against the ideological influence of the Soviet Union, the document urged that the party now increase its efforts against the penetration of "bourgeois" ideology and decadence, which, it said,

> is being carried out with careful bowing to political slogans of socialist democracy and is characterized as the victory of that democracy. Ideologically, however, it attacks first of all the philosophical bases of [M]arxism. Dušan Matić writes, for example, that 'there is no [M]arxist aesthetics just as there is no [M]arxist physics or agronomy . . . " Dušan Nedeljković teaches 'The Philosophical Synthesis of Materialism and Idealism' in the Kolarčev People's University and *Svedočanstvo* praises him for it, criticizing only the fact that he is nonetheless too exclusivist toward domestic idealists. Belgrade's *Mladost* and *Svedočanstvo* defend the ideology of anti-heroism in literature and are reviving surrealism. Zagreb's *Krugovi* declared abstract art to be 'the only contemporary art.' And [Edvard] Kocbek in Slovenia is publishing a book of novellas which are really reactionary social criticism in literary form and which have a clearly marked personalistic existentialist position."[27]

Such concerns were particularly evident among communist leaders of the People's Youth (PY). To some extent their reaction reflected only a long history of extremism in the party's youth contingent. In this case, however, youth leaders may reasonably have felt particularly pressured, since it was youth who seemed most vulnerable to the influence of western culture and ideology but who were also expected to provide the basis for the new socialist culture. Finally, the outraged response of youth leaders to the onslaught of western culture reflected a growing generation gap between those leaders—who were, in fact, no longer so young—and their truly youthful constituents.

Thus, already in January 1951 a meeting on the work of the PY with young writers bemoaned the growing tendency of youth to support and imitate prewar decadent poetry in direct opposition to "progressive" literary art. The split with the Soviet Union, one speaker explained, while broadening peoples' perspectives, had also contributed to the idea that "various lines" of culture were acceptable and that only decadent poetry was real poetry. Even agreeing that young people always aspire for something new, the speaker nonetheless worried that so many were running from reality into subjectivism, while so few continued the tradition of "fighting poetry."[28]

Far more numerous, however, were those documents from the PY concerned about the proliferation of wild jazz music, "amoral black dances," and "bad" American films that, one said, distract youth from "our" problems and difficulties and create a myth of the West as a place where people "work very little and live very well." Others complained about the western-inspired inclinations toward extravagant fashions and tastes, slang, and cheap entertainment. One noted the formation of various "decadent," "reactionary," and "immoral" youth clubs that called themselves "teksas-klapen" bands or "sheri-brandi" brigades whose members engaged in such outrageous activities as adopting nicknames like Bimbo, Jumbo, Dedi, Fredi, and Judi, excitedly discussing idiotic American films, and exchanging old comic books about gangsters, detectives, love, or adventure.[29]

The main characteristic of such western deviations was, of course, that they were popular and designed to entertain the masses. They stood as proof that the gap between high and popular culture was as wide as ever and that the latter was not losing its appeal. Faced with repression in the late 1940s, popular culture had simply gone underground; now in the new and more tolerant atmosphere of the early 1950s it was back out in the open, sauntering down the street in a tight red dress, wearing spike heels, and gaudy lipstick. It showed up at parties and dances where, to the horror of CPY leaders, young people would "drink brandy, roast meats, swear etc."[30] It also appeared in the youthful fascination with movie stars and pop musicians (especially western ones), and with fashion fads. Djilas has recalled, for example, that in 1949-1950 the western fashion of wearing multicolored socks with tight pants hit Yugoslavia, causing great consternation among PY leaders who resented its implication that ideology wasn't important.[31]

Worst of all, however, it showed up on the pages of the new, financially independent press. CPY demands that the media become financially self-sufficient had placed an enormous new burden on editors, forcing them to seek out and walk the fine line between popularity and political reliability. This new financial requirement, combined with a serious paper shortage in 1951, now plainly revealed contradictions within the party's cultural policies, forcing people to choose sides in a battle among ideology, aesthetics, and accessibility.

Thus ideological purists shuddered and writers sneered at an article that suggested literary journals achieve solvency through higher customer satisfaction following the example of a Sarajevo stockings factory.[32] The editors of those newspapers and journals, however, facing strict financial constraints and having read reports that showed entertainment and sports newspapers reaping substantial profits while political and ideological journals operated in the red, sought to boost the popularity of their political and literary organs by lightening their tone and including more varied types of material.[33] These materials were not, however, always consistent with the party's ideological agenda. A document from the Central Committee of the PY, for example, complained that the editors of the central youth journal, *Omladina*, had clearly gone too far in their efforts to enrich the content of the paper, especially with regard to increased coverage of entertainment where, it said, the journal did not differ at all from petty bourgeois newspapers.[34]

Likewise, many publishers began creating original comic strips that were then either sold separately or inserted within other newspapers and journals. This innovation made a certain amount of sense, both financially and ideologically. Despite the party's revulsion toward them as media of bourgeois decadence and vulgar pop culture, western comic strips had remained immensely popular in postwar Yugoslavia and were a regular feature of youth underground culture and black market activity. By creating new Yugoslav comic strips, publishers could argue that they were simultaneously meeting the natural demands of youth for entertainment, providing strips that were more ideologically and politically correct than those published in the West, and increasing the circulation and profitability of their newspapers and journals. The latter claim was certainly true; the new Yugoslav strips sold out quickly and clearly contributed to publishers' financial independence. Yet CPY and especially youth leaders were far from satisfied with the strips. They worried incessantly about their criminal content, poor artistic and linguistic quality, adventurist, mystical, and sensationalist tendencies, and "vulgar" themes about the struggle for love, honor, revenge, and wealth. The editors of these strips, one author concluded, clearly did not understand issues of ideology and did not connect the strips to the problem of instilling socialist and communist qualities in youth. He cited the example of a new strip entitled "Our Beginnings" about athletic competitions in the Stone Age that, he said, included half-animal people and "impossible" animals, unknown to zoologists, but who wore modern sports outfits and used modern sports equipment. "How can such nonsense pretend to have ideology in its content?" he asked.[35]

That author accepted the possibility that domestic strips might be improved if based on events from Yugoslavia's history that, he insisted, "are much more interesting and dramatic than the impossible ideas copied from the West." But he warned that editors must guard against vulgarizing or warping those events. By way of example, he referred to a strip called "The Marriage of Maksim Crnojević," based on an event from Serbian history. The problem here, he said, was that Maksim looked more like a Hollywood film star or Tarzan than a hero from Serbia's medieval struggle against the Turks.[36]

While the author did not further elaborate on this issue, his arguments seemed to cast doubt on the party's ability to use popular culture for its own ends. Yugoslav youth might indeed read "The Marriage of Maksim Crnojević" because its form was appealing and its hero reminiscent of Hollywood superstars. Yet whatever they then learned about Serbian history and its glorious revolutionary traditions, he seemed to imply, would be overshadowed by the more potent message promoting light culture and western values. The medium, in other words, was the message. The CPY not only could not create new culture that was popular, it could not use the existing popular culture for its own purposes.

Despite such concerns, the CPY did not rehabilitate the more restrictive cultural policies of the 1940s. And however rancorous the debates and public attacks, agitprop leaders were now generally forced to rely on persuasion, only rarely resorting to old methods of censorship, intimidation, or arrest.[37] After all, those policies had also failed. Moreover, top CPY leaders remained convinced of communism's ultimate victory and the accompanying cultural transformation. Thus they downplayed the deleterious effects of western culture on youth. One author, for example, reassured his public that while youth of a certain age would always seek out adventure films and try to imitate them, they would later find them stupid and cliched. "The Magic Sword," he admitted, had inspired many boys to play at being knights with wooden swords but, he continued, "on that basis should we really prevent the film from being shown and forbid children under 16 from seeing it?"[38]

Djilas, meanwhile, reiterated his arguments about the importance of ideological debate and cultural freedom for the proper socialist education of youth. It was both natural and necessary, he said, for young people to have an entertainment, sports, and cultural life, for how else could they become broad and educated people? "They must pass through it," he insisted, "or they will become dried up people, who at the age of forty resemble some shaved official who understands only what has been ordered from above or a blinkered horse who cannot see to the right or left."[39] Serbian agitprop leader Bora Drenovac also now argued in favor of greater struggles among youth. There is nothing so terrible, he suggested, about the possibility of four answers to one question. "For me, it isn't important if a question creates chaos in the youth organization, it is good, and we should let it be discussed. . . . If some youth is excited by a theory which seems terribly important to him or if he thinks that there is no more horrible beast than a cat, let him be excited and speak out, that isn't dangerous for our youth. What is dangerous is when the struggle about such things ceases . . . what is dangerous is stagnation."[40]

Proof that the new less restrictive policies toward culture would not be reversed but continued came at the November 1952 Third Congress of the Yugoslav Writer's Union in Ljubljana. In a speech previewed and approved by top CPY leaders, the renowned Croatian author, Miroslav Krleža, openly denounced the dogma of socialist realism and the entire utilitarian approach to culture. In a conflict between a work's political or ideological content and its aesthetic form, Krleža now spoke out firmly for the latter.[41]

CONCLUSION

Yugoslavia's reformist policies in the political and ideological sphere reached their high point by the spring of 1953 and began slowly to be reversed in the following years. Yet the party's liberal policies toward culture and the arts remained. Indeed over time, CPY efforts to influence the form and content of culture gradually declined. Certain nonnegotiable restrictions and taboos certainly remained, especially with regard to the national question and Tito's personal reputation. Otherwise, however, although party and youth leaders still occasionally ranted and raved about the negative impact of vulgar pop culture, they did so no more forcefully or effectively than do those in the U.S. who decry the degenerate values promoted by Hollywood and expressed in pop music. Thus it appears that by the end of the 1950s, CPY leaders had not only abandoned their direct efforts to manipulate culture, but had given up altogether on its value as a means of indoctrination. Creative activities and consumer responses could neither be controlled nor accurately predicted. Cultural personnel—if artists—could not or would not create in accordance with party dictates, and—if party hacks—could not imbue their politically correct creations with artistic value. Likewise, cultural consumers, whether high-brow or low-brow, stubbornly refused to modify their tastes and interests to suit party expectations.

The party's response to social pressures from below meant that culture would play a very different role in Yugoslavia than in the other communist-dominated states of Central and Eastern Europe. For CPY leaders could have and, in the absence of the 1948 Cominform split, perhaps would have maintained their Soviet-style voluntaristic and restrictive cultural policies. To do so, however, would have meant accepting that the official culture would have a limited and often counterproductive impact, while alternative and underground culture would become increasingly politicized and serve as a form of protest. In contrast, CPY leaders after 1950, by depoliticizing culture, generally prevented it from becoming a form of political opposition. Only when the party sought to demonize a particular cultural manifestation—as, for example, punk music in the 1980s—did it take on importance in the political sphere. Yet even when left to its own devices, popular culture still served to undermine the communist program by rejecting its emphasis on the predominance of ideology over aesthetics or entertainment. The failure of the communist ideology to penetrate the Yugoslav consciousness was evidenced over the course of later decades by the persistence of popular culture and even more so by the appalling growth of pornography starting with the introduction of *Playboy* and *Start* in 1969 and leading ultimately to the proliferation and public display of *Hustler*-type magazines on every newspaper stand in the country.[42] Even such distasteful culture, inasmuch as it reflects the interests and values of consumers, is a means of social communication and pressure from below and discredits any notion of impotence and passivity among the populace.

Interestingly, since the dissolution of Yugoslavia several successor states have established new campaigns against popular culture. The Croatian Radio-Television Council and the Serbian minister of education have both spoken out against rock music and films with violence and sex, while Belgrade's mayor has banned pornographic magazines from being displayed on news stands.[43] Those hoping for change in these regimes may now take comfort in the certainty that such moves will not stifle consumer demands for culture that reflects their interests and may, in fact, by politicizing such culture, help create an opposition movement. On the other hand, one must admit that the idea of an opposition movement based on the demand for pornography is cold comfort indeed.

Notes

1. Research for this chapter was made possible by grants from the International Research and Exchanges Board (IREX) and the American Council of Learned Societies (ACLS). Thanks are due also to Charles Hanson, Mark Eifler, and all the participants of the Albuquerque conference for their comments and suggestions on earlier versions. The work is based largely on periodical literature and on archival documents in both Belgrade and Zagreb. In Belgrade I used the Arhiv Centralnog Komiteta Saveza Komunista Jugoslavije (hereafter ACKSKJ) and the Arhiv Jugoslavije (AJ); in Zagreb I used archives at the Institut za historiju radničkog pokreta Hrvatske (AIHRPH).

2. Most studies of propaganda in general have also concluded that to be effective it must rely on extant values and beliefs. See for example, Jacques Ellul, *Propaganda: the Formation of Men's Attitudes* (New York: Alfred A. Knopf, 1965), 295; Oliver Thomson, *Mass Persuasion in History: An Historical Analysis of the Development of Propaganda Techniques* (Edinburgh:

Paul Harris Publishing, 1977); Ian Kershaw, "How Effective Was Nazi Propaganda?" in David Welch, ed., *Nazi Propaganda: the Power and the Limitations* (Great Britain: Croom Helm Ltd., 1983), 180-205.

3. See Jane De Rose Evans, *The Art of Persuasion: Political Propaganda From Aenas to Brutus* (Ann Arbor, MI: University of Michigan Press, 1992); Garth S. Jowett and Victoria O'Donnell, *Propaganda and Persuasion* (Newbury Park, CA: Sage Publications, 1986); James Leith, *The Idea of Art as Propaganda in France, 1750-1799* (Toronto: University of Toronto Press, 1965); Michael Schudson, *Advertising, The Uneasy Persuasion: Its Dubious Impact on American Society* (New York: Basic Books, Inc., 1984); Phillip M. Soergel, *Wondrous in His Saints: Counter-Reformation Propaganda in Bavaria* (Berkeley, CA: University of California Press, 1993); and Thomson, *Mass Persuasion in History*.

4. On the difficulties of evaluating propaganda's effect see Ellul, *Propaganda*, 260-302; Leif Furhammar and Folke Isaksson, *Politics and Film* (New York: Praeger, 1971), 244; Jowett and O'Donnell, *Propaganda and Persuasion*, 25-26; Kershaw, "How Effective Was Nazi Propaganda," 180-81.

5. For a clear and unapologetic expression of both views see the introductory chapters by Bernard Rosenberg and David Manning White in their edited volume, *Mass Culture Revisited* (New York: Van Nostrand Reinhold Co., 1971), 3-21. For a more recent discussion of the issue, see the articles by Lawrence W. Levine, Robin D.G. Kelley, Natalie Zemon Davis, and T. J. Jackson Lears in *American Historical Review*, 97 (December 1992): 1369-430.

6. For information on Soviet cultural policies see Peter Kenez, *The Birth of the Propaganda State: Soviet Methods of Mass Mobilization, 1917-1929*, (Cambridge, MA: Cambridge University Press, 1985); James von Geldern and Richard Stites, eds., *Mass Culture in Soviet Russia: Tales, Poems, Songs, Movies, Plays, and Folklore, 1917-1953*, (Bloomington, IN: Indiana University Press, 1995); and Denise J. Youngblood, *Movies for the Masses, Popular Cinema and Soviet Society in the 1920s* (Cambridge, MA: Cambridge University Press, 1992). Youngblood's monograph includes a particularly interesting section on the "entertainment or enlightenment" debate of the 1920s.

7. Ivan Curl, "Muzika za ples," 16 December 1946, AIHRPH-CKKPH; and Dušan Timotijević, "Naš budući domaći crtani film," *Film*, 2 (March 1947): 31-35.

8. M. M., "Uloga filma u odgoju omladine," *Republika*, 4, 1 (1948): 95-98.

9. See Lawrence Levine, *Highbrow/Lowbrow: The Emergence of Cultural Hierarchy in America* (Cambridge, MA: Harvard University Press, 1988) and the excellent introduction by James von Geldern in Von Geldern and Stites, *Mass Culture in Soviet Russia*, xi-xxvii.

10. "Referat o ideološkom odgoju komunista," 8 December 1946, AIHRPH-CKKPH.

11. For example, Serbian agitprop leader, Radovan Zogović, was clearly one of socialist realism's most rigid and unyielding supporters. Yet, one observer has noted that Zogović's best poems were far from dogmatic socialist realism and ultimately stood in denial of his concept of art as only a handmaiden of ideology and politics. Josip Pavičić, "Uz smrt Radovana Zogovića," *Vjesnik*, 7 (January 1986), 11.

12. Milo Gligorijević, *Odgovor Mica Popović* (Beograd: 1984), 39-40, 49-53.

13. Vladimir Dedijer, *Novi prilozi za biografiju Josipa Broza Tita*, 3 (Beograd: Rad, 1984): 218-19.

14. "Nalik gajde na muziku," *Jež*, 27 April 1946.

15. Sergej Petrović, "Kulturno-umetnička društva treba da posvete veću pažnju radu svojih dramskih grupa," *Prosvetni radnik*, 1 January 1948; Curl, "Muzika za ples;" "Problemi muzičkog odeljenja Radio-Beograda," 22 December 1947, ACKSKJ, VIII II/4-d-2; "Zapisnik sa savjetovanja sa članovima žiria za nagradjivanje naših umjetnika," 2 February 1948, ACKSKJ, VIII II/4-d-5.

16. "Resultat konkursa Ministarstva prosvete NR Srbije za dramsko delo," *Naša književnost*, 1, no. 12 (December 1946): 591; Natko Devčić, "Gotovčev Kamenik u Zagrebačkoj operi," *Borba*, 5 February 1947; "Završetak sezone Zagrebačkog narodnog kazališta," *Vjesnik*, 3 July 1947.

17. Louis Adamic, *The Eagle and the Roots* (Garden City, NY: Doubleday and Co., Inc., 1952), 115. See also "Rezultat konkursa časopisa Mladost," *Mladost*, 4, no. 1-2 (Jan.-Feb. 1948): 97-98; M.P., "Skupština Udruženja književnika Srbije," *Književnost*, 5-6 (May-June 1948): 394-98.

18. "Izveštaj o organizaciji i problemima aparata KP Srbije"; "Izveštaj o ideološkom vaspitanju članova Partije," 1948, ACKSKJ, VIII II/6-13.

19. Veljko Vlahović, "Pitanje agitacije i propagande," 20 April 1949, ACKSKJ, VIII IV/a-8, 1-2; Veljko Vlahović; "Rad Partije na ideološkom vaspitanju partiskog članstva," 21 April 1949, ACKSKJ, VIII IV/a-9, 14-16.

20. "Izveštaj o umetničkom, idejnom, i političkom stanju u poeziji i prozi mladih kniževnika," 1949? ACKSKJ, VIII II/8-c-23; "Savetovanje mladih književnika i kritičara u prostorijama časopisa 'Mladost,'" 15 November 1949, AJ-Savez socijalističke omladine Jugoslavije (SSOJ) F76; "Zaključci savetovanja uredništva omladinskih časopisa i njihovih saradnika," 14-15 Nov. 1949, AJ, SSOJ F76.

21. "Govor druga Edvarda Kardelja na svećanom zasedanju Slovenačke akademije znanosti i umetnosti na dan 12 XII 1949. godine, *Nauka i priroda*, no. 1,(1950) 4 cited in Ratko Peković, *Ni rat ni mir, Panorama književnih polemika, 1945-1965* (Beograd: Filip Višnjić, 1986), 73, n.33.

22. Milovan Djilas, "Problemi školstva u borbi za socijalizam u našoj zemlji," Speech at the Third Plenum of the Central Committee of the CPY, in Branko Petranovič, Ranko Končar, and Radovan Radonjić, eds., *Sednice Centralnog komiteta KPJ (1948-1952)* (Beograd: Izdavački Centar Komunist, 1985), 289.

23. "Informacija o problemima u vezi sprovodjenja odluka III plenum CK KPJ u organizacijama Narodne omladine na univerzitetima," June 1950, AJ, SSOJ F330; "Report on the tasks of the People's Youth in schools," (n.d., mid 1950s?), AJ, SSOJ F101.

24. "Izveštaj o pitanjima kulturnog rada i života u organizaciji NO Beograda," [1949-50?], AJ, SSOJ-78.

25. Memo about distribution of the press, 10 October 1950, ACKSKJ, VIII II/5-b-50; Memo to all CKs from Milovan Djilas, 10 October 1950, ACKSKJ, VIII I/1-a-11; Olga Biljanović, "Kvalitet štampe—osnovno merilo u njeno rasturanju," 5 November 1950, ACKSKJ, VIII II/5-b-51; "Zapisnik sa sastanka o štampi," 2 December 1950, ACKSKJ, VIII II/2-b-41.

26. "Moralno vaspitanje omladine," 1951, AJ, SSOJ F76.

27. "Problemi kulturno-prosvetnog rada," 1952, ACKSKJ, VIII II/8-d-61.

28. "Zapisnik sa savetovanja o radu organizacije Narodne omladine sa književnim početnicima," 15 January 1951, AJ, SSOJ F76.

29. Informacija o Narodnoj omladini," 19 January 1952, AJ, SSOJ F330; Milorad Pešić, "O nekim pitanjima ideološko-vaspitnog rada u organizacijama Narodne omladine," 5-7 January 1950, AJ, SSOJ F29.

30. Pešić, "O nekim pitanjima ideološko-vaspitnog rada"; "Izveštaj o omladini," 1951, ACKSKJ V-KII/27.

31. Author's interview with Milovan Djilas, 6 August 1991, Belgrade.
32. Miroslav Djordjević, "Varijacije na jednu novu temu," *Književne novine*, 26 June 1951, IV/26, 1; Isak Samokovlija, "Ko je protiv borbe mišljenja," *Književne novine*, 17 July 1951, IV/29, p.1; Zoran Gluščević, "Nove varijacije na stare teme," *Književne novine*, 24 July 1951, IV,/30, 3.
33. "Pregled mjesečnog financijskog poslovanja listova *Narodne štampe*," 23 September 1947, AIHRPH, CKKPHAP.
34. "Zapisnik sa sastanka Biroa CK NOJ," 3 October 1951, AJ, SSOJ F56.
35. Report about youth illustrated newspapers and comic strips, 1951, AJ, SSOJ F79.
36. Ibid.
37. For example, although Branko Ćopić was called in to the agitprop department for a private meeting with Djilas, threatened by security officers, and publicly denounced by Tito himself for his 1950 satire of the party bureaucracy, Tito publicly insisted that there would be no legal repercussions and Ćopić was permitted to continue publishing. Edvard Kocbek, on the other hand, was apparently blacklisted as a result of his 1951 collection of "decadent" and "individualistic" war stories. Peković, *Ni rat ni mir*, 83-86, Milovan Djilas, *Rise and Fall* (New York: Harcourt, Brace and Jovanovich, 1985), 270-71: Dedijer, *Novi prilozi za biografiju Josipa Broza Tita*, 520-22.
38. "Moralno vaspitanje omladine."
39. Milovan Djilas, "O Partiji," 6 June 1952, ACKSKJ, CKKPJAP VIII IV-a-20.
40. Bora Drenovac, "Stenografske beleške Savetovanja članova Centralnih komiteta NO republika po pitanju rada u srednjim školama u narednoj godini," 16 August 1952, AJ, SSOJ F58. Drenovac, like Djilas, had previously confirmed his ideological credentials in a series of attacks on modernist and "sensationalist" deviations in *NIN*, *Mladost*, and *Svedočanstvo*.
41. Peković, *Ni rat ni mir*, 147-50.
42. Between 1985 and 1989 there was a virtual explosion of pornographic materials, which included the following new magazines: *Erotika* (1985), *Dvoje plus Erotikon* (1986), *Erotski dodir* (1988), *Extra erotika* (1988), *Sex club* (1989), *Sexpress* (1989), and *Sexy erotika* (1989).
43. *Vreme* (English-language version), no. 148, 25 July 1994.

6

Socializing the State:
Civil Society and Democratization from Below in Slovenia

Jozef Figa

INTRODUCTION:
CIVIL SOCIETY AND SLOVENE CULTURE[1]

Slovenia's independence was a culmination of the process in which civil society subverted a totalitarian state. At the beginning of that process leaving Yugoslavia was not an alternative under consideration. Rather until 1988 the focus was on expanding the space available for free expression.

Civil society is a sum total of groups and organizations that operate autonomously from the state. Some definitions see it as a distinct collective entity.[2] Students of communist societies tend to focus on grassroots initiatives emerging as the result of loosening governmental constraints.[3]

Civil society in Slovenia emerged from what became known as the "alternative scene."[4] The precise point of its discovery was a seminar/happening entitled "What Is the Alternative" organized by the Slovene alternative scene in 1983.[5] The discussion was significantly influenced by the military coup in Poland and by the repression of Slovene punks by the party-state.[6]

Communist doctrine calls for the party's control over every facet of individual life. Anything that operates outside of that control poses a challenge to the party-state authority and may emerge as a component of a civil society. What makes the Slovene development unique is that civil society emerged out of its cultural life and that its development was from the very beginning supported by a key institution of the communist-dominated political system: The League of Socialist Youth of Slovenia (LSYS).

The history of Slovene civil society is the opposite of the history of its Polish counterpart. The Polish equivalent of the LSYS did not sympathize with the demands of its youth.[7] Slovene civil society was not underground as in Poland. Nor was it Vaclav Havel's "parallel polis."[8] Rather it was a marginal phenomenon existing within the continually expanding margin of what was acceptable. In East Germany the Lutheran Church fulfilled a function analogous to that of the LSYS in Slovenia by offering its space and support to loosely structured groups of social activists that became known as New Social Movements (NSMS).[9] East Germany also created an alternative culture in the form of rock and roll.[10] But this alternative did not have the sanction of the state. In the development of civil society in Eastern Europe Slovenia is unique because its first brush with autonomous action outside of the state was generationally and culturally driven.

THE ALTERNATIVE:
PUNKS, LAIBACH, AND VISUAL ARTS

Punk rock was the first manifestation of civil society in Slovenia.[11] It appeared in Slovenia as a youth subculture in 1977. Its music was quickly disseminated by an independent radio station, which had its start in 1969. Punk rock was for Slovene youth a manifestation of a discontent with the official ideology and accepted lifestyle. Its impact was rooted in its marginality. It challenged the all-encompassing state control and the ideology of mass consumerism. It showed that culture could and even should happen outside of the party-state framework. By deliberately positioning themselves outside of the mainstream social order, the proponents of punk paved the way for other manifestations of "alternative culture." They argued that creative behavior and thinking is possible only on the margins of the society[12] and with this position they began the process of challenging the party's monopoly over defining what is allowed. The groups leading that process have been described by social scientists as NSMs. In a roundtable discussion in March 1981, journalist Dušan Rogelj observed:

> Alarms around Punk appear above all because Punk events place themselves as an alternative to other organized forms. And between Punk manner of expression and organized manner of expression (cultural organizations, youth organizations) there is emptiness and as a matter of fact, these organized structures of manners of expression do not know what to say about what takes place spontaneously. A Spontaneous event is probably the only constructive form of searching for one's own identity. Second, it alarms that we have an alternative culture . . .[13]

In the same discussion Gregor Tomc, a member of a punk group named Bastards, answered the accusation that punk is "foreign" to Slovenia. On the contrary, he argued, "Punk is problematic because out of all the music it is the least foreign."[14]

Punk was a young people's movement that transcended all class divisions.[15] Its texts talked about the opportunism of aspiring young politicians, monotonous and dehumanizing work, indifference to human suffering, and alienation from all authorities. Saying such things outside of the approved framework indicated that young people found it impossible to express themselves through the organization that was supposed to represent them, the LSYS.

Of course, as in the rest of Europe, punk constituted a loud minority, whereas the silent majority preferred disco.[16] The best policy for the party-state would be ignore the movement. Why this did not happen can be explained by the nature of Yugoslav politics.

Expressing criticism was consistent with the official ideology of self-management, but contrary to the praxis of the rulers. The latter demanded the monopoly over determining what can be said, where, and when.[17] Violations were interpreted as manifestations of hostility to socialism; a counterrevolutionary activity that needed to be thwarted with the available means.

The excuse for attacking the punk movement came from its graffiti, which often parodied official slogans. The slogan "Mi So Titovi", became "Mi So Sidovi."[18] Other slogans were deliberately provocative, for example, "Down with the Red Bourgeoisie," and "Down with the State."[19] On some walls swastikas appeared. Such provocative slogans and symbols gave the police, courts, and juvenile authorities a reason to claim that the punk movement contained fascist components.

Attacks on punks began following a newspaper article that linked punk to fascism and anarchism.[20] Subsequent harassment of punkers included arbitrary arrests, beatings in police stations, pressure on parents of punk groups' members, banning various symbols of punk, and harassing punkers in their schools and at work. A number of places where punkers used to meet were closed, some permanently, some for renovations. In several places, in a true self-managerial manner, waiters refused to serve people suspected (usually because of their dress) of being punkers. In a few cases people involved in punk were arrested for insulting the national and patriotic feelings of citizens. The Slovene students' radio station, Radio Student, was accused of playing the anthem of the Third Reich during one of its programs. Police claimed to actually discover a fascist punk group as well as an anarcho-fascist group.[21]

Attacks on punks mobilized a number of young artists and writers who enjoyed the support of the LSYS. They pointed out that there is a major difference between anarchists and fascists, and that there was no proof of fascist links or sympathies among Slovene punkers.[22] Repressions of the autonomous movement and the defense of it by state-sanctioned writers and artists politicized punk and transformed it into a seed for the future civil society.

Operating outside of the framework of approved sociopolitical organizations was a major innovation in socialist Yugoslavia. This was inadvertently confirmed in 1982 by an army delegate to the Eleventh Congress of the League of the Socialist Youth of Yugoslavia. Criticizing a statement by a Slovene delegate who "fights for the existence of the Punk and criticizes our society"[23] he suggested: "Against our negative phenomena we have to struggle by working through organizations already well known to us, youth, party, trade union, pioneer, veteran, and other socio-political organizations, not by creating new, organizations and movements foreign to our society."[24]

However, punk now had space within the political establishment. The LSYS began to tolerate punk music and the punk movement in places under its control, especially in Ljubljana. Punk and then other manifestations of the Slovene alternative scene were able to express themselves openly over the Radio Student, in the FV Disco in the student housing complex in Ljubljana, and in the Student

Cultural Center (SKUC). In 1983 all of these groups moved into the Center for Interest Activities of Young People. As a further show of tolerance in 1984 the center opened a gay disco.

By 1985 there were roundtable discussions about punk, its music was played on a number of TV and radio programs, and punk clothing became commercialized. By the mid-1980s punk was mainstreamed and tamed. What was left of it evolved into hard rock, which found a niche, was not harassed, and, partly because of that, had no political impact.

Punk initiated the process of the uncoupling of the LSYS from other official organizations. Eventually the LSYS became an organizational framework for all of the manifestation of the Slovene "alternative scene." The scene began with a group named Laibach.[25] It started an important trend in Slovene "anti-culture:" subverting totalitarianism by mimicking it. Its technique of using totalitarian texts and images in their performances was eventually adapted by other components of the Slovene alternative scene. The ultimate goal of Laibach and its spinoffs, notably a group of artists named Neue Slovenische Kunst, was to sensitize people to their totalitarian surroundings by deliberately using totalitarian symbols and iconography—both German Nazi and Soviet Stalinist Communist.[26] When Laibach was accused of wearing costumes that looked like Hitlerjugend uniforms, they answered that the uniforms were based on those of Yugoslav soldiers.[27]

Authorities fought Laibach by banning its performances. One of the excuses was that Laibach is a German name for Ljubljana. And they accused Laibach of disseminating fascist ideas.[28] But visual arts and multimedia political theater were left alone. They continued with their antimodernist and antitotalitarian messages through multimedia techniques and mimicry and kept on transcending the limits of what was acceptable. They were joined in it by the NSMs.

There is an argument that civil society, by virtue of its autonomy from the state, enables those who participate in it to reach such elusive goals as freedom and authenticity.[29] It does so by freeing organized social behavior from numbing state-sponsored rituals. In Slovenia this quest for freedom and authenticity (as opposed to careerism and opportunism facilitated by repeating increasingly meaningless slogans and conforming to rigid rules and rituals) began with punk rock. It was followed by Laibach that, in turn, influenced new forms of visual arts, drama, and, finally, groups and movements that sought to move beyond the state in other spheres as well. All of this challenged the status quo by destroying accepted models of culture, expression, and societal behavior. By the mid-1980s intellectuals, and a few years later, politicians, began to challenge party-state authority.

NEW SOCIAL MOVEMENTS

The NSM's key characteristics were their loose organizational structure and postmodern interests and values.[30] They were concerned with Slovenia, but focused on the quality of life, rather than on territorial dimensions of the national question.[31]

NSMs addressed issues not faced by the political establishment. They posed a dilemma for the rulers: By permitting NSMs to operate, the party-state allowed them to expand into the space for free expression, thereby giving up control over certain social and political processes, even though the party-state at any time could lay claim to that space if they were prepared to use violence. By clamping down on them it would arrest the process of democratization. Yugoslavia in general, and Slovenia in particular, were very proud of their progressive and democratic nature vis-à-vis the USSR and its allies. An antidemocratic purge would be embarrassing when Soviet totalitarianism was on the verge of collapse. With Tito and Kardelj dead such a purge would be perceived as being imposed from Belgrade, that is, as inherently anti-Slovene, and interfering with Slovene autonomy. No political organization in Slovenia could afford creating such an impression.

NSMs did not raise any taboo issues except for the pacifists. Nor did they ask for something that was unacceptable within the framework of self-managerial, socialist Yugoslavia. Further, their insistence on operating informally, that is, without a formal, organizational framework, made it difficult to accuse them of organizing anti-state plots.

NSMs were concentric circles of sympathizers and activists, a stable nucleus surrounded by circles of friends and fellow travelers. Most of the participants were young people with a university education, usually employed in the areas that focused on humanities, human relations, and human services.[32] Since NSMs were issue- not ideology-oriented, anybody was welcomed regardless of his or her political affiliation. Those issues were rooted in postmodern concerns and included opposition to using violence in any form of human interaction, peace, minority rights, environmental issues, alternative forms of psychotherapy, and gay rights.

The societal background of the participants determined the specific groups they chose. Groups focusing on civil rights, opposition to the death penalty, abolition of Article 133 of the Yugoslav Constitution, and those focusing on protecting cultural heritage consisted of educated middle-class, and middle-aged activists. Pacifists, ecologists, spiritualists, and sexual minorities were younger, with roots and experience in the youth subculture.[33] Members of various groups interacted socially. Thus the NSMs created a *network* of alternative groups that operated outside of the official organizational framework. For example, feminists, environmentalists, and pacifists co-organized protest "celebrations" in 1986 and 1987. The latter event coincided with the anniversary of Chernobyl.[34]

The event commemorating Chernobyl and its effects also demonstrated that NSMs were rooted in Slovene cultural tradition and recent fears. The pride over their landscape is a very important contributor to the Slovene sense of uniqueness and self-worth. Environmentalists linked those values to problems rooted in (socialist) industrial development that resulted in environmental catastrophes both outside of Slovenia, notably in Chernobyl, and in Slovenia, notably the poisoning of several rivers. The Krško nuclear power station in earthquake-prone Slovenia proved particularly troubling to most Slovenes.

The techniques NSMs used to accomplish their goals varied according to those goals. In general they preferred various forms of peaceful, direct actions, for example distributing leaflets, to appeals for action through the official channels. NSMs's attitudes to those channels and to traditional politics varied with their goals. They were essentially consciousness-raising movements. But some groups found it necessary to enter the official political scene in order to influence legislature. The distinction between groups staying out of official politics and those joining into it was a matter of the issue as well as strategy. Groups focusing on spiritual transformation did not need the state. On the other hand, groups interested in changing existing laws had to deal with the political establishment. All of the NSMs enjoyed the LSYS's support and as the result of this support NSMs were the major catalyst in the process of activization and democratization of the LSYS.[35] Pacifists offer an example of this process.

THE PEACE MOVEMENT

The significance of the Slovene peace movement lies in its impact on Slovene-Yugoslav relations. By not suppressing it and by accepting some of its demands Slovene republican authorities found themselves in opposition to the federation and its army. Also, the pacifists contributed to the evolution of the LSYS into an independent political force.

We need to compare pacifists to Slovene punks. The latter were suppressed and repressed by local authorities in spite of their reliance on the LSYS for the protection and sponsorship. But, while punks' only explicit political demand was to be left alone by the authorities, pacifists openly challenged political order by calling for specific legislative changes. Since that challenge involved an all-Yugoslav institution, the army, it was impossible to *contain* the Slovene social movement within the confines of Slovenia—short of brutal repressions. The pacifist movement became an important contributor to the process of the transformation of the conflict between civil society and the state into one between Slovenia and Yugoslavia.

The pacifists' challenge took place in a new political climate. Tito was dead. Therefore the ultimate authority that could have been invoked to justify any repression was gone. With his death the army lost the key supporter of its all-Yugoslav role. There was also a change of leadership in Slovenia. The new authorities, both in the party and in the government, were far more liberal than their predecessors. Finally, Slovene pacifists were in touch with a Europe-wide pacifist movement operating in an information-dominated environment. Any form of repression would have reverberated throughout Europe.

Pacifists and the army clashed over laws concerning conscription. Mass conscription was the key component of the doctrine of the Total People's Defense and of the Yugoslav constitution. Religion and conscience were not recognized by authorities as legal reasons for avoiding the draft. Jehovah Witnesses routinely served multiple prison terms for refusing to serve in the army. Pacifists demanded introducing alternative service in social or humanitarian institutions such as hospitals or hospices. This was to include not only Jehovah Witnesses, Nazareans, or Adventists, but also anarchists, conscientious objectors, and anybody else whose conscience forbade him to carry weapons.[36]

The official name of the group was The Working Group for Peace Movements. Formally, it operated under the overall umbrella of the republican committee of the LSYS.[37] However, the initiative belonged to the working group. Since the working group wanted to change the law, it needed an entry into the official decision-making and political bargaining process. But this group was not represented in the delegate system and needed somebody to represent it in the legislature. In short, they needed the LSYS.

The working group "used the alternative youth media,"[38] which operated under the LSYS's umbrella, to present its initiative in 1985. It was the beginning of a serious and open debate of a previously taboo subject. An openly rebellious Krsko congress of the LSYS in 1986 authorized its leadership to present the initiative to the Socialist Alliance. Its official document suggested amendments to existing laws: a single, rather than multiple sentences for those refusing to serve, unarmed service in military units, and service outside of military units.[39] None of this was acceptable to the army. And the army had the decisive influence on *federal* authorities as far as military matters were concerned. Since this was not the case at the *republican* level, a conflict between the republic and the army over the federal legislation emerged.

The chairman of the Socialist Alliance, Joze Smole, stated in 1986 that alternative initiatives were acceptable, if they did not question one of six taboos: self-management, nonalignment, general people's resistance, social self-protection, the Yugoslav People's Army, and the federation as the way Yugoslav nations are united.[40] Thus the official reaction in Slovenia was ambiguous, since the working group's initiative did not challenge the need for the army, but rather the army's monopoly over decisions concerning the nature of the military service.

At the republican level, pacifists' demands were actually discussed and addressed. In fact, commissions and committees that were dealing with defense matters in the central committee of the League of Communists of Slovenia and of the Socialist Alliance of Working People of Slovenia found the initiative fit for discussion and, in some cases, actually supported some forms of alternative services for religious sects. Major criticism came from the media outside of Slovenia. They, by and large, voiced official positions to the initiative—except for the youth media.[41] Slovene media gradually began to look at the entire affair more objectively.

The Slovene Socialist Alliance sent to the Yugoslav Socialist Alliance a suggestion to abolish repeated sentences and offer alternative service in army units to members of religious sects.[42] In this manner, a group that was not a component of the official political scene acquired legitimacy. Notwithstanding the death of the initiative at the federal level, pacifists and members of other NSMs continued to demand publicly alternative service for all conscientious objectors. The student Cultural Club (SKUC) was the permanent forum for such discussions.

Pacifists's reliance on the LSYS as their representative in the Socialist Alliance contributed to the change of the role of LSYS. Rather than being a mouthpiece of the party, it actually became a mediator and the source of an important legislative initiative. Slovene pacifists therefore effectively challenged the army's monopoly over issues involved in defending the country. They also contributed to enhancing the status of the magazine *Mladina*. Finally, they challenged the army's monopoly over a number of decisions, notably over the control of the draft.

Other challenges followed. *Mladina* and other journals began to publish articles about harassment of Slovene conscripts in the army. Thus the army-pacifists conflict resulted in enhancing the status of *Mladina*. When *Mladina* was defending punks, it represented the LSYS as the whole and it positioned itself against local authorities in Slovenia. This was an important moment. *Mladina* was becoming a journal opposed to what amounts to be the conservatism of *local* authorities. In 1977 it was not yet critical of *republican* authorities. By taking pacifists under its wings it became a critic of *federal* authorities. It bypassed the criticism of Slovene Communists. This enabled *Mladina* to survive, because only republican authorities were in a position to silence it, and there was no one to order them to do so. It became the voice for Slovenia *against* the Federation and the Army.

Pacifists facilitated the crystallization of the status of *Mladina* as the journal that would stand up for Slovenia in any dispute. In particular, it positioned itself as the chief critic of the army.

In the spring of 1987 *Mladina* took up this particular task with a vengeance. It attacked the overall militarization of the state, the selling of weapons to Ethiopia, and the Minister of Defense Admiral Branko Mamula's use of state military funds for the construction of his private country house. When *Mladina* published a document suggesting that the army was preparing a coup, four people responsible for it were put on trial.

The alternative service initiative resulted in the increased focus of the media on the army—beyond ritual descriptions of the glory of the service, its holidays and anniversaries. It ceased to be a taboo subject for journalists. Furthermore, Slovene journals other than *Mladina* began to write about the peace movement's initiative in particular, and about NSMs in general, with either sympathy, or at least without a bias that would reflect the official party (and army) line. The weekly *Telex* came quite close to sharing the ideas and sympathies presented by *Mladina*.[43] The journal *Problemi* contributed to the growing legitimacy of NSMs by becoming a forum for a number of their members and by systematically publishing theoretical analyses that looked at NSMs as a distinctly postmodern phenomenon. At the same time major journals outside of Slovenia, such as *Danas* and *Nin*, took the side of the army. The conflict between Slovenia and Yugoslavia began.

The pacifist initiative was accompanied by two other conflicts between Slovenia and the JNA: the use of Slovene language in the army and the control over Slovene territorial defense and its weapons. They exploded with full force as the result of the democratization of the official Slovene politics and provided the final stimulus for Slovenia's leaving Yugoslavia.

TITO RELAYS AND THE POSTER AFFAIR

In 1987 LSYS decided that Tito's relays and celebrations of the Youth Day ought to focus on specific concerns of Slovene youth, such as unemployment or environmental pollution. The Tito Relays and the poster affair enabled LSYS to define itself as a democratic force struggling against a totalitarian opposition.

A poster produced for the relay by an artist group called New Collectivism turned out to be based on a Nazi poster.[44] The Belgrade daily, *Večernje Novosti*, which was the first to break the news on 28 February 1987, stated that, while all of those involved in approving the poster could not have been aware of its original source, it is difficult to believe that linking socialist and Nazi symbols was a coincidence.[45] New Collectivism argued that the poster was an example of the retro principle in art and that "emotional impulse can engender irrational reactions in broader cultural and political space."[46]

The ensuing debate over the poster pitted leaders of the Youth League's central leadership against LSYS leadership and *Mladina*.

Federal leaders called for the criminalization of the poster alleging that it amounted to an attempt to smuggle fascist ideas into the Day of the Youth.[47] *Mladina* saw these calls as evidence of the conflict between democracy and the totalitarian state. It was also criticized by the president of the League of the Socialist Youth of Yugoslavia, Hašhim Rexhepi, who called for the use of "Yugoslav language" during the first stage of the relays, that is, the one taking place in Slovenia.[48] Other initiatives supported by LSYS's were also attacked, for example the LSYS organizing a congress of homosexuals and lesbians. There was also strong criticism of the Slovene democratic media, especially of *Mladina* and *Tribuna*. The political scientist and journalist Pavle Gantar observed that the official Yugoslav ideology saw fascist consequences in everything they could not comprehend. But accusations of fascism pointed to the threat of the use of the state apparatus to suppress Slovene democratic movements.[49]

Several Slovene intellectuals explained their perspective on the entire affair in an open letter entitled "The Call to Reason." Its authors pointed to growing tendencies to use conspiracy theories by some authority figures to explain normal societal developments that they did not initiate. They were a product of the "logic of totalitarian ruling." Hence the call to reason that was directed to "all democratic forces in Yugoslavia."[50] This statements is significant because it did not contain any anti-Yugoslav rhetoric. Rather it juxtaposed democratic and antidemocratic forces. The latter revealed their totalitarian essence by calling for banning the poster and prosecuting people responsible for it. *Mladina* answered that the poster's critics were not interested in a legal procedure, but in a political trial and in retarding the process of democratization.[51]

In a subsequent roundtable debate Gantar stated that fascist tendencies characterized not the New Collectivism but those who attack them. Journalist Rastko Močnik added that the coalition ruling Yugoslavia was not able anymore to endure the integration of the country on a "healthy basis," so it was necessary to "consciously organize a democratic front of Yugoslav forces."[52] The latter were present in the political establishment and in the agencies of the state.[53] The "poster affair" proved that the line separating the "bureaucratic totalitarianism" and democratic forces cut across the entire sociopolitical structure of Yugoslavia.[54] At this point the hypericonoclastic *Mladina* thought that Yugoslavia might survive the transition to democracy.

Ultimately the affair proved that the LSYS did not consist of obedient political opportunists. Further, the LSYS embraced as its own those initiatives that came from NSMs. Civil society began to socialize the state. The LSYS also accepted the idea that in Slovenia one has to debate Slovene problems. This was a shift from worshiping the all-Yugoslav icon to focusing on issues that were defined in national terms.

SOCIALIZATION OF THE STATE

Public opinion surveys indicate that the NSMs' initial place among the public and in the media was marginal. Their impact grew because of Slovene concern with the environment, following several ecological catastrophes. The result was the increase of the support for environmentalists, and subsequently, for other NSMs.[55] By 1986, surveys indicated that most Slovenes were aware of the NSMs' activities. By 1988, as the result of the growing threat of the army's intervention in Slovenia, issues of national security began to dominate Slovene public opinion. Also, the Slovene political establishment positioned itself against the army. This led to the marginalization of the NSMs.[56] They lost their antiestablishment edge because the Slovene political establishment joined the growing anti-Yugoslav consensus.

Slovenes did not accept NSMs as an alternative to the official political system. They supported their autonomy (about 55 percent of respondents), but while 25 percent supported their total autonomy, 30 percent supported their autonomy in the framework of the Socialist Alliance.[57]

But NSMs were the key catalyst in the emergence of conflicts between Slovenia and the Yugoslav Army and between Slovenia and Serbia. These conflicts, in turn, facilitated democratization of the political establishment. The 1986 and 1987 public opinion surveys indicated that the majority of both members and functionaries of the LSC were willing to cooperate with the NSMs. In fact, functionaries were more interested in it than LSC members.[58] The party elite was willing to accept democratization of politics, without necessarily accepting the principle of political pluralism based on competition among various political parties.

THE FINAL STAGE: THE TRIAL OF "THE FOUR"

By 1985 there were no taboo issues in Slovene public debates. In the field of culture, language became a point of contention in a debate between the Montenegrin writer Miodrag Bulatović and his Slovene counterpart, Josip Vidmar. In a 1985 speech in Ljubljana, Bulatović stated that Slovene national consciousness and language amounted to separation from Yugoslav patriotism and in subsequent interviews insisted that Yugoslav patriots speak only Serbian. Vidmar a bonafide Titoist and Yugoslav patriot answered that the Slovenes's path into European culture lies in their own language. This clash and subsequent attacks on Vidmar resulted in Slovene writers' opposition to Bulatović's candidacy for the post of the president of the Union of Yugoslav Writers.[59]

Around that time the most respected of Slovene economists, Alexander Bajt, publicly stated that a market system is superior to self-management.[60] He followed with the argument that the latter was a major obstacle in the process of modernization of the Yugoslav and Slovene economy. He also pointed out that Yugoslav economic policies favored less-developed economies over those that were more effective exporters.

In 1986 two key journals devoted entire issues to the Slovene national question: *Revija 2000,* a Catholic journal representing the liberal Catholic tradition rooted in writings of Mounier and Maritain, known as personalism, and *Nova Revija*. *Revija 2000* began the process by publishing a series of articles about national issues that inter alia included discussion of small nations under socialism, and Leninist principles of depriving nations of their culture, a relatively modest beginning of what was to come next.

All of it culminated in *Nova Revija,* which appeared in January 1987. To a certain extent it was a response to the memorandum of the Serbian Academy of Science. The response explicitly raised the subject of Slovenia's status in Yugoslavia and its right to self-determination. It was the catalyst for the growing conviction that Yugoslavia in its Titoist, socialist, self-managerial version could not contribute anything anymore to the cultural, political, economic, and social developments of Slovenia.[61]

This conviction was increasingly supported by Slovene Communists. It put them on a collision course with the defendants of the old order, a status that to a certain extent was claimed by Serbian Communists around Slobodan Milošević. Moreover, the army emerged as the key Yugoslav institution. In this way the conflict between civil society and the state was redefined in nationalist terms as one between Slovenia and the army. It culminated in the affair known as the Trial of the Four.

What interests us here is not the chronology of that historical event, but rather its impact.[62] It was an attack by an agency of the Yugoslav state on the process of opening, on democratic forces and the process of democratization. The use of Serbo-Croatian in the proceedings that took place in the military court in Ljubljana was treated not only as an insult, but as an attack on the Slovene language. Milan Kučan summarized the reaction in a speech during the meeting of Slovene Singing Societies. He stated that the Slovene nation cannot treat as its own the state that curtails its right to use its own language.[63] The president of the League of Slovene Communists positioned himself and his party as defenders of Slovenia against Yugoslavia.

The trial united all the groups of Slovene civil society. They formed the Committee for the Protection of the Rights of Janez Janša. It soon became the Committee for the Protection of Human Rights. It became a de facto political opposition supported by republican authorities.[64] This resulted in the final redefinition of the conflict: The forces facing each other were Slovenia and the only remaining Yugoslav institution—the army.

CONCLUSION

The independence of Slovenia was a culmination of a process of transformation of Slovene politics that began in the early 1980s. The initial goal of that process was to expand the space available for free expression primarily in the sphere of culture. This goal involved an important ambiguity. The level of decision making was always quite problematic in Yugoslavia. The post-1974 self-managerial decentralization put the emphasis on local authorities and on those who were directly affected by decisions. Formally, decision-making rights of the central government were quite limited. However, Tito's charismatic authority enabled him to directly or indirectly influence local affairs and to impose his will on them. With Tito's death the key vestige of central authority disappeared and the ambiguity remained.

The resulting political order consisted of pluralism of political elites at the federal level and a one-party system at republican levels. Republican ruling elites were in charge of dealing with dissent. The scope of freedom was dependent on those elites.[65] With a vacuum of power at the center the army tried to assert itself as the central authority. This attempt united Slovenes in opposition to the army and to Yugoslavia.

The process that culminated in the independence of Slovenia began with the state politicizing an independent movement—the popularity of punks. The fact that this movement, and later other groups that formed a Slovene alternative culture, found its umbrella organization in a component of the political establishment, the League of Socialist Youth of Slovenia, resulted in the democratization of that particular component and then the rest of the establishment. Since the democratization was perceived as increasingly anti-Yugoslav, the result was the clash between Yugoslavia and Slovenia. Since the legal and political arrangement of Yugoslavia put local authorities in charge of maintaining political order, the clash resulted in a crystallization of an anti-Yugoslav consensus across the entire Slovene society. By democratizing republican politics, civil society in Slovenia began the process that culminated in the collapse of Tito's Yugoslavia.

Notes

1. I am grateful to the IREX for its Short Term Travel Grant (GIST), which immensely facilitated research for this article. I would like to thank the Director of the Institute of Sociology in Ljubljana, Dr. Vojko Antončić, for his overall help in conducting the Ljubljana part of my research. I also would like to thank Drs. Veljko Ruš, Gregor Tomc, Pavle Gantar, Matjaž Klemenčić, and Miso Jezernik for their help and advice. Preparing the final draft of this article was helped by the advice and criticism of both reviewers and Dr. James Seroka. Finally, I am very grateful to Dr. Melissa Bokovoy for her editorial suggestions.

2. Adam B. Seligman, *The Idea of Civil Society* (New York: Free Press, 1992), 5.

3. For example see Vladimir Tismaneanu, *Reinventing Politics: Eastern Europe from Stalin to Havel* (New York and Toronto: The Free Press, 1992).

4. The term *alternative scene* denotes a network of social movements that operated outside of the party-sponsored organizational network. The scene included pacifists, gays, environmentalists, feminists, and seekers of "new spiritualism." It also included groups of young artists and several rock groups. See Tomaž Mastnak, "From Social Movements to National Sovereignty," in Jill Benderly and Evan Kraft, eds., *Independent Slovenia; Origins, Movements, Prospects* (New York: St. Martin's Press, 1994), 94.

5. See Tomaž Mastnak, "Civilno Društvo u Sloveniji: od Opozicije do Vlasti," *Sociologija*, XXXII, no. 4 (1990): 438; Tomaž Mastnak, "Civil Society in Slovenia: From Opposition to Power," in Jim Seroka and Vukasin Pavlović, eds., *The Tragedy of Yugoslavia: The Failure of Democratic Transformation* (London: M.E. Sharpe, 1992); Pavel Gantar and Tomaž Mastnak, "Civilna Družba na Slovenskem: Prva Petletka," *Problemi*, XXVI, no. 10/302 (1988): 71. Zoran Pokrovac, "Razlika Gradansko Društvo-Država i Nova Vlast," *Sociologija*, XXXII, no. 4 (1990): 459-77.

6. Gantar and Mastnak, "Civilna Družba na Slovenskem," 71-72.

7. For Polish developments see Roman Laba, *The Roots of Solidarity: A Political Sociology of Poland's Working-Class Democratization* (Princeton, NJ: Princeton University Press, 1991); see also Jan Jozef Lipski, *KOR* (London: Aneks, 1983).

8. This term refers to a network of social and civic organizations operating underground, in defiance of the party-state monopoly over organized social life. See Vaclav Havel, "Power of the Powerless," in John Keane, ed., *Power of the Powerless: Citizens against the State in Central-Eastern Europe.* (Armonk, NY: M.E. Sharpe, 1990), 23-96.

9. For a definition of New Social Movements see pages 261-63, which discuss NSMs in Slovenia.

10. See Sabrina Ramet, *Social Currents in Eastern Europe: The Sources and Meaning of Great Transformation* (Durham and London: Duke University Press, 1991), Chapter 2.

11. See Mastnak, "Civilno Društvo u Sloveniji," and "From Social Movements to National Sovereignty."

12. See Gregor Tomc, "Apokaliptični Paradiž," *Punk Problemi*, no. 7 (1988): 6-16.

13. Reprinted in *Punk pod Slovenci* (Ljubljana: Univerzitetna Konferenca ZSMS, 1985), 180.

14. Ibid., 181. Bastards were the premier group of Slovene punk. Tomc quickly emerged as one of the key spokespeople for Slovene punk.

15. Bastards were followed by groups named O!Kult, Ljubljana Dogs, Children of Socialism, and Rotten Souls, to mention a few.

16. *Mladina* journalist Darko Strajn, quoted in *Punk pod Slovenci*, 182.

17. Rastko Močnik, "Razum Zmaguje," in *Punk pod Slovenci*, 61-81. 18. Sid Vicious was the most notorious member of the British punk group the Sex Pistols.

19. Bastards' second album, after some negotiations with its producers, was issued under the title *Bastards—Lovers of the State*. See Sabrina Ramet, *Social Currents in Eastern Europe*, 217.
20. Zlatko Šetinc. "Kdo Riše Kljukaste Križe?" in *Punk pod Slovenci*, 222-26.
21. Ibid., 224. The sources of his data were police sources. See "Zmage in Porazi," *Mladina*,1, no. 1 (January 1990): 224. We need to compare the political impact of the harassment of Slovene punks to the repressive tolerance of their western counterparts. The alleged fascist punk group never performed in public. The suspects spent three months in jail. The 1983 trial of two of them proved their innocence. See Aleš Erjavec and Marina Gržinic, *Ljubljana: Osemdeseta Leta v Umetnosti in Kulturi* (Ljubljana: Mladinska Knjiga, 1991), 60.
22. The Anarchy graffiti was borrowed from the Sex Pistols.
23. *Punk pod Slovenci*, 359.
24. Ibid.
25. For a description of Laibach see Mark Thompson, *Paper House: The Ending of Yugoslavia* (New York: Pantheon Books, 1992), 42-44. See also Sabrina Petra Ramet, "Shake, Rattle and Self-Management: Making the Scene in Yugoslavia," 118-21 in Sabrina Petra Ramet, ed., *Rocking the State, Rock Music and Politics in Eastern Europe and Russia* (Boulder, CO: Westview Press, 1994).
26. That dadaist politics offers an analogy to Poland's Orange Alternative. But the latter's texts were recent communist symbols and slogans and focused on absurdities of the system. See Ramet, *Social Currents in Eastern Europe*, 85-86.
27. *Punk pod Slovenci*, 320-21. On occasion Laiback appeared on stage wearing brown shirts, black ties, and black arm bands.
28. Gregor Tomc, "Spori in Spopadi Druge Slovenije," in *Punk pod Slovenci*, 9-27.
29. For example, see George Kolankiewicz, "The Reconstruction of Citizenship: Reverse Incorporation in Eastern Europe," in Kazimierz Z. Poznanski, ed., *The Remergence of Civil Society and Liberal Economy in the Post-Communist World* (Boulder, CO: Westview Press, 1992), 142-43.
30. These values focus on quality of life, rather than on maximizing consumption. They include concerns with the environment, peace, nonviolent conflict-solving, and work satisfaction. For the analysis of the shift toward those values in Western Europe, see Ronald Inglehart, *Culture*

Shift in Advanced Industrial Societies (Princeton, NJ: Princeton University Press, 1990). For the review of NSMs in Eastern Europe, see Janusz Bugajski and Maxine Pollack, *East European Fault Lines; Dissent, Opposition and Social Activism* (Boulder, CO: Westview Press, 1989), chapter 7. Also see Ramet, *Social Currents in Eastern Europe*.

31. Dimitrij Rupel, "Slovenia in Post-Modern Europe," in Henry R. Huttenbach and Peter Vodopivec, eds., "Voices from the Slovene Nation," *Nationalities Papers*, XXI, no. 1 (spring 1993): 51-60.
32. Danica Fink Hafner, *Nova Družbena Gibanja—Subjekti Politične Inovacije* (Ljubljana: Fakulteta za Družbene Vede, 1992), 26-28.
33. Gregor Tomc, "Alternative Politics: Example of the Initiative for Civil Service," in Vera Gathy, ed., *State and Civil Society: Relationship in Flux* (Budapest: Ventura, 1989), 119.
34. Ramet, *Social Currents in Eastern Europe*, 203.
35. See the interview with the president of the republican conference of the LSYS in *Delo*, 29 March 1986, 18.
36. Danica Fink Hafner, *Nova Družbena Gibanja*, 209.
37. Tomc, "Alternative Politics," 119.
38. Ibid., 120.
39. Ibid., 121.
40. Ibid., 113-14.
41. Ibid., 122.
42. Ibid., 123. For a detailed analysis, see Danica Fink Hafner, *Nova Družbena Gibanja*, 201-15.
43. Ibid., 224-25.
44. *Mladina*, no. 10 (1987), 5. The poster was supposed to be based on partisan graphics.
45. Ibid.
46. Ibid., 12.
47. Ibid., 9.
48. Rastko Močnik, "Demokratične Sile in Poskus Vpeljave Izjemnega Stanja," *Mladina*, no. 11 (1987), 8.

49. Pavel Gantar, "Afera in Nauk," in ibid., 9.
50. "Klic k Razumu," in ibid., 8.
51. See Mastnak's statement in "Tvoj Je Vstajenja Dan," *Mladina*, no. 10 (1987), 13.
52. Ibid.
53. Ibid., especially the statement by Močnik. See also the "Call to Reason."
54. Ibid.
55. Danica Fink Hafner, *Nova Družbena Gibanja*, 75.
56. Ibid., 76.
57. Ibid., 77. The data are from 1986 and 87 public opinion surveys.
58. Ibid., p. 92.
59. Janko Prunk, *Slovenski Narodni Vzpon: Narodna Politika, 1768-1992* (Ljubljana: Državna Založba Slovenije, 1992), 408.
60. Aleksander Bajt, "Trg kot Podlaga Gospodarskega Sistema," *Teorija in Praksa* 22, no. 12 (1985): 1487-513.
61. Ibid., 414,
62. The four were three journalists from *Mladina*, Janez Janša, David Tašić, and Franci Zavrl, and an officer who worked for the Ljubljana District Military Command, Ivan Borstner. They were arrested in May and June of 1988 and accused of revealing military secrets. See Janez Janša, *Premiki: Nastajanje in Obramba Slovenske Države 1988-1992* (Ljubljana: Mladinska Knjiga, 1992). See also Dimitrij Rupel, "Slovenia's Shift from the Balkans to Central Europe," in Jill Benderly and Evan Kraft, eds., *Independent Slovenia*, 187-89.
63. Prunk, *Slovenski Narodni*, 416.
64. "Samoorganiziranje Civilne Družbe," *Teorija in Praksa*, 25, no. 11-12 (1988): 1453-457.
65. Josip Županov, "Samoupravni Socializam—Konec Neke Utopije," *Teorije in Praksa*, 26, no. 11-12 (1989): 1387-399, especially 1396.

7

Feminist Movements in Yugoslavia, 1978–1992

Jill Benderly

Yugoslavia in the 1980s was home to an outspoken feminist movement, the strongest women's movement in Eastern Europe. Yugoslav feminism began in the 1970s as a critique of self-managed socialism articulated by women in the academy and the media. By the mid-1980s, feminism had turned into a New Social Movement (NSM) functioning within an expanding Yugoslav civil society. As such the women's movement acted as an autonomous social force that simultaneously challenged the party-state and created its own alternative culture and network of initiatives. Feminist discourse and activism had a notable impact on Yugoslav society, bringing attention and limited reforms (laws punishing marital rape and upholding reproductive rights). In fact, the autonomy of the feminist movement and that of other NSMs was in itself a challenge to the party-state's claim to represent all social interests. Unlike other NSMs, however, feminism held out little hope that society could be reformed at a deep level; the ideology believed that patriarchal control of women would persist in either a socialist or a capitalist system.

In the moment when the NSMs anticipated the advent of pluralism, the breakup of the Yugoslav federation and the nationalization of its successor states occurred. Like other NSMs, feminism in Yugoslavia failed to transform the state's values; in fact, the successor states boded worse for women's rights than did socialist Yugoslavia. The ensuing war redefined women not only as enemies to be raped, but also as bearers of the nation.

Feminists in the Yugoslav successor states organized across national lines to protest the war's impact on women, and provided small-scale but significant opposition to the war. They also provided social services for its women survivors. However, a rift developed between those feminists who opposed nationalism and those who became more patriotic as they drew parallels between the victimization of women and the victimization of their nation. The new states marginalized the nonnationalist feminists and attempted to coopt the patriotic ones.

For this chapter, I define feminism as an ideology that exposes and rejects female subordination in society, and as a social movement that seeks to transform society to empower women. I will describe the development of this feminist movement, briefly tracing its links to earlier women's movements in the Yugoslav region in the twentieth century. I will compare three periods of Yugoslav feminism: the period of feminist discourse (1978-85), the period of feminist activism (1986-91), and the period of feminist opposition to the war (1991-92). The goals and strategies of Yugoslav feminism differ for each of the three periods.

Feminism became a New Social Movement (NSM) and as such part of civil society in Yugoslavia in the 1980s. By locating the 1980s women's movements in the rise of Yugoslav civil society, I will examine the state's reaction to feminism and the impact of feminism on the state as well as explore the relationship of feminism to national, regional, and republican interests. Unlike the other NSMs, feminism was not incorporated into the moment of transition in 1990. While greens and students entered the political contract of the new states, women's interests were remarginalized. I will then consider feminist activity during the war, through 1992. I will look at the effects of nationalism on the feminist movements, and the way nationalism bifurcated the women's movements into nonnationalist and patriotic camps.

THE HISTORY OF YUGOSLAV FEMINISM

Yugoslav feminism did not evolve out of the official communist women's organizations but rather grew independently. In their pursuit of Yugoslav women's studies, contemporary feminist historians unearthed sources describing the existence of South Slav women's movements in Belgrade, Novi Sad, Zagreb, Trieste, Klagenfurt, Ljubljana, Sarajevo, and elsewhere before the creation of the first Yugoslavia.[1] These historians documented a "first wave" of Yugoslav feminism beginning in the 1890s and continuing through the establishment of the first Yugoslav monarchy (1918) and afterwards, until World War II. This movement worked to increase women's education and legal rights, including suffrage, which was finally granted in 1945. (Yugoslavia was one of the last European countries to give women the right to vote.) The feminist historians tracked the ways these independent movements were subsumed into the anti-fascist and Partisan struggle of 1941-45. They also explored the ways autonomous women's organizing was stifled by communist Yugoslavia after 1945, and the ways that the self-managed socialist system claimed to have emancipated women "from above" and indeed legislated certain aspects of women's equality, but failed to seriously incorporate women's demands into the system.[2]

In the early 1940s the Communists transformed feminism into the Antifascist Women's Front (AWF), a strong movement of women Partisans. The late Yugoslav feminist historian Lydia Sklevicky argues that the AWF ran the risk of becoming an autonomous feminist organization in the Partisan struggle, and that the CPY took strong steps to rein it in, denying women a strong organizational voice in the formation of the postwar state.[3] Communist ideologue Vida Tomšič was quite frank in her account of this period: "The rapid growth of the Antifascist Front of Women, however, carried away by the enthusiasm of the awakened masses of women, was attended by instances of excessive independence and of the women leaving the common political organizations."[4]

After the war, the AWF transmogrified into the official Union of Women's Societies and later into the Conference for the Social Activity of Women (CSAW), which monopolized the women's movement for 30 years. Again, Tomšič explains:

> In the belief that the further existence of the Antifascist Front of Women as the comprehensive and sole women's organization, evenly organized from top to bottom, would at the present level of social development tend to keep women from taking part in the joint efforts to solve social problems, maintain the false idea that women's status was a separate women's issue and not an issue of our social community and of all the fighters

for socialism, The Fourth Congress of the Antifascist Front of Women adopts the decision to set up the Union of Women's Societies in its place.[5]

Under self-managed socialism, women were "emancipated from above." While the regime used women's issues for its own legitimation, and to contribute to the economy, a significant number of women's rights were codified and social services benefiting women provided, including reproductive rights, formal equality under law, the right to retain one's maiden name after marriage, parental leave, and child care. In Slovenia, a law was enacted allowing prosecution for marital rape.

While the independent women's movement was effectively silenced for more that 20 years of socialist Yugoslavia, a deeper exploration might elicit what Verta Taylor calls "abeyance structures" of feminism, which allowed it to reemerge in the late 1970s.[6]

Latter-day Yugoslav feminism began in the late 1970s in Belgrade and Zagreb as a critique of Yugoslav socialism's failure to liberate women, a critique expressed mainly through scholarly publications and the media. The feminist pen provoked a fierce backlash in the academy, the media, and the organs of the Yugoslav state, including the official communist women's conference. By the mid-1980s, feminists in Zagreb, Belgrade, and Ljubljana launched a small but radical new social movement. This feminist activism centered around two new types of activity: public forums and protests and provision of independent self-help services for women, plus continuation of the academic and media work. In addition, lesbian groups began to meet in all three cities. The feminist movement interacted with other emerging new social movements, especially the peace, ecology, and gay movements.

After the 1990 republic multiparty elections, feminists organized direct pressure on the newly elected republic governments by means of women's parties, women's "parliaments," mass protests, and constitutional commissions. Women's movements became the backbone of opposition to the war in 1991. The feminist initiatives transformed into centers to help women survivors of war-related rape and violence.

The public space for Yugoslav feminism was opened in part by a change in both state and society in the 1980s; that is the rise of civil society possibilities and the NSMs that sprung up in Eastern Europe. A key theme for observers of the women's movements in the United States and Western Europe is the relationship between the radical consciousness and community-building of the women's liberation movement and the impact of feminism on state policy. Drude Dahlerup generalizes that "the new women's movement wanted first and foremost to reach women, not the state." She identifies the uniqueness of the feminist social movement as "an intersection between personal and social change."[7]

In Yugoslavia, it was extremely difficult to influence the one-party state directly until it reached the stage where it was falling apart. The Yugoslav feminists had thus even more reason to reach women and to change their lives. The ability to directly lobby for change in the political system began only when the state began to collapse, but the ability of feminists to influence the post-Yugoslav, post-communist regimes has been minuscule—with the exception of Slovenia, where feminists led the successful struggle to preserve the legal right to abortion.

1978–85:
THE EFFECT OF FEMINISM ON DISCOURSE

What I call the "second wave" of Yugoslav feminism, launched in 1978, began as an ideology that used the academy and the media to make public its critique of self-managed socialism's failure to fulfill its promise of women's emancipation. In this period, the goals of Yugoslav feminism were to raise women's consciousness and to press the party-state to make good on its promises to women. Though the state polemicized fiercely against feminism, the women's critique came at a period of decentralization and when more open discussion within the Marxist framework was occurring. By 1982, it appears that some forces within the League of Communists were willing to see these issues debated in Marxist publications such as *Žena* and *Naše Teme*.

Yugoslav neo-feminism dates from 1978, when an international feminist conference was held in Belgrade. Women at the conference found that feminism explained so much of why women's "emancipation," as mandated by Yugoslavia's unique form of "self-managed socialism," did not feel like freedom. Yugoslav women were free to be workers, mothers, heroines of the Partisan war and shoppers all rolled into one. But they were not free to ask the question, "What do we women want our lives to be?"[8]

Croatian feminist sociologist Silva Mežnarić explored these issues in her article, "Theory and Reality: The Status of Employed

Women in Yugoslavia." She describes passages from Tomšič's book about sexual equality and women's emancipation under self-managed socialism as illustrative of "legitimative emancipatory rhetoric," which demonstrate the confusion of what "is" and what "ought" to be. In Yugoslav doctrines of emancipation, discussions of the status of women lead to the characteristic error of utopian and dogmatic social thought, the confusion of legitimations with the real attributes of concrete social institutions.[9]

Gordana Crnković, in discussing the political contribution of Yugoslav women fiction writers, describes writing about individual women's lives as a challenge to Yugoslavia's failure to allow the development of individualism as a problem of women's subjectivity. She details how Yugoslav individualism differs from that in the United States:

> [In Socialist Yugoslavia] the economic base, ideology and/or discourse of individualism has always been more or less absent, and what Yugoslavia has had instead was a group-oriented discourse—of family, nation, peasants, intelligentsia, the proletarian class. Therefore, when I say that the absence of individualism in Yugoslav women's lives has always been negative, I think of individualism as the articulation of those aspects of a women's lives which cannot be expressed by the speech of a group. . . .
>
> "The negation of people's individualities can be taken as one of the many causes of the current Yugoslav crisis. Bringing women's subjectivities into life in Yugoslavia is in itself a political project of primary importance."[10]

At first, the feminist critique of women's social role was developed in the academy and the press. In 1978, feminists in Zagreb organized the Žene i Društvo (Women and Society) section of the Croatian Sociological Society. In 1981, a similar group was founded in Belgrade (Feministička Grupa Žene i Društvo) under the auspices of the Student Cultural Center. Both groups continued to meet through the 1980s for discussions, and for sponsoring sporadic public forums. One of their key strategies for spreading feminist ideas was getting feminist articles published in mainstream newspapers and magazines. As Rada Iveković wrote in 1984, "Theory is so far confined to the work of a few serious authors—plus the slight but constant awakening of a feminist sensibility in women's awareness—and is still far more prominent than practice or political activity."[11]

Slavenka Drakulić, the most widely published of the Yugoslav feminist journalists, chronicled the party's antifeminist backlash.

Branka Lazić, president of the CSAW, denounced feminism in her speech to the Twelfth Congress of the LCY in 1982:

> Such ideas as are foreign to our socialist, self-management society, especially the feminist ones which are imported from developed capitalist countries... demand an organized fight for [their] suppression and elimination in daily actions by our subjective forces, especially the League of Communists.... There is only one question I would like to ask our feminists: do they want women above society or inside our self-management socialist society?[12]

The six mortal sins of feminism, as Drakulić counts them, are imported ideology, love for power, elitism, noninstitutional activity, apoliticization, and excluding the women's question from class.

The early 1980s were characterized by continuing exposure of feminist ideas, and continuous condemnation by the Communists. Disapproval did not produce direct repression of any sort, however, not even censorship of journal articles. Perhaps the attitude could be considered "repressive tolerance."

In the search for ways out of Yugoslavia's unfolding crisis in the early 1980s, the Slovenes led the way by accommodating NSMs, including feminists, lesbians and gays, Greens, pacifists, and punks. Ljubljana peace activist Marko Hren explains, "The Communists have made space as civil society and political structure have become separated. The number of party members was dropping. They had to do something to regain their legitimacy."[13]

The Croatian Communists in the 1980s were much less hospitable to alternative lifestyles and groups than were their Slovene counterparts. But intellectual liberalization—within the bounds of "critical Marxism"—meant that political journals, mass market magazines, and even the daily newspapers reflected a wider discourse.

Two party-linked journals, *Žena,* published by the Croatian branch of the official women's organization, Conference for the Social Activity of Women, and *Naše Teme,* a thick Marxist journal, co-sponsored and published a 1982 debate on "Social consciousness, Marxist theory and women's emancipation today."[14] In that debate, party functionary Stipe Šuvar called feminism "one of the forms of conservative social consciousness."[15] Feminist Blaženka Despot rebutted Šuvar by justifying the need for an autonomous women's movement outside of the Communist Party.[16] Feminist Rada Iveković argued that Šuvar's comments were symptomatic of patriarchal consciousness.[17]

In the mid-1980s, as intellectual liberalism developed, feminists penetrated the media. They succeeded there due to a cautious mixed approach that made them seem nonthreatening. Croatian feminists Drakulić, Vesna Kesić, Jasmina Kuzmanović, Alemka Lisinski, Ines Sabalić and others were editors and prominent reporters at the mass-market magazines *Start, Danas,* and *Svijet*. This can be explained as the convergence of Yugoslav feminism's strategic effort to spread its ideas through the media and the liberalization of the Croatian mass media in an effort to market itself to the western-oriented tastes of its readers.

Kuzmanović and Lisinski explained their success by their striking a delicate balance between "straight reporting" and the introduction of feminist themes. Kuzmanović comments that "feminism survived in Yugoslavia because it was considered unthreatening."[18] Lisinski put it this way: "The male editors considered us good professional journalists. 'So let them have their feminism once a month,' the editors figured."[19]

Meanwhile in Belgrade, feminist access to the media waxed and waned depending on the political climate of the moment. But overall, writings by feminists including sociologist Žarana Papić, psychologist Lepa Mladjenović, philosopher Nadežda Četković, and others appeared fairly often in the weekly newsmagazine *Nin*, the daily *Politika*, and the mainstream women's magazine *Duga*.

In Ljubljana, feminist publicist Vlasta Jalušič, sociologist Silva Mežnarić, and others saw their work published frequently in *Teleks, Mladina, Delo,* and elsewhere. Feminist writings were well-tolerated in the pages of student publications and certain theoretical journals throughout the federation.

The window of opportunity for feminist journalism—and other critical media perspectives—began to open after the socialist system sought a limited degree of intellectual pluralism to foster a discussion of the crisis in Yugoslav socialism, and reached its peak in 1989-90 as Croatia traveled the road to political pluralism in its catchup version of the East European revolutions. By 1990, some even went so far as to accuse Croatian feminists of taking over the media. "We get letters from pro-lifers saying, 'Feminists control the Croatian media,' and I think that's great," said Jasmina Kuzmanović, columnist for the Croatian independent newsweekly *Danas*.[20]

The decrescendo for feminist journalism began even before the Yugoslav war, for political and economic reasons. Not long after the Croatian Democratic Union (CDU) ascended to power in April 1990, it began to purge the media and remove the supports for youth movements. Simultaneously, on the economic front, what had promised to be the breakup of the Vjesnik media monopoly looked more like the nationalization of the most profitable publications and attempts to bankrupt the less successful ones, including three where feminists had made inroads.

Thus, the "second wave" of Yugoslav feminism started as an intellectual current, carried through the media, book publishing, and academia. The feminists of this period succeeded in their goal of raising public consciousness of feminism by articulating their critiques. Some elements of the LCY appeared to sanction at least the discussion if not explicitly the feminist position itself. However, verbal backlash emanated from the state, and especially from the official women's organization, which did not like its turf trod upon and could not tolerate the suggestion that women's emancipation was incomplete in Yugoslavia. Despite this backlash, the feminists of the late 1970s through the mid-1980s were generally considered a part of the critical Marxist current, who kept their jobs and continued to influence a younger generation whose activities came to be more radical.

1986-91: ACTIVISM, THEN PLURALISM

The late 1980s in Yugoslavia was the growth period of civil society and NSMs. The differences between the meaning of NSMs in Eastern Europe and in Western Europe and the United States parallels the regional differences in the meaning of "civil society." In the United States and Western Europe, "civil society" is a broad political science term meaning those social institutions and currents that are not under the aegis of the state. However, in communist Eastern Europe, the phrase "civil society" carried a particular meaning, with a range of components formulated. According to Slovene sociologist and activist Tomaž Mastnak:

> "Civil Society" is the concept that normatively summarizes the reinvention of democracy in Eastern Europe and describes a wide range of empirical democratic struggles. It was the ruling idea of the democratic opposition and was understood as a sphere distinct from, independent of, and opposed to the sphere of state action. As a social reality, civil society was initially conceived of as creating "parallel structures," independent public spheres and an alternative culture. As social action, it primarily meant gradual

and self-limited (re)construction of social reality "from below," legalistic and non-revolutionary in principle. Its principal actors were citizens' groups and initiatives and new social movements who adopted "anti-politics" as their ethos."[21]

For Mastnak, civil society was the stage on which citizens' groups and NSMs acted. What were the key ideas of civil society that shaped the roles of its actors, the NSMs?

Czech dissident writer Vaclav Havel described the emergence of the "independent life of society" in "The Power of the Powerless."[22] Hungarian democratic opposition writer George Konrad dubbed this stance and activity "antipolitics."[23] These notions of civil society described the elements of changing conditions and consciousness in Eastern Europe in the 1980s that set the stage upon which grassroots initiatives and NSMs began to act. The initiatives and movements began to be viewed synonymously with civil society itself in Eastern Europe, as was succinctly encapsulated by Vladimir Tismaneanu: "Civil society can thus be defined as the ensemble of grassroots, spontaneous, nongovernmental (although not necessarily antigovernmental) initiatives from below that emerge in the post-totalitarian order as a result of the loosening of state controls and the decline of the ideological constraints imposed by the ruling parties."[24]

Why didn't the regimes destroy the NSMs? Hungarian writer Janos Kis spoke in 1987 of "the decomposition of power . . . which is the context of the emergence of the New Social Movements. On one hand the feeling that is it necessary to engage in public affairs is much stronger than it was. On the other hand, the power of the state is much weaker than it was. Power in crisis is unable to check social initiatives in the same way as well-entrenched, successful power can."[25] The NSMs themselves can be grouped roughly into five categories: Green, peace, feminist, gay and youth/punk/counterculture. It is possible to add human rights movements (such as then-Czechoslovakia's Charter 77). I exclude nationalist and religious movements, and proto-parties organized along traditional ideological/political lines, as I consider these "old" movements.[26]

In Yugoslavia, the strongest site for the growth of NSMs was the republic of Slovenia.[27] The movements arose in the 1980s, and in Slovenia one had the feeling that pluralism wasn't far behind. Their counterparts in other Yugoslav republics were emboldened by the apparent tolerance of the Slovene state toward the NSMs.[28]

Yugoslav civil society and NSMs included not only feminism but also independent publishing and other NSMs, including ecology (which actively opposed the construction of nuclear power plants), peace (which demanded civilian alternatives to military service), gays (who wanted civil rights and an end to homophobia), punks (who pursued an alternative lifestyle, a subculture rather than a subpolitics),[29] and others. The feminist movement interacted with these other NSMs, were protected under the umbrella of the Socialist Youth Organization (SYO)(which gave them meeting space, funding, and access to other resources without exercising control over the content of their work), and came to experience repressive tolerance from a state increasingly struggling to maintain its authority over its citizens.

By 1986, a new generation of feminists had arisen. Many had been tutored by feminist academics at the universities, but few had jobs; in the 1980s, unemployment and underemployment were highest among university graduates. Perhaps they experienced the profound economic and social crisis and extensive unemployment as "nothing left to lose." Their feminism took a different tack from their predecessors; they put their primary efforts into grassroots activism and self-help for women. For them, the women's movement was about action. For three years, Belgrade feminists spent March 8, International Women's Day, going to the open-air markets to conduct "action research" in which they surveyed women on how they felt about their lives. They opened their doors to Gypsy women who came to drink coffee, tell fortunes, and speak about the difficulties of homelessness. They dared one another to spray-paint the walls of the housing blocks with "Women neighbors of the world, unite!"[30]

In the late 1980s, groups in Zagreb, Belgrade, and Ljubljana started SOS telephone hotlines to assist women survivors of domestic violence and rape. Feministička grupa Trešnjevka, founded in Zagreb in 1985, focused at first on consciousness-raising. By 1988 it formed Ženski Pomoć Sada (Women's Help Now) and initiated the first SOS hotline in Yugoslavia. The Zagreb hotline received more than 9,000 calls in its first two years.

Before long, Belgrade and Ljubljana had followed suit. "Our SOS is a great witness to what happens in a society where Balkan men feel that women get what they deserve," said Belgrade activist Sanja Milojević, "but the authorities say we always lie" on behalf of women.[31]

The state's centers for social work cooperated with the hotlines, and in a number of locations provided some assistance to the feminists, who helped battered women navigate through the maze of legal, police, health, and social work systems. Based on the notion of women volunteer counselors providing active listening and self-help for other women, the SOS projects provided help much appreciated by abused women who had never thought about feminism. Yet the three antiviolence projects shared a dilemma, "how to come out as feminists within the SOS projects." With new volunteers arriving all the time, how would it be possible to instill feminist principles and an analysis of male violence as part of patriarchy? Ljubljana SOS founder Mojca Dobnikar commented in 1990, "At first we were too quiet about the fact that we do this because we're feminists." After a few months, Slovene SOS workers separated into two competing groups with two phone numbers, one made up of feminists and one of "professional experts" who set out to help all powerless people, elderly, women, children, and men.[32]

Soon the hotline groups began plans for establishing shelters where women and their children could find refuge. Zagreb's Autonomous Women's House was started the hard way in 1990—by occupying an apartment that had been promised to the project but never delivered.

Groups in the three cities formed the Yugoslav Feminist Network in 1987, which held annual gatherings to share ideas and link projects, especially the hotlines. The declaration by the first gathering declared that "various feminist initiatives and groups in Yugoslavia are legitimate and legal." It opposed all forms of population control, especially the measures to reduce the Albanian birth rates in Kosova and in Tetova, Macedonia, which the women saw as racially discriminatory and nationalistic on the part of the dominant nationalities of the republics in question. The document also demanded constitutional equality of all citizens regardless of sexual orientation.[33]

The first lesbian group was organized in Ljubljana in 1987, as a subsection of the feminist group Lilit, and was followed by similar groups in Zagreb and Belgrade. These groups began later to cooperate with gay males, publishing magazines, holding social events and occasionally political ones.

In 1991, radical feminists from Zagreb produced one issue of *Kareta*, the first glossy feminist magazine in Yugoslavia. Published in March 1991 with support from the U.S.-based Global Fund for

Women, it featured news from the first Croatian women's parliament held in December 1990, and account of feminist antimilitarism in Yugoslavia in 1917, and interviews with Yugoslav and Swedish feminist filmmakers. Other articles in the 35-page magazine covered news shorts, reviews, law, economics, and women's studies. Beograd and Ljubljana women also put out mimeographed feminist bulletins on a sporadic basis.

Feminists cooperated with other social movements, particularly peace and ecology groups, all under the protective umbrella of the Socialist Youth Alliance of Yugoslavia, which provided office space and small amounts of funding. These joint efforts transformed the youth organization into an organ of civil society. In Slovenia, women from Lilit cooperated with the Peace Movement Working Group in a successful 1986 campaign against mandatory military training for women. The argument was that women would not gain equality by further militarization of society. The military scuttled its proposal for the training. In April 1987, women's, peace, and ecological groups in Ljubljana co-sponsored a march on the Slovene parliament to demand a moratorium on the construction of a nuclear power plant at Krško. Nearly 4,000 people took part in the protest.

Feminist participation in Yugoslav political life reached a peak in 1990 as the first multiparty elections were held in each republic. Feminists saw the democratic elections as an opening where they could move the feminist agenda into the political arena. Political parties from communist to center tried to recruit outspokenly feminist candidates for the 1990 elections. Some women signed on the various tickets, hoping to gain a platform for feminist ideas. Croatian feminists ran as communists, Greens, and the Coalition for National Understanding (the centrist party of the Croatian Spring leaders from 1971). In Slovenia, feminists supported the independent social movements ticket. None of the feminist candidates in either republic made it into parliament, with the exception of Slovene Communist Sonja Lokar of the Party of Democratic Renewal. The failed efforts showed the limits of state cooperation. The broader public preferred more radical change of the nationalist sort and virtually disregarded women's issues.

As the political landscape was transformed throughout Eastern Europe and for a brief moment civil society initiatives were in the spotlight, feminist groups sought strategies to heighten their visibility. The older generation of feminists, led by Slavenka Drakulić, attempted to organize an Independent Women's Alliance in 1990 as an umbrella for all women's groups, including professionals, feminists, and even remaining members of the official Conference for the Social Activity of Women. However, at the founding meeting April 16, 1990, grassroots activists from the Yugoslav Feminist Network expressed their frustration because they had not been asked to serve in the leadership, which they termed hierarchical and elitist.

The year 1991 saw the mushrooming of women's initiatives, which were affected by two simultaneous but contradictory conditions. On the one hand, there arose wider possibilities to organize autonomous activity in a pluralistic system. On the other hand, women seemed to suffer rollbacks of rights, status, and opportunities under the new governments and increasing privatization. The Catholic church influenced conservative ruling parties, such as the CDU in Croatia and Christian Democrats in Slovenia, to campaign for dropping women's rights to abortion and contraception from the new constitutions. In all republics, rising nationalism meant demographic pressure for women to bear more children for their nation. Women's participation in the new parliaments decreased[34] (from nearly 20 percent, although these women were generally tokens) to 11 percent in Slovenia, 5 percent in Croatia, and 1.6 percent in Serbia after the 1990 republic elections. Unemployment had a disproportionate effect on women, whose presence was high among never-employed college graduates.[35]

The nationalist revival in Serbia and Croatia sang hymns to women as "mothers of the nation." The inauguration of Croatian president Franjo Tudjman climaxed in a ceremony in which he tucked a feather into an empty cradle to honor unborn Croatian babies.[36]

Feminists responded with women's parliaments to propose initiatives concerning women and to react with a women's perspective to all relevant measures in the "male parliaments." In Serbia, women organized a women's party, ŽEST (an acronym for Women, Ethics, Cooperation and Tolerance), whose platform calls for "democracy and against all forms and aspects of discrimination and authoritarian power and authority in society, for peace, tolerance and cooperation among nations and peoples, and for the quality of life as the crucial aim of development."[37] Programmatic goals included creation of a mixed economy, an independent judiciary, health-care reform, clean technology and alternative energy, radical reform of the educational system especially regarding sex role stereotypes, and equality of family life including individual freedom to choose. ŽEST, the Beograd Women's Lobby, and Women and Society organized a "women's parliament" that called for the formation of a women's ministry, and new laws on marriage and the family.

In Croatia, a Women's Parliament convened by feminists on International Women's Day, March 8, 1991, proposed a similar plank to the drafters of the new Croatian Constitution.[38] In Slovenia in 1991, some two thousand people demonstrated in front of the parliament to demand the protection of reproductive rights within the new constitution. They fought and won the right to retain the paragraph (inherited from the 1974 Yugoslav constitution) regarding the "human right to decide on the birth of one's own children," albeit in a weakened form, as a freedom, not a right.[39]

Not all the efforts of Yugoslav feminists were defensive. They successfully introduced women's studies courses into the university curriculum in Ljubljana and Zagreb, and in 1993 started a women's studies center in Belgrade.

Until the outbreak of war in 1991, feminist movements showed little interest in independence of the republics, calling these questions "male politics," anticipating that new states would not be any more gender-neutral than Yugoslavia. In fact, between 1988 and 1991, feminists gave increasing attention to opposing nationalism (whether present among Communists such as Slobodan Milošević in Serbia or their opponents such as the CDU in Croatia or Demos in Slovenia). Feminists asserted that the construction of any nation, be it Yugoslavia or one of the republics, manipulates women. In critiquing the impact of nationalism on women, Yugoslav antinationalist feminists developed an analysis that followed the typology, explicated by Floya Anthias and Nira Yuval-Davis, of the five ways women have tended to participate in ethnic and national processes and state practices:

1. as biological reproducers of members of ethnic collectivities;
2. as reproducers of the boundaries of ethnic/national groups;
3. as participating centrally in the ideological reproduction of the collectivity and as transmitters of its culture;
4. as signifiers of ethnic/national differences—as a focus and symbol in ideological discourses used in the construction, reproduction, and transformation of ethnic/national categories; and
5. as participants in national, economic, political, and military struggles.[40]

Feminist theorists in Zagreb, Beograd, and Ljubljana alike traced the pressures on women in increasingly nationalized civil society to fulfill the above roles. As the new nations emerged, the feminist argument extended. Ljubljana sociologist Renata Salecl argues that

> When the problem of patriarchal domination officially ceased to exist [under socialism], patriarchal domination became officially invisible—which also means that it became much more difficult to recognize its effects. As with nationalism, which officially did not exist, but nevertheless remained at work in a concealed way, patriarchal domination, although officially overcome, remained a surmise of political discourse. Thus, it was not difficult for the post-Socialist moral majority to articulate patriarchy in a new way: to present the return to "natural" sexual roles as an attempt to introduce morality into a previously "immoral" social regime, and to reinterpret the moral majority ideology in a nationalist way."[41]

Feminism posed a strong challenge to rising nationalism in Yugoslavia by linking women's groups across republic lines, and by critiquing the manipulation of reproductive rights for nationalistic demographic purposes. Anti-abortion "right-to-life" initiatives were successfully blocked.

The activist period of feminism set the goal of organizing women autonomously into a NSM, to empower or transform women. In a certain way, autonomous feminist projects helped the state by doing its job in the social sector, providing services for survivors of rape and domestic violence. On the other hand, and in linkage with other NSMs under the rubric of the Socialist Youth Organization, feminism challenged the party-state by criticizing population policy. Before 1989, feminism attempted to improve the status of women under the Yugoslav system, not to create a pluralist system. (This was true for other NSMs as well, which sought to end nuclear power, to allow civilian alternatives to military service, allow gay rights, and so on.) In fact, many feminists preferred the socialist system to its successor regimes. Ultimately, however, Yugoslav feminism in essence makes a deep criticism of any patriarchal system, whether communist or capitalist.

1991–92: WOMEN AGAINST WAR

The new national entities had even more instrumentalist approaches to women than did the Yugoslav socialist state. Under Croat, Serb, and even Slovene national states (I only consider republics where feminist movements existed before the war), women's roles were as symbol of the nation and mother of the nation. In the war, women's roles were as contested terrain, for one side the object of rape, conquest, and ethnic cleansing by a national army, for the other side the victim of such atrocities, both as "women" and as a national symbol.

Sociologist Žarana Papić from Beograd describes women's position in all of the new states:

> With such totalitarian domination of nationalist ideologies the first victim is civil society itself. With civil society in danger, all human rights (and especially women's rights are in danger. . . . All nationalist ideologies in their political and military strategies are constructed and based on purposefully provoked, dominantly aggressive, openly violent and deadly oriented type of masculinity . . . .
>
> And its victims are not only the Other Enemy-Nations but equally Women as war-target, war-weapon, war-threat, war-revenge, war-pleasure-reward—as rape-objects. . . . Every aggressive, war-oriented nationalism (of which we are all victims) is, as a rule, based and primarily functions on the specific form of an undignified, violent patriarchal system, and strictly gendered order, in which men and women are separated into opposite zones: battle fields and shelter fields."[42]

Feminists in the former Yugoslav republics were among those best positioned to help women survivors of rape and ethnic cleansing in the wars that consumed their region since 1991; they were already providing social services for women through anti-violence hotlines and battered women's shelters. Feminists were also among those most actively involved in documenting the abuses, and amassing evidence for the prosecution of war crimes. These small-scale, women-run self-help projects for refugees attempted to reconstruct some elements of civil society in the midst of an uncivil war.

As Slovenia and Croatia declared independence in the summer of 1991, and the war broke out, the peace movements across former Yugoslavia had their work cut out for them. Young men deserted the army in droves. Mothers and soldiers marched on parliaments and army headquarters to demand that their sons be sent home from army duty. At first, mothers from Serbia, Croatia, Bosnia, and elsewhere held coordinated antiwar protests.[43] But as the war ravaged Croatia, cooperation—and even communication—between antiwar efforts in the various republics dwindled.

As the experience of a war replete with massacres and occupation shaped a defensive Croatian consciousness, it became easy for the Croatian government to coopt popular "peace" sentiment, such as that of the mothers' movement "Wall of Love" (Bedem Ljubavi). These mothers opposed their sons' draft into the Yugoslav People's Army (YPA), but did not oppose their draft into the Croatian Defense Forces of President Franjo Tudjman.[44]

The Croatian peace and feminist movements also suffered bitter divisions between those who felt themselves to be part of a victimized Croatian nation and those who still opposed all nationalism. Those with the first view were more likely to cooperate with the government. The nonnationalists, grouped around Antiwar Campaign—Croatia in Zagreb, and its affiliates in other Croatian cities, had more trouble gaining public exposure, as the government had done an effective job of throttling "disloyal" independent media.[45]

The issues of nationalism and nonnationalism were further complicated by the spread of the war into Bosnia. While the Serbs were the most blatant ethnic cleansers there, local Croatian militias and the Croatian government also pursued their thirst for Bosnian and Hercegovinian territory.

In Belgrade, the number of draft resisters was estimated in 1993 to be in the hundreds of thousands.[46] A significant portion of the capital city's populace—albeit a small proportion of the inhabitants of the rest of Serbia, out of reach of the political opposition and the independent media—grew tired of the war and the government of Slobodan Milošević. On the first anniversary of the war, Belgrade feminists led a crazy quilt of marchers—students, royalists, and intellectuals—ringing alarm clocks and bells in front of Parliament to warn the regime to wake up to the truth.[47] Cigarettes and gasoline disappeared from the stores as international economic sanctions were imposed. Weapons, however, were still on the market. And the Serbian second economy was run by war profiteers, a mafia of paramilitary and military men.

Since the war began, a small band of Belgrade feminists dubbing themselves Women in Black held silent vigils against the war. Standing in Belgrade's main street every week, they grew familiar with being spat upon and called traitors and whores.[48] In August 1993, Women in Black organized an antiwar protest in Vojvodina, which drew 200 women from all over ex-Yugoslavia as well as Western Europe.

NATIONALISM DIVIDES FEMINISTS

Feminists in the Yugoslav successor states split over their understanding of nationalism and patriotism. Two clusters of feminists in Zagreb worked on the issues of war-raped women. Croatia sheltered most of the war refugees from its own republic and from Bosnia-Hercegovina, so it became the most feasible site for work on this issue. The war severely exacerbated already existing conflicts among the Zagreb feminist groups. Not long after the war began in 1991, the Croatian feminist movement had indeed become a political movement, with one part coopted by the nationalist regime, and the other part an open opposition movement, termed traitorous by the government and no longer tolerated.

Four organizations—the radical feminist group Kareta; a Croatian women's group, Bedem Ljubavi (Wall of Love); a Bosnian refugee women's group, Žene BiH; and the International Initiative of Women of Bosnia-Hercegovina, or Biser, all of which have retained the counsel of U.S. feminist attorney Catharine MacKinnon—took a stand that as Croatian women they viewed rape as a distinctly Serbian weapon for which they held all Serbs (even feminists who oppose the war) culpable. They seemed to draw an analogy between nation as victim and women as victim.

An excerpt from an "Open Letter" from these four groups gives a sense of their blanket condemnation; the effect of nationalism on this cluster of women's groups:

> to place Muslim and Croatian women in forums which force on them women of the group committing the genocide, who do not even acknowledge that genocide is going on and who are trying to convince Muslim and Croatian women that it isn't happening, is to commit further violence against these women. This might be something like forcing Jewish women to "debate" with German women while the holocaust was still going on ... [49]

At the June 1993 U.N. Human Rights Conference in Vienna, U.S. feminist attorney Catharine MacKinnon, going public with her hostility to Serbian feminists, made the following comment in response to a question posed by Belgrade feminist activist Nadežda Četković: "If you are in opposition to the regime in Serbia, why aren't you already dead?" MacKinnon wrote that the abundance of pornography in the Balkans induced genocidal rape in the war.[50] While there is evidence that videotapes of genocidal rape have been marketed, this shows porn as an effect, not a cause of rapes.

This patriotic, moralistic turn in feminism is somewhat reminiscent of the "sexual purity" movement of the early twentieth century. Striking parallels with the present movement in Croatia can be detected in George L. Mosse's description of an earlier period in Germany and England: "The transition from the advocacy of women's rights to a crusade against all forms of vice helped reconcile the feminist movement with both respectability and nationalism. Once again the outsiders were co-opted, lending new strengths to the dominant norms."[51]

In contrast to the influence of nationalism on the actions of the aforementioned women's group, the Zagreb Women's Lobby (Center for Women War Victims, et al.) took a public stand against Croatian nationalism. In December 1992, the Zagreb Women's Lobby sent "a letter of intention" to international women's and peace groups discussing strategy and explaining what kind of help they needed. Lobby members wrote that

> we fear that the process of helping raped women is turning in a strange direction, being taken over by governmental institutions. . . . We fear that the raped women could be used in political propaganda with the aim of spreading hatred and revenge, thus leading to further violence against women and to further victimization of survivors.[52]

The climate in Croatia brought severe attacks on these feminists who oppose nationalism. Five Croatian women writers and journalists, who questioned Croatian nationalism and its effects on women, were targets of a hate campaign whipped up against them in Zagreb's yellow press. These "five witches," who included well-known feminist writer Slavenka Drakulić, feminist philosopher Rada Iveković, and feminist editor/journalist Vesna Kesić, found their photos on Zagreb's front pages, under headlines screaming that they were feminists, quislings, and communists.[53]

Nonnationalist politics made it possible for a working relationship to be re-established—delicately—among Croatian, Bosnian, and Serbian feminists, who frequently met at international conferences and communicated with one another via electronic mail.

However, nationalism also took its toll on feminists in Serbia. Women in Black activists Lepa Mladjenović and Vera Litričin shared some of their deepest feelings about the effect of the war in a paper entitled "Belgrade Feminists 1992: Separation, Guilt and Identity Crisis":

> When the war started, nationalist hatred increased dramatically and the Serbian government began to produce propaganda and the notion of the Enemy. All of a sudden Slovenians became an enemy, then Croats, then Muslims, then Americans, Albanians and so on. Deep conflicts emerged in families, in work places, and women began to separate on that basis. Completely new questions appeared in women's groups. Can a feminist be a nationalist chauvinist? Can a pacifist be a nationalist? Is a weapon an instrument of defense? Should the groups take clear attitudes toward nationalist questions (and therefore the war) and in that way lose some women? Should the groups avoid the issue of nationalism altogether? Should the women merely sit down and confront their beliefs and see what happens?
>
> So nationalism made some women split within [sic] themselves. It also caused painful scars to Zagreb-Beograd feminist relationships.[54]

CONCLUSION

Feminism in Yugoslavia has a long history. Developments in the feminist movement have been linked to those in the European women's movement since the first women's organizations were founded in the South Slav provinces of the Hapsburg empire and in Serbia in the 1890s. The relationships among autonomous feminist organizations and communist or social democratic parties have long been complex and conflictual. Women's active participation in Yugoslav Partisan struggle, particularly in the Antifascist Women's Front, created the possibility of a semiautonomous feminist organization influencing the newly established socialist Yugoslavia. Instead, the women's organizations were reined in, and independent Yugoslav feminist voices were not heard again until the late 1970s.

From 1978 to 1986, feminism articulated a critique of self-managed socialism's unfulfilled promise of women's emancipation. This critique theorizes that all states constitute the "state subject" in a gendered way, so that citizenship is essentially a male project. Under Yugoslav socialism, while "the woman question" was purportedly solved by incorporating women into production and self-management, and by providing services to make this "social activity" of women possible, the unequal citizenship of women was never addressed, nor was the patriarchal nature of all states. The LCY (at various levels) polemicized against this feminist position, but did not attempt to silence it.

After 1986, feminist activism took shape as a NSM. While the feminist movement cooperated with other NSMs (especially where they were most developed, in Slovenia) and attempted to have an impact on "politics" as far as women's citizenship and rights were concerned, it also had a life of its own, building its own alternative culture, community, and network of initiatives in three Yugoslav republics.

Thus it appears that the Yugoslav feminist movement was a small beacon of opposition to nationalism before 1991. Women's groups from various republics built up a long-term cooperative relationship that endured longer than the Yugoslav federation. The basis for this antinationalism lay in the analysis that nationalism (whether in the form of nationalist movements or a nationalist state) manipulates women to become "mothers of the nation," and to relinquish any other form of agency.

Feminist activism in the period of 1989 to 1991 was focused to a great degree on identifying and resisting the effects of rising nationalism on women, particularly in the area of population and reproductive policy.

Women's solidarity above and beyond national identity made feminism a fairly unique social movement in the period when most other movements had, to varying degrees, become nationalized by 1991. However, under pressure of war, some feminists ultimately reflected the nationalism of their states. Of course, there are varying types of nationalism in each Yugoslav successor states. The roles of Serbia and Croatia in the ensuing war looked at first to be aggressor and victim, but certain feminists on both sides warned that the nationally constituted identities of both states were aggressive (as later was their taste for Bosnian-Hercegovinian territory).

I have described here the divisions in the Croatian feminist movement on their view of women in war. Those who saw Croatia as a national state manipulative and dangerous to its women citizens located themselves in an oppositional position not only to the war, but to the Tudjman regime, and as "witches" they suffered the same sort of attacks as did their equally disloyal sisters in Belgrade. Those who conflated "women as victim" and "nation as victim" moved toward a sort of feminist nationalism, the patriotism of the victimized, a stance that appeared to be well tolerated by the Croatian regime.

Notes

1. See especially the works of Lydia Sklevicky, "Karakteristike organiziranog djelovanja žena u Jugoslaviji u razdoblju do drugog svjetskog rata (I and II)," *Polja* (Novi Sad, 1984), 308 and 309; and "Organizirana djelatnost Žena hrvatske za vrijeme NOB 1941–1945," *Povijesni prilozi*, 3:1(1984): 85-127.

2. The "first wave" of Yugoslav feminism flourished in the 1920s and 1930s, in synch with demands of international feminism (suffrage, peace, and employment issues). The Yugoslav Women's Union encompassed 205 affiliated groups in 1921, with a total membership of 50,000. The women's movement in Ljubljana in 1933 held meetings demanding the right to legal abortion, alimony, and pay equity. The Alliance of Women's movement organized massive demonstrations for women's suffrage in 1939; it claimed to have gathered 30,000 signatures on a suffrage petition.

   The Communists were deeply involved with women workers on strike, but the party at this time shunned the women's rights movement, considering it "bourgeois" (following the earlier line of Alexandra Kollontai in Russia as well as others).

   But under the "united front from below" the Yugoslav Communist Party (CPY) began to "bore from within" the feminist movement. When the Comintern line shifted to the strategy of "united front from below" (1931-35), the CPY—unable to function aboveground under Alexander's dictatorship—began to send its women cadre to explore the feminist movements. (The CPY had been banned since after the elections of 1921 and had begun to look for "front groups" whom it could lead behind the scenes.) The united front from above (1935-41) soon followed. In this front the CPY guided the work of women who attempted to takeover the Alliance of the Women's movement and the Little Entente of Women and ultimately succeeded.

3. Lydia Sklevicky, "Karakteristike" (I and II), and "Organizirana djelatnost."

4. Vida Tomšić, *Women in the Development of Socialist Self-Managing Yugoslavia* (Beograd: Jugoslavenski Pregled, 1980), 77.

5. Resolution on the establishment of the Union of Women's Societies of Yugoslavia, in September 1953, quoted in Tomšić, *Women in the*

Development, 80. There were about 2,000 women's societies established to provide assistance to mothers, housewives, women farmers, and so on, at all levels from federal to communal. All were united into the Union of Women's Societies, as part of the Socialist Alliance of Working People. Commissions for women's social activity were also formed "to incorporate women into political life." By 1961, the Union of Women's Societies and these commissions were fused into the Conferences for the Social Activity of Women.

6. Verta Taylor, "Social Movement Continuity: The Women's Movement in Abeyance," *American Sociological Review*, 54 (October 1989): 761-776.

7. Drude Dahlerup, *The New Women's Movement: Feminism and Political Power in Europe and USA* (London: Sage Publishers, 1986), 14.

8. Slavenka Drakulić-Ilić, *Smrtni Grije i Feminizma: Ogledi o mudijologije* (Zagreb: Znanje, 1984); Rada Iveković and Slavenka Drakulić-Ilić, "Yugoslavia: Neofeminism and Its 'Six Mortal Sins,'" in Robin Morgan, ed., *Sisterhood is Global* (New York: Anchor Books, 1984), 734-39.

9. Silva Mežnarić, "Theory and Reality: The Status of Employed Women in Yugoslavia," in Sharon L. Wolchik and Alfred G. Mayer, eds., *Women, State and Party in Eastern Europe* (Durham, NC: Duke University Press, 1985), 215.

10. Gordana P. Crnković, "That Other Place," *Stanford Humanities Review*, 1, no. 2-3 (fall 1990): 135-37.

11. Iveković and Drakulić, "Yugoslavia," 736.

12. Quoted in Iveković and Drakulić, "Yugoslavia," 736.

13. Marko Hren, interview with author, February 1987, Ljubljana.

14. "Društvena svijest, marksistička teorija i emancipacija žena-danas," *Žena*, 2-3 (1982): 44-91.

15. Ibid., 71.

16. Ibid., 78.

17. Ibid., 82.

18. Jasmina Kuzmanović, interview with author, June 1991, Zagreb.

19. Alemka Lisinski, interview with author, June 1991, Dubrovnik.

20. Jasmina Kuzmanović, interview with author, June 1991, Dubrovnik.

21. Tomaž Mastnak, "The Powerless in Power: Political Identity in Post-Communist Eastern Europe," *Media, Culture and Society*, 13 (1991): 402.

22. Vaclav Havel, "The Power of the Powerless," reprinted in Gale Stokes, ed., *From Stalinism to Pluralism: A Documentary History of Eastern Europe since 1945* (Oxford: Oxford University Press, 1991), 173-74.

23. George Konrad, *Antipolitics: An Essay* (New York: Harcourt Brace Jovanovich, 1984), 230-31.

24. Vladimir Tismaneanu, *Reinventing Politics: Eastern Europe from Stalin to Havel* (New York: Free Pres, 1992), 170-71.

25. Pat Hunt, "Interview with Janos Kis," *European Nuclear Disarmament Journal*, 28/29 (Summer 1987): 25.

26. These categories are complicated by the nature of East European opposition, which functioned in a variety of forms (or amorphousness) in response to varying degrees of repression (and, at the end, imitation and cooptation). Polish Solidarity is a particularly confusing case, given its multiple identity. To the extent that it was an independent trade union, I consider it an "old" (class-based) social movement. But, of course, it became much more than that. Solidarity became in idea, a critique, a set of values, even a functioning "second society," one that set an example for the many NSMs that followed in the region. A helpful discussion is that of David S. Mason in "Solidarity as a New Social Movement," *Political Science Quarterly*, 104, 1 (1989): 41-59.

27. Jozef Figa, "Socializing the State: Civil Society and Democratization from Below in Slovenia," paper presented at "Partisans to Patriots: State-Society Relations in Yugoslavia, 1945-1992," conference in Albuquerque, New Mexico, May 1994, 11.

28. Tomaž Mastnak, "From Social Movements to National Sovereignty," in Jill Benderly and Evan Kraft, eds., *Independent Slovenia: Origins, Movements, Prospects* (New York: St. Martin's Press, 1994), 93-111.

29. Gregor Tomc, "The Politics of Punk," in ibid., 113-34.

30. Information gathered from author's participant-observation in 1986-87, Belgrade, Zagreb, and Ljubljana. See Jill Benderly, "Yugoslav Feminists Organize," *New Directions for Women*, 16 (July/August 1987); and "Do Croatian Feminists Control the Media?" paper presented at the American Association for the Advancement of Slavic Studies, Phoenix, Arizona, 1992.

31. See Jill Benderly, "Yugoslav Women Pull Together," *New Directions for Women*, 19 (Sept./Oct. 1990): 3.
32. Mojca Dobnikar, presentation at Yugoslav Feminist Network gathering, Beograd, April 1990.
33. Ženski skup, "Declaration," 13 December 1987.
34. Yugoslav women's participation in parliamentary bodies has always been lower than the rest of Eastern Europe—17 percent of federal chambers in 1981, compared to 33 percent in East Germany and 30 percent in Hungry. At the local level in 1978, women composed only 7.2 percent of the self-management organs of local communities, in comparison to more than 35 percent in Bulgaria, Albania, and East Germany. Joni Lovenduski, *Women and European Politics* (Amherst: University of Massachusetts Press, 1986) 236-3.
35. Yugoslav women have never achieved the employment levels of the Soviet bloc countries, with 1980 averages around 33 percent of the workforce, rather than half in Eastern Europe. Susan Woodward chalks this up to the market economy, a postwar labor surplus and direct employment discrimination against women. See Susan Woodward, "The Rights of Women: Ideology, Policy, and Social Change in Yugoslavia," in Wolchik and Meyer, eds., *Women, State and Party in Eastern Europe*, 35.
36. Jill Benderly, "East European Diary," *On the Issues* (Spring 1990):16.
37. ŽEST charter, 1991.
38. Kareta, 1991.
39. Vlasta Jalušič, "Troubles with Democracy: Women and Slovene Independence," in Benderly and Kraft, eds., *Independent Slovenia*, 135-57.
40. Nira Yuval-Davis and Floya Anthias, eds., *Women-Nation-State* (New York: St Martin's Press, 1989).
41. Renata Salecl, "Nationalism and the Disavowal of Patriarchal Domination in Post-socialism," paper presented at Gender, Nationalism and Democratization: Policy Initiatives for Central and Eastern Europe, Washington, D.C., October 1993.
42. Zarana Papić, "Nationalism, War and Gender: Ex-femininity and ex-masculinity of ex-Yugoslavian ex-citizens," paper presented at Gender, Nationalism and Democratization, Washington, D.C., October 1993.

43. *Žene za mir* (Belgrade: Žene u crnom, 1993); "Koliko su puta prevarene," *Danas,* 9 July 1991.

44. Slavenka Drakulić, interview with author, December 1991, Zagreb.

45. Issues of *Arkzin,* 1991; Slavenka Drakulić, interview with author, December 1991, Zagreb; Marko Hren, interview with author, July 1993, Ljubljana; Lynne Jones, interview with author, July 1993, Ljubljana; Tomaž Mastnak, interview with author, July 1993, Ljubljana.

46. Vesna Pešić, director of the Center for Anti-War Action, interview with author, summer 1993, Belgrade.

47. *Vreme,* July 1992; letter from Lepa Mladjenović, July 1992.

48. Lepa Mladjenović and Vera Litricin, "Belgrade Feminists 1992: Separation, Guilt and Identity Crisis," *Žene za Mir* (Belgrade: Žene u crnom, 1992).

49. Fax received by author, signed by Kareta, Biser, Bedem Ljubavi, and Žene BiH, March 1993.

50. Catharine A. MacKinnon, "Turning Rape into Pornography: Postmodern Genocide," *Ms.* (July-August 1993): 24-31.

51. George L. Mosse, *Nationalism and Sexuality: Respectability and Abnormal Sexuality in Modern Europe* (New York: Howard Fertig, 1985), 111.

52. Zagreb Women's Lobby, "Letter of Intentions," circulated by e-mail, December 1992.

53. "Croatia's Feminists Rape Croatia," unsigned article, *Globus* (Zagreb), 11 December 1992, 1.

54. Lepa Mladjenović and Vera Litričin, "Belgrade Feminists 1992: Separation, Guilt and Identity Crisis," in *Žene za Mir* (Belgrade: Žene u crnom, 1992).

8

The Role of Religious Communities in the Development of Civil Society in Yugoslavia, 1945–1992

Paul Mojzes

The religious communities did not play a significant role toward the development of a civil society since a genuine civil society has not yet emerged on the territory of the former Yugoslavia. Nor is there any hope for the flourishing of one in the foreseeable future.

An initial clarification is needed as to what I mean by a civil society. A civil society is one in which there is a free proliferation of autonomous organizations and expression of ideas outside of and not dependent upon or even approved by the government, meaning that it is the antipode of totalitarianism. Instead of enforcing the control of all activities by a single agent—the Communist Party of Yugoslavia—a civil society would mean a plurality of centers of decision making in a variety of human activities ranging from politics to sports.

In the case of Yugoslavia from 1945 to 1953 an absolute concentration of control by the Communist Party took place. From 1953 to the late 1980s this control was less visible yet nevertheless was ultimately effective and was gradually being replaced at first by the more nationalistically inclined Communist Party elites of the various republics. Neither the CPY nor any of these republican Communist Parties were interested in promoting the growth of a civil society nor did they show any willingness to permit the religious communities to contribute toward the growth of such a civil society. The religious communities were, however, an exception to the general communist ambition to subsume everything under their control, for they allowed the religious organizations—with great misgivings on the part of the Communists—to maintain organizations and worldviews not consistent with the Marxist interpretation of reality. In 1945 a mighty struggle ensued in which the CPY attempted to control and penetrate religious organizations, which, to some degree, succeeded. That it did not need to succeed completely and that it later, in the 1960s, eased off from such attempts has more to do with its effectiveness to politically neutralize religious leaders and its sensitivity to international concerns about religious liberties, which forced it to make modifications, than it does with the achievement of religious communities.

If a contribution to the creation of a civil society means merely this minimal dissonance with the otherwise firm communist control of societal phenomena, then, indeed, the religious communities did contribute, by their very existence, and by every continued activity, toward the development of such a civil society and my thesis is not fully substantiated. But, I am assuming that civil society is much *more* than a minimal permission for the continuance of religion, which the Communists in any case assumed to be moribund. The religious practices in the former Yugoslavia were not consciously aimed by the religious leaders or membership toward the development of a civil society, although the religious communities continued to hope for a day when communism might fail. The most influential religious leaders envisioned the replacement for communism not by a democratic civil society but by the return of the age-old symbiosis of their religion with the traditional ethnonational formation.

From 1945 to 1989 the social system in Yugoslavia was a revisionist Bolshevik-style communist monopoly of societal decision making. That system was fairly flexible and yielded to decentralization and small-scale democratization with prospects that further democratic trends might lead toward a civil society. But instead of the emergence of a civil society a number of competing nationalistic societies (not dissonant with the hopes of some religious leaders) emerged in which the dynamic force in society became *ethnos* rather than *demos*. The emergence of a civil society during nationalistic fighting among the states, which took place in the early 1990s, is not very likely, though it is not entirely excluded, especially on the fringes of war (that is, Slovenia, and perhaps Croatia).

The reason that the largest religious communities, namely Eastern Orthodoxy, Roman Catholicism, and Islam (Judaism and Protestantism played very minor roles and are partially an exception to the mainstream) were not likely to contribute to the creation of civil society in Yugoslavia is that it was alien to their tradition as practiced in the Balkans. If anything, they are likely—even under conditions of greater opportunities for democratization—to impede this process. The reason for this is that the creation of civil society would tend to diminish rather than strengthen the social role of the religious communities as compared to ethnoreligious social constellations that asserted themselves in the late 1980s and early 1990s. Therefore the large religious communities are not likely to move in this direction since they cherish the opportunity that they obtained after 1989 to play, for the first time since 1945, a significant social role.

THEORETICAL FRAMEWORK

A fourfold typology of church-state relations regarding religious liberties[1] is being proposed here.

1. Ecclesiastic Absolutism

The exclusive power vested in a single religious option or one religious institution is given preferential treatment while others are discriminated against. Only one religious organization is supported by the state and in return that religion supports the national state. The government provides preferential treatment and extends freedom only to those who fully comply with the beliefs and practices of the "state church." In Eastern Europe it was in the not-too-distant past when churches like the Eastern Orthodox Church, Roman Catholic Church, or the Islamic community were in a distinctly privileged position.

2. Religious Toleration

Theoretically the state is separated from the religious organizations, which are treated equally before the law; yet the state remains benign toward all religions. In reality such states give practical preferences to the stronger churches and discriminate against nonbelievers, either legally or by various manipulations of public opinion. The amount of religious liberties is much greater than in Ecclesiastical Absolutism.

In history there are frequently situations that do not fit clearly given categories, often because states and religions are in transition. This seems to have been the case in Yugoslavia before World War II. At that time the Serbian Orthodox Church in the eastern and southern regions of the country and the Catholic Church in the western regions of the country were established churches. Some religious communities, such as the Lutherans, Muslims, and Jews, had certain legal standing and protection, while groups like Baptists and Methodists were tolerated but with distinctly limited rights. Certain religious groups were outlawed; as were the Communists after a brief period of legality. The first Yugoslavia was a society in transition between Ecclesiastic Absolutism and Religious Toleration.

3. Secularistic Absolutism

All religious expressions are hindered while the state favors a single brand of secularist worldview. Religion as such is rejected by the state. In this model all religions suffer various degrees of restrictions, while nonbelievers, especially militant atheists, often receive privileges. Not infrequently this alleged atheist state promotes the adoration of the state and its leadership, which renders it a secular religion.[2] Secularistic Absolutism arises as a result of dissatisfaction with Ecclesiastic Absolutism, but the exclusivist mentality remains the same. In later stages of Secularistic Absolutism in Yugoslavia there was evidence of some vestiges of Ecclesiastic Absolutism and of Secularistic Absolutism as well as a tendency to tolerate some features of Religious Toleration or Pluralistic Liberty type societies.

4. Pluralistic Liberty

Pluralistic Liberty connotes the full exercise of freedom in a context of a variety of truth claims. The state is really indifferent and neutral toward religion or nonreligion. This type is a human possibility but is rarely a historical achievement, though it has been experienced at least in rudimentary form in some areas of the world. In such a state religious organizations and the government will be truly separated with no intention on part of either to dictate or mix into the affairs of the other.

There are close linkages between Ecclesiastic and Secularistic Absolutisms on the one hand and Religious Toleration and Pluralistic Liberty on the other. In their pure form Ecclesiastic Absolutism and Secularistic Absolutism are both intolerant toward all except those whom the state decides to favor. Secularistic Absolutism was more problematic from 1945 to 1992 but Ecclesiastic Absolutism appears to be making a recovery. Secularistic Absolutism came into existence in the twentieth century when the totalitarian and manipulative power of the state had reached unprecedented scope. Hence the inquisitorial practices and religious wars that characterized Ecclesiastic Absolutism seemed to pale into insignificance when Secularistic Absolutism made its brutal appearance. Just when it seemed that with the implosion of Communism Secularistic Absolutism would disappear, the nationalist explosion resulted in the bloody conflicts between nationalistic states in which the ethnoreligious unity was enthusiastically welcomed. This makes it likely that much blood will be shed in the collisions among Ecclesiastic Absolutist societies in the Balkan peninsula—and elsewhere.

If civil society is a society that distributes power to a wide range of competitive sources then Religious Toleration and Pluralistic types would be conducive to a positive role of religion in creating and maintaining a civil society, the other two types would not. Ecclesiastic and Secularistic Absolutist types are autocratic and totalitarian structures in which the dominant religion or ideology refrains from sharing its power. The tragedy of the successor states of Yugoslavia is that their development seems to favor a retreat from Secularistic to Ecclesiastic Absolutism rather than to either Religious Tolerance or Pluralistic Liberty.

HISTORICAL DATA

The Communist Party of Yugoslavia was originally a loyal follower of the Communist Party of the Soviet Union and shared all of its ideals and approaches. Two well-known Leninist principles dominated this approach.

One was the legal separation of church and state, declaring that religion is the private affair of every citizen. This had the effect of relegating religion out of the public sphere into the private spiritual domain of individuals. Religious liberty was understood narrowly as the freedom to worship or not to worship.

The second principle was that it is the task of the Marxist party as the avant-garde of the working class to assist in what is considered the inevitable fading away of religion, thus assisting the process of individual and social liberation from superstitious and exploitative religious practices that are surviving merely as vestiges of the past.

In theory these two principles can be separated by stating that the government applies the first principle, while the Communist Party advocates the second. That theoretical distinction is futile, for in practice the government consisted of the leaders of the Communist Party, and the second principle became decisive in interpreting the first. This conflict of approaches prevailed from 1945 until nearly 1989 despite some efforts to modify it by emphasizing legal aspects of the principles of separation of church and state, which would tend to diminish state intervention in religious matters and thereby provide for greater religious liberty.

Several discernible stages mark the period from the communist takeover in 1944-45 to 1992[3] that broadly correspond to the situation of human rights in general within the state.[4] A brief summary of each period follows.

1. Radical restriction of religious liberty, 1945-1953.
2. Gradual relaxation of restrictions, 1953-1965.
3. Significant liberalization, 1965-1971.
4. Selective restrictions reimposed, 1971-1982.
5. On the threshold of full freedom; new opportunities and new pitfalls, 1982-1989.
6. The Great Transformation, including the beginning of Balkan warfare, 1989-1992.

1. Radical Restriction of Religious Liberty, 1945–53

The government and the Communist Party mounted an all-out attack on the churches despite a claim of religious liberty during these years. Marxist scholars and even government leaders admitted in the 1960s and 1970s that harsh measures were undertaken against religious institutions and individuals, including imprisonment, murder, nationalization, destruction of property, and so forth. From 1945 to 1948 the country was under direct Soviet influence and the government attempted to implement the Soviet model. The Yugoslav Constitution of 1945 was a "carbon copy" of Stalin's Constitution of 1936. To the Yugoslav Communists it seemed that their own dealing with the multinational, multireligious Yugoslavia should be analogous to Stalin's dealing with the multinational, multireligious Soviet Union.

The government intervened heavily in the internal affairs of the churches. The Secretariat of Internal Affairs had to give its approval for the appointment of the clergy to specific parishes. In order to split up the lower and the higher clergy and to gain closer control of the clergy the government forcefully promoted the creation of unions or associations of clergy in the Orthodox, Catholic, and Muslim communities.

Church buildings were expropriated; some were destroyed. Church assets were frozen, monasteries and religious schools were closed, religious processions and public ceremonies were generally forbidden, and clergy were prevented from visiting their charges.[5] Several show trials, the most spectacular against Alojzije Cardinal Stepinac, demonstrated the government's resolve to break any religious opposition.[6] Often no such propaganda or legal procedures were deemed necessary; many religious leaders, clergy and lay, were murdered or imprisoned by executive order or arbitrary local initiative. Some were simply brutally murdered, beaten, mutilated, or incarcerated, while others simply vanished, never to be seen again.[7]

The constitution of 1946 separated the church from the state, guaranteed freedom to worship, forbade the abuse of religion for political purposes or for spreading religious hatred and intolerance, and declared all citizens equal regardless of ethnicity, race, sex, and religion.[8] Such constitutional principles were a sound basis for liberty, but there was no recourse to legal protection when the government itself violated the constitution.

Contrary to expectation, after Yugoslavia broke off with the Soviet Union and other Informbureau countries in 1948 and until Stalin's death in 1953 the conflict between the churches and the state and oppression of religious communities by the Yugoslav Communists actually sharpened. On the one hand, it seems that the general pattern in socialist societies is to crack down against religion a few years after gaining power. On the other hand, the Yugoslav Communists were trying to show to the Soviet leadership that they were still real Marxists-Leninists by repressing the intellectuals, peasantry, and religion.[9] What is paradoxical about the situation is that in other areas of life, especially in the economic sphere, since 1952, greater freedom was being achieved under the policy of workers' self-management, but there were simply no political and civil rights.[10] Some of the most well-organized persecutions of religion took place between 1950 and the first part of 1953.

2. Gradual Relaxation of Restrictions, 1953–65

Since the second half of 1953 the persecutions and harassments slowly abated. Contrary to some who posit erroneously that this was due to the strength of the religious communities I attribute it to the need of the Yugoslav government for approval by western and Third World countries with which Yugoslavia had developed increasingly good relations. Thus religious communities were the beneficiary of political considerations without having made a reciprocal impact upon politics. One of the landmarks in the changing relations between the government and the religious communities was the passing of The Basic Law on the Legal Position of Religious Communities. This law reflected the 1946 constitution's separation of church and state. One of the constitutional provisions fostering religious liberty was that it allowed the formation of new religious communities. This was utilized over the years so that the sum total of religious denominations in Yugoslavia grew to about 50. But while the law formally improved the status of religious communities, the CPY simultaneously sharpened its ideological attacks against religion. Hence this was a classical case of taking away with one hand what was given with the other. Amidst all these ambiguities a gradual reduction of the pressure against churches and religious individuals continued until 1965. Excesses—such as torture, imprisonment on false charges, and even murder by the secret police—were still practiced from time to time, more in some parts of the country than in others.

Despite the republican CPs learning from the same Marxist-Leninist script, over time how each party actually treated the religious communities came to vary. This feature that continued to characterize Yugoslav church-state relations has increasingly been handled by the republican and provincial rather than the federal government. What this means is that in one region of the country, for example, in Slovenia and Croatia, the authorities may have shown a great deal more tolerance and permissiveness toward religious activities, while in another part, for example, in Macedonia or Kosovo, clergy and believers, especially of certain denominations, were openly harassed and intimidated by the police, usually where news of the greater liberties in the other parts of the country rarely reached the public. The greater historical strength of Catholicism as an institution (including a better educated clergy, church attendance, support by the Vatican and other western churches) also contributed to greater freedoms, though paradoxically it also caused sharper verbal attacks and harassment by the government on account of that very vitality.

3. Significant Liberalization, 1965-71

This was the most liberal period in the treatment of the churches, the "golden age" in church-state relations. The system had opened up to such a degree that many religious practices were unobstructed. Government interference in internal church matters was minimalized and in some instances was almost completely removed. The churches were permitted to publish journals and books again; theological schools were allowed to expand; clergy could travel almost freely in and out of the country; religious education on church premises was sanctioned again; and so forth. In order to impress Tito's Third World allies the Muslims were showcased as beneficiaries of the government's benevolence.

A growing concern, however, was expressed by the government and the press at the simultaneous increase of politization of the few larger religions, particularly the Roman Catholic but also the Islamic and Serbian Orthodox. To some degree the government was itself responsible for this politization. The Muslims, previously a religious designation, were proclaimed by the Communist Party as a nationality. Previously the contention was that there were *muslims* who were either Croats, Serbs, or Yugoslavians. But since the nationalistic tensions were exacerbated it seemed that by creating a Muslim nationality the rivalry between Serbians and Croatians in regard to the muslims' ethnic affiliation would be alleviated. Instead, Islam started functioning as a civil religion. Since the Muslim nation did not have the same secular institutions as the others, the Muslim nationality affirmed itself in the existing muslim religious institutions. Political questions were now raised in mosques, and this led to more open conflicts between the state and Islam than with other churches. This situation will continue at least for the duration of the war in Bosnia and Herzegovina until other forms of expressing Muslim nationalism can be found. The trend is toward the solidification of such ethnoreligious identity rather than its weakening.

Another new situation was the creation of the autocephalous Macedonian Orthodox Church by means of a schism from the Serbian Orthodox Church. This schism was blessed by the CPY and Macedonian CP but resented by the Serbian CP. There is no evidence that this schism created conditions for development in civil society in Macedonia.

After 1968 a significant number of humanistic Marxists became interested in religious issues in a much more objective manner than their predecessors. Many became not only sympathetic to certain religious issues, values, and persons but engaged both publicly and privately (though more in print than in public forums) in a Christian-Marxist dialogue, just when this dialogue was waning in some other European countries. Many of these Marxists were significant contributors, theoretically and practically, for the increased liberties granted by the more cautious bureaucratic Marxists.[11]

4. Selective Restrictions Reimposed, 1971–82

The fourth period, from 1972 to 1983, was characterized by an attempt to install more controls over church life and the suspension or privatization of the Christian-Marxist dialogue. A complete reversal of the concessions made during the previous period did not take place, however. Certain aspects of church life did not suffer at all, but rather, developed steadily, thereby giving additional weight to certain freedoms (for example, noninterference in the curricula and teaching staff of theological schools, and fairly easily obtained permissions for repairs of church buildings). Regression took place in a few areas—for example, longer periods of prior notification of authorities required if a foreign visitor was to preach in a church. The situation altered not qualitatively but quantitatively; an overall increase of confrontational practices could be felt.

Radovan Samardžić, then the secretary of the Commission for Relations with Religious Communities of the Federal Executive Council of Yugoslavia wrote:

> The de-politicization of the church is a condition sine qua non for its freedom of activity in the Yugoslav political system. Religion is a non-political element of society and hence an individual's private affair. . . . [T]he church itself determines the dimension of its freedom to the extent to which it adjusts the interests of believers to all other interests of Yugoslav self-managing socialist society.[12]

Freedom thus understood is conditional rather than an inherent right; namely, one will be free to the degree that one accepts or adjusts to the social system; opposing the social system would bring a reduction in *religious* freedom.

Religious communities continued to be the focus of the kind of discontent that could not be expressed in another manner, especially nationalistic or separatist tendencies. Some people in the churches welcomed this; others were wary. The political authorities had no effective way of dealing with this because if they wanted to repress such threats it would seem that they are repressing religious freedom. The authorities expressed the willingness to use administrative and legislative restrictions but on the whole shied away from it[13] as they had become much more sensitive to the role of world public opinion and were eager to maintain the reputation of being the most open of socialist societies.

A segment of the domestic religious press, which was growing by leaps and bounds (from nearly total absence in 1950s to about 40 religious journals and newspapers in 1977, and nearly 200 by the 1980s) claimed that there was insufficient religious freedom to which administration officials responded defensively by citing the large number of religious leaders, students, and the total number of publications.[14] It was obvious that religious people were by then able to raise their voice in self-defense more publicly and effectively and that government officials, many of whom did not abandon old attitudes resorted to more verbal (rather than violent) attacks. The humanistic Marxist scholars continued the sociological study of religion that charted the way toward greater tolerance and favored the Christian-Marxist dialogue, but many of them during this period had to lay low because Tito feared loss of leadership and the demise of socialism and tightened the screws within the Communist Party. Some of the most liberal Communists were repressed and others feared the loss of their positions and decided to bide their time and wait for better times—presumably when Tito, the "Old Man," would die. He did in 1980.

5. On the Threshold of Full Freedom; New Opportunities and New Pitfalls, 1982-89

From 1981 the people had to start adjusting to the absence of a charismatic leader acceptable to all Yugoslavs, though for a while the communist leadership behaved as if he had not died. Confused as to which direction to take after Tito's death, they nevertheless vouched to follow in his path. The country was entering a period of a long and profound crisis. National conflicts increased, leading occasionally even to violent conflict.

The large religious groups were implicated in the conflict by virtue of their close identification to ethnicity. National conflicts became again religious conflicts.[15] Religious institutions did not consciously seek to diminish the conflict, perhaps because their newfound popularity among those seeking national affirmation provided broader opportunities for their activities. A new openness was being experienced—at least with regard to the freedom to discuss in the press, other media, and at conferences certain formerly taboo subjects pertaining to earlier and present failures of the leadership. This period contained not only possible pitfalls (especially from the Communists seeking to divert the attention away from economic problems by attacking the churches as scapegoats), but also new opportunities for the expansion of liberties in a country that is without a long democratic tradition.

The increased participation in religious practices was interpreted by the institutions as either a larger number of people "coming out of the closet" as the repressions eased, or as a genuine religious revival, particularly among the young. This necessitated at least a reassessment of the role of religion in the particular circumstances of Yugoslav history. Many humanistic Marxist scholars advocated more tolerant attitudes toward religion, providing religious people did not spearhead a revolt against the government. The basic concession asked from the churches was not to oppose the socialist system but rather to recognize it at least tacitly. However, explicit endorsement of the socialist system by church leaders was very rare. Therefore, the slogan changed from "if you are not with us you are against us" to "if you are not against us you are with us." This called for a less-doctrinaire approach to religion, which became a hallmark of the Yugoslav communist attitude toward religion. Srdjan Vrcan, the well-known sociologist of religion from Split, captured the changing role of religion with the title of his book, *From the Crisis of Religion to the Religion of Crisis*. Indeed, many people formerly uninvolved or uninterested, including many young people, became much more active participants in the life of the churches and were generally not stigmatized for doing so. The visions of the Virgin Mary in Medjugorje, Herzegovina, became an international sensation after 1981, with more than 5 million visitors in less than a decade. After some feeble attempts to foil these pilgrimages the government yielded and even tried to take advantage of the commercial windfall created by the phenomenon.

Secularist Absolutism was receding rapidly in favor of Religious Toleration but with some ominous signs that Ecclesiastical Absolutism claims could reappear on the scene if the conflicts between the ethnoreligious groups were to get sharper.

6. The Great Transformation, Including the Beginning of Balkan Warfare, 1989-92

Yugoslavia had the possibility but not the probability of transforming itself into a Pluralistic Liberty society. The need was there because of the multiconfessional nature of the country and the history of intolerance. But remnants of Ecclesiastic or Secularistic Absolutist mentality remained strongly entrenched and intertwined. Milovan Djilas warned about the dangers of the conflict between these two monopolistic tendencies. Djilas wrote:

> The evidence is that society itself passes into stagnation and illiberality once the conscience of its individual members—religion, in other words—comes under the control of monopolistic ideologies, with church and state constantly sparring for supremacy.... Freedom has bounds; but it cannot become a piece of property. Any attempt to appropriate freedom for a particular doctrine or social group can only result in a loss of freedom for them too.[16]

The responsibility for the conflicts and ambiguities of the Yugoslav situation in regard to religious liberties rests not only on the government; the churches themselves have frequently initiated or contributed to the tension. To proclaim religious liberty and human rights when until very recently the same institution denied it to others and still shows disrespect for the rights even of some of its own members sounds hollow and hypocritical. The past behavior or misbehavior of many of the religious communities was one of the serious obstacles to a successful affirmation of such rights in recent times. The very narrow scope of the religious concern for human rights weakened the effectiveness of any church's witness. The churches have not shown any great creativeness in broadening the notion of religious liberty. The link with nationalism gave some of the churches the clout to defend their own minimal rights, and, regretfully, most have been satisfied to continue to travel this route. They felt that an ever greater claim of being the defender of a certain nationalism would increase their freedom and influence, possibly to the position of a favorite status. This turned out to be correct from a narrow ethnoreligious perspective. Very few churches sought to find in their own religious treasure some creative responses or initiatives that would not at the same time threaten the liberties of other churches and find ways for a constructive cooperation. As long as the government continued to be the guarantor of at least legal equality among the religious groups, the churches continued to be fairly ineffective as authentic embodiments of the proclamation and practice of religious liberties and human rights for all and not only for themselves.

With the unraveling of the Yugoslav federation in the early 1990s and the resulting warfare, both of which are not within the scope of this chapter, the religious situation changed dramatically. The *new* Balkan wars were not religious in their inception or motivation but as I have tried to demonstrate in my book, *Yugoslavian Inferno: Ethnoreligious Warfare in the Balkans*,[17] the wars took on an ethnoreligious character due to the reassertion of a blending of church and state in which the two fused elements cannot be disentangled. This becomes very apparent when certain politicians and religious leaders favor this symbiosis.

CONCLUDING OBSERVATIONS

The first five periods were various phases of Secularistic Absolutism with the gradual introduction of features of Religious Toleration. The direction of the sixth phase is as yet unclear. Originally it seemed that it would be a clear assertion of Religious Toleration, and perhaps even some movement toward Pluralistic Liberty, but instead a powerful thrust toward Ecclesiastic Absolutism took place as Yugoslavia headed toward disintegration.

During the first five periods religions did play a role of providing alternatives to a totalitarian concept of society. Totalitarianism was imposed to different degrees during the entire period from 1945 to 1989. In an oversimplified manner it can be conceptualized along Milovan Djilas's "new class" approach, namely the concentration of power in all aspects of life (political, economic, legal, social, cultural, educational, sports, recreational, and mass communications) in the hands of the new class. The only real exception were religious communities. During the earlier periods (especially the first) the CPY sought to impose full-fledged totalitarianism by either attempting the elimination of the religious communities altogether (and that was its long-range aim to the end), or by subverting them to communist control when they realized that the first option was impractical. The latter was carried out by cutting off foreign contacts and by subverting their activities (by means of spying, coercion, restriction, harassment, and intimidation), while externally portraying the situation as one of freedom. The religious communities were not terribly effective in countering the communist totalitarians except by the mere fact of survival. It was the tenacity of the believers, including their leadership, to maintain their faith and practices that ultimately made them play a role of providing the diversity that usually characterizes civil society. Namely, by their very existence in the midst of a totalitarian society that tried to monopolize the right to interpret reality, religious communities that offered different interpretation of reality were left as practically the only alternative worldviews available to the population.[18] The existence of a single religion would have already provided an alternative to totalitarianism but since in Yugoslavia there were a number of religions people were aware of alternate visions, albeit each with an authoritarian bent of its own, each claiming the monopoly of truth. Thus it would be erroneous to assume that the conflict between religion and Communism in Yugoslavia was a conflict between those who espouse pluralism and democracy against those who espouse totalitarianism. Rather it was a conflict of several visions of reality each of which claimed to be the only correct one.

Yugoslav Communism was somewhat like a chameleon; able to adapt its color according to needs to survive. As external and internal pressures forced Communists to make accommodations it seemed that the nature of the beast changed. But the events surrounding the disintegration of Yugoslavia showed that it did not. It only disguised itself more effectively and therefore many did not realize its resiliency or extent of control.

In regard to religion the Yugoslav Communists followed a line more enlightened than its Eastern Europe and Soviet neighbors and the religious communities benefited by the fewer restrictions imposed upon them (with the possible exception of Poland). Yet on the other hand the religious communities in Yugoslavia did not have the same social role in fomenting dissatisfaction with Communism as did the religious communities of some of their neighbors (such as Catholicism in Poland and Protestantism in Eastern Germany). Yugoslav Communists were in a better position to exercise effective social control, while the religious communities did not have the same internal strength as those communities. Religious communities wasted much of their energies in mutual conflict, feared the Partisans, and were too vulnerable to the charge that they had collaborated with the enemy during World War II.

It is accurate, however, to say that those who were actively affiliated with religious communities in Yugoslavia did represent a large segment of the population that did not buy into the vision of the Communist Party, though active dissent was rare. Most religious people in Yugoslavia placed more hope in the gradual reform of Yugoslav communism, which would lead to greater freedoms, than in actual opposition to the system itself.

In the last period since 1989, another aspect familiar to all who know Yugoslavia, the ethnoreligious identity of most of its people, reasserted itself. This ancient symbiotic union offered itself as a useful tool to politicians (mostly former Communists but also some of the nationalistic opposition) when socialist slogans no longer had the ability to appeal to the electorate. Having collapsed elsewhere in Eastern Europe it showed little promise as a vision for Yugoslavia, though in Serbia and in Montenegro it is showing some adaptability.

The tendency toward ethnoreligious homogenization is more easily observed taking place in rival states and religious communities than in one's own. Elsewhere I have demonstrated[19] that several Roman Catholic theologians have pointed to the Serbian Orthodox Church leaders' propensity to identify themselves entirely with the Serb national cause. These authors claim that the Roman Catholic leaders in Croatia did not fall into the same trap. I attempted to show that there are greater similarities than differences in the behavior of these two great communities and the same may be said of the Islamic community. Using the data by some of these Catholic authors I pointed out that what seemed to them as a wise leadership by Croat Roman Catholic leadership appears to be a very similar (if not the same) phenomenon that they rejected in the Serbian Orthodox. On the other hand the Serbian Orthodox Church has occasionally distanced itself from certain concrete Serb governmental policies that it fears will harm the Serb people. Similarly, the Roman Catholic leadership occasionally opposes the Croat (or Slovene) leadership when they judge their national interest is threatened.

The religious leaders of all three religious communities see themselves not as prophets but as pastors and thus protectors of the national interest only of their own ethnic group (only occasionally bemoaning the suffering of others and almost never admitting the atrocious behavior of the most belligerent representatives of their own people, who are condemned in the vaguest of terms). No war criminal of their own nationality has yet been excommunicated by their church—no more than Hitler or Stalin were.

Formally since 1989 a great degree of legal freedom is being experienced by nearly all religions. Although not too many religious laws were enacted the police stopped restricting religious groups and whatever restrictive legislation remained on the books was no longer applied. Religious leaders changed from persona non grata to persona desiderata. Religion is experiencing a veritable process of rehabilitation, both in the legal and medical meanings of the term. Numerous efforts have been made to find the rightful place for religion in the new social circumstances. In searching for the rightful social position there is much more looking backward and sideways than looking forward. The general tendency is to try to forget the 45 years under communism as soon as possible and return the former privileges and status of the predominant religious community. Sideways glances are also cast. Many Serbian and Macedonian Orthodox look toward the Greek model of church-state relations and many of the Slovenian and Croatian Roman Catholics look toward Austria and Germany for inspiration. The American model of separation of church and state is not considered viable, except by Protestants, Jews, secular thinkers, and a small number of adherents of the dominant communities.

This does not mean that there are no protagonists of a civil society. It would not be surprising if many were not in favor of it in a general manner. But when it comes to implementing the social vision of the respective religious communities each strains to have its own legally enacted. Thus in Slovenia and Croatia the Roman Catholic Church strives for the establishment of Catholic catechetical education in schools, the return of their previously nationalized church properties, and the inclusion of their own moral vision in national legislation irrespective of the feeling of other religious communities.

Representatives of each religious community raise their voices on behalf of the aggrieved of their nationality and bless the troops of their state going to battle. The Islamic religious leaders do the same within the scope of their influence, dreaming of the establishment of a state in which Islamic precepts would be carried out. Serbian and Macedonian leaders would also like to see themselves as constitutionally recognized as the church of their nation-state. They want to play the same crucial role in determining the formulation of state policies as has been previous ascribed to Roman Catholics. Thus the trend is away from religious tolerance (except in a very narrow sense of the word) and toward ecclesiastical absolutism.

The Protestant and Jewish membership and leadership as well as secularists may be said to be in favor of a civil society, not out of the conviction that this is the best model but rather in self-defense. The former Marxist secularists, seeing that their vision of secularistic absolutism has failed, prefer a civil society because it promises to provide the least amount of coercion toward themselves and their children. The minorities stand to be protected in their religious and civil rights far more greatly in a civil society than in a nationalist sacral one and therefore they represent dissent toward the trend of the ethnoreligious symbiosis (though some of the Protestants and certainly the Jews are colored by the same symbiotic relationship).

The greatest pressure toward the creation of a civil society—provided that the Balkan wars cease, which is an absolute precondition in that direction—will be the large number of nominal members of religious communities and those who have no firm convictions as a result of the rise of apathy under Communism. They have been alienated by both the communist and nationalist ideology and by the absolutist claims of their religions. Many of them had had some experience of western-style civil societies. Some of the intelligentsia have embraced that model due to their exposure to it.[20] A number of these people are affiliated religiously but it is not clear how many. It is they rather than the formal leadership of religious communities who are likely to spearhead the drive toward civil society. If war conditions prevail for an extended time civil society will not have much chance to develop.

To use the imagery of the conference, the religious communities showed less affinity to the Partisan paradigm than to the patriot paradigm. The Partisan paradigm was rejected as it was later rejected by the entire society. There is less likelihood that any of the large religions are going to be able to resist the patriot paradigm. Should ethnic cleansing be successful and lead to the virtual disappearance of rival religious communities from a given area, the ethnoreligious symbiosis would be strengthened. The religious community of each state would become an impediment to the establishment of a civil society of their respective state. Rather they would gravitate in the direction of the establishment of several blocs of ecclesiastical or sacral absolutist societies (Orthodox, Catholic, Islamic) standing in confrontation with other blocs of ecclesiastical absolutist societies and with the bloc of civil societies as observed by Samuel P. Huntington.[21] The war in Bosnia is already creating pressures toward the creation of such constellations, most of which will not be favorable toward the creation of civil societies.

Notes

1. The typology was developed for my book, *Religious Liberty in Eastern Europe and the USSR: Before and After the Great Transformation* (Boulder, CO: Eastern European Monographs and distributed by Columbia University Press, 1992).

2. A very strong case is made, especially in regard to the religious nature of Soviet Communism by Giovanni Codevilla, "The Limits of Religious Freedom in the USSR" in Dennis J. Dunn, ed., *Religion and Communist Society* (Berkeley, CA: Berkeley Slavic Specialties, 1983), 67-84, see esp. 68-74.

3. For a detailed description of church-state relations from 1945 to 1972, see Stella Alexander, *Church and State in Yugoslavia since 1945* (London; New York; Melbourne: Cambridge University Press, 1979). A more elaborate discussion of the periodization is found in Paul Mojzes, "Christian-Marxist Dialogue in the Context of a Socialist Society," *Journal of Ecumenical Studies,* 9, no. 4 (winter 1972): 25. The most recent attempt at periodizing the post-World War II Yugoslav approach to religion is in Mojzes, *Religious Liberty in Eastern Europe and the Soviet Union,* chapter 13.

4. See other periodizations, for example, Zdenko Roter, "Razvoj odnosov med katolisko cerkvijo in deržavo v socijalistični Jugoslaviji," *Teorija in praksa,* no. 7 (September 1970): 1280-282; and Pedro Ramet, "Catholicism and Politics in Socialist Yugoslavia," *Religion in Communist Lands,* 10 (winter 1982): 257.

5. J. Hutchinson Cockburn, *Religious Freedom in Eastern Europe* (Richmond, VA: John Knox Press, 1953), 94-96.

6. Alexander, *Church and State in Yugoslavia,* 95-120.

7. Such measures were not directed only against religious people. During these violent times Tito's forces were establishing totalitarian control. The brunt of their suppression was leveled not only at real enemies but even at Communists who stepped out of line or who were scapegoated though innocent of charges leveled against them.

8. Trevor Beeson, *Discretion and Valour* (Glasgow: Collins Fontana Books, 1974), 264. There is an error in Beeson's text "... declared that all citizens are equal in spite of national, racial or religious hatred and intolerance..." which I state in its correct form in the text.

9. Dr. Zdenko Roter, professor of sociology at University of Ljubljana, interview with author, 19 November 1987, West Chester, Pennsylvania.

10. Tito and his cohorts were under great pressure from the Soviet Union and its East European allies. Tito's elite maintained itself in power against all real and potential threats by summary suspension of all human rights, for which they had little inherent respect in the first place. After all, they had no respect for bourgeois law during old Yugoslavia when they had been declared illegal, nor could they respect orderly procedures under the conditions of Nazi occupation and a civil war during World War II. Certainly they were not about to give up power gained in such a bloody manner so quickly. Hence the notion of respect for human rights was alien to them and the idea would emerge only gradually, mostly by the increasing contacts with various Social Democrats from Western Europe, usually via dissidents such as Milovan Djilas and Vladimir Dedijer.

11. Paul Mojzes, *Christian-Marxist Dialogue in Eastern Europe* (Minneapolis, MN: Augsburg House, 1981), 128-58.

12. Radovan Samardžić, *Religious Communities in Yugoslavia* (Belgrade: Srboštampa, 1981), p. 24 quoted in Horak, 480.

13. Gerald Shenk, "The Social Role of Religion in Contemporary Yugoslavia," (Ph.D. diss., Northwestern University, 1987), 107.

14. Todo Kurtović, *Crkva i religija u socijalističkom samoupravnom društvu* (Belgrade: Rad, 1978), 353-54. This book is a collection of essays and speeches written by the author while he was the head of the Bosnia and Herzegovina and later federal commission for religious affairs. The book may well be the worst book on religion published in Yugoslavia. The author is the representative of a self-congratulatory approach by members of the Communist Party of Yugoslavia who see all errors as made by the churches and a few "sectarian" Communists while the Party was always on the right path.

15. Zdenko Roter, "Yugoslavia at the Crossroads: A Sociological Discourse," *Occasional Papers on Religion in Eastern Europe* 8, no. 2 (May 1988): 20.

16. Milovan Djilas, *The Unperfect Society: Beyond the New Class*, trans. Dorian Cooke (New York: Harcourt, Brace & World, Inc., 1969), 39.

17. Paul Mojzes, *Yugoslavian Inferno: Ethnoreligious Warfare in the Balkans* (New York: Continuum, 1994).

18. Knowledge of what took place in the West increasingly played a role and has been a significant factor in striving toward a civil society, at the same time the religious communities within their own structures and worldviews did not espouse pluralism, which characterizes civil society.

19. Paul Mojzes, "The Role of Religious Communities in the War in Yugoslavia," *Religion in Eastern Europe* XIII, no. 3 (June 1993): 13-31. Also see Mojzes, *Yugoslavian Inferno*, 125-51.

20. I have in mind people in Croatia such as Prof. Vesna Pusić, the people gathered around the journal *Erasmus* in Zagreb, Reverend Vinko Pulić, a Catholic parish priest in Vinkovci, or Reverend Jovan Nikolić, a retired Serbian Orthodox priest in Zagreb. In Serbia one can mention Professor Vesna Pešić and the people gathered in the Citizen's Alliance, the Belgrade circle in Serbia, or independent intellectuals such as Professor Svetozar Stojanović of Belgrade. In Slovenia, Professors Zdenko Roter and Niko Toš and Marjan Smrke in Ljubljana. In Bosnia Reverend Marko Oršolić, a Franciscan from Sarajevo now a refugee in Munich who is trying to organize a dialogue center for the great religions and who published a journal entitled *Zajedno* [Together]. These are the kind of people I have in mind. They are far more numerous than these examples would indicate.

21. Samuel P. Huntington, "The Clash of Civilizations?" *Foreign Affairs*, 72, no. 3 (summer 1993), 22-49.

Part III

Nation and State

Introduction

Jill A. Irvine

This final section of the book examines the way in which the Socialist period in Yugoslavia reshaped the national question. While acknowledging the historical roots of national conflict in Yugoslavia, it reveals the ways in which this conflict was redefined during the period of state socialism. The focus upon state and nation is intended to signify that they are not coterminous in the multinational Yugoslav context and to highlight the changing character of their relationship throughout the socialist period. It is also intended to capture the salient features of the Yugoslav case where party authorities engaged actively in efforts to order and reorder the relationship between nation and state for their own political purposes. The state-building activities of socialist elites during the founding period and in subsequent decades were closely linked to the question of how to distribute power among Yugoslavia's several national groups. The successes and failures of these strategies have left an enduring legacy for the character of post-socialist politics in this area.

One consistent feature of these strategies (both before and after the decentralization of the late 1960s) was the effort to balance the various national groups through the federal structures. The Tito regime sought to provide a balance of power within the federation chiefly through two means. One, it sought to restrict Serb and Croat national sentiments, which it perceived as threatening to the party-state. And two, it attempted to strengthen the national consciousness and sentiments of Macedonians, Albanians, and Muslims as a counterbalance to these two more powerful republics in the federation. The result of these efforts was to create a new set of grievances among perceived losers in the Yugoslav federation, and to reinforce claims of a greater number of national groups to sovereignty over a particular territory.

The four chapters in Part III provide a rich picture of this process of creating winners and losers within the Yugoslav federal system and its ultimately disintegrative effects. Chapters 9 and 10—Stefan Troebst's "Yugoslav Macedonia, 1944-1954, Building the State and Nation," and Francine Friedman's "The Bosnian Muslims: The Making of a Yugoslav Nation"—as their titles suggest, both examine nations that were the subject of state- and nation-building enterprises by Socialist authorities. In a sense, both were winners within the Yugoslav Socialist state with important ramifications for the postsocialist period. Chapters 11 and 12—Nicholas Miller's "Reconstituting Serbia, 1945-1991," and Lenard Cohen's, "'Serpent in the Bosom': Slobodan Milošević and Serbian Nationalism"—examine attempts to reverse what many Serbs viewed as the nation-destroying effects of the LCY's state-building strategy.

Stefan Troebst begins his discussion of Yugoslav Macedonia by describing the ways in which the Macedonian case diverged in timing though not sequence from Miroslav Hroch's three phases of national awakening. He focuses on the third phase of mass mobilization that occurred during World War II, when the Communists came to play a large part in this process through the Partisan resistance movement. Troebst outlines the Partisan strategy of allying itself with individuals and groups of non-Communists fighting for national liberation, a strategy that was applied with much success elsewhere in the country. There were two major strands in the CPY's support for national liberation in Macedonia. The first was the creation of an autonomous Macedonian political unit within the Yugoslav federation—a particular state-building strategy; the second was the reinforcement of a separate Macedonian national consciousness and identity through the codification of a new Macedonian language—a particular nation-building strategy. Troebst seeks to explain how the CPY carried out both.

The CPY's state-building strategy allowed it to cooperate with non-Communists until the movement began to centralize during 1944 and 1945. At this point, Tito's followers Svetozar Vukmanović-Tempo and Lazar Koliševski came into conflict with the Anti-Fascist Council's president and popular Partisan leader Metodi Andonov

Čento who desired more autonomy for the Macedonina party and state structures. After a struggle for control over these institutions (a struggle that resembled similar measures taken against party leader Andrija Hebrang in Croatia), the central party leadership neutralized and finally imprisoned Čento in 1946. Troebst also documents the CPY's struggle against other groups who opposed the Partisan state-building strategy because they desired either unification with Bulgaria or an independent state. These were mostly IMRO splinter groups that began to appear in 1945 and were finally eradicated in 1948.

The CPY's nation-building strategy encountered less resistance since the dissemination of the new Macedonian language was extremely popular with the public. The new Macedonian language, which represented a compromise between Serbian and Bulgarian, was finally settled upon in the spring of 1945. The Communist Party of Macedonia (CPM) immediately set about propagating the new language in schools, new universities, films, books and especially radio broadcasts. Troebst attributes the success of the CPM's nation-building enterprise to the fact that Macedonian Communists functioned as ethnic entrepreneurs with bureaucratic and state tools at their disposal. He makes it clear, however, that this success rested in large part upon powerful popular support for Macedonian cultural activity. Although Troebst does not argue this himself, it is also clear that the CPY's nation-building strategy has had a profound effect on the second round of state-building occurring in Macedonia. Current efforts to consolidate the new Macedonian state would have been immensely more complicated without five decades of state- and nation-building efforts by Yugoslav party elites.

Another national group that found itself in an increasingly advantaged position within the federal system was the Muslim population of Bosnia-Hercegovina. Francine Friedman's chapter highlights how the position of Bosnian Muslims changed as a result of the federal restructuring of the late 1960s, and the designation of "Muslim" as a separate nation. As Friedman illustrates, the Muslim population had initially possessed an ambiguous status in Socialist Yugoslavia because it lacked its own federal unit and formal designation as a separate national group. The decision to introduce Muslim as a legal national category was motivated by a combination of factors including Tito's wish to enhance his status in the Non-Aligned Movement and to mitigate Serb-Croat squabbling over Bosnia-Hercegovina. Its effect was to open up a new front of national conflict in Yugoslavia after 1971 as Muslim party elites responded to institutional incentives to present their demands for resources and political goods in ethnic terms. At the same time, the Muslim populace, under the tutelage of Muslim intellectuals in Bosnia-Hercegovina, began to display an increased sense of a separate national identity and religiosity, partially, Friedman argues, because many more Bosnian Muslim children were sent to Islamic schools abroad.

In the mid-1980s the regime found itself forced to respond to what it perceived to be growing Muslim nationalism and launched an assault on Bosnian Muslim opposition leaders such as Alija Izetbegović. Nevertheless, the institutional position of Bosnian Muslims continued to improve in the decade after Tito's death. Herein lies the source of tragedy for this group, Friedman concludes, because the Muslim's newly enhanced status as a nation under the Tito and post-Tito regime is a main cause of its difficulties today. The strengthening of the Bosnian nation in an effort to restructure and balance relations between nation and state in socialist Yugoslavia increased the likelihood that Bosnian Muslims would become the target of competing claims for political control over parts of Bosnia-Hercegovina.

While the political liberalization and redefinition of the federal structure enhanced the status of Bosnian Muslims in the Yugoslav political system, Serbs perceived this process as inimical to their national interests. Indeed, the designation of Muslims as a separate national group represented, as Nicholas Miller describes it in chapter 11 on political developments in Serbia during this period, "a huge setback for the national mythology of the Serbs." As power was increasingly devolved from the center, the perception increased among Serbs that they had been punished in the Yugoslav socialist state. Many Serbs felt that Tito had wanted to weaken Serbia in the new Yugoslav federation and complained that the settlement of the national question during World War II had resulted in a "parcelization" of Serbia. The CPY had established two autonomous provinces within the borders of Serbia and had formed two new republics—Bosnia-Hercegovina, which had a large Serb population and Montenegro, many of whose inhabitants considered themselves Serbs. This arrangement may have been tolerable when a highly centralized state order was in effect and republic borders were virtually meaningless. But with the decentralization of power to the republics after the federal reforms of the late 1960s, it became increasingly unacceptable. By the late 1970s the sentiment had grown even within the League of Communists of Serbia (LCS) that the dispersal of Serbs could not continue. The LCS's response of simply relying on institutional engineering, such as the revision of the 1974 constitution, however, was seen as inadequate by many Serbs outside the party. After Tito's death, this opposition drew increasingly upon older, pre-partisan ideologies that were anti-communist and anti-Muslim. As concern about the situation of Serbs in Kosovo increased, consensus grew that the most important objective was to undo the legacies of socialist Yugoslavia and reconstitute the Serbian state.

This consensus on Serbian national aims was formulated by intellectuals from two main groups: the members of the Serbian Academy of Sciences and Arts (SANU) and members of the Praxis group. The importance of the Memorandum of the Serbian Academy in 1986 has been well-documented. This memorandum articulated the view that had emerged during the de-Titoization campaign of the previous several years. For SANU intellectuals, Tito, Kardelj, and the system they had created were responsible for Serbia's present ills. Their solution was the complete national and cultural integrity of the Serbian nation, regardless of the republic in which it was located. SANU intellectuals were joined in their aims by members of the Praxis group, who had achieved a certain amount of notoriety both within Yugoslavia and abroad by their opposition to the regime during 1970 and 1971. As proponents of a more democratic form of self-managing socialism, their turn toward nationalism at first seems perplexing. Miller argues, however, that their concept of democracy, rooted in a collective conception of social rights, made easy the move from one homogenizing collective ideology to another. A similar observation can be offered about other opposition groups in Eastern Europe, whose orientation was based primarily on collective as opposed to individual rights. In any case, the several strands of opposition to the Titoist treatment of the Serbian population—from Ćosić to LCS leaders, to more overt nationalists outside the party—came together under the leadership of Slobodan Milošević, who achieved a "historic fusion" of party and non-party oppositionists.

Slobodan Milošević is the focus of the last chapter of Part III. In chapter 12, Lenard Cohen examines Milošević's rise to political preeminence and some important features of Serbian political culture that assisted in his consolidation of power. A vivid picture emerges of Milošević's adeptness in exploiting the patron-client networks characteristic of Yugoslav patrimonial socialism. Until 1986, when he became president of the CC LCS, Milošević adhered closely to the line of Ivan Stambolić, his patron and the most powerful man in Serbian politics. Thus he pushed for constitutional reform as a solution to the Serbian question and denounced nationalism as a "serpent in the bosom of the Serbian people." Indeed, Stambolić promoted Milošević's career in the belief that Milošević would help him achieve a moderate solution to the constitutional paralysis of Yugoslav politics.

What interests Cohen is what he labels as Milošević's metamorphosis after he assumes the presidency of the LCS, and Cohen makes two interesting arguments about this process. First, he places a great deal of emphasis on Milošević's famous trip to Kosovo Polje in April 1987 when Milošević encountered the intense frustration and anxiety of Serbs in Kosovo. According to Cohen, Milošević was profoundly affected by the depth of Serbian national sentiments and sensed their political potential, though he was still uncertain how to use it. Prior to this time Milošević had said little about the situation in Kosovo; now he spoke of it frequently. And, while he attacked the Memorandum in a closed meeting shortly thereafter, Milošević was "a master of political guile who was willing to both attack and forecast his own course of action." Milošević's break with Stambolic came at the Eighth Session of the CC LCS in October 1987, when he attacked Belgrade party chief, Dragiša Pavlović. Cohen rejects the argument that Milošević had already established a close alliance with SANU intellectuals before this meeting. This interpretation has significant implications for Milošević's subsequent political position, for he was not beholden to this group in his climb to power.

Cohen then turns to the question of why Milošević's message was so appealing to the general populace and concludes that Milošević's rise to power had more to do with the cultural underpinnings than the structural features of the Serbian polity. Milošević's message was appealing because it resonated with the Serbian political culture. Although he cautions against extrapolating directly from the historical conditioning of the Serbian mindset to current conditions, survey research reveals popular attitudes among Serbs congruent with such cultural expectations and values. Milošević responded to these cultural underpinnings in two important ways. First, his populist style resonated with the strong leader tradition in Serbian politics and the patron-client, limited pluralism of Tito's Yugoslavia. Moreover, his nationalist message corresponded closely to the unity of national themes in Balkan political culture in which national ideologies have provided the defining features of collective identity.

Cohen's chapter leaves us with the strong impression that conflict over the relation between nation and state, which became the defining feature of Yugoslav political life in the last decade of its existence, was not the result exclusively or even primarily of manipulation from above. Indeed, all of the contributions in Part III point to the complex interaction between republic party elites and the populace over the articulation and pursuit of national interests. Within the changing parameters of the Yugoslav federal system, party elites often responded to the national aspirations of mass publics and opposition intellectuals and modified their state-building strategies accordingly. That these strategies increasingly reflected the aims of traditional national ideologies speaks to the endurance of particular themes in South Slavic political culture. That they became expressed in struggles over the distribution of power within the Yugoslav state was a mark of both the success and the failure of socialist attempts to reconfigure the relationship between nation and state.

9

Yugoslav Macedonia, 1943–1953:
Building the Party, the State, and the Nation[1]

Stefan Troebst

> A bre Makedonce,
> *kade se spremas?*
> —Partisan song in the Prilep area, 1942[2]

In describing the ethnopolitical situation in Macedonia, the Swedish right-wing politician and scholar Rudolf Kjellén stated in 1916: "Here a people are living . . . who themselves do not know whether they are Serbs or Bulgars, . . . [who] are in fact like a flour with which one can bake every cake one wishes once the question of citizenship has been decided."[3] As it turned out during the next three decades things were not *that* easy in Macedonia: While the Slavic-speaking, Christian-Orthodox majority of the population in Vardar Macedonia had to accept successively Serbian, Bulgarian, Yugoslav, and then Bulgarian citizenship again, it did *not* accept the underlying national programs and ethnopolitical concepts of these citizenships. Instead, from 1943 onward, it readily embraced a new national concept, that of a separate South Slav nation called Macedonian. While the "historical roots" of this concept were rather thin and went back in time only to the turn of the century, the prospects for the future of the new national ideology looked bright from the very beginning. Already in the mid-1950s, after an only ten-year "Macedonization" process, ethnopolitical dissent in Yugoslav Macedonia—be it "Greater Bulgarianism" or "Serbianizing"—was no topic any longer: the foundations of the new Macedonian nation were laid. The two most important reasons for this stunning success story were undoubtedly the parallel erection of a semi-independent Macedonian state in the form of a Yugoslav republic, and the transformation of the Macedonian branch of the Communist Party of Yugoslavia (CPY) into the sole center of power *and* simultaneously into the main ethnic entrepreneur.

"FIRST *ILINDEN*" TO "SECOND *ILINDEN*": THE PRE-HISTORY OF THE IDEA OF A MACEDONIAN NATION, 1903–44

According to Miroslav Hroch's model of the "national awakening" with "smaller European nations," three successive phases can be distinguished: Phase A is characterized by a still purely academic interest of some individuals in the folklore, oral tradition, history and so on of their ethnic group; in phase B a small group of determined "patriots" then develops a program of national agitation aiming at the mobilization of the whole target group; and during phase C this mobilization process turns into a mass phenomenon, thereby achieving the final goal, that is, their own nation-state.[4]

Leaving aside the interesting question of the motives guiding the "patriots" in the development of their propaganda, it is obvious that this model does not work too well in the Macedonian case. While around the turn of the century there had been some sort of an A phase—theoreticians such as Krste P. Misirkov indeed collected historical, ethnic, and linguistic arguments for the existence of a separate Macedonian ethnic group—culminating even in a militarily organized uprising on St. Elias's Day (*Ilinden*) in 1903, no B phase followed. This was mainly due to the fact that the first protagonists of a Macedonian nation in the nineteenth century either lost their lives fighting the Ottomans, or—more frequently—were sucked away by the career offers made by the competing nation-states of Bulgarians, Greeks, and Serbs.[5] Consequently, there was little maneuvering room for Macedonian nationalism during the interwar period. From 1941 on, it even seemed as if the ideas of the first protagonists of a Macedonia national mobilization had completely withered away. Parts of Aegean Macedonia now fell under the Bulgarian military administration, while Vardar Macedonia was incorporated into Bulgaria—a political change initially welcomed by most of the Vardar Macedonian population. Several prominent members of the avantgarde of Macedonian nationalism now (re)converted to Bulgariandom.

By 1943, however, three major political factors had brought about a radical change and thereby initiated the B phase of Macedonian nationalism: First, The new Bulgarian authorities in Vardar Macedonia did not act as liberators, but rather as occupiers. They did so in spite of the Bulgarian propaganda topos of "daughter Macedonia" being freed from her "Serbian abductors" and returned into "mother Bulgaria's" lap. Second, the German Axis partner Italy dropped out of the war in the summer of 1943, leaving Western Macedonia unguarded; thus, the Tito Partisans now were able to set up a bridgehead in Macedonia, too. In Western Macedonia the Partisans met with the support of a rapidly growing non-communist partisan force that was aiming primarily at a "reunification" of all of Macedonia and the founding of a Macedonian state, preferably linked to one or several western powers. And, third, to make its new military position in Macedonia also politically safe, the CPY reiterated a decision taken back in 1937, that in a future Communist Yugoslavia Macedonia should be granted the status of a sixth republic next to Yugoslavia's "historic" parts—Slovenia, Croatia, Bosnia-Hercegovina, Serbia, and Montenegro—and that its inhabitants should be regarded as Macedonians instead of "southern" or respectively "Mountain Serbs."

In the summer of 1944 then, with the victory of the Partisans over the Bulgarians and Germans in sight, mass support for the new Partisan Movement triggered off what was clearly a C phase in Hroch's terms. For several years to come, in Vardar and in Yugoslav Macedonia the B phase and the C phase of nation-building, that is, mobilization efforts and mass response, took place almost simultaneously.

In 1943-44, the leadership of the CPY had at least four good reasons for its decision to constitute Macedonia as a sixth republic of the new federal Yugoslavia and for simultaneously encouraging the process of building a separate nation there. First, this considerably helped the Belgrade party and state leadership to establish and maintain control over this geographically and strategically exposed southern border. Second, by this decision Vardar Macedonia was tightly tied to Yugoslavia, since Bulgarian aspirations toward this region and its population were effectively warded off.[6] Third, it gave Yugoslavia the possibility to gain a certain degree of *mitbestimmung* in Bulgarian Pirin Macedonia and thus provided an efficient tool to interfere directly into Bulgarian politics. And fourth, the idea of a Macedonian nation supplied the Belgrade leadership with an equally effective tool toward Greece and its Slavic minority in Aegean Macedonia. The conditio sine qua non of the CPY's Macedonian policy was, of course, the close affiliation and integration of the new republic and its nation-in-progress into the Yugoslav federation and its peoples' "brotherhood and unity."

While the ultimate decision on the foundation of a Macedonian republic was proclaimed on November 29, 1943, by the Anti-Fascist Council of the National Liberation for Yugoslavia (AVNOJ) at Jajce, it took more than seven months until the Macedonian Partisans and Communists had formed *their* AVNOJ-like republican parliamentary representation called ASNOM (Anti-Fascist Assembly of the National Liberation of Macedonia) on August 2, 1944—again St. Elias's Day. In the ASNOM presidium, all key positions were held by those representatives of the Partisan Movement who aimed at Macedonian unification, meaning reunification and autonomy, while the Communists had so far no particular influence. At the end of November 1944, when Vardar Macedonia was finally cleared of German and Bulgarian troops, the ASNOM presidium uncontestedly represented the highest political authority in the new Yugoslav republic. In late December 1944, however, things began rapidly to change. First, the Communists took over some key positions inside ASNOM, then transferred almost all executive power onto the new government. By mid-April 1945, when ASNOM was transformed into a regular parliament, this body had lost its political weight completely. Now the prime minister and key cabinet ministers, all members of the Central Committee of the Communist Party of Macedonia (CPM), were in charge. This communist conquest of all formal and informal power in Macedonia was carefully planned and directed by the "mother party" in Belgrade, the local Macedonian party functionaries being no more than tools of the CPY and its inner circle around Tito.

BUILDING THE NEW MACEDONIA: "WHITE SPOTS" IN HISTORIOGRAPHY AND AGENDA OF RESEARCH

While the process of state-building in Macedonia was directed from outside, the parallel and much more difficult task of nation-building—being, to be sure, also planned from the outside—necessarily had to be carried out by the Macedonian Communists and the new Macedonian state authorities themselves. While the erection of the new state structures and a planned economy can be rather convincingly explained by the unchallenged political dominance of the Communists in Macedonia, the success story of the creation of a new nation presents more problems for explanation. So far the only serious attempt to do so is a book published in 1971 by the American diplomat Stephen E. Palmer, Jr., and the Radio Free Europe analyst Robert R. King on *Yugoslav Communism and the Macedonian Question*.[7] Since the publication of Palmer and King's book, in the West not much on developments in Vardar Macedonia during the decisive years from the end of the war in 1944 to 1953, when Yugoslav Stalinism began to erode, has been published.[8] From the 1970s on, however, Yugoslav Macedonian authors—in particular, legal specialists, political scientists, sociologists, economists, and to an insignificant degree historians as well[9]—have done more extensive research. In the beginning, this research concentrated on the legal and administrative development of the new republic, in the 1980s analyses on political, economic, and educational problems were produced, and in the 1990s taboo topics and "white spots" were finally touched upon.

The main intention of this chapter is to compare the state of knowledge in Stephen Palmer and Robert King's work of 1971 with the recent findings of Macedonian academia, and to outline those research results that confirm or even go beyond Palmer and King's framework. I shall concentrate on three of the many factors of Macedonian nation-building. First, the internal divisions of the group of Hroch's "patriots"—in the Macedonian case the leaderships of the Partisan Movement and the Communist Party—shall be given short treatment. Second, some aspects of "cultural Macedonianism" which according to Palmer and King, "has given greater impetus to Macedonian nationalism than any other aspect of the communist program to develop a Macedonian consciousness"[10] shall be highlighted.

And third, the so far neglected question of the destruction of those political forces that opted for another, that is a non-Yugoslav orientation of the new state, and also those ethnopolitical factors that opposed the new nation-building process, will be taken into consideration.

THE PARTY AND THE ISSUE OF POWER

As Palmer and King have observed, in wartime "the CPY played its cards with consummate skills in Vardar Macedonia."[11] An embryonic party organization not only succeeded in steering a victorious Partisan Movement, but also in remaining at its head after the war. It was, however, this particular period—the final phase of war—when the antagonism between the tiny party and the bulk of basically non-communist and often anti-communist Partisans threatened to become too wide. This gap opened up particularly over two topics of the Macedonian national agenda, namely the internal organization of the emerging new state in the once again Yugoslav part of Macedonia, and the international problem of completing state-building and nation-building in Vardar Macedonia by carrying out what was termed as the "liberation of Aegean and Pirin Macedonia" in order to "reunite" these two territories with the nucleus in Skopje. Up to early 1945, by carefully identifying the various camps and groupings inside the Macedonian movement, Tito, his chief aide in Macedonian matters, Svetozar Vukmanović-Tempo, and his Skopje representative Lazar Koliševski,[12] managed to avoid such conflict. In their rhetoric at least, they also made the basic concession of not giving up the unification scheme. Thus, they succeeded in making the "nationalists" in the Macedonian movement pledge allegiance to the Yugoslav federation.

There was, however, one current inside the Macedonian Partisan Movement that the Communists had difficulty in controlling. That was, as it turned out, the politically most potent group around the popular partisan leader Metodi Andonov called "Čento." In the summer of 1944, Čento, one of the very few charismatic figures in Macedonia at that time, succeeded in getting hold of what was then the most important political post, the presidency of ASNOM. In the following nine months, up to the formation of the first Macedonian government, a bitter power struggle took place between on the one side the Central Committee of the CPM with the CPY and on the other side the ASNOM president and his group of followers—Bogoja Fotev, Panko Brašnar(ov), Kiril Petrušev, Mihailo Apostolski, Venko Markovski, Petre Piruze, Mane (Emanuil) Čučkov, Lazar Sokolov, Kiro Gligorov, and others.

While historians in Macedonia and Bulgaria have recently published some new information on Čento,[13] the power struggle so far has not been the object of systematic research. Judging from ASNOM documents, especially those published since 1984, Čento opposed the communist policy in almost all vital fields. In particular, he was strictly against sending Macedonian troops in a northern direction to fight the Germans, fervently arguing instead for a campaign of the Partisans toward the Aegean port of Solun (Thessaloniki), which in his eyes was the true historical capital of Macedonia. Čento also violated a great number of new political taboos. For example, in the spring of 1945 he suggested the foundation of a separate Macedonian Orthodox Church instead of resurrecting the Serbian church organization in the Vardar region—a suggestion that was implicitly anti-Serbian. Decidedly anti-Serbian then was his resistance against the return of those Serbs that the Bulgarian occupiers had deported in 1942 from Macedonian to Old Serbia. And equally anti-Serbian was his refusal to agree to the stationing of Yugoslav troops from Serbia in Macedonia. But the Communists were also infuriated by Čento's proposal not to use the services of the new TANJUG news agency but to build Macedonia's own Telegraph Agency of Macedonia (TAM), and by his expression of dislike of the new alphabet because of the Serbian outlook of some of its letters (j, lj, nj). From Belgrade, the Skopje Communists were advised to take action when the anti-Serbian and Greater Macedonian tendencies by Čento and his followers took forms that were considered politically alarming. This was the case with a riot of the Macedonian Partisan brigade—the Goce Delčev—in late November and early December 1944. The brigade's artillery platoon stationed at Skopje, and one of its infantry platoons at Štip revolted against the order to be sent to the Srem front to fight the Germans. Instead they demanded to be sent immediately "down to Solun." While this riot itself was quickly dealt with by the new Yugoslav secret service OZNA (from 1946 on called the UDB),[14] the communist measures against Čento took some more time. The first step was the installation of Lazar Koliševski as Čento's first deputy in the ASNOM presidency during the second session of this assembly on 28-31 December 1944. Then on 22 January 1945, inside the ASNOM presidency a special "Working Body" was created that functioned as a *de facto* government and was led also by Koliševski.[15] And in mid-April 1945, shortly before the end of World War II in Europe, the wartime parliament was transformed into a regular republican parliament—Narodno Sobranie—handing over its executive functions to the new official Government of Macedonia of Koliševski.[16] Now Čento had lost his influence completely; he was, however, allowed to stay on for one more year as the politically powerless president of the new National Assembly of Macedonia until March 1946.[17] After his deposition from this post he announced in a public speech in Prilep that he would leave the country in order to present the cause for an independent and united Macedonia to the United Nations. Immediately afterwards, however, he was arrested, and at the end of 1946 tried and sentenced to 11 years of forced labor.[18] Čento's arrest provoked disturbances of an unprecedented scale throughout Macedonia, and there is evidence that during a protest demonstration in the Macedonian town of Resen near the Greek border 37 pro-Čento demonstrators were killed by the militia.[19] In 1946 a wide-ranging purge of real and alleged Čento followers in the government service throughout all of Macedonia was carried out, leading to an unknown number of arrests and executions.

LANGUAGE, CULTURE, AND EDUCATION IN THE NATION-BUILDING PROCESS

According to a Macedonian social scientist "the essence of the new state was the Party"[20]—an observation that should not be stated without emphasizing that this party was at least as new as the state. While in 1941 there had been only some 400 members of the CPY, with the foundation of the CPM in mid-1943 this number had not changed much.[21] It rose to some 800 members at the end of the war. Then, however, membership figures increased considerably, as table 9.1 shows.

The CPM, however, did not only provide the basic preconditions to the Macedonization of Vardar Macedonia by setting up the new state and its educational and cultural authorities, but also participated also more directly in the nation-building process. This was done by mobilizing large segments of the Macedonian society for political and ideological, as well as but also for national aims. A crucial role in this mobilization effort, which encompassed as much as one sixth of the country's adult population,[22] was played by various communist front organizations. The coordinating roof institution

Table 9.1
CPM Members 1945–54

Year	Number	Index
1945	6.077	100
1946	11.570	190
1947	14.405	237
1948	27.029	445
1949	30.984	510
1950	37.068	610
1951	46.736	769
1952	49.595	816
1953	45.166	743
1954	43.595	717

Source: Lazar Lazarov, "Organizacioniot razvoj i sostav na partiskata organizacija (KPM) vo periodot na socijalističkata izgradba na NR Makedonija do 1954 godina," in Red. Ljupco Arsov, et al., *Osnovanjeto i razvojot na Komunističkata partija na Makedonija: Materijali od Naučniot sobir održan na 1, 2 i 3 noemvri 1979 godin,* vol. 2. (Skopje: Komunist, 1980), 1085-106.

of these organizations was the United National Front of Macedonia (Edinstven Naroden Front na Makedonija or ENOF), founded on November 26, 1944 in Skopje, which was headed by Dimitar Vlahov as its president and led by Lazar Koliševski as its secretary. It was the successor organization of the National Liberation Front of the war days.

The successful effort undertaken by the CPM to mobilize the population of the new republic to a considerable degree and of the new state structures to encompass more and more citizens points to the crucial role of language in this process. It was therefore a stroke of genius that the leadership of the Macedonian Partisan Movement had decided already in wartime to use and later to codify a virtually new Slavic language. Until 1944, the Slavic-speaking, Eastern Orthodox majority of the population of Vardar Macedonia was bilingual, insofar as regional dialects were used for everyday communication, while the official language in written communication, particularly with state institutions, was at first Turkish, then Serbian and Bulgarian respectively.[23] The local and regional dialects were perceived by their speakers neither as belonging to any known codified language nor as being a separate Macedonian language. If at all, these speakers referred to their idiom as "naški," "našenski," or "našinski," meaning simply "our idiom."[24] This fact paralleled the ethnic indifference of the majority of the population in question. That, however, meant that the language was one of the most promising keys to ethnic determination in a Macedonian sense. Someone who acknowledges that he speaks the Macedonian language is more easily convinced that he belongs to the Macedonian nation, too.[25] Thus, one of the ASNOM decisions of August 2, 1944, reads as follows:

> Art. 1 In the Macedonian state the colloquial Macedonian language (narodniot makedonski jazik) will be introduced as the official language.
> Art. 2 This decision becomes effective immediately.[26]

But the colloquial Macedonian language so far was a spoken idiom used in writing only by the Partisans, and this in dozens of regional varieties. Its transformation into an official language required, first of all, a codification of the orthography. This necessity, however, confronted Macedonian language politicians with a difficult twofold question: First, how to codify a Macedonian language in such a way that it would be accepted by its potential speakers as their mother tongue and not as a foreign language. And second, how to carry out this codification without running the risk that the final product resembled too much the two large neighboring South Slav languages—Bulgarian and Serbian—and allowed these neighbors to go on bolstering their aspirations with linguistic arguments.

The body set up to grapple with these problem was the Commission for Language and Orthography, that is—to be more exact—three successive commissions with that name that operated between the summer of 1944 and the spring of 1945. They consisted of philologists, writers, military persons, party functionaries, and educators. While the general framework of these commissions and their work are known from previous publications,[27] this knowledge is by now considerably enhanced by a monograph published in 1988 by the Macedonian philologist Stojan Risteski.[28] The result of the commission's deliberations was a rather innovative compromise between the Serbian and Bulgarian language. As Risteski's study shows, this compromise was not the result of the work of the various expert commissions but of interference by the emerging new political leadership, in particular the CPM. The recommendations of the first and the second commission were flatly rejected by Koliševski and his colleagues. In both cases they dissolved the commission and installed a new one. The third commission, a small ad hoc body put together under time pressure, then produced recommendations amenable to Koliševski, who was then the head of the first postwar government.

On May 3, 1945,[29] the new alphabet and the first regulations for spelling were officially proclaimed.

The government decision on the new orthography was popularized immediately in a brochure entitled "Macedonian Orthography"[30] and implemented in the first textbook, *Dictionary with Reading Materials for the First Grade*.[31] In January 1946, 16,000 copies of the first short grammar book of the new language were published.[32] The next important step in language policy was the foundation of the Kiril i Metodij University of Skopje in 1946. From the beginning its philosophical faculty included a "Catheder for South Slav Languages," to which a "Seminar for Macedonian Language" belonged.[33] Also in late 1946 the Writers' Union of Macedonia was founded, and in that same year the first piece of fiction in the new language, a collection of short stories, was published.[34]

Language, of course, was also an important aspect in other fields of culture. On April 3, 1945, the newly founded Macedonian National Theater had opened with a play by the Soviet Ukrainian Oleksandr Kornyjčuk (Aleksandr Kornejčuk). The equally new Macedonian opera gave its first performance on May 9, 1945, in Italian. It took until May 1954 for the first Macedonian opera—Goce by Kiril Makedonski—to be written and performed.[35] Yet more important from a political point of view was another medium. On May 29, 1946, the first film with Macedonian titles was shown in Skopje. While this was, of course, a Soviet film, shortly afterward a new governmental Committee for Cinematography (Komitet za kinematografija) was set up,[36] and in 1952 the first movie produced in Macedonia went into the cinemas.[37] A more traditional way of simultaneously popularizing the new language and the new ideology was musical folklore—a medium used with considerable success by the Partisans during the war. In particular, the genre of comitadji songs—anti-Ottoman guerrilla fighters' songs—was adapted to suit contemporary needs.

Nonfiction, however, is more important for the creation of a standard language than fiction, as Heinz Kloss has observed in a different context[38] and as Karl W. Deutsch has demonstrated.[39] Especially in a largely illiterate society as Macedonia during the mid-1940s—in 1944 as much as 67.5 percent of the population over the age of ten years was not able to read or write[40]—the spoken word reached much larger target groups than the written one. The conclusion the Macedonian Communists drew from these two facts was to concentrate their linguistic popularization efforts on the medium that had proved successful for their wartime propaganda—the radio. On December 28, 1944, Radio Skopje broadcast its first program in Macedonian, and in January 1945 regular broadcasting began.[41]

In Yugoslav Macedonia, print media too played its role in popularizing the new language and enforcing the new national identity. The most important was the republic-wide daily *Nova Makedonij*, which began on October 29, 1944 and by June 1953 had a circulation of 16,000 copies. The Yugoslav press—first of all Serbian-language papers from Serbia, Montenegro and Bosnia—was also available in Macedonia, something quite a few Communists regarded as a potential threat to their intensive Macedonization efforts. This general dilemma was not to be solved in the Yugoslav context: The Macedonian leadership had to accept that parallel to their campaign of cultivating a new Macedonian national identity, a Yugoslavization of Vardar Macedonia was unavoidable. And in the Macedonian case "brotherhood and unity among the peoples of Yugoslavia" meant a revival of Serbian linguistic, cultural, and also political influence. The strongholds of Serbs coming from Serbia into Macedonia were first of all the army, then the economy, and only to a lesser degree the party.[42] But in the cultural sphere as well Serbs were active in Macedonia, not the least because many of the most reliable and skillful new Macedonian cadres were needed for the Macedonization of the Pirin region in neighboring Bulgaria.[43]

The most important medium to transmit not only the new language and the newly propagated cultural forms but the idea of a separate Macedonian nation was the educational sector. While the role of education in the process of Macedonization is not yet researched, at least the organizational history of setting up a new educational system in Vardar Macedonia on different levels—elementary education, higher education, alphabetization campaigns—is by now well known. The curricula of the new educational institutions clearly show the predominance of subjects such as the new mother tongue, national literature, national geography, and above all, national history.

A good indicator of the effectiveness of the school system in its national function is the fact that the first postwar emigrants from Macedonia expressed a clear-cut national consciousness. In particular, miners and tobacco farmers from Vardar Macedonia, who in the mid-1950s emigrated to the mining and tobacco-growing areas of western Australia due to high unemployment,[44] defined themselves as ethnic Macedonians and immediately engaged in squabbles with Greek and Bulgaro-Macedonian emigrant groups.[45] In other words: Even sporadic attendance at the one-year, four-year and/or seven-year elementary schools in the Macedonian republic had made these "peasants into Macedonians."[46] This, of course, could have worked only because, in contrast to other political and nation-building measures of the new regime, its language policy did indeed have popular support. And the decision to propagate the new language did not cause criticism inside Yugoslav Macedonia, either in the 1940s or later, even by stout anti-communists. It may therefore be assumed with some degree of plausibility that the decision to codify the new language was *the* decisive measure that functioned as a key to the creation of the new national identity.

THE LIQUIDATION OF ANTI-"MACEDONIANISM"

The power struggle between the Čento group and the Communists under Koliševski, however bitterly fought, still had no ethnopolitical connotation, since both poles shared the view of the existence of a separate Macedonian nation. That, however, did not mean that the propagation, popularization, and strengthening of the new ethnic concept was carried out smoothly. To the contrary, the Macedonian leadership met with fierce opposition on ethnopolitical grounds. This opposition came from two groups that were often difficult to distinguish from each other. The first group was the camp of what at that time was called "Greater Bulgarian chauvinism," meaning people whose ethnic consciousness was clearly Bulgarian and whose political sympathies went into the direction of an *anschluss* of Vardar Macedonia to Bulgaria. The second camp was perceived as being even more dangerous because it was more violent: the group of the followers of the Internal Macedonian Revolutionary Organization led by the exiled Ivan Mihajlov. While the latter also defined themselves as Bulgarians in ethnic terms, in political terms they were opting for a united, independent, and pro-western Macedonia outside Yugoslavia. Both groups were classified by the party and state as being politically anti-communist ("fascists") and ethnopolitically anti-Macedonian ("Greater Bulgarian chauvinists"). But what the Communists perceived as even more alarming than the mere existence of these currents and organizations was the fact that between them and the Greater Macedonian nationalists of the Čento variety, as well as some of their own functionaries, personal and traditional political links also existed.[47]

The Greater Bulgarian opposition was rather soon dealt with. In 1944 a large number of sympathizers with the Bulgarian occupation regime and, in particular, persons who had held official functions in the Bulgarian bureaucracy during the period 1941-44 were arrested. While some were executed without legal procedures, the more prominent ones were put on trial. The first trial of late May to early June 1945 was against three high-ranking functionaries of the pre-war IMRO, then of MANAPO, and later high Bulgarian officials in Vardar Macedonia, Dimitar Gjuzelev, Dimitar Čkatrov, and Spiro Kitinčev, the first two of which were executed.[48] To make sure that not only those sympathizers of the Bulgarian orientation who had committed war crimes would be held responsible, the new crime of "violation of the Macedonian national honor" was introduced and a special court set up. According to a Macedonian historian, "this court . . . put on trial those violations of national honour which cannot be qualified as treason, or as support of the occupier in his war crimes."[49]

Having thus cleansed all of Vardar Macedonia of the political remnants of Bulgarian rule, the secret police of the new Macedonian republic soon faced a new type of "Bulgarian danger": In 1945 the first IMRO-inspired formation, the secret separatist Democratic Front of Macedonia, Ilinden 1903 (DFM), was founded.[50] At the beginning of 1946, a second secret group by the name of IMRO—Independent Democratic Republic of Macedonia under the Protectorate of America (VMRO-SDRMA)—was organized by a group of young people at Prilep.[51] During the same year it started to function as the coordination center for similar IMRO student groups in Strumica, Štip, Skopje, Bitola, Veles, Kičevo,[52] and in 1947 more groups started to operate in Ohrid, Kumanovo, and Gevgelija. Most of them were discovered by the UDB within several months and some 400 people were arrested, out of which roughly 150 were tried.[53] After a short pause, however, IMRO in Vardar Macedonia recovered and in 1948 was resurrected as IMRO-Truth (VMRO-Pravda). The new organizational net covered not only most of the towns of Vardar Macedonia, but also remote areas such as Debarca and Maleševo. But what made IMRO-Truth even more dangerous from the perspective of the regime, was the fact that its members called themselves čentovci—followers of Čento. Still UDB was efficient in discovering the cells of this organization, too.

During the years 1948 to 1950, some 300 members were arrested, out of which about 150 were sentenced.[54] This was definitely the end of the "old" IMRO in Vardar Macedonia, one of the reasons being that after the Tito-Stalin break western support for some of these anti-communist formation ended.[55]

A new wave of pro-Soviet agitators that secretly crossed the border into Macedonia from Bulgaria[56] and Greek Cominformists, who operated from bases in Albania,[57] were neither a serious threat to the republic nor to the process of Macedonization. The same was true for the followers of Stalin inside the CPM and, in particular, for NKVD collaborators like the ASNOM veteran Panko Brašnar and the first minister of justice, Pavel Šatev.

By the beginning of the 1950s, UDB was in control of political and ethnopolitical dissent in Macedonia. The secret police effectively safeguarded the new nation-building process against adverse influences by external and internal factors alike. Pro-Bulgarian agitation had ceased to exist as had Greater Macedonianism in its Čento and Mihajlov varieties, and thus Macedonization and Vardarization were promoted.

CONCLUSION

The success story of Macedonian nation-building of the 1944-53 period rests on several pillars, the precise impact of which is not yet determined in every singular case. Undoubtedly one of the most important pillars is the territorial factor, given the military and then political control over Vardar Macedonia (at certain periods also over Pirin Macedonia) by the new main protagonists of Macedonian nationalism, that is, the Macedonian (and Yugoslav) Communists. This political control took more permanent shape in the form of a republic inside the new federation, whereby the Macedonian Communists in their function as "patriots" or ethnic entrepreneurs, set up a bureaucratic apparatus that they then could instrumentalize for their nation-building project. Of particular importance was the fact that in addition to the Yugoslav state the Yugoslav Communist Party was also organized at least formally on a federal basis. Thus, the Macedonization could be carried out exclusively by Macedonians, while non-Macedonian party functionaries played at least no visible role. The parallelism of party and state also produced the advantage that political mobilization was used partly, if not wholly, to accomplish ethnopolitical aims too. Therefore, in Macedonia, the traditionally communist campaigning and volunteer system had a strong ethno-consolidatory note.

The main state instruments of Macedonization could be used for both active and defensive measures. For defensive purposes mainly the security apparatus—UDB and militia—and the judiciary were activated, for active purposes the educational system, the print media, the new electronic medium of the radio, and those cultural sectors that were under direct and indirect control of the state, such as the theaters, operas, film production, the Writers' Union, and so on were utilized. The new language soon guaranteed the effectiveness of these activities.

Still the experiment of building a new nation in Yugoslav Macedonia was an enterprise whose results in 1944 were by no means foreseeable. In particular, the effective warding off of the two most dangerous political and ethnopolitical alternatives, a re-Bulgarization and a re-Serbianization, was probably more due to the Tito-Stalin split than to the abilities of the CPM "patriots." The closing of the Yugoslav-Bulgarian border in 1949 isolated the population of Vardar Macedonia from the Bulgarians to a degree, which the pre-1949 conditions did not allow. And the systemic liberalization of Yugoslav Stalinism from the early 1950s on provided the communist leadership in Skopje with at least some minimal room to maneuver. Thereby the Macedonian Communists even succeeded in getting rid of their image as being mere agents of a Serbian-dominated Belgrade.

But there is yet another reason for the stunning success of the new Macedonian national ideology. In sharp contrast to the main ideological components of the nation-building processes of the Greeks, the Serbians, the Bulgarians, and others in the nineteenth century, mid-twentieth-century Macedonian nationalism did not focus in the first place on a "glorious past," but on an equally "glorious future." The absence of what Anthony D. Smith has called a "mythomoteur" was due to the fact that "historical" knowledge of the pre-history of the new Macedonian nation was still weak. At that time, the Ilinden Uprising of 1903 was the "most ancient" event in Macedonian national history, and that obviously was perceived as being too recent to function as a founding myth. Thus the stress on the future. The innovative and almost revolutionary impulses and the dynamics of the anti-Bulgarian, anti-Italian, and anti-German resistance movement of the war years were at least partly preserved and—in a very peculiar way—transformed into a movement toward a new national identity. To most Macedonians in 1944 "the past" was more appalling than appealing, whereas "the future" as a separate nation in a semi-independent nation-state under the roof of a larger South Slav federation seemed far more attractive.

While Tito's legacy to southeastern Europe as a whole is a negative one—Kosovo, Sandžak, Montenegro, and Vojvodina under Serbian hegemony, a Serb-Croat *Ausgleich* never achieved, Bosnia disrupted, Yugoslavism bankrupt—the man from Kumrovec's solution to the Macedonian problem worked and still works. The propagation of Macedonianism as a new national identity was highly successful; the foundation of a new Macedonian nation-state considerably stabilized international relations in one of Europe's most sensitive areas; and the remnants of authoritarianism in the form of Stalinism and later Titoism proved, at least in the Macedonian case, to be flexible enough to adapt to a more democratic political system.

Notes

1. From an abridged version of an article originally published in *Berliner Jahrbuch für osteuropaeische Geschichte*, 1, no. 2 (1994): 103-39. A special thanks goes to Jochen Hellbeck for assistance with the translation.

2. Blaže Ristovski, "Kako e nastanata pesna 'A bre makedonče'?" in *Makedonskiot folklor i nacionalnata svest. Istražuvanja i zapisi*, 1 (Skopje: Studentski zbor, 1987), 353.

3. Rudolf Kjellén, *Die Politischen Probleme des Weltkrieges. Leipzig-Berlin 1916*, 3d ed. (Leipzig and Berlin, Germany: B.G. Teubner, 1916), 52-53.

4. Miroslav Hroch, *Social Preconditions of National Revival in Europe: A Comparative Analysis of the Social Compositions of Patriotic Groups among the Smaller European Nations* (Cambridge, England: Cambridge University Press, 1985).

5. Fikret Adanir, *Die Makedonische Frage. Ihre Entstehung und Entwicklung bis 1908,* Frankfurter Historische Abhandlungen, vol. 20 (Wiesbaden: F. Steiner Verlag, 1979); Fikret Adanir, "The Macedonians in the Ottoman Empire, 1878-1912," in Andreas Kappeler in collaboration with Fikret Adanir and Alan O'Day, *The Formation of National Elites,* Comparative Studies on Governments and Non-Dominant Ethnic Groups, 1850-1940, no. 6 (Aldershot, Hampshire: Dartmouth 1992), 161-91; Jutta de Jong, *Der nationale Kern des makedonischen Problems. Ansaetze und Grundlagen einer makedonischen Nationalbewegung (1890-1903),* Ein Beitrag zur

komparativen Nationalismusforschung, Europaeische Hochschulschriften, III/174 (Frankfurt/M., Bern: Peter Lang Verlag, 1982); Ivo Banac, *The National Question in Yugoslavia: Origins, History, Politics* (Ithaca, NY: Cornell University Press, 1984), 307-28; and Duncan M. Perry, *The Politics of Terror: The Macedonian Revolutionary Movement, 1893-1903* (Durham, NC; London: Duke University Press, 1988).

6. As an anthropologist recently put it: "It was an effective way for Yugoslav officials to integrate Vardar Macedonia securely into the Federal Republic of Yugoslavia, since it served to delegitimate both Serbian and Bulgarian claims to the area." Loring M. Danforth, "Claims to Macedonian Identity: The Macedonian Question and the Breakup of Yugoslavia," *Anthropology Today,* 9, no. 4 (1993): 5-11, see page 8. See also the similar explanation by Stephen E. Palmer and Robert R. King, *Yugoslav Communism and the Macedonian Question* (Hamden, CT: Archon Press, 1970), 199.

7. This book was based on a manuscript by Stephen Palmer written anonymously for the U.S. Department of State. Stephen Palmer, *Macedonian Nationalism and the Communist Party of Yugoslavia* (Washington, DC: State FD, October 11, 1954), Library of Congress, call no. DR 701 M4 U62. The 1971 version has been criticized in a somewhat hysterical way in a review by the Harvard Slavist Horace G. Lunt, an eyewitness of the "birth" of the new nation. See Horace G. Lunt, "Review of *Macedonian Nationalism and the Communist Party of Yugoslavia,*" *Slavic and East European Journal,* 16, no. 1 (1972): 132-33. Earlier undertakings were written by Evangelos Kofos, "The Making of Yugoslavia's People's Republic of Macedonia," *Balkan Studies,* 3, no. 2 (1962): 375-96; and Djoko Slijepčević, *The Macedonian Question: The Struggle for South Serbia* (Chicago, IL: American Institute for Balkan Affairs, 1958) are difficult to use due to heavy Greek and Serbian bias. Short, but interesting accounts, however, are found in the articles by H.N. Brailsford, "The New Yugoslavia—Macedonian Renaissance," *The New Statesman,* 41 (13 January 1951): 31, and H. R. Wilkinson, "Yugoslav Macedonia in Transition," *Geographical Journal,* 118, no. 4 (December 1952): 389-405.

8. For some minor exceptions, see Stefan Troebst, "Makedonische Antworten auf die 'Makedonische Frage' 1944-1992: Nationalismus, Republiksgruendung, Nation-building," *Suedosteuropa,* 41 (1992): 423-42; Hugh Poulton, *Who Are the Macedonians?* (Bloomington, IN: Indiana University Press, 1994) and Danforth, "Claims to Macedonian Identity."

9. For the notorious neglect of the post-1944 period by Macedonian historians, see Stefan Troebst, *Die bulgarisch-jugoslawische Kontroverse um*

Makedonien 1967-1982, Untersuchungen zur Gegenwartskunde Suedosteuropas, 23 (Munich: R. Oldenbourg, 1983), 219; and Lazar Lazarov, "Kon istoriografijata na Makedonija meǵu dvete svetski vojni, Narodnoosloboditelnata vojna i Socialističkata revolucija (1941-1945) i socijalističkata izgradba na zemjata (1945-1985)," *Glasnik na institutot za nacionalna istorija (GINI)* 31, 2 (1987): 195-206.

10. Palmer and King, *Yugoslav Communism and the Macedonian Question*, 153.

11. Ibid., 113.

12. Although Koliševski had been the strongman in Macedonia not only in the 1940s but up to the late 1980s, no memoirs by him nor a biography on him has been published. Instead, his collection of speeches and articles, *Aspekti na makedonskoto prašanje* (Skopje: Kultura, 1962) has been reprinted over and over again. The title of a recent book by Dragan Kljakić, *Sovjetizacija balkanske zone: Ispovest Lazara Koliševskog* (Beograd: Radnička stampa, 1992) is somewhat misleading, since it does not contain any confessions of the former Macedonian party chief, it contains very little new information. See also the critical review of this book by Iso Rusi, "Koliševski go vraḱa udarot," *Puls*, 3, no. 113 (18 March 1993): 26-27.

13. On Čento, see Fidanka Tanašskova, *Metodija Andonov Čento* (Skopje: NIP Nova Makedonija, 1990); Kosta Tsurnushanov, *Makedonizmut i suprotivata na Makedoniia sreshtu nego* (Sofiia: Universitetsko izdatelstvo, Sv. Kliment Okhridski, 1992), 275-82 and 378-402; and a rather poorly organized and edited collection of articles and memoirs: Orde Ivanoski, et al., eds., *Čento— Čovek, revolucioner, državnik, Zbornik na materijali od Trkaleznata masa održana na 26. 11. 1991 godina vo Prilep,* (Prilep: Institut za nacionalna istorija, Društvo za nauka i umetnost, 1993).

14. Cvetko Uzunovski, "U[prava za] D[ržavna] B]ezbednost] moken organ na našata narodna revolucija," *Socijalistička zora* 1, no. 3 (May-June 1949): 1-20, see pages 11-12.

15. Novica Veljanovski, "Prezidiumot na ASNOM meǵu negovoto Vtoro i Treto zasedanie," *GINI*, 32, no. 2 (1988): 103-18, see page 108.

16. See Aleksandar Hristov, "Vladata na NR Makedonija (1946-1953)," in *Sozdavanje na makedonskata država,* Državnopravniot razvitok na Socijalistička republika Makedonija 1946-1978, vol. 4 (Skopje: Misla, 1985), 49-74.

17. For the CPM, having Čento stay on as the head of parliament was the safest decision since after the third ASNOM session of April 1945 it took

a whole year before the parliament convened again in April 1946. Novica Veljanovski, *Administrativno-centralističkiot period vo državnopravniot razvoj na Makedonija (1945-1953)* (Skopje: Institut za nacionalna istorija, 1992), 72n; and Aleksandar Trajanovski, et al., *Zlatna kniga 100 godini VMRO* (Skopje: Glas na VMRO-DPMNE, 1993), 241.

18. After having been released from the notorious Idrizovo jail near Skopje in September 1955, Čento died in June 1956. See Stojan Risteski, *Sudeni za Makedonija (1945-1985)* (Skopje: Vreme, 1993), 37-66.

19. Palmer and King, *Yugoslav Communism and the Macedonian Question*, 137.

20. Lazar Lazarov, *Opštestveno-ekonomski razvoj na NR Makedonija: Periodot na obnovata e industrijalizacijata (1944-1957)* (Skopje: Institut za nacionalna istorija, 1988), 318.

21. Palmer and King, *Yugoslav Communism and the Macedonian Question*, 135.

22. In 1959, Koliševski mentioned the figure of 120,000 citizens more than 14 years old as being members of various official political organizations. Palmer and King, *Yugoslav Communism and the Macedonian Question*, 141.

23. In addition, the majority of the South Slav–speaking Orthodox Christians had a command of one or more of the minority languages of the region, for example, Albanian, Vlach, Judeospanish, and Greek. On language policy in neighboring Bulgaria, see Maria Todorova, *Language in the Construction of Ethnicity and Nationalism: The Bulgarian Case*, working paper, 5.5 (Berkeley, CA: Center for German and European Studies, 1992); "Language as Cultural Unifier in a Multilingual Setting: The Bulgarian Case During the Nineteenth Century," *East European Politics and Societies*, 4, no. 3 (1990): 439-50.

24. Norbert Reiter, "Das mazedonische Glied in der Suedslavenkette," in Karl Gutschmidt, Helmut Keipert, and Hans Rothe, eds., *Slavistische Studien zum XI: internationalen Slavistenkongress in Pressburg/Bratislava* (Cologne; Weimar; Vienna: Boehlau, 1993), 351-62, see page 359. For a general overview, see Leopold Auburger, "Ueberblick ueber die aeussere Geschichte makedoslavischer Ausbausprachen (Altkirchenslavisch und moderne makedonische Standardsprache)," in *Sprachen und Staaten: Festschrift für*

Heinz Kloss. Pt. II: Nationalitaeten- und Sprachenfragen in weltpolitischer Perspektive (Hamburg: 1976), 9-123.

25. For a somewhat Macedonophile treatment of this question, see Peter Hill, "The Political Significance of the Macedonian Standard Language," *Australian Slavonic and East European Studies*, 1 (1987): 53-60.

26. See the facsimile in ASNOM. Dokumenti od Prvoto, Vtoroto i Tretoto zasedanie na ASNOM, vol. I, part 1 (Skopje: Institut za nacionalna istorija, 1984), see pages 160 and 161.

27. Blaže Koneski, "Za donesuvanjeto na makedonskata azbuka i pravopis," *Makedonski jazik*, 1, no. 5 (1950): 99-104; Krum Tosev, "Die mazedonische Schriftsprache," *Suedost-Forschungen*, 15 (1956): 491-503; Nikolaos P. Andriotis, *Der foederative Staat von Skoplje und seine Sprache* (Athens: 1966), 49-51; Palmer and King, *Yugoslav Communism and the Macedonian Question*, 154-59; Trajko Stamatoski, "Trieset godini na makedonskata azbuka i pravopis," *Literaturen zbor*, 22, 2 (1975): 3-9, reprinted in *Borba za makedonski literaturen jazik* (Skopje: Misla, 1986), 189-99; "Thirty Fifth Anniversary of the Creation of the Macedonian Alphabet and Spelling," *Macedonian Review*, 10, no. 3 (1980): 312-16; Stojan Kiselinovski, *Statusot na makedonskiot jazik vo Makedonija (1913-1987)* (Skopje: Misla, 1987), 78-86; Victor Friedman, "The First Philological Conference for the Establishment of the Macedonian Alphabet and the Macedonian Language: Its Precedents and Consequences," in Joshua A. Fishman, ed., *The Earliest Stage of Language Planning* (Berlin; New York: Mouton, de Gruyter, 1993); and Olivera Jašar-Nasteva, "Soziolinguistische Aspekte des makedonischen und der anderen Sprachen in der Republik Makedonien," *Die Welt der Slaven*, 37 (1992): 188-210.

28. Stojan Risteski, *Sozdavanjeto na sovremeniot makedonski literaturen jazik* (Skopje: Studentski zbor, 1988).

29. Hristo Andonov-Poljanski et al., eds., *Dokumenti za borbata na makedonskiot narod za samostojnost i za nacionalna država*, vol. 2, no. 296 (Skopje: Univerzitet Kiril i Metodij, 1981), 647-48.

30. *Makedonskiot pravopis* (Skopje: 1945), 20.

31. *Bukvar so čitanka za prvo odelenie* (Skopje: Goce Delčev, 1945).

32. Krum Kepeski, *Makedonska gramatika* (Skopje: Državno knigoizdatelstvo, 1946), 80. See also "Kako se zafativ so pišuvanje na prvata makedonska

gramatika," in Risteski, *Sozdavanjeto na sovremeniot makedonski literaturen jazik*, 458-60.

33. On March 1, 1953, this seminar combined with the Section for Folk Literature which was part of the Institute for Folklore founded in 1950, to form an Institute for Macedonian Language.

34. Jovan Boškovski, *Rastrel* (Skopje: 1947). On literature in general, see Blaže Koneski, *Makedonskata literatura vo 19 vek. Kratok pregled i tekstovi* (Skopje: Državno knigoizdatelstvo na NR Makedonija, 1950); Blaže Koneski, *Makedonskite učebnici od 19 vek. Eden prilog kon istorijata na makedonskata prerodba* (Skopje: Glaven odbor na Narodniot front na Makedonija, 1949),99; Haralampie Polenakovik, *Stranici od makedonskata kniževnost* (Skopje: Kočo Racin, 1952); and Horace G. Lunt, "A Survey of Macedonian Literature," *Harvard Slavic Studies*, 1 (1953): 363-96. The first larger literary success, however, was Slavko Janevski's 1952 novel *The Village behind the Seven Ash-Trees*. See Slavko Janevski, *Selo zad sedumte jaseni* (Skopje: 1952); and Detlev Kulman, "*Selo zad sedumte jaseni*," Kindlers Literaturlexikon im dtv. vol. 24: Nachtraege (Munich: Deutscher Taschenbuchverlag, 1974): 10918-919.

35. Kiselinovski, *Statusot na makedonskiot jazik vo Makedonija*, 85.

36. Veljanovski, *Administrativno-centralističkiot period vo državnot pravniot razvoj na Makedonija*, 246.

37. Kiselinovski, *Statusot na Makedonskiot jazik vo Makedonija*, 84-85.

38. Heinz Kloss, "Moeglichkeiten und Grenzen einer nichtdichterischen Prosa (Sachprosa) in "plattdeutscher" Sprache," in *Jahresgabe der Klaus-Groth-Gesellschaft*, (1972), 166-71, see page 166.

39. Karl W. Deutsch, *Nationalism and Social Communication: An Enquiry into the Foundations of Nationality* (Cambridge MA: MIT Press, 1966).

40. Nada Jurukova, *Osnovnoto vospitanie i obrazovanie vo Makedonija (1944-1950)* (Skopje: Institut za nacionalna istorija 1990), 151. During the very first postwar year this number even increased. While in late 1944, there were 229.170 analphabets, in 1946 their number was 265.236, among them two-thirds were women. Only in 1947 did the alphabetization campaign gain momentum, and by the end of 1950, as many as 185.099 former analphabets were now considered to be literate, ibid., 151, 159, 163. It should be remembered that around the year 1900 the rate of illiteracy in Ottoman Macedonia was down to less than 20 percent. Adanir, *Die Makedonische Frage*, 177.

41. Kiselinovski, *Statusot na makedonskiot jazik vo Makedonija*, 85. By 1953, next to the 20 KW station at Skopje, a small 0.5 KW station at Bitola functioned. See "Rundfunk in der FVRJ," in Werner Markert, ed., *Osteuropa-Handbuch Jugoslawien* (Cologne-Graz: Boehlau, 1954), 351.

42. Trajanovski, *Zlatna kniga 100 godini VMRO*, 240.

43. Palmer and King, *Yugoslav Communism and the Macedonian Question*, 137.

44. For figures on the notoriously high unemployment rate in postwar Macedonia, see Palmer and King, *Yugoslav Communism and the Macedonian Question*, 15.

45. Peter Hill, *The Macedonians in Australia* (Carlisle, WA: Hesperian Press, 1989), 33-34.

46. On the rapidly expanding system of elementary education, see Boro Kitanovski, *Prvite makedonski učilišta vo NOB*, Bibiblioteka "Naše revolucionerno minato" (Skopje: Naša kniga, 1973); and Jurukova, *Osnovnoto vospitanie i obrazovanie vo Makedonija*.

47. Like the IMRO, Čento and Vlahov also opted for the unification of Vardar Macedonian with the Aegean and Pirin parts—if need be by seceeding from the Yugoslav federation—and although both Čento and Vlahov supported the new concept of a separate nation, Čento expressed his aversion against orthographically de-Bulgarizing the new language, while Vlahov made it clear that he considered himself in linguistic terms not as speaker of the newly constructed language, but of well-established Bulgarian. Until 1924 Vlahov was a regular member of IMRO, and during the last years of the old Yugoslavia, local Macedonian Communists of the younger generation in Vardar Macedonia cooperated with the remnants of IMRO's youth organization within a legal political formation, founded in 1935 and called the Macedonian People's Movement (MANAPO—Makedonski naroden pokret). The history of MANAPO is neglected by official Skopje historiography in a way that raises suspicion. There is, however, a short account of it by the leading CPM functionary Kiril Miljovski, *Makedonskoto prašanje vo nacionalnata programa na KPJ (1919-1937)* (Skopje: Kultura, 1962), 140-54. From the Bulgarian side, see Dimitur G. Gotsev, *Mladezhkite natsionalno-osvoboditelni organizatsii na makedonskite bulgari 1919-1941* (Sofiia: Bulgarska akademija na naukite, 1988), 64-70.

48. Tsurnushanov, *Makedonizmut i suprotivata na Makedoniia*, 248-74.

49. Mile Todorovski, "The Second Session of ASNOM," *GINI* 31, no. 3 (1987), 21-34, see page 31. See also Veljanovski, *Administrativno-centralistickiot period vo državnopravniot razvoj na Makedonija*, 165.

50. Tsurnushanov, *Makedonizmut i suprotivata na Makedoniia*, 283-87; and Trajanovki, *Zlatna kniga 100 godini VMRO*, 243-44.

51. On this organization and the trials against it, see Trajanovski, *Zlatna kniga 100 godini VMRO*, 244; and Risteski, *Sudeni za Makedonija*, 67-128.

52. Trajanovski, *Zlatna kniga 100 godini VMRO*, 244-45.

53. For a treatment of some of these trials see Tsurnushanov, *Makedonizmut i suprotivata na Makedoniia*, 288-99 and 308-13; and Risteski, *Sudeni za Makedonija*, 141-333.

54. See Tsurnushanov, *Makedonizmut i suprotivata na Makedoniia*, 301-07 and 314-23; and Risteski, *Sudeni za Makedonija*, 334-448 and 467-512.

55. On IMRO-Pravda, see Ilija Maksimovski, *Političeskiot zatvornik za Makedonija* (Skopje: Makedonska radio televizija [Makedonsko Radio], 1991); Ristevski, *Sudeni za Makedonija*, 128-40 and 449-66; and Trajanovski, *Zlatna kniga 100 godini VMRO*, 245-47.

56. Evangelos Kofos, *Nationalism and Communism in Macedonia* (Thessaloniki: Etaireia Makedonikon Spojdon, 1964) 191-92.

57. Kljakić, *Sovjetizacija balkanske zone*, 186. This Belgrade journalist speaks of a Soviet "plan Vyshinskii" aiming at instigating guerilla warfare in Yugoslav Macedonia.

10

The Bosnian Muslims:
The Making of a Yugoslav Nation

Francine Friedman

The purpose of this chapter is to explore the development of the Bosnian Muslim nation, focusing on the post–World War II years. This topic is problematic for a number of reasons. First, scholars disagree about whether the Bosnian Muslims can even be deemed a "nation" in a broadly accepted meaning of that term. Second, many differ about the origins of this group, their role in the history and development of the South Slavs, and their responsibility for the tragedies that have befallen Yugoslavia in recent years. Finally, depending on one's stance regarding these issues, widespread disagreement exists about what should be "done" with the Bosnian Muslims. The daunting task of sorting out these problems requires more space than is permitted here. Nevertheless, a brief overview of the process of the creation of national status for the Bosnian Muslims, the reasons behind the process, and the ramifications for the future of the Bosnian Muslims, may indicate how their promising outlook degenerated into today's televised war.

THE BOSNIAN MUSLIM NATION

Explicitly delineating what is a nation has frustrated many an analyst. For the purposes of this chapter, while the *state* is a juridical concept signifying the political organization of a sovereign, territorially based group of people, the *nation* signifies the psychological affinity of a group.[1] In post-World War II Yugoslavia, nation *(narod)* came to mean South Slavs in Yugoslavia numerous enough to occupy their own titular republics—initially Serbs, Croats, Slovenes, Montenegrins, and Macedonians.[2]

Depending upon whom you consulted, the Bosnian Muslims were a religious group with roots in either the Serb or the Croat nations, or a nation *(narod).* Many Serbs and Croats, of course, asserted the former, while many Bosnian Muslims emphasized the latter, especially after World War II, arguing on the basis of history, common language, common religion, and psychological affinity. But this chapter will contend that it was this claim of nationhood, which was supposed to legitimate their position during the Tito era on a par with the other nations, that made the Bosnian Muslims vulnerable to the current depredations.

Was there something about the history of the South Slav peoples or their twentieth-century institutions or regimes that made ethnic cleansing in the name of ethnic homogeneity inevitable? In attempting to confront the questions of the viability of the Bosnian Muslims as a nation and to understand why they have suffered at the hands of their compatriots, it is necessary to search for clues throughout their singular history.

THE HISTORICAL DEVELOPMENT OF THE BOSNIAN MUSLIMS

At the nexus of Occident and Orient, the former Yugoslavia also provided the line of bifurcation between Rome and Byzantium. It was frequently crossed by traders, soldiers, and missionaries on the way to the Middle East, which also enticed Islam into the area. Sources indicate that the ancestors of today's Serbs and Croats, who entered the Balkans during the sixth century as part of the larger Slav movement westward, may have been of the same stock originally, becoming differentiated only when the Serbs occupied eastern parts of the Roman Empire while the Croats went westward. Christianity developed divergently in each part of the Empire, creating among different branches of the South Slavs, as among different parts of the Roman Empire, an unhealable breach.

As the Serbs and Croats settled in the Balkans, they were subject to the political maneuvering of their neighbors. However, the Croats eventually were able to throw off Byzantine and Frankish influence. They built an independent Croat state lasting for 200 years until it fell under Hungarian suzerainty at the beginning of the twelfth century. The Hungarian reign endured until the end of World War I.

The Serbs, too, became politically and militarily active in the region at about the same time that the Croats' fortunes were ebbing in the early tenth century. The Serbs engaged in alliance manipulations with the Byzantines, Ottoman Turks, and Bulgars, until Serbian leader Stefan Dušan was crowned Emperor of the Serbs and Romans by the Serbian Patriarch in 1346. Dušan's territory then extended "from the Danube to the Gulf of Corinth and from the Adriatic to the Aegean."[3]

The existence of the Croat and Serb medieval kingdoms have received historical acceptance, but what of Bosnia? Historians have uncovered relatively little documented evidence about Bosnia and Herzegovina's early history, only acknowledging that many peoples, including the Serbs, Croats, Hungarians, and Byzantines, controlled it at various times. Nevertheless, Bosnian Muslim historians assert the legitimacy of the contemporary Bosnian Muslim nation on the basis of the existence of an independent medieval Bosnian state.[4] Serbs and Croats, however, have generally dismissed Bosnian manifestations of state authority as mere tribal unions.[5]

With the hard evidence to clarify Bosnian history decidedly lacking, we can nevertheless make out some outlines. The era of Ban Kulin (1180-1204) was significant for Bosnia, as he may have been an important actor in the region.[6] Still later, Bosnia may have been fairly powerful if, as some Bosnian historiographers claim, its state under King Tvrtko encircled neighboring territories, allowing Tvrtko to style himself King of the Serbs, Bosnia, and Primorje, as well as Dalmatia and Croatia, at the end of the fourteenth century.[7] Thus, for Bosnian historians Bosnia was clearly an independent entity until its conquest by the Ottoman Turks in 1463, although Serb, Croat, and other historians bicker over sources and their significance.

Nationalist inclination also infuses the scholarly discussion of another phase in the development of the Bosnian Muslims—the existence of a schismatic, dualist religious sect, the Bogomils. Bosnian Muslim historians claim that the members of this sect, who were persecuted as heretics by the surrounding established churches and became Muslims in self-defense when the Ottomans invaded the Balkans, were the forebears of today's Bosnian Muslims.

Yugoslav scholars, supported by some British scholarship, called the "heretical" Christian faith *Bogomilism*. Those who insisted on a separate and distinct nationality for the Bosnian Muslims thus argued that the unique character of the religion in that area indicated that their direct descendants were originally separate from either the Serbs or the Croats. Equally forcefully, many Serb and Croat nationalists maintained that Bosnia was originally part of one or the other cultural, religious, and geographic legacy.

John V. A. Fine and others, however, have persuasively argued that the "heresy" was an indigenous but generally unrecognized schismatic Bosnian Church (*Crkva Bosanska*) entirely separate from the Bogomil sect yet often confused with Bogomilism. The Bosnian Church, Fine argued, was an independent church "established after the emigration to Slavonia of the Catholic hierarchy,"[8] which retained its Catholic ideology but altered some of the mainstream rituals. The Bosnian Church was thus considered flawed by the Catholic Church, but its members did not consider themselves Bogomils or heretics. The question of medieval religious rituals may seem arcane in this century, yet it is central to the identity claims made by various Yugoslav nationalists, and thus to the problem of the political and national status of the Bosnian Muslims.

The general thrust of the argument of Bosnian Muslim historiographers is that the Bosnian Muslims comprise a notably unique national entity, which was recognizable as such even during the prefeudal era when the Serbs, Croats, and other South Slavs were also becoming unified national entities. The emphasis on when the various medieval states formed is due to the perceived link between the formation of the state organization and the simultaneous formation of the nation.[9] The strong implication, of course, is that Croats and Serbs have no claim to Bosnian territory or that Bosnian Muslims are not really Serbs or Croats, as Serbs and Croats would have the world believe. Instead, if Bosnia had an independent status during the Middle Ages similar to the Croats and Serbs and followed different rituals and behavioral patterns, then one could not conceive of awarding Bosnian territory to anyone but the contemporary descendants of the autochthonous Bosnians, that is, the Bosnian Muslims. Furthermore, while Bosnian Muslims did not necessarily follow the nationalistic path of the Serbs and Croats, nevertheless their sense of their own uniqueness was not absent.

Bosnian Muslim historians paint a compelling portrait of their national development through the many periods of the history of the South Slavs. For example, it may be safely stated that the Bosnian Muslim elites experienced many prosperous years under the Ottoman regime in return for their staunch support of the empire.[10] While the conquered peoples labored to support the ruling Turkish nation, those who had converted to Islam became influential and were able to control property.

The gradual weakening of the Ottoman Empire was manifested by nationalistic stirrings, particularly among the subject South Slavs. But the unease that was felt in other parts of the Ottoman Empire did not radically manifest itself in Bosnia and Herzegovina until the early to mid-nineteenth century. Simultaneous with the nineteenth-century independence struggles of the Ottoman Empire's Christian subjects, Bosnian Muslim elites, too, found themselves often in direct opposition to the centralizing tendencies of the Ottoman administration. Rebellions against the Porte (the Ottoman administration) were led by the Bosnian beys in 1821, 1828, 1831, and 1837. By the mid-nineteenth century, when 19 of 23 Turkish battalions stationed in Bosnia were composed almost entirely of Bosnian Muslims, the loyalty to the Porte of many of these army units was questionable.[11]

The weakness of the Ottoman Empire encouraged the South Slavs in the Austro-Hungarian Empire to seek some kind of union with the South Slavs under Ottoman rule so that together they could escape the imperial experience. The Bosnian Muslims were in a rather anomalous position, being part of the ruling class in the Ottoman Empire and yet not of Turkish ethnicity. Yet the evidence does not strongly indicate the existence of a deep-seated national identification by Bosnian Muslims. One might observe the development of some common traits and attitudes that were distinguishable from the Bosnian non-Muslim population. Furthermore, the Ottoman period may have encouraged a consolidation of Bosnian Muslim interests and the decline of the Ottoman Empire through an understanding by Bosnian Muslim landowners that their best interests lay with local patriotism rather than continued loyalty to the Porte. Nevertheless, this does not qualify the Bosnian Muslims to be classified as a distinct national entity at this point in history, although communal responses to collective problems and stimuli were notable.

Meanwhile, with the weakening of the great multinational empires, possession of Bosnian territory had become an object of a number of political programs, such that Bosnia became a pawn in the great power game. Simultaneously, national yearnings in the Balkans reached a fever pitch during the nineteenth century, expressed in part through the territorial aspirations of other South Slav nations. Both

Croats and Serbs eyed Bosnian territory and hoped to control it by claiming that the Bosnian Muslims were really Islamized Croats or Serbs, respectively.

During the late nineteenth and early twentieth centuries, the Bosnian Muslims lost their ruling status as Bosnia and Herzegovina was annexed by Austria-Hungary. Able to express only weak nationalist aspirations of their own, the Bosnian Muslims felt forced to play coalition games—supporting Croat, Serb, or Habsburg policies, depending on which group's goals were closest to the Muslim elite's determination of communal self-interest. Being a numerical minority, the Bosnian Muslims realized that there was no hope that a political solution for that area would grant them much autonomy or permit them to retain the influence they had commanded within the Ottoman Empire. Those Muslims who elected to remain in Bosnia would be dependent upon whatever ties they could forge with the Serbian, Croatian, or Austro-Hungarian politicians active in settling the question of Bosnia's future. Some people have termed this practice opportunism, but Bosnian Muslims considered it a question of political survival.

Although the Muslims acquired little political influence under Austro-Hungarian rule, the Habsburg monarchy was able to ensure Muslim acquiescence by realizing that the major concern of Muslim leaders under Austria-Hungary was to maintain as before their economic-political position and their way of life. The Austro-Hungarian Empire attempted to fight the rising tide of South Slav nationalism by trying to entice Muslim support for the monarchy. "Bosnianism" *(bošnjaštvo)*, the concept of one indigenous people living in Bosnia, was officially popularized to replace any South Slav nationalistic feelings within Bosnia and Herzegovina. It was also meant to discourage any irredentist challenges mounted by Serbia, which claimed Bosnia as part of its patrimony. In return for the Muslim elite's acceptance of *bošnjaštvo*, the monarchy put the question of agrarian relations into abeyance. The Habsburgs did not destroy the feudal land ownership system, even though this move might have boosted Bosnia and Herzegovina's economic development, and thus retained Bosnian Muslim acquiescence to their rule until World War I.

In the wake of World War I, South Slav nationalism was finally realized with the creation and recognition of the Kingdom of the Serbs, Croats, and Slovenes in 1918. However, the vagueness of the terms of organization of that Kingdom would become a major problem, as many of the involved national groups believed that they were deprived of even minimal rights within the state and that the Serbs were attempting to form a Greater Serbia out of the South Slav lands.

From the beginning, the Bosnian Muslims were wooed by both Serb and Croat nationalists. The basic issue surrounding possession of Bosnia and Herzegovina was that the nation that retained the loyalty of Bosnia and Herzegovina would dominate the South Slav state. Both the Serbs and the Croats cited historical imperatives to justify their claims. The Serbs pressured the Muslims to support the existing political order while the Croat nationalists aggressively emphasized that "the Serbs and the Serb-dominated government were responsible for their plight and that Muslims were, in fact, Croats."[12] Vladko Maček, leader of the Croatian Peasant Party, stated in 1936 that his party, "as the political organization of the entire Croatian nation, considers the Bosnian Muslims the purest part of the Croatian nation by origin, by history and by dialect."[13]

Yet despite these insistent courtships, the Muslims were more or less excluded from the political influence their numbers should have ensured in the Kingdom. Thus, contrary to the vociferous and aggressive statements of the Serbs and Croats, the Bosnian Muslims were fairly reserved. Progressive Islamic leaders decided that Serb and Croat chauvinism was inimical to the improvement of the economic and social position of the Bosnian Muslims. Such policies fostered the threat of a partition of Bosnia and Herzegovina that would make of the Bosnian Muslims a permanent and ineffectual minority. Therefore, they continued to participate in the Constituent Assembly and followed the official doctrine of Yugoslav unitarism. Bosnian Muslim actions were in line with the theory of Dr. Mehmed Spaho, leader of the Yugoslav Muslim Party, that "support for the government, whatever its complexion and policy, would always bring greater benefits to a small minority than pointless defiance."[14]

However, the Muslims in Bosnia and Herzegovina found themselves in an unenviable position. The 1929 reorganization of Yugoslavia partitioned Bosnia and Herzegovina into four *banovinas* (provinces) each with a Muslim minority. During the tense days preceding the signing of the 1939 *Sporazum* (agreement), with which the Yugoslav government granted Croatia greater autonomy, Spaho and most of the Muslim leaders went on record as opposing the partition of Bosnia and Herzegovina between Serbia and Croatia.[15]

Out of their interwar experiences, the Bosnian Muslims began to evolve into a legitimate political group in a modern nation-state. As a result of the pressures they faced from both Serbs and Croats, the Bosnian Muslims reaffirmed that their most secure policy would be support of the central government from which patronage, protection, and other benefits would flow. This policy, practiced throughout their history, stood them in good stead. Only when the Bosnian Muslims abandoned this policy in the 1990s (or, to be more precise, when it was removed as an option), did their misfortunes begin.

Thus, in characterizing the uniqueness of the Bosnian Muslims, their historians have emphasized the transformation of this group from ruling cadre under the Ottomans to a position of less influence under Austria-Hungary, their attractiveness to Serbs and Croats who wished to commit them to a national identity they could not wholeheartedly embrace in order to possess the Bosnian Muslim land, the absence among their elites of a strong ideological stand, and a willingness to go along with the ruling government's policies as long as they were not inimical to Bosnian Muslim interests. They further emphasized that, while the Bosnian Muslims did not throughout the ages trumpet their cohesion and sense of self-identification, nevertheless, it did exist and, as was only proper, was finally recognized more than 20 years after World War II.

THE BOSNIAN MUSLIMS UNDER COMMUNISM

The ambivalent position of Bosnian Muslims during World War II, when many members of their community participated in genocidal Ustaše atrocities against the Serbs while many other Muslims supported Tito's multinational Partisans, was reflected in their status in post–World War II Yugoslavia. The often mutually exclusive claims of Serbia and Croatia to the lands between them were denied altogether by Tito's creation of the republic of Bosnia and Herzegovina, designed to be a multinational unit consisting of Serbs, Croats, and other Bosnian inhabitants, but "belonging" to none of them.

The second indicator of the Bosnian Muslims' ambivalent position within communist Yugoslavia was reflected in the various post–World War II censuses. The 1948 census demonstrated Bosnian Muslims' lack of equal status with other national groups by forcing them to declare themselves as Serbs, Croats, or "Muslims nationally undetermined." Reflecting the apparent lack of Bosnian Muslim self-identification as either Croats or Serbs, 875,609 Muslims used the last category while less than one-tenth of that number used the Serb or Croat designation.[16]

During the peak of the ideological campaign for *Jugosloventsvo* (Yugoslavism), meaning one Yugoslav nation, the category of "Yugoslav undetermined" was introduced into the 1953 census. Presumably, those who chose this category were mostly Bosnian Muslims,[17] who again did not wish to declare themselves as either Serbs or Croats, as well as members of mixed marriages and their offspring and those who simply did not wish to declare for any nation. Significantly, Muslims in areas other than Bosnia and Herzegovina felt no compunction against declaring themselves to be members of the major national group in their republic.[18] It would not be unrealistic to assume that here was one indication of the early differentiation of the Bosnian Muslims from other Yugoslav Muslims, as, perhaps, at least a fledgling national group.

The introduction of self-management in the 1950s was considered necessary for the achievement of equality and concord among the national groups. Conceptually, self-management was meant to introduce direct democracy and decentralization into the workplace, as well as into society as a whole. Self-management thus signified that the republics and local units of government would also receive expanded political control at the expense of the federation. This transformation of the Yugoslav bureaucratic system thus created a new set of significant political actors. Self-management recognized, indeed enshrined, nation-based politics at all levels of the federation. Battles over the federally-controlled means of development inevitably were perceived as national questions, and the individual protagonists at the republic, district, and local levels and even in the various enterprises took on the mantle of defenders of the national interest.

The Bosnian Muslim situation in Yugoslavia was not radically altered by these changes, for their access to the political system even at the republic level was limited. Individual Bosnian Muslim politicians could serve and garner economic or political rewards in the newly decentralized system. But the Bosnian Muslim community as a whole, not being recognized as a corporate national group in the census or through any other mechanism, was denied the access to the republic and federal levers of power that recognized national groups enjoyed.

This situation changed as the domestic conception of decentralization became mirrored in Yugoslav foreign affairs through the policy of nonalignment. With bipolarism beginning to recede during the 1950s and with the lessening of aggressive Soviet hegemony,

Yugoslavia's version of national communism (its *separate roads to socialism*), which rejected Soviet economic and political colonialism, encouraged communist bloc national communism. And its independent foreign policy, beholden neither to the communist nor the capitalist blocs, inspired the former colonial countries of Asia and Africa, such that Tito was considered a founder of nonalignment, along with India's Jawaharlal Nehru and Egypt's Gamal Abd'el Nasser. Tito's prestige in the Non-Aligned Movement increased the salience for him of world affairs and concomitantly in nonalignment in general and Middle East affairs in particular. Consequently, he also evinced greater interest in the fortunes of the Bosnian Muslim community.

Tito first signaled this interest officially in the 1961 census with the appearance of the category of "Muslim (ethnic membership)."[19] This designation attracted almost 850,000 adherents.[20]

However, the full integration of the Bosnian Muslims into Yugoslav society was eased only by the political defeat in 1966 of Aleksandar Ranković, vice-president of Yugoslavia, head of security, and Tito's presumed heir apparent, who used his position to abet Serb interests in Bosnia to the detriment of the Croats and Muslims living there. Subsequently, the Bosnian Muslims were able to secure more influence within Yugoslav society.

When chauvinistic nationalism emerged in Yugoslavia in the 1970s, an official counterattack decimated the ranks of Croat, Serb, Slovene, and Macedonian officialdom during 1971 and 1972. While the Bosnian and Montenegrin parties and governments apparently escaped the kind of housecleaning visited on the other republics, nevertheless, Tito also inveighed against Muslim nationalism and "pan-Islamism" as early as 1972. Yet at the same time as the Communists were squelching nationalist challenges, Bosnian Muslim national self-identification was being encouraged by the formal recognition of the Bosnian Muslims as a Yugoslav nation at the Fifth Congress of the League of Communists (LC) of Bosnia and Herzegovina in January 1969.

Reflecting their new status, more than 1,700,000 people used the category "Muslims in the sense of nationality" in the 1971 census. The Bosnian Muslims became the third largest national group in the country and the largest nation in Bosnia and Herzegovina.[21]

Bosnian Muslim demographics became vitally important as the 1974 constitution turned Yugoslavia into a de facto confederation. Confederal status conferred the bulk of decision-making power (except for foreign policy, defense, and a few other areas) on the republics (and autonomous provinces). Most high-ranking jobs in the republics as well as in the federal government, and the security and armed forces, were filled according to an ethnic key (apportionment according to proportion of the nation [*narod*] in the total population). Therefore, the fact that the Bosnian Muslims were accorded national status opened up important avenues of access to levers of influence, although the representation remained skewed against the Muslims in party and government positions. Bosnian Muslims were also underrepresented in the military and security services, which contained traditionally high levels of Serbs and Montenegrins.[22]

The 1974 constitution has been blamed for the disintegration of the Yugoslav market and for the consequent mutual dissatisfaction of the various ethnic groups. The confederalism that it imposed encouraged the republics and even the localities to shoulder much of the decision making heretofore reserved to the federal government. Therefore, regions and localities were forced to go head-to-head for the limited resources of the Yugoslav state. Such constant, unremitting conflict could only exacerbate ethnic particularism. Furthermore, the LCY was abdicating power to the republican parties, which, in effect, turned Yugoslavia into a multiparty political system, each republic controlled by its own party organization.

While the republics were being strengthened by the reforms to the detriment of the central government, the Bosnian Muslims were being recognized as a separate Yugoslav nation with all the prerogatives attaching to that designation. Therefore, for the first time in history the Bosnian Muslims were part of the "in crowd," legitimate players with real access to a significant proportion of Yugoslav resources.

BOSNIAN MUSLIMS IN THE POST-TITO ERA

The recognition of the Bosnian Muslims as a nation (*narod*) was intended to have four major effects on the political affairs of Yugoslavia, three domestic and one international. First, as we have seen, Bosnian Muslim ethnic identification had historically been a bone of contention between Serbs and Croats. National recognition of the Bosnian Muslims meant that they would no longer be the targets for attempts by Serbs and Croats to force allegiance toward either national group. Tito had expected that this move would quell Serb and Croat nationalist passions and aspirations aimed at Bosnia and Herzegovina.

The second effect Tito strove for in recognizing the Bosnian Muslims was to mobilize their leadership to active support of Yugoslavia in order to preserve for their own nation any gains accruing to Bosnia and Herzegovina from a more cohesive country. This point arose from the 1974 constitution's assignment of sovereign rights to each nation and nationality in its own republic or autonomous region. Since all titular nations had their own republic, and since the Bosnian Muslims had become an officially recognized nation, at least some of the Bosnian Muslims could logically have concluded that Bosnia and Herzegovina had become "their" republic, since the Serbs and Croats each had a home republic. To protect their new status and perhaps an implicit, if never explicitly mentioned, homeland, the Bosnian Muslims would become even more loyal to the Yugoslav federation.

Indeed, upon the public recognition of their nationhood, Bosnian Muslims immediately sought to justify it with a historical record equal to the Serbs and Croats. To promote a national separation from the Bosnian Serbs and Croats, Bosnian Muslim historians during the 1980s were busily attempting to prove beyond all doubt that their people had always retained a sense of their own distinctiveness. They stressed that official recognition of Bosnian Muslim nationhood was simply recognition of an already extant Bosnian Muslim national identity, not just religious affiliation.

The third reason Tito had elevated the status of the Bosnian Muslims was to end the Serb-Croat squabbling over resource distribution within Bosnia and Herzegovina. By adding a third group to the situation, perhaps more rational, less nation-based policies would be crafted within the republic and even perhaps at the federal level. However, adding the Bosnian Muslims to the equation did not erase national arguments over purely regional economic or political decisions in Bosnia and Herzegovina.

Confederalization as promoted by the 1974 constitution altered the way the Yugoslav market operated and even the characteristics of Yugoslavia's state sovereignty. While Tito was alive, of course, procedures worked well enough. He remained the ultimate arbiter and, until his death, all power except his was relative. But no one was really satisfied with his system, which became evident after his death. Much of the economic and political decision making moved to the republics and localities, which were now expected to compete with one another for the state's limited resources. The lessening of centralization lowered the federal government's ability to ameliorate regional conflict because of its declining influence at all levels of decision making. The result of this change in emphasis was the exacerbation of national particularism, both in regard to political as well as economic decisions.

The League of Communists of Yugoslavia (LCY), too, had abdicated power to the republic parties. There was greater political advantage in being part of the republican, not the federal, party elite. In effect, then, Yugoslav turned into a multiparty political system with the elites of each republic vying for influence and for resources for their own party structure. This, too, encouraged national chauvinism. Increasingly, party and state decision making was based on nationalism, rather than coherent, federally conceived initiatives. In Bosnia and Herzegovina, because of the power-sharing conditions established by Tito when he inserted the Muslims into the equation, coalitions drove the decision making. The Bosnian Muslims, of course, had played that role throughout their history. Nevertheless, during the 1980s the Bosnian Muslims began to widen their power base and legitimacy within the republic and the federation, at the expense of the formerly dominant Serbs. The Serbs were increasingly frustrated with having to play coalition politics in Bosnia and Herzegovina in the post-Tito era. And, indeed, much mistrust in the federation was at least partially because leadership positions and, in fact, staffing of Yugoslav political institutions as a whole depended upon ethnic definition rather than some more ascriptive elements. The heterogeneity of many regions of the country was in conflict with politically supported national particularism, a volatile mixture that could produce national conflict.

Finally, with an eye to the international scene, Tito had hoped to coopt potential Bosnian Muslim enchantment with the militant international pan-Islamic movement, while increasing his own prestige within the Non-Aligned Movement. Tito wanted to encourage the Bosnian Muslims to abjure international adventures by offering them a greater stake in what was happening at home. Simultaneous with the numerical growth of Bosnian Muslims, as portrayed by the census figures, and contrary to the secular aims of Bosnian Muslim intellectuals, however, there occurred a growth of religious identification and sentiment within the Bosnian Muslim community. Of course, this was not supposed to happen in a communist country, where religion was discouraged. Recognition of Bosnian Muslim nationhood was expected to have only secular implications, since previously the Bosnian Muslims had shown no real religious predilections. However, once they gained national recognition and increased communal self-identification, their religiosity was concomitantly reinforced.[23] Indeed, as soon as the nationhood of the Bosnian Muslims was officially recognized, the Bosnian Muslim religious hierarchy began to pursue a more active and public role in the life of the Bosnian Muslims.

However, Tito's foreign policy was able to turn this increased religiosity and elevation of the Bosnian Muslims to national status into a positive factor. These advances increasingly endeared Yugoslavia to Middle Eastern and North African Arabs who were discovering their own augmented power through worldwide Islamic activism. In furtherance of Yugoslavia's foreign policy aims, Yugoslav delegations to Islamic states usually included a Muslim representative from Bosnia; foreign Islamic leaders were generally taken to Sarajevo for a visit with local Muslims. Furthermore, the greater status for Yugoslavia such an action engendered among the nonaligned Muslims increased Tito's leverage in the movement at a time when he needed it most—when he was attempting to prevent Castro from coopting the Non-Aligned Movement for Cuban imperialism masquerading as representation of the socialist commonwealth.[24] All in all, Tito cleverly used "his Muslims" to advantage by acting as if "Yugoslavia was the second-strongest Moslem country in Europe, after Turkey."[25]

The increasingly open political and social climate permitted the flowering of religious institutions in Yugoslavia.[26] More than 1000 mosques and buildings dedicated to Islamic education were built in Yugoslavia between 1945 and the mid-1980s.[27] Furthermore, Yugoslavia was the only European country that could boast an Islamic theological school, 3000 mosques, and several Islamic middle schools, as well as a number of Muslim periodicals.[28]

The Bosnian Muslims also increased their contacts and links with foreign Muslims. For example, the Bosnian Islamic Council, which supervised all affairs of the Islamic religious community in its region, began to distribute literature discussing Islamic concerns and Arabic-language literature from the Middle East. Hajj figures indicated increasing participation by Bosnian Muslims.[29] Nevertheless, the Islamic religious hierarchy was not permitted to assume the role that an Islamic religious hierarchy would normally play in a Muslim-dominated society. The LCY was uncomfortable with rising Islamic activism among the Bosnian Muslims. The risk in Bosnia's case was that its Muslims would begin to pursue their political interests more as members of a Muslim religious community than as one of the Yugoslav nations. The religious implications of the national designation for the newest Yugoslav nation—Muslim—were not subtle and were not lost on the population. For instance, there was a noticeable increase of Bosnian Muslim youth being educated in Muslim centers throughout the world during the 1980s. Those that returned "had ceased to be Communists and had become instead fanatic Moslems, not only in the ethnic sense, but, what was even more dangerous for the regime, in the religious sense as well."[30] The Yugoslavs were thus caught in a contradiction of the recognition of a nation whose dominant factor was religion, an anti-Marxist paradox to say the least.

The Muslim national challenge was taken very seriously in Yugoslavia throughout the 1980s. Islam was the only total ideology/theology that could, like (or instead of) Marxism, regulate the entire life of its citizens. Christianity and other mobilizing theologies did not present as full a challenge to Marxism as did Islam, with its cradle to grave and sunrise to sunrise prescriptions of how to live and its centrality and universality in the lives of Muslims. Even more than Marxism, Islam from its inception *was* the state, with religion and government united so that there was no difference for Muslims between religious and political authority. Therefore, although the Yugoslav leaders were bound to give the Bosnian Muslims as many privileges and as much latitude as possible in coming to their self-realization, the Bosnian Muslims were likely closely watched during the 1980s to prevent any pan-Islamic manifestations from arising to further exacerbate national relations in that country.

THE RISE OF NATIONALISM IN BOSNIA AND HERZEGOVINA

Until Tito recognized the national status of the Bosnian Muslims, "*republic* nationalist manifestations were not severe" in Bosnia and Herzegovina.[31] Tito's acknowledgment of their nationhood in his pursuit of a political agenda, however, opened up a new front for nationalist conflict in Yugoslavia. As the former Yugoslavia discovered, there was no small paradox in a communist country taking steps to ease the plight of a religious group in order to obtain its cooperation in achieving other, political goals.

Despite the uses to which Yugoslav leaders could put rising Bosnian Muslim nationalism and its manifestations in Bosnia and Herzegovina, Bosnian Muslim nationalism was discouraged. Following the rather lukewarm attempts to control Bosnian Muslims nationalism in the 1970s, the Yugoslav leadership in the 1980s launched a major salvo starting on April 10, 1983, against what was perceived to be chauvinistic Bosnian Muslim nationalism. Thirteen Muslims, including current Bosnian President Alija Izetbegović, were arrested and later (beginning July 18) tried in the Sarajevo District Court on charges of "hostile and counter-revolutionary activities."[32] The defendants were described as "active Muslims" who had used Muslim nationalism "in order to destroy the brotherhood, unity, and equality of the nationalities and national minorities in the Socialist Republic of Bosnia-Herzegovina."[33] Their crimes, aside from having described communism as a threat to Islam, welcomed anti-Yugoslav turmoil in Kosovo, criticized Yugoslav nationalities policy as aimed at the Serbianization of the Muslims, plotted to eliminate the Serbian and Croatian populations in Bosnia-Herzegovina, and manipulated the religious feelings of others in an effort to mobilize support for a militant Islam,[34] were the alleged illicit links with reactionaries abroad and the spread of hostile propaganda within Yugoslavia. The latter claim dealt in particular with the dissemination of a document written in 1970 by Izetbegović called *The Islamic Declaration: A Programme for the Islamization of Muslims and the Muslim Peoples*. This document was certainly provocative from the point of view of Yugoslav authorities in that it appeared to preclude Muslim allegiance to a non-Muslim ruler.[35] However, the defendants denied that anything in the treatise referred particularly to Yugoslavia or to Bosnian Muslims.

Aside from the fact that most Muslims were not stirred to action in Yugoslavia by the publication of the declaration, that document "became obsolete after the Islamic revolution in Iran in 1979."[36] Nevertheless, even a whisper of such thoughts and actions must have stunned the Yugoslav leadership. The fragility of the ethnic balance in Yugoslavia had become even more delicate with the burgeoning of Bosnian Muslim nationalism. That such nationalism should occur in a national/religious form reminiscent of the Serb and Croat variants would appear doubly dangerous to Yugoslav authorities. In fact,

Fuad Muhi, characterized as "an ardent defender of the Moslem nationality in Yugoslavia,"[37] described Muslim nationalism in Yugoslavia as the most dangerous nationalism of all. This was so because the Muslims have created "some sort of spiritual union with Moslems all over the world, 'from Gibraltar to Indonesia,'" based on the Koran.[38]

The arrest and conviction of the 13 Bosnian Muslims for hostile propaganda was only one in a series of campaigns against nationalism undertaken throughout the 1960s and 1970s beginning with the purge of Ranković in 1966. These campaigns had been launched against Croatian nationalism, Kosovar nationalism, "punk nationalism," and nationalism in Vojvodina and Slovenia, for example.[39] The Muslims, however, had every reason to be paranoid with regard to the potential of their persecution within Yugoslavia, particularly since the death of Tito, who was regarded as the guarantor of their national prerogatives and security.[40]

Furthermore, the Serbs believed there was a good reason to crack down on Bosnian Muslim nationalism—to prevent the Croats and the Bosnian Muslims from making common cause based on mutual geographic and economic interests, not to mention what some considered strong historical, ethnic, and linguistic connections. Their coalescence would have made a union of 60 percent of Bosnia and Herzegovina's population, which would undermine Serb power in Bosnia and Herzegovina.

Nevertheless, the position of the Bosnian Muslims improved during the 1980s. Muslims simultaneously seemed to have been integrated into Yugoslav life while developing a new sense of either religiosity or national consciousness. The Bosnian Muslim elite and the Islamic religious community no longer appeared to be totally without influence in the decision-making spheres of the government, although they certainly were not equal in power to the other nations either in Bosnia and Herzegovina or in Yugoslavia as a whole.

THE TRAGEDY OF THE 1990s

Yugoslav leaders had carefully crafted a set of institutions to replace Tito upon his demise. The institutions were created to insure as much continuity and as much pressure to maintain a united federation as possible without undermining Tito's own power.

However, after Tito's death, the operation of the institutions, in fact, encouraged narrowly national rather than Yugoslav aspirations. The complexities of the issues and the ramifications of the decentralization and liberalization of the LCY, the economy, and the political system were not readily apparent at Tito's death. Gradually throughout the 1980s, however, the dynamics of the machinery inevitably produced policies based on distinctions among nations (and nationalities). When the political unit for economic and political decision making (the republic or the autonomous province) coincided with ethnic boundaries, it was inevitable that economic and political decisions would be infused with nationalism.

The destructiveness of this nationalistic emphasis was shown most poignantly in the case of the disintegration of Bosnia and Herzegovina. Caught in the inherent contradiction between Croat aspirations of autonomy and Serbia's desire to regain its interwar hegemonic position in Yugoslavia, the options of the Bosnian Muslims became more and more circumscribed. Their main post-Tito protector, the LCY, collapsed, and nationalism replaced communism as a legitimating ideology in Yugoslavia. Nor was the international arena able—or willing—to take on the role of protector of the Bosnian Muslims. In the end, their homeland was to fall victim to Croat and Serb aspirations, as well as to the indecision and flawed decision making of the international community, which was too absorbed in dealing with the ramifications of the sudden implosion of the communist system as well as with Saddam Hussein's challenge in the Persian Gulf to spend much time or treasure on Yugoslavia.

With the collapse of the much-touted institutions set up during Titoist times to propel a cohesive Yugoslavia into the post-Tito era, the only chance that the South Slavs had of maintaining any unity, short of the notoriously lacking goodwill among the nations, was a vigilant, aggressive western alliance. Through a variety of misjudgments, badly formed policies, and unfortunate goals, the West failed Yugoslavia even as Yugoslav chauvinists captured the system from reasonable, Yugoslav-oriented policymakers.

The Bosnian Muslims were not permitted to realize their aspirations for a pluralistic, democratic state that would accommodate the political, social, economic, and cultural needs of Muslims, Serbs, and Croats. Instead, their erstwhile Bosnian compatriots—both Serbs and Croats—have rejected their goals and are displacing and murdering them. What alternatives remain for the survivors?

Could the common origins of the South Slavs serve as the basis for a newly reconstituted Yugoslavia? Could a new Bosnia and Herzegovina arise from the bitterness left by the memories of ethnic cleansing? Will future generations seek to redress the wrongs they have observed and suffered? Will the institutionalized international community succeed in crafting a program or series of policies to encourage the peaceful settlement of outstanding ethnic disagreements so that the lands of the former Yugoslavia will not continue in turmoil? These questions will tax international policy makers for years to come. But, unfortunately, their solutions may come too late to preserve in any meaningful way a golden future for the Bosnian Muslims.

Notes

1. Anthony D. Smith, ed., *Ethnicity and Nationalism* (Leiden: Brill, 1992), 1.

2. Other specifically Yugoslav concepts were the nationality (*narodnost*), denoting those populations whose majority inhabited states bordering Yugoslavia, such as the Hungarians and Albanians, and ethnic minority *(etnički manjine)* for the remainder of groups scattered throughout Yugoslavia that did not fit into the classification of *narod* or *narodnost*.

3. Enno Franzius, *History of the Byzantine Empire: Mother of Nations* (New York: Funk & Wagnells, 1967), 390.

4. See, for example, Nada Klaić, *Srednjovjekovna Bosna: Politički položaj bosanskih vladara do tvrtkove krunidbe (1377 g.)* (Zagreb: Grafički zavod hrvatske, 1989), 8.

5. Enver Redžić, "O posebnosti bosanskih muslimana," *Pregled*, 60 (April 1970): 459.

6. Ibid.

7. Ibid.

8. John V.A. Fine, *The Bosnian Church: A New Interpretation: A Study of the Bosnian Church and Its Place in State and Society from the 13th to the 15th Centuries* (Boulder, CO: East European Quarterly, 1975), p. v. Atif Purivatra finessed the disagreement between the two schools when he wrote about "members of the socio-historical phenomenon known as the 'Bosnian Church,' popularly called 'Bogumils,'" in "The National Phenomenon of the Moslems of Bosnia-Herzegovina," *Socialist Thought and Practice*, 12 (December 1974), 30.

9. Muhamed Hadžijahić, *Od tradicija do identita: Geneza nacionalnog pitanja bosanskih muslimana* (Sarajevo: Svjetlost, 1974), 16.

10. See Salim Ćerić, *Muslimani srpskohrvatskog jezika* (Sarajevo: Svjetlost, 1968), 100-1044, for a catalog of incidents where Bosnian Muslims played significant roles in furtherance of Ottoman imperialism.

11. Robert Donia, "Imperial Occupation and Its Consequences: The Army and Politics in Bosnia and Hercegovina, 1878-1914," (Liman, OH: Ohio State University, 1979), 3.

12. Wayne S. Vucinich, "Yugoslavs of the Moslem Faith," in Robert J. Kerner, ed. *Yugoslavia* (Berkeley, CA: University of California Press, 1949), 270-71.

13. Cited in Stephen L. Burg, "The Political Integration of Yugoslavia's Muslims: Determinants of Success and Failure" (Pittsburgh, PA: Carl Beck Papers in Russian and East European Studies, University of Pittsburgh, 1983), 14.

14. Cited in Raymond Pearson, *National Minorities in Eastern Europe 1848-1945* (London: Macmillan, 1983), 148. Other Muslim leaders criticized Spaho. They were particularly incensed by his vow not to make public statements without prior government approval. Spaho's critics claimed that he was jeopardizing the equal representation of Muslims by signing away the Muslim right to public protest. Atif Purivatra, *Jugoslavenska muslimanska organizacija: Organizacija u političkom životu Kraljevine Srba, Hrvata i Slovenaca* (Sarajevo: Svjetlost, 1974), 31-32.

15. Spaho thus remarked during preliminary negotiations to the *Sporazum*, "If Bosnia and Herzegovina cannot get autonomy, then we cannot at any price allow the region to be divided, but let the whole of it go to Serbia." Cited in Vucinich, "Yugoslavs of the Moslem Faith," 270-71.

16. Dennison I. Rusinow, "Yugoslavia's Muslim Nation," *Universities Field Staff International Reports* (Europe: 1982). 4. Further data from Yugoslav statistical accounts for 1948, 1953, 1961, and 1971 may be found in George Schöpflin, "Nationality in the Fabric of Yugoslavia," *Survey*, 25 (Summer 1980): 13.

17. Rusinow, "Yugoslavia's Muslim Nation," 4.

18. Stephen L. Burg, "The Political Integration of Yugoslavia's Muslims," 22.

19. Note that in Yugoslavia "ethnic membership" was not the same thing as "nation" or "nationality."

20. An interesting and perhaps unwelcome phenomenon occurred as a result of the appearance of this new census designation. The category "Yugoslav

undetermined" was a major loser to the Muslim category, indicating that some citizens had used the Yugoslav category to reject being put into a repugnant ethnic box (either Serb or Croat). But even more arresting is that "most of these remaining 'Yugoslavs' (87 percent) were still recorded in Bosnia-Hercegovina, indicating that a considerable number of communist and other nonreligious members of the Slav Muslim community continued to regard 'Muslim' as a religious and not an 'ethnic' category." Rusinow, "Yugoslavia's Muslim Nation," 4-5.

21. Schöpflin intimated that the attainment of Muslim plurality in Bosnia and Herzegovina in the 1971 census was due to a statistically significant Muslim switch in national self-determination from Serb to Muslim. "Nationality in the Fabric of Yugoslav Politics," 9.

22. For figures illustrating Bosnian Muslim underrepresentation in important sectors of Yugoslav society, see Slobodan Stanković, *The End of the Tito Era: Yugoslavia's Dilemmas* (Stanford, CA: Hoover Institution Press, 1981); Slobodan Stanković, "On the Eve of the 12th Yugoslav Party Congress," Radio Free Europe Research (June 25, 1982); and Schöpflin, "Nationality in the Fabric of Yugoslav Politics," 9.

23. Little reliable data exists concerning the number of faithful and the intensity of religious beliefs among the Bosnian Muslims. However, a dramatic decline in intermarriage by Yugoslav Muslims was noted as early as the mid-1960s. Milan Andrejevich, "The Position and Activities of the Religious Communities in Yugoslavia: With Special Attention to the Serbian Orthodox Church," in Bohdan R. Bociurkiw and John W. Strong, eds., *Religion and Atheism in the U.S.S.R. and Eastern Europe* (Toronto: University of Toronto Press, 1975), 364-65. Also noticed was a slow but steady rise in the degree of Muslim affiliation in the Yugoslav population at large. Sergej Flere, "Denominational Affiliation in Yugoslavia 1931-1987," *East European Quarterly*, (June 1991): 154. On the other hand, the Belgrade weekly magazine *NIN* found that the proportion of young Yugoslavs who claimed to be religious dropped 14 percent in 1983 from the 1969 total of 40 percent (29 July 1984), 18. These contradictory findings suggested no "recent increase in the number of faithful in Yugoslavia, but an increase of the number of those who freely express their religious beliefs." See Esad Ćimić, *Socialističko društvo i religija: Ispitivanje odnosa izmedju samoupravljanja i procesa prevladjavanja tradicionalne religije* (Sarajevo: Svjetlost, 1966), 125.

24. I am grateful to Robin Alison Remington for suggesting this point to me.

25. Slobodan Stanković, "Tito's Successors Fear 'Moslem Nationalism,'" *Radio Free Europe Research/RAD Background Report/82* (Yugoslavia: 1983), 3.

26. Reis-ul-ulema Hadži Naim Effendi Hadžiabdić in 1977 mentioned that "the material basis of our religious employees has never been better. All imams are covered by health, pension and invalid insurance. A large number of very beautiful mosques have been built—there are more than 500." See "Muslims in Yugoslavia: Adaptation and Accommodation," *Impact International*, 7 (June 24-July 7, 1977), 14.

27. "Anti-Moslem Feelings Denied," *Yugoslavia: Situation Report, Radio Free Europe Research*, 1 (Yugoslavia: November 30, 1984), 29.

28. Slobodan Stanković, "Islamic Revival in Yugoslavia Hailed," *Radio Free Europe Research/RAD Background Report* (Yugoslavia: April 26, 1984), 1, citing Nenad Ivanković, in *Danas* (March 27, 1984).

29. For data on Bosnian Muslims taking the hajj, see H.Hfz. Husein Mujić, "Ovogodišne putovanje na hadž," *Glasnik VISa*, 30 (May-June 1967): 233; H. Alija Kusturica, "Osvrt no ovogodišnje hodočašće," *Glasnik VISa*, 31 (April-May-June 1968): 237; David Edwin Long, *The Hajj Today: A Survey of the Contemporary Makkah Pilgrimage* (Albany, NY: State University of New York Press, 1979), 134; H.Hfz. Sinanuddin Sokolović, "Hadž 1971. godine (2211 hadzija iz SFRJ)," *Glasnik VISa*, 34 (March-April 1971), 135; Ibrahim Lisovac, "Ovogodišnje putovanje na hadž," *Glasnik VISa*, 37 (May-June 1974): 224; Zejnil Fajić, "Putovanje na hadž u 12398./1978. godini," *Glasnik VISa*, 41 (November-December 1978): 632-34. See also Kingdom of Saudi Arabia, *Statistical Yearbook* (Ministry of Finance and National Economy, Central Department of Statistics).

30. Stanković, "Tito's Successors Fear 'Moslem Nationalism,'" 3.

31. Fred Warner Neal, "Yugoslav Approaches to the Nationalities Problem—The Politics of Circumvention," paper presented at the annual meeting of the American Association for the Advancement of Slavic Studies, Washington, October 16, 1982, 11.

32. Other defendants were well-educated, professional people ages 26 through 61. They included two Muslim clerics, two lawyers, two teachers, and four engineers. Two of the defendants were women; one defendant was a former party member and another a former Partisan. See "The Trial of Moslem Intellectuals in Sarajevo," *South Slav Journal*, 6 (Spring 1983): 5.

33. Stanković, "Tito's Successors Fear 'Moslem Nationalism,'" 2, citing *Borba* (11 April 1983).

34. Sabrina Petra Ramet, *Nationalism and Federalism in Yugoslavia, 1962-1991* (Bloomington, IN: Indiana University Press, 1992), 155.

35. "Just like an individual, a people that has accepted Islam is thereafter incapable of living and dying for any other ideal. It is unthinkable (sic) that a Muslim should sacrifice himself for any king or ruler, no matter who he might be, or for the glory of any nation or party, becase the strongest Islamic instinct recognizes in this a king of paganism and idolatry." From Alija Izetbegović, *The Islamic Declaration*, published in the *South Slav Journal*, 6 (Spring 1983): 6.

36. Fuad Munić, "Paranoične ideje o 'muslimanskoj republici,'" *Borba* (30 April—1-3 May 1983), 13.

37. Slobodan Stanković, "Campaign Against 'Khomeini-Inspired' Moslems in Yugoslavia," *Radio Free Europe Research* (Yugoslavia: May 24, 1983), 3.

38. Muhić, "Paranoične ideje o 'muslimanskoj republici,'" 13.

39. Stanković, "Tito's Successors Fear 'Moslem Nationalism,'" 3, citing *Vjesnik* (11 April 1983).

40. Muhić, "Paranoične ideje o 'muslimanskoj republici,'" 13.

11

Reconstituting Serbia: 1945–1991

Nicholas J. Miller[1]

By now it is clear that the claim of Yugoslav Communists that they solved the national question was invalid. In fact, the opposite was certainly true: rather than solve the national question, the communist regime demonized it, which allowed negative mythologies to develop within and about each of the nationalisms of Yugoslavia. Rather than search for reasons why the state collapsed so violently, one might better seek reasons for the minor miracle of its 46 years of peaceful survival. It seems now that Yugoslavia served different purposes for each of the state's different ethnic groups. For Serbs, Tito's Yugoslavia provided protection (as did the first Yugoslavia from 1918 to 1941). Any threat to Yugoslav unity equalled a threat to the unity of Serbs, who were dispersed through each of the Yugoslav federal units except Slovenia.[2]

When the Yugoslav state began to unravel, and after clearly stating their preference that Yugoslavia remain a single state, the desire for unity led many Serbs to take up arms not in the interests of a united Yugoslavia, but for a strictly Serbian state. With the prospect of Croatian and Bosnian (not to mention Macedonian, Albanian, and potentially Montenegrin) separatist movements in the 1990s, Serbs in each of those regions feared complete separation from the core Serbian state. The demand of Serbian unity in the face of Croatian and Bosnian secession movements prompted the wars of Yugoslav succession beginning in 1991.

To understand Yugoslavia's collapse, it is vital to understand how each of the Serbian communities of Yugoslavia—Serbia proper and the intra-Yugoslavian Serbian diaspora in Kosovo, Croatia, Bosnia and Hercegovina, Montenegro, Vojvodina, and Macedonia—fit into the larger picture of Serbian national ideology and mythology. This brief chapter has several goals: to examine in institutional and political terms how the Serbian nation was treated in a federal Yugoslavia after 1945 and then after 1966, when the federal structure of the state began to change; then, to analyze the response of the spectrum of Serbs, politicians as well as intellectuals, to the status of Serbs in Yugoslavia; and finally, to determine whether there was a national(ist) consensus among Serbs in Yugoslavia, which elements it was composed of, and how it conceived of Serbia. The strength of Serbian nationalism might seem exaggerated now, but in light of the long-term commitment of Serbian intellectuals, politicians, and even mainstream communist politicians to maintaining a united Serbia, it is perfectly understandable—even inevitable.

THE SERBS IN A FEDERAL YUGOSLAVIA

Serbs traditionally conceived of Serbian lands in loose rank order: the modern core of Serbia was Šumadija (the Belgrade region southward); Kosovo (known by nationalists as "Old Serbia") farther south was integral to Serbia in spite of its predominantly Albanian population; Macedonia, known before 1945 as "Southern Serbia," was among the lands of the medieval Serbian kingdom; Vovjodina to the north (really Baranja, Bačka, and part of Banat) was the location of the nineteenth-century cultural revival of the Serbian nation, but Serbs there suffered from cultural biases against those who had left the heartland. Thus, Croatian and Vojvodinian Serbian communities were included in the category of Serbs from "across the river" (the Sava and the Danube), known as *prečani*. Bosnian Serbs also occupied an ambiguous place in the Serbian spectrum. Serbs from south of the rivers still proudly call themselves Srbijanci whereas all other Serbs are called Srbi—a critical distinction. *Prečani* have periodically been resented for their "European" culture and pretensions and for the fact that they had, allegedly, unheroically abandoned the homeland to the aggressor Turks by emigrating to the Habsburg lands.

During World War II, the Serbs of these regions suffered to varying degrees. Serbs constituted approximately half of the war deaths: 530,000 of 1,027,000.³ The Serbs of Bosnia and Croatia had been exposed to the atrocities of the Independent State of Croatia and its Ustaša supporters. The Serbs of Serbia proper fell under the regime of the German puppet ruler, Milan Nedić; significant numbers of them died as Partisans, Četniks, or victims of German reprisals. The Germans administered the Banat, and Kosovo had been given by its Italian occupiers to Albania, which placed Serbs under an alien and hostile regime. In Macedonia, which Serbs always considered a Serbian land, Yugoslav Partisans, Bulgarian occupation authorities, and others competed for its ultimate control. Serbs thus suffered greatly during the war.

Serbia brought more than suffering to the postwar table, however. The Yugoslav Communists believed that the strength and position of Serbia in the interwar state had alienated other nationalities in Yugoslavia, leading to its collapse in 1941. Thus Serbia's legacy of suffering was to some degree offset by its history of intolerance in the interwar state. Serbs were in essence punished after the war for their role in the first Yugoslavia. In the course of the war and its aftermath, several basic assumptions (often in mutual contradiction) formed in the minds of the Partisans: that Serbia could not be allowed to dominate the second Yugoslavia, because of its role in the first; that certain nationalisms would be discouraged after the war (namely, Croatian and Serbian), while others would be tolerated or even encouraged (Macedonian, later Albanian); and that decisions regarding borders would be manipulated according to the need to balance national aspirations in the postwar state. Even with such general guidelines, the tally of territorial winners and losers after the war was unclear. Clearly enough, however, Serbs considered themselves losers.

The Serbia of 1913, that Serbia which Serbian nationalists considered minimal, disappeared in 1944-45. Macedonia became a republic, the now-nurtured Macedonian nation its lord. Portions of Baranja, Bačka, and Banat became the Autonomous Province of Vojvodina—autonomous from the Socialist Republic of Serbia. Kosovo became the Autonomous Region of Kosovo and Metohija—a slightly lesser status, also autonomous from Serbia. In addition, other territorial decisions affected Serbian communities: the Serbs of Croatia were not given autonomous status, which had been considered by the communist leadership;[4] Bosnia and Hercegovina, instead of being divided between Serbia and Croatia (an impossible task in any case), became a republic. And Montenegro retained its independence.

In 1948, 14.47 percent of Croatia's population was Serbian (543,795 total Serbs); by 1981, that percentage had fallen to 11.55 percent, for a total of 531,502. In 1948, 41.48 percent of Bosnia and Hercegovina's population was Serbian (not including those designating themselves as Serb-Muslims in that year's census), for a total of 1,064,125 Serbs; by 1981, the percentage had fallen to 32.03 percent, but there were 1,320,644 Serbs total. Kosovo's ethnic composition, always a contentious topic, was 76.9 percent Albanian in 1981, leaving 368,445 non-Albanians, nearly all ethnic Serbs and Montenegrins. In 1981, of 8.1 million Serbs in Yugoslavia, 6.5 percent lived in Croatia and 16.23 percent lived in Bosnia. A further 14 percent lived in Vojvodina. A much smaller percentage lived in Kosovo, but that region's importance transcended the population figures. Only about 58 percent of Serbs lived in Serbia proper in 1981.[5] From the Serbian perspective, Tito's Yugoslavia was founded and organized on a series of unhappy ironies. Arguably the most persecuted nationality in Yugoslavia during the war, Serbs provided the core of the original Partisan units. Yet after the war their Serbia was all but dismembered. The perception that Serbs were punished after the war grew over the postwar period, as power in the new Yugoslavia devolved ever more to the republics and provinces at the expense of the center.

There was certainly a different logic to the federalization of Yugoslavia than the desire to destroy Serbian nationhood. At the risk of repetition of some of the truisms of postwar Yugoslav politics and power: the Partisans came to power on a dual wave of social revolution and anti-nationalism. Furthermore, they recognized that Yugoslavia could only survive if some sort of mechanism could be implemented to control nationalism. The result was a Yugoslavia federalized according to the Soviet model, but with variations. Self-management, for all of its revolutionary character as an alternative to Marxism-Leninism, was envisioned as a transformative means to eliminate bourgeois cultural identifications like nationhood in favor of class identifications. Moreover, until the early 1960s, Yugoslav leaders attempted to create a new supranational "Partisan" Yugoslav patriotism. In a self-managed Yugoslavia, it was conceivable (if visionary) to imagine the elimination of older national loyalties. This confidence lasted until the early 1960s, when the state's economy slowed down significantly.

Through this early era in the history of the second Yugoslavia, Serbs did not fear their status in the state in spite of the demonization of their interwar role and regardless of their dispersion throughout the republics and provinces of Yugoslavia. One reason for this was the position and influence of Aleksandar Ranković, a Serb, one of the "big four" Yugoslav Communists (with Tito, Edvard Kardelj, and Milovan Djilas), the head of the UDBa (internal security) and, from 1963, vice-president of Yugoslavia. Ranković provided both symbolic and real comfort for Serbs, especially due to the role he and his security service played in maintaining the dominance of Serbs in the nomenklatura of Kosovo, which then as now was by far the most critical territory in the minds of Serbian nationalists. Although it is unclear exactly how Ranković's position and influence reassured Serbs, it is quite clear that his removal, which would come in 1966, would have the effect of disorienting many Serbs, from the top communist leadership through the intelligentsia and including the general public.

REVISING THE ETHNIC SOLUTION: THE LIBERALIZATION OF THE 1960s

The early 1960s were a time of rapid change in every sphere of Yugoslav political life. With the economy stalled, much of the Yugoslav leadership determined that the administration of both the state and the economy needed to be decentralized to facilitate market-oriented reforms. That point of view opened the door to the gradual devolution of power to the republics and provinces in Yugoslavia at the expense of the center in Belgrade; it therefore also opened the door to evermore fragmentation of the Serbian community of Yugoslavia. Not coincidentally, Aleksandar Ranković and his supporters in the federal government were those most resistant to economic reform—because such reforms would involve decentralization of decision making and thus a weakening of the only guarantee that Serbs had of continued, if circumscribed, unity. The implications of economic reform were thus in direct contradiction to the political and administrative interests of Serbian unity.

The success of the liberal reformers, who included many of the leaders of the Slovenian and Croatian parties and relatively few Serbs, radically altered the path that Yugoslav federalism had taken until the mid-1960s. Hitherto, federalism had been less fact than fiction. After the victory of the reformers, Yugoslav leaders began to implement true decentralizing features, and federalization gained substance. With decentralization, the old emphasis on producing a new, "Partisan," identity receded. The nurturing of benign forms of national self-definition would take the place of the demonization of individual nationalisms. Now each republic and province would be considered the territory of one of the major nations of Yugoslavia in an effort to balance and harmonize the relations of the various groups. The adoption of this strategy foreshadowed the turnover of Kosovo to its Albanian majority, and the recognition of a Muslim nationality among the South Slavic-speaking religious Muslims of Bosnia-Hercegovina and the Sandžak of Novi Pazar.

The years 1966 to 1971 were filled with the aftershocks of Tito and Kardelj's decision to decentralize. In many ways the most important symbolic change in the Yugoslav administrative system was the removal of Ranković in 1966. In order to eliminate Ranković's faction from the federal government, where it was providing much resistance to decentralization, the leadership removed Ranković from his positions in 1966 for a variety of stated reasons that included the claim that he had spied on Tito himself.[6] His removal was also motivated by the desire of the rest of the ruling class in Yugoslavia to stigmatize, finally and completely, centralism and Serbianism as one and the same ill in Yugoslavia. Without question, it was a purge of the periodic type that accompanied major changes in orientation in communist regimes. Serbs could only view his removal as an affront to them, while others, especially in Kosovo, breathed a sigh of relief at the fall of the Serbian watchdog.

Other events served notice to Serbia that its comfortable position in a firmly controlled Yugoslavia could not last. After Ranković's fall in 1966, Tito handed Kosovo over to its Albanian majority, effecting a massive overhaul of the *nomenklatura* and making it resemble an Albanian mini-state. The police forces in Kosovo, hitherto dominated by Serbs, were fired, and Albanians replaced them. In 1968, the first of several phases of unrest hit Kosovo. In order to quell the disturbances, further concessions were made to the Albanians of the region: the University of Priština was founded in 1969 as an Albanian-language institution; in official business, the term "Albanian" replaced the pejorative "Šiptar"; the province's official designation,

Kosovo-Metohija, was shortened to Kosovo, since Metohija was a Serbian place name with no cultural validity for the Albanian majority of the region. It seems likely that the demonstrations of 1968 represented a demand for further liberalization of the regime in the area, a reflection of the principle that violent opposition to a situation only occurs as that situation begins to improve.[7] Serbs reasonably perceived the fall of Ranković and the Albanian assumption of predominance in Kosovo as part of the same process.[8]

Additionally, between 1968 and 1971, Muslim South Slavs gradually moved from an unclear position as a religious minority to full status as a constituent nation in Yugoslavia.[9] Those Muslims who spoke Serbo-Croatian (that is, not Albanian or Turkish-speaking Muslims) were, as of the 1971 census, a nation—fully equal to Serbs, Croats, Montenegrins, Slovenes, and Macedonians among Yugoslavia's ruling nations (not nationalities, such as the Albanian, Hungarian, and others, which fell beneath nations in the Yugoslav hierarchy). Muslim attempts thereafter to designate Bosnia-Hercegovina the republic of the Muslims failed,[10] but for the Serbs and Croats of Bosnia, recognition of a Muslim ethnicity represented a huge setback to national mythology. Previously, all had assumed (and Muslims had been forced to acknowledge) that Muslims were simply Serbs or Croats of the Islamic faith.[11] Once again, the revised approach to national relations in Yugoslavia appeared to work to the detriment of Serbs.

Finally, the Croatian Spring, whose origins dated to 1967 but which peaked in 1971, saw a rapid rise in open Croatian nationalism. It followed the victory of the liberal reformers of the mid-1960s. The movement involved many issues, but focused on the sovereignty of the Croatian people in Croatia. In light of the fate of Croatia's Serbs during World War II, Serbs viewed the movement as a threat to them.[12] The writing of a new constitution for Croatia most directly affected Serbs. Proposals emanating from the Croatian cultural organization, *Matica Hrvatska*, did not include recognition of the Serbian nation in Croatia. As such, the key issue of 1971 for Serbs in Croatia would be mirrored in the crisis of 1990-91: Would Serbian individuality in Croatia be respected under Croatian authority? In 1971, the Serbian cultural organization *Prosveta* presented the Serbian position, while within the Croatian League of Communists, the only Serb, Dušan Dragosavac, did the same. When Tito decided to crush the mass movement, the Serbian question played a prominent role in his calculations.

The ultimate expression of the decentralization that proceeded apace after 1966 was the constitution of 1974, with which self-management decision making was shifted almost entirely to the republics and autonomous provinces. Furthermore, the ultimate logic of the concept of "one republic, one nation" was unveiled, as Kosovo and Vojvodina both achieved near-republican status—the only notable remaining condition being that they did not have the right to secede from the federation. However, they did now occupy the unique constitutional position of being parts of both Serbia and the Yugoslav federation simultaneously. As if to prove again the maxim that upheaval under repressive regimes gathers steam as the repression declines, demonstrations again erupted in 1981 in Kosovo for republican status for the province. Only then did the issue of fully and constitutionally reconstituting Serbia arise with a vengeance among Serbs.

THE BIRTH OF SERBIAN DISSENT

> We can no longer fail to recognize how much the conviction spreads in Serbia regarding the intensification of relations between Šiptars and Serbs, regarding the feeling of endangerment of the Serbs and Montenegrins, regarding the pressures for emigration, regarding the systematic removal of Serbs and Montenegrins from leading positions, regarding the desires of specialists to abandon Kosovo and Metohija, regarding inequality before the courts and lack of respect for legality, regarding blackmail in the name of national identity.[13]
>
> —Dobrica Ćosić, 1968

It took very little time for the cumulative effect of the Albanian, Muslim, and Croatian exploitation of the new nationalities orientation of the regime to provoke an unsuppressed but isolated Serbian response. On May 29, 1968, at the Fourteenth Plenum of the Central Committee of the League of Communists of Serbia, Dobrica Ćosić, a member of that committee and a favored member of the postwar Partisan intelligentsia, spoke. His speech established the foundation for Serbian complaints about the devolutionary tendencies of Yugoslav communism for the following two decades. Several things were notable about his presentation.[14]

First, Ćosić echoed the familiar communist claim that the national question could only be solved through modernization. The path to "human liberation" for Ćosić was socioeconomic development so that "national identification [*pripadnost*] is a matter for the private sphere, an existential possibility for the enrichment of human creative originality."[15] To assure such development, Ćosić became the first strident Serbian voice in opposition to the "bureaucratization" of Yugoslav society, asserting that the federalization of Yugoslavia contributed not to the modernization of the state but to the growth of distinctly antimodernizing local bureaucracies in every republic and province. The idea that modernization would solve the national question was hardly new among Communists; nor was the proposal that bureaucracy was an enemy of progress in communist states. However, to underscore the persistence of the Yugoslav national question, the debate regarding modernization and bureaucracy in the 1960s followed national lines: the reformist Slovenes and Croats assuredly believed that market processes would accelerate modernization, and that those processes could only be implemented in a decentralized state; Serbs sincerely felt the opposite.[16]

More than a sociologist's eye informed Ćosić's overall exposé, however. Also implicit in his presentation was a vision of what constituted Serbia, and the ways that current changes in Yugoslavia affected Serbs. His vision was not narrow. He rejected the notion that Serbia was nothing more than Šumadija, the nineteenth-century heartland of Serbia: *srbijanstvo* (Serbianism that diminished the importance of the *prečani*) was "an essentially primitive and anachronistic political mentality." In fact, when pressed, Ćosić discovered Serbian nationalism only among believers in this narrow definition of Serbdom—which thus placed all nationalisms, which were doctrinarily negative for him, in corresponding categories: bureaucratic, narrow, based in new federal units.[17] Serbs, in his view, should not be particularists but universalists. Only a universal perspective could resolve Yugoslavia's national and developmental questions successfully. In the behavior of the Vojvodina and Kosovo leagues of Communists (emboldened by the reforms of the 1960s and moving away from the Serbian center), Ćosić saw the destruction of Serbia: "Will the Sava and the Danube indeed be for our generation the border between Belgrade and Novi Sad, Mačva and Srem, Banat and Danubia? Do in fact some Communists really continue to view the socialist autonomous Vojvodina as their own vojvodstvo?"[18] Ćosić feared that Vojvodina would become Magyarized, or its Serbs separated from their Šumadijan anchor, by its bureaucracy. Ćosić's fear of the growth of a Vojvodinian (Magyar) identity was more than matched by his fear that Kosovo, "the ancient and original homeland of the Serbian people,"[19] would also abandon its Serbianness.

Perhaps the strongest impression left by Ćosić's speech is of his obvious disdain for Albanians and fear of Albanian nationalism. And it is here that one senses finally the ultimate logic of his (and later) attacks on bureaucracy, decentralization, and nationalism. Ćosić feared the creation of an Albanian Kosovo. He relied on the old Marxist fictions: "To me the favoring of any nationality at the expense of the class perspective, at the expense of general social worth, at the expense of knowledge and capabilities, work and morals as fundamental human values in the socialist community is unacceptable in social and Marxist terms." But in Kosovo, the Albanian nationality was favored in his view—in fact, "nationality is obviously favored and the first characteristic of an expression of autonomous rights," a critical reversal of classic Marxist teachings, and a critical reversal for the Serbs of Kosovo. The new treatment of Kosovo was "bureaucratic-etatist," and "[could] not but end in irredentism, in the deepening of political differences between the nations of Kosovo and Metohija and Albania and Yugoslavia, in a permanent and open conflict."[20] Thus, with regard to Albanian nationalism, Ćosić asserted that "the only way that [Albanian irredentism] can have no serious political effect is if economic progress, democracy and social relations in Yugoslavia are always and in every way dominant over Albanian reality."[21] A dual logic informed Ćosić's position: Decentralization clearly allowed the "Albanian reality" to predominate over all others in Kosovo, and it did indeed enable the growth of huge bureaucracies that eventually hindered economic development. The missing element is the human one—Kosovo's population was Albanian, but the land was Serbian. Thus the Albanian reality was irrelevant.

Ćosić was the first, but has not been alone, in asserting that the character of Kosovo is not to be determined by its demographic makeup but by its history. The starting point for many Serbs in discussions of Kosovo is their assertion that Kosovo is, in simplest terms, a Serbian land. There is no room for discussion of that point. Mihailo Marković would later note in 1990 that "[t]he region which was invaded and eventually conquered by islamized Albanians, also happened to be the cradle of Serbian culture. . . . That is why Serbs cannot give it up."[22] This statement ignored the fact that, at the time of its writing, more than 80 percent of Kosovo's population was Albanian. It reflects the blinders that hinder dialogue between Serbs and outsiders regarding Kosovo.

Ćosić's presentation, Marxist in its pretensions and rhetoric, reflected deep-rooted fears among Serbs that they were to be made second-class citizens in their own lands. Such a fear was, on the surface, not unreasonable. But the speaker's Marxist structure gave way to an ethnic nationalist superstructure when he defined that which was Serbian in expansive terms. The structure of the populations of Kosovo, where Serbs were vastly outnumbered, and Vojvodina, where they coexisted with a large Magyar minority, did not alter for Ćosić the fact that they were Serbian lands. And while there were rays of hope in his exposition ("the freedom-loving and revolutionary Serbian people has the consciousness, strength and desire to democratically understand the national feeling of the Šiptars of Kosovo and Metohija, and to support all of their demands if they are democratic in content and form"), it is rooted in an uncompromisingly collective vision of equality. Thus the offer is conditioned by the demand that Albanian "national sovereignty [not be] founded on nationalistic forms and on the endangerment of the survival, freedom, and integrity of the very Serbian nation in Kosovo and Metohija. Because Serbs and Montenegrins did not annex Kosovo and Metohija, they did not conquer it from the Šiptars by war, therefore they are not occupiers and conquerors. Kosovo and Metohija are the ancient and original homeland of the Serbian nation."[23] Ćosić viewed the rights of nations (not individuals) as a zero sum equation. If Albanians had them, Serbs would not. But if Serbs were predominant, not only would it be historically just, but it would be morally progressive, since only the Serbian nation had the requisite consciousness.

Dobrica Ćosić spoke in 1968, and was immediately excluded from the Serbian League of Communists along with a like-thinking colleague, Jovan Marjanović. Their outburst reflected the growing assertiveness of other national groups in Yugoslavia: the Croatian Spring got its start with the uproar surrounding the publication of a common dictionary for Serbian and Croatian languages in 1967; the first productive movements toward the recognition of a Muslim nation in Yugoslavia began in 1968; and Serbs feared the demonstrations in Kosovo in 1968. One could view the three-year period from 1966 to 1968 in either of two ways: It was an expression of hitherto repressed nationalisms and was a healthy response to the decentralization of power in Yugoslavia; or it represented an insidious assertiveness on the part of national groups in Yugoslavia who saw in the decentralizing reforms an opportunity to dominate their neighbors once again. Either way, it appeared to threaten Serbs of Ćosić's mind, and such Serbs would continue to use his 1968 speech as a cornerstone. In the late 1980s, Slobodan Milošević used the idea of opposition to bureaucracy to focus his own revisionist communist movement, which he artfully labeled the "anti-bureaucratic revolution." By the 1980s, in very changed circumstances, it reflected not merely fear of empire-building local bureaucracies, but the desire for a complete turnover in the Titoist party, which had, in their view, become weak and uncreative—and consequently anti-Serbian.

THE CREATION OF A SERBIAN NATIONALIST CONSENSUS

The 1974 constitution made official the confederation of the party and the atomization of economic decision making in Yugoslavia, and thus represented the culmination of the tendencies of the 1960s. Before that, however, Tito made certain that nationalist passions, unleashed in the late 1960s and best represented by the Croatian Spring of 1970-71, could not challenge the ultimate authority of the center. Along with the Croatian leadership (Miko Tripalo, Savka Dapčević-Kučar, and others), Tito removed members of the leadership of the Serbian party whom he claimed to view as too nationalistic, although there is general agreement that Marko Nikezić and Latinka Perović (the best-known victims in Serbia) were sacrificed in the president's quest to achieve ethnic symmetry in his persecutionary measures. Today, there is significant support for the thesis that Serbia lost its best and brightest in 1972, leaving the field open to talents like Milošević in the 1980s.[24]

Tito thus granted Yugoslavs the 1974 constitution after purging those "nationalists" who he assumed might take republican liberties too far. The constitution made immutable all of the best and worst of confederation: the one nation, one republic-province equation, which represented an attempt to allow each major ethnic group in Yugoslavia a home of its own; the entrenchment of republican, provincial leaderships that might have become national leaders, but instead developed into corrupt *apparatchiks*. For Serbs, the constitution made the situation of Kosovo and Vojvodina ridiculous. Each province now occupied a dual constituent status: simultaneously part of

Serbia and the federation, they played a republican role in the federal context, where their powers were almost identical to the republics with the exception of the right to secede.

The standard Serbian response to the situation was acquiescence. Such a response is completely understandable—the strength of the Titoist ideology, the pervasiveness of the myth of self-management, and the intense antinationalistic rhetoric of the regime and popular culture made it so. Until the late 1970s, the Serbian party doctrinarily ignored or persecuted those like Ćosić who claimed anti-Serbianism was integral to post-1966 Titoism. This era gave birth to real disillusionment with Titoism among Serbs. By the late 1970s, however, within the Serbian party, a subtle consensus grew that the dispersion of Serbs could not continue. From that point on, quiet agitation for a revision of the 1974 constitution began. For loyal Serbian Communists, there was only one way to take advantage of Titoism and still support a reconstitution of Serbia: attack Albanian nationalism (as well as others) while asserting that "progressive forces" (Serbian, socialist) existed that could eradicate it.[25] Those progressive forces could only be adequately utilized in a reunified Serbia, in which the excesses of Albanian nationalism could be tackled.[26] To the frustration of many Serbs, this approach was self-limiting: Ivan Stambolić, the head of the Serbian party until 1987, accused those Serbs who went beyond assertions of Albanian counter-revolution and denied the ability of the Serbian and Kosovo parties to solve the problem institutionally of having "already begun to swim in the waters of a different nationalism [Serbian]."[27] That was the limit, set by the system itself, on expression of Serbian unhappiness. All energies devoted to the reconstitution of Serbia had to be channeled through the party's initiative to revise the constitution of the republic. The source of tension in Serbian society in the 1980s, however, would be precisely the growing belief of Serbs outside the party that Titoist methods were no longer useful. The party no longer served Serbs.

Until the mid-1980s, outside of the party, little could be said. Until Tito died in 1980, open Serbian pining for the return of Kosovo or Vojvodina was muted. But after he died in May 1980, the Serbian nationalist movement grew outside of the party, among historians, writers, and other intellectuals. That movement embodied the true expression of anti-Titoism, the deepest sense of opposition to the regime—in effect, the energies of the Serbian opposition were totally focused on re-creating Serbia. What's more, new demonstrations in

Kosovo occurred in 1981. Those events, more violent and challenging than the 1968 demonstrations, reminded all Yugoslavs that Albanian nationalism was a potent force in Kosovo. As of 1981, the older, more restrained methods of questioning the division of Serbdom were outpaced by the development of extra-party movements that were overtly nationalistic, that utilized old, pre-partisan mythologies, and that mined the depths of anti-Titoism in Serbia, reviving older nationalist cultural images, especially those which were anticommunist and anti-Muslim. Whereas in other countries of Eastern Europe, opposition took the form of "living in truth," "antipolitics," or "the new evolutionism," all of which described attempts to create a "civil society" parallel to the regime, in Serbia attempts to create space for the individual were rare indeed. Instead, the re-creation of a Serbian "ethnic society" was the goal.

Dobrica Ćosić, the herald of the original antibureaucratic revolution, also heralded the opening of the second front, the non-party, intellectual uprising against Titoism, with his 1977 speech to the Serbian Academy of Sciences and Arts, which has come down to us under the name "Literature and History Today."[28] Ćosić's vehicle was a speech on the relationship of the novel to history—specifically, the ability of the novel and the novelist to characterize the history of a people where historians fail. However, the true theme of the presentation is to be found in the history he claims has inadequately been served by historians. And that is the history of the Serbian people in the nineteenth and twentieth centuries. Ćosić establishes here the litany of grievances that Serbian historians and intellectuals would carry forward in the name of the return of history and truth. Here we discover that "in Europe there is not a small nation which in the past two centuries, and especially in the twentieth, has expended so much in the name of history . . . as the Serbian nation."[29] His exposition betrays a petulance that would characterize the next ten years of Serbian attempts to revise the verdict of Yugoslav historiography. Thus outsiders were to blame for Serbian failures; Serbs are not accorded enough credit for their suffering in the name of civilization.[30] He approvingly notes the command of Tolstoy: "Write the real, true history of this century! There is your life's task!" Ćosić's call would be taken up in the 1980s by historians seeking the truth. In the process, the pendulum would be dragged too far in the direction of a new false orthodoxy—nationalist this time.

The first area in which the new search for truth would be practiced was with regard to Kosovo, the Albanian land that provided Serbia with its vast pantheon of heroes, anti-heroes, and sacred grounds. The absence of Tito emboldened an enormous range of people to attack the Titoist solution to the Albanian "counter-revolution." In the course of the period from 1981 to 1986, an opposition to the way the Serbian party dealt with Albanian nationalism would coalesce around several specific points: the fact of Serbo-Montenegrin outmigration; the immense economic drain that Kosovo represented; and the alleged revisitation of ancient crimes (rape, murder, and even impalement) against Serbs perpetrated earlier by Turks, now by Albanians. The overarching theme of this new opposition was the argument that Kosovo was a Serbian land. Thus, not only were crimes being committed against Serbs in Kosovo, they were being committed in a land that was Serbian by definition, regardless of the demographic facts. Given the long-term Titoist commitment to seeing Kosovo develop in the hands of Albanians, the Serbian League of Communists came to be viewed as a virtual traitor to the Serbian nation.

The developing consensus was spurred by regular demonstrations of Serbs who left Kosovo after 1981. These manifestations of Serbian discontent became more open, more publicized, and more poignant as it became clear that the party could not answer the demands of these demonstrators. In time, however, the justified (or at least understandable) complaints of migrants from Kosovo took on surreal dimensions. The theme of migration of Serbs from Kosovo has a relatively long pedigree in Serbian national thought. Perhaps, then, it was inevitable that linkage of the distant past and the present would continue and even escalate. In May 1985, when a Serbian farmer from Kosovo named Djordje Martinović was found with a broken bottle in his anus, the story inflamed a Serbian public that was convinced that he had been "impaled" by Albanians.[31] Regardless of the truth of the story, the episode took on religious dimensions when the painter Mića Popović produced his "1. May 1985," depicting the suffering of Martinović. The importance of all of this for our purposes is not in the details (it does not matter whether Martinović impaled himself or was impaled); it is in the nature of the reaction to the event and the nationalist consensus that developed outside of the party as a result and the role that the idea of a reunited Serbia played in that consensus.

The consensus was prompted by intellectuals, the majority of whom represented two factions in Serbian society: one centered in the Serbian Academy of Sciences and Arts, the other in members of the Praxis Group, which consisted of a group of Serbian philosophers best known for their socialist-humanist opposition to Titoist Marxism-Leninism. Of the two groups, the first seemed far more likely to forge or join a nationalist consensus. Together, however, these intellectuals entered the fray regarding Kosovo in early 1986, when 200 of them produced a petition to the Serbian and Yugoslav national assemblies. The petition asserted that genocide (the word was used for the first time in this context) was being perpetrated against Serbs in Kosovo (and, meaningfully, Metohija)—the "ancient hearths" of the Serbian people.[32] Given the ethnic makeup of Kosovo, it is clear that for these intellectuals Kosovo was a constituent part of Serbia because of its history rather than its population. The response of the party to this petition and others signed by residents of Kosovo at the same time only confirmed to these outsiders that the party was still Titoist in every way.[33] And in fact, the party, in its insistence on "self-managed" solutions based on increased efficiency, missed the point. The issue was that change was "unimaginable without changes likewise in the relationship between the Autonomous Provinces and the Republic of Serbia. . . . [g]enocide cannot be prevented by the politics that had led to it in the first place: the politics of gradual surrender of Kosovo and Metohija—to Albania."[34]

There was little surprise that a portion of this new opposition would emerge from the Serbian Academy. Led by Antonije Isaković, the vice-president of the Academy and a leading Serbian author, whose work *Tren* 2 (Moment 2) had already established its author as an outsider and critic of Titoism, the Academy would in 1986 produce the well-known "Memorandum of the Serbian Academy."[35] A long document, the final section concerns the position of Serbia in Yugoslavia. The Memorandum blamed Tito, Kardelj, and the system they created for all of Serbia's ills. It was the crystallization of the thesis, first proposed by Ćosić in 1977, that the Serbian nation had suffered more and been rewarded less than any other.

If the general point of the Memorandum was that Titoism mistreated Serbs, then the way Titoism did this is equally crucial. The answer was simple: "[f]irst of all, it is the Serbian nation and its state that are being discussed." "[A]fter four decades in the new Yugoslavia, she alone does not have her own state."[36] Like Ćosić in 1968, the authors rejected the notion of a division between Srbijanci and prečani.[37] The main focus of the authors was Kosovo, but Croatia followed closely behind. If the "physical, political, legal, and cultural genocide of Serbs in Kosovo and Metohija" was one extreme in the continuum of Serbian suffering, then the belief that "excepting the period of the existence of the NDH [Independent State of Croatia], Serbs in Croatia have never in the past been so endangered as they are today" was the other.[38] The solution was "the establishment of a complete national and cultural integrity of the Serbian nation, regardless of which republic or province it is in, is its historical and democratic right."[39] "In order to satisfy the legitimate interests of Serbia, revision of the constitution is inescapably imposed [on us]. The autonomous regions must become true integral parts of the Republic of Serbia."[40]

The Memorandum, which was never openly released (only leaked to the public), met with a predictably weak response from the Serbian party leadership. Ivan Stambolić, the president of the presidency of the Serbian party, asserted that "we [communist party leaders] do not accept the Memorandum's call for Serbia to turn its back on its own future and the future of Yugoslavia, for it to arbitrarily accuse the proven leaders of the revolution and of socialist development, for Serbian Communists to be seen as the illegitimate leaders of the working class and people of Serbia."[41] The decline of the party's legitimacy in the eyes of the Serbian public could only accelerate in the face of such a weak response.

Where the party missed the point, others did not. Ćosić approved the Memorandum and defended the integrity of the academy.[42] But in many ways the Memorandum opened up new vistas. This was particularly true of its condemnation of the treatment of Serbs in Croatia. The opening of a Croatian front met with a strong response from Serbian historians, including Vasilije Krestić, Dragoljub Živojinović, Veselin Djuretić, Milan Bulaić, and Vladimir Dedijer, all of whom produced crude, ahistorical, yet influential works purporting to prove the existence of a Catholic conspiracy (or even, in Krestić's case, a genocidal determination) among Croats to eliminate Serbs.[43] The attack of Belgrade's intellectuals on Croatia was unprovoked and unfair, and led to an escalating series of polemics with Croats that eventually proved the Serbian prophecy correct: Croats did come to fear and despise the Serbia of the late 1980s.

The other half of the non-party opposition consisted of members of the Praxis group. Their position outside of the party had been long-established. Yet their opposition to the party had always been essentially Marxist. The fact that they now joined a nationalist consensus is thus intriguing and somewhat shocking. Four members of the group, Ljubomir Tadić, Zagorka Golubović,[44] Mihailo Marković, and Milan Kangrga had signed the January 1986 petition that first labeled Albanian behavior in Kosovo as genocidal. Their gravitation from Marxism to nationalism was abrupt. Their anti-Titoism was of long pedigree, and their democratic inclinations were well publicized. Their transition can be explained in two ways: their democracy, like that of other Serbs (and Croats, as well as others) was not rooted in a belief in individual liberties, rather it was founded on a collective conception of society and rights; and they found it easy to move from one homogenizing, collective ideology (class-based Marxism) to another (cultural-based nationalism). By the early 1990s, Marković was Milošević's intellectual alter-ego.[45]

Several intertwined oppositions to Titoist treatment of the Serbian population of Yugoslavia have been loosely delineated in this chapter. One, which was pioneered by Dobrica Ćosić in 1968, paved the way for all others, focusing on the need to reconstitute Serbia because its division opened the door to antiSerbian nationalisms as well as emphasizing some hoarier myths from Serbia's nationalist past. The Serbian party adopted portions of Ćosić's approach when, from 1974 to 1986, it supported a constitutional revision of the status of the Serbian republic, but rejected the notion of accomplishing that outside of a Titoist framework. Others outside the party adopted those elements of Ćosić's dissidence that were more than "revisionist": as we have seen, it included (despite his own protestations) elements that were overtly nationalistic. His fear/loathing of Albanians, his reliance on historical arguments for the reattachment of Kosovo and Vojvodina to Serbia, and his espousal of a broad Serbianism all foreshadowed another major faction in the Serbian opposition to Titoism, that which arose outside of the party in the mid-1980s after the president's death.

Both general approaches reached their fullest development in Slobodan Milošević's "anti-bureaucratic revolution," which began in 1988 and played on Serbs' hatred of the Titoist party and demanded a complete turnover in the party elite. Milošević took advantage of the general Serbian belief that the party did not have the capability to "end the terror in Kosovo."⁴⁶ Instead of droning on using Titoist phraseology about the ability of "self-management" to produce solutions, he took the old Ćosić idea of anti-bureaucracy and made it his own. This "anti-bureaucratic revolution," by cleansing the party, allowed Milošević to install his own men, who supported his new nationalist proclivities, whether cynically or not. Milošević thus achieved a historic fusion of the attitudes of the party and of the non-party oppositionists. From late 1987 forward, the now "revolutionary" party incorporated more and more of the ideas of the Serbian Academy nationalists and their non-party allies. The fusion could best be seen in the celebrations of the 600th anniversary of the Battle of Kosovo in June 1989. With the backdrop of the "field of blackbirds," on which the Battle of Kosovo was fought and which is considered by Serbs one of their sacred places, Milošević pronounced his determination to redress the balance of history. The Battle of Kosovo was lost due to "lack of unity and betrayal." "Therefore," he continued, "words devoted to unity, solidarity, and cooperation among people have no greater significance anywhere on the soil of our motherland than they have here in the field of Kosovo, which is a symbol of disunity and treason."⁴⁷ By linking the fate of a disunited Serbia in 1389 with that of the allegedly disunited Serbia of 1989, Milošević bridged the subtle revisionism of the Serbian party with the overt nationalism of the Memorandum authors.

CONCLUSION

This chapter demonstrates the existence of a long-term opposition to Titoism both in and out of the Serbian League of Communists based on the desire to see the divisions of Serbia eliminated; a movement, in other words, dedicated to the "reconstitution" of Serbia. Given that long-term commitment, and given the inability of the League of Communists to satisfy that demand in a thoughtful and methodical way, an aggressive nationalist movement was bound to emerge in Serbia. Beginning in 1968 and growing until 1991, opposition to the communist regime in Serbia focused most commonly on the dispersion of the Serbian people among a variety of federal units. And the ironies are endless (to outsiders, national mythology is always full of ironies): Kosovo, the one area of Yugoslavia with few Serbs, became the central goal of nationalists. Croatia, with its large Serbian population, remained a secondary problem (and remains so today).

Today in Serbia, the unanimity with which the major political parties treat the Serbian national question mirrors the strength of the idea over the previous 20 years. Today, it is impossible to conceive of a popular politician or party, and nearly impossible to conceive of a truly popular intellectual, who does not support the consensus that developed over the period from 1968 to 1991. It is true that today's consensus also reflects three years of war. But the fact remains that there were indeed few options to such a nationalist consensus. Dissidence in Serbia focused its hostility on the regime (just as dissidence did in other societies). The regime, for Serbs, meant the power that had punished Serbs when they should have been rewarded; meant the power that had divided Serbs ever more, and more importantly, divided Serbian lands. Reconstituting Serbia in an "ethnic society" was the goal.[48]

Notes

1. In the preparation of this chapter, the author was aided greatly by his participation in a National Endowment for the Humanities Summer Research Seminar in College Park, Maryland, entitled "Democracy and Ethnic Conflict in Eastern Europe," headed by Professor Vladimir Tismaneanu. I would like to thank several readers for their comments, including some strong and justified criticism that I could not respond to adequately at this point.

2. As Dennison Rusinow wrote in 1981, "concern for the fate of fellow-Serbs living as minorities in Croatia and also in Bosnia-Herzegovina, Montenegro, Kosovo, and elsewhere can and often does make the Serbs the most genuinely 'Yugoslav' of Yugoslavs." See Rusinow, "Unfinished Business: The Yugoslav 'National Question,'" American Universities Field Staff, Inc., *Field Staff Reports*, 35, (Europe: 1981), 11.

3. Sabrina Petra Ramet, *Nationalism and Federalism in Yugoslavia, 1962-1991*, 2nd ed. (Bloomington, IN: Indiana University Press, 1992), 255. Ramet uses the figures of Vladimir Zerjavić. It goes without saying that all figures for wartime demographic losses are debated endlessly by Serbs, Croats, and others. Aleksa Djilas borrows the numbers of another researcher, Bogoljub Kočović, who asserts that 869,000 South Slavs died in the war, 487,000 of them Serbs; see *The Contested Country: Yugoslav Unity and Communist Revolution, 1919-1953* (Cambridge, MA: Harvard University Press, 1991).

4. Ivo Banac, *With Stalin against Tito: Cominformist Splits in Yugoslav Communism* (Ithaca, NY: Cornell University Press, 1988), 106.

5. Ramet, *Nationalism and Federalism in Yugoslavia*, 20-21, 180, 206; see also Zdenko Antić, "The Dangers of Increasing Serbian Nationalism," *Radio Free Europe Research/RAD Background Report*, 63 (Yugoslavia: March 24, 1983), 2.

6. On Ranković's fall, see in English Steven L. Burg, *Conflict and Cohesion in Socialist Yugoslavia: Political Decision Making since 1966* (Princeton, NJ: Princeton University Press, 1983). For a Croatian perspective (by one of the members of the commission that built the case against Ranković), see Miko Tripalo, *Hrvatsko proljeće* (Zagreb: Globus, 1990), 69 ff.

7. On the situation in Kosovo before and after 1968, see Ramet, *Nationalism and Federalism in Yugoslavia*, 187-201.

8. By the late 1980s, this perception had become doctrine among Serbian nationalists. For one example, see Zoran Sekulić, *Pad i ćutnja Aleksandra Rankovića* (Belgrade: Dosije, 1989), 337: "Because it is hard to escape the impression that it was in fact the Sixth Plenum of the Central Committee of the League of Communists of Serbia [following the removal of Ranković] that opened the door widely to Albanian nationalism and separatism."

9. Dennison Rusinow, "Yugoslavia's Muslim Nation," Universities Field Staff International, *USFI Reports*, 8 (Europe: 1982).

10. Ramet, *Nationalism and Federalism in Yugoslavia*, 184-85.

11. For a discussion of the census categories that denied the existence of a separate Muslim group in Bosnia/Yugoslavia, see Dennison Rusinow, "Yugoslavia's Muslim Nation," *USFI Reports*, no. 8 (Europe: Universities Field Staff International, 1982) 4-5.

12. Jill Irvine, *The Croat Question: Partisan Politics in the Formation of the Yugoslav Socialist State* (Boulder, CO: Westview Press, 1993) 265-72.

13. Dobrica Ćosić, *Stvarno i moguće: Članci i ogledi*, 2d ed. (Ljubljana: Cankarjeva založba, 1988), 31.

14. This speech can be found in Ćosić, *Stvarno i moguće*, 27-38.

15. Ibid., 37.

16. The Croat Communist Miko Tripalo explained that "at that time, in the opinion of many people, Ranković personified the conception of bureaucratic-etatist socialism and the centralistic system in Yugoslavia." Thus both sides in the debate could claim to be fighting the effects of bureaucratism. See Tripalo, *Hrvatsko proljeće*, 69.
17. Ćosić, *Stvarno i moguće*, 31.
18. Ibid., 33.
19. Ibid., 36.
20. Ibid., 32.
21. Ibid., 35.
22. Mihailo Marković, "Tragedy of National Conflicts in 'Real Socialism': The Case of the Yugoslav Autonomous Province of Kosovo," in *Praxis International*, 9, no. 4 (January 1990): 409.
23. Ćosić, *Stvarno i moguće*, 36.
24. See Slobodan Inić, "Serbia's Historic Defeat," in *New Politics*, IV, no. 3 (summer 1993): 161-66; see also Burg, *Conflict and Cohesion in Socialist Yugoslavia*, 167-78.
25. For a series of good examples of such an approach, see the collection of speeches by Ivan Stambolić, *Rasprave o SR Srbije, 1979-1987* (Zagreb: Globus, 1988).
26. See Stambolić, "Za jedinstvo SR Srbije," in *Rasprave o SR Srbije*, 113 ff. Slobodan Milošević, of course, began his political career as a protege of Stambolić, and he could be heard to echo similar sentiments: "The working class and people of our republic . . . rightly expect from us, from the League of Communists, that we will eliminate disagreements in political relations and devote ourselves to the economic, cultural and general socialistic self-managed development of the republic and land as a whole"; Milošević, *Godine raspleta* (Belgrade: Beogradski izdavačko-grafički zavod, 1989), 126.
27. Stambolić, *Rasprave o SR Srbije*, 27.
28. This speech can also be found in Ćosić, *Stvarno i moguće*, 121-33. Also see Slobodan Stanković, "Conflict over 'Serbian Nationalism' Sharpens," in *Radio Free Europe Research/RAD Background Report*, 198 (October 4, 1977); and Zdenko Antić, "The Danger of Increasing Serbian Nationalism."

29. Ćosić, *Stvarno i moguće*, 126.
30. Ibid.
31. See Christopher Cviić, "A Culture of Humiliation," *The National Interest*, no. 32 (summer 1993): 79-82; and Atanasije Jevtić, *Stradanje Srba na Kosovu i Metohiji od 1941. do 1990* (Priština: Jedinstvo, 1990), 59-61, for two diametrically opposed renditions of this story.
32. The text of this petition can be found in English in Branka Magaš, *The Destruction of Yugoslavia: Tracking the Break-Up, 1980-92* (London: Verso, 1993), 49-52.
33. "Serbian Residents of Kosovo Sign Petition," FBIS Daily Report (9 Jan. 1986); "Serbian LC Reviews Events," FBIS Daily Report (9 Jan. 1986); "Serbian Presidency Discusses Problems in Kosovo," FBIS Daily Report (30 Jan. 1986).
34. Magaš, *The Destruction of Yugoslavia*, 51.
35. The memorandum has been reprinted in Bože Ćović, ed., *Izvori velikosrpske agresije* (Zagreb: školska knjiga, 1991), 256-300. In spite of the tendentious title, this is one of the few accessible copies of the memorandum, which has never been translated into English to this author's knowledge.
36. *Izvori velikosrpske agresije*, 287.
37. Ibid., 286.
38. Ibid., 288, 293.
39. Ibid., 297.
40. Ibid., 298.
41. "Stambolić Criticizes 'Memorandum' Authors," FBIS Daily Report (31 Oct. 1986).
42. Ćosić, *Stvarno i moguće*, "O memorandumu srpske akademije nauka i umetnosti," 155-61.
43. The crudest examples of this literature included Vasilije Krestić, "O genezi genocida nad Srbima u Nezavisnoj državi Hrvatskoj," in *Srpsko-hrvatski odnosi i Jugoslovenska ideja*, 2nd ed. (Belgrade: Nova knjiga, 1988) 339-68; and Dragoljub Živojinović and Dejan Lučić, eds., *Varvarstvo u ime Hristovo: Prilozi za Magnum Crimen* (Belgrade: Nova knjiga, 1988). On this literature, see Ivo Banac, "Historiography of the Countries of Eastern Europe:

Yugoslavia," in *American Historical Review*, 97, no. 4 (October 1992): 1100-103.

44. It should be mentioned that Golubović has been a harsh critic rather than an intellectual or political ally of Marković and other nationalist leaders in Serbia.

45. For an illuminating English-language example of Marković's ideas, see his "Tragedy of National Conflicts in 'Real Socialism.'"

46. Milošević, *Godine raspleta*, 267-68.

47. "Milošević Delivers Speech," FBIS Daily Report (3 July 1989).

12

"Serpent in the Bosom": Slobodan Milošević and Serbian Nationalism

Lenard J. Cohen

> Why did the Serbian people desire this great illusion named Slobodan Milošević? . . . I emphasize the Serbian people wanted the illusion. And it has been living quite long under this illusion, as you can see, despite all that has happened to them, and is happening.
>
> —Ivan Stambolić, 1995

Slobodan Milošević's manipulation of Serbian nationalism as a political tool during the late 1980s and early 1990s had a significant influence on the collapse of the "Second Yugoslavia," and also on the horrendous warfare that followed in its wake. In the context of the emotional political controversy surrounding the assignment of responsibility for the savage fighting in the Balkans, Milošević has frequently been described as an ultranationalist adherent of "Greater Serbianism," or even less generously pilloried as a "demagogue," "fascist," "war criminal," "butcher," or "bully." Considering the heated political climate and tendency to oversimplification prompted by the recent Balkan conflict, it is important to carefully reconsider and evaluate how and why Slobodan Milošević first achieved power during the twilight of the communist regime. This analysis will revisit the fascinating story of Milošević's emergence as a major figure in Serbian political life during the waning years of the Titoist regime, and also some important features of Serbian political culture that assisted his consolidation of political power.[1]

PRELUDE TO POWER:
THE AMBITIOUS YOUNG TITOIST

Slobodan Milošević was politically spawned and shaped by the very Yugoslav communist regime that he would eventually help destroy. Indeed, the features of Milošević's early political socialization, and his profound political metamorphosis during the second half of the 1980s, illustrate the internal dynamics, serious defects, and tortuous disintegration of the now defunct Yugoslav socialist experiment. The collapse of the communist regime, and the emergence of Milošević as the leader of the rump Yugoslav state, are two separate, but closely related stories.

Raised in a communist family—both his mother, a schoolteacher, and his father, a Serbian Orthodox priest, were party members[2]— Milošević's formal commitment to the values and organizational structure of the Yugoslav socialist regime had been nurtured well before his teenage years. Indeed, Milošević was literally a "child of the revolution." He was born on August 29, 1941, in the provincial city of Požarevac (about 100 kilometers southeast of Belgrade), only four months after Yugoslavia's dismemberment by Nazi Germany and its allies, and two months after Tito and the Yugoslav Communist Party began a guerrilla struggle against the fascist occupation and various anti-communist nationalist groups. During the period of Milošević's secondary education (1953-58), Tito's maverick model of communism evolved into a political amalgam comprised of a one-party oligarchy, a conservative police apparatus, a spurious federal system, and a novel structure of promising, but politically powerless, workers' councils. Young people during those years were expected to imbibe the values of "Yugoslav socialist patriotism," a belief system premised on the expectation that ideological bonds among "producers" would gradually transcend traditional ethnoregional forms of identity.

In 1959, at the age of 18, Milošević joined the League of Communists (until 1952 the Communist Party of Yugoslavia). A year later he entered law school at Belgrade University; the faculty that excelled in preparing educated officials for service in Serbia's communist establishment. While studying law in Belgrade during the first part of the 1960s, Milošević served as a secretary for ideological political work in the League of Communists' Belgrade University Committee, and subsequently became president of that committee's Ideological Commission. It was at law school that Milošević forged a close friendship with another young Communist, Ivan Stambolić. Stambolić, five years older than Milošević, was the nephew of Petar Stambolić, one of Serbia and Yugoslavia's leading communist officials. By the time he had met the well-connected Stambolić, Milošević was married to his high-school sweetheart, Mirjana ("Mira") Marković, whose father and uncle were prominent communist officials. The postsecondary education of the young Milošević couple, and their early working life, coincided with a decade of steady Titoist reform. It was also a phase when the regime officially recognized that the "national question" had reemerged as a major problem in Yugoslavia, and that social conflicts constituted a normal facet of a socialist society.

Milošević's friends from his law school days generally point out that the young Slobodan's commitment to Marxism was rather superficial, and that he tended to view adherence to communist orthodoxy primarily as a vehicle for career advancement.[3] In this regard, Milošević was not atypical of political activists from his particular generation and milieu. Indeed, he exhibited an exceptionally high aptitude for exploiting one of the most characteristic features of Titoist Yugoslavia (and other one-party states), namely, the use of patron-client networks for early career advancement. Milošević's major patron was Ivan Stambolić. Thus, during the two decades after Milošević's graduation from law school in 1964, Stambolić generously helped the younger Slobodan assume a succession of jobs that had already been pretested and successfully occupied by Stambolić himself. As Stambolić advanced up the economic and political ladder in Yugoslavia, the ambitious Milošević eagerly took advantage of posts offered to him by his successful comrade and friend. For example, after holding some minor posts in the Belgrade city administration, Milošević served (1970-73) as Assistant General Director under Stambolić at the enterprise, "Tehnogas," which manufactured industrial gases. He then followed Stambolić to become the firm's General Director (1973-78). In 1978, Stambolić, who had become the president of the Belgrade City Chamber of Commerce, also helped

Milošević to get appointed president of UBB (Udružena beogradska banka), one of Belgrade's leading banks.

ENTERING THE POLITICAL FRAY: SERBIAN POLITICS AND THE STAMBOLIĆ LINE

In 1982, after spending more than a decade as a political manager in the economic sector, Milošević followed Stambolić into the sharply factionalized and hardball world of Serbian politics. Stambolić, already a member of the communist establishment due to his family ties, had actively joined the Serbian political elite near the end of Tito's life. Serving as Prime Minister of Serbia in the late 1970s and early 1980s, Stambolić had responsibility for managing a large and important republic. Mastering the game of musical chairs among political professionals, referred to by Yugoslav communist officials as the "rotation of cadre," Stambolić made sure that his close friend, Slobodan, was not left standing idle. In 1982, while still a bank president, Milošević became a member of the Presidency of the Serbian League of Communists. That post, although a nonprofessional political position, served as an important vantage point from which to observe and become involved in the dynamics of his republic's power structure. He was also the president (another avocational position) of the Communal Committee in Belgrade's biggest commune, Stari Grad, a post that provided an important power base for his future political career. In spring 1984, Milošević assumed his first solo role as a leading Serbian political functionary when he became President of the City Committee of the League of Communists in Belgrade (a post that had been held by Stambolić from 1982 to 1984). Bound closely by ties of friendship and common perspectives, Stambolić and his friend Slobodan formed a unified team in Serbian political life. The younger and less visible Milošević was, however, clearly the team's junior partner.

During the early 1980s the Serbian communist leadership was preoccupied with three closely related negative legacies of the Tito era: first, an economic crisis growing out of structural problems in the economy and economic mismanagement; second, an internationality crisis traceable to the persistence of deep inter-ethnic conflicts; and, third, a political crisis arising from the general delegitimation of the long-ruling League of Communists. The political and economic crises were interdependent, and both crises stimulated, and in turn were exacerbated by the problem of ethnonationalism in the perennially fragile country. During the mid-1980s, the Serbian political scene was still dominated by the same clique of passive, obedient, and uninspired political leaders whom Tito had foisted on the republic a decade earlier. Tito's move had been connected with a purge of regional liberal leaders that began with the removal of independent-minded Croatian Communists in late 1971, and had subsequently spread to other republics. Thus, the political delegitimation of the Serbian communist leadership was well underway in 1981, when, only a year after Tito's death, the republic was hit by growing economic difficulties and a serious escalation of tensions between Albanians and Serbs in the province of Kosovo.

Lacking a strategy to deal with its multiple crises, the republic's weak communist establishment turned to its seasoned tactics of repression and drift in order to maintain power. Indeed, throughout the last decade of Tito's life, Serbian leaders had avoided taking any innovative steps with regard to the issue of politicized ethnicity. Thus, all non-socialist forms of ethnic participation were officially prohibited, while extreme or vocal expressions of nationalism on the part of any ethnic group were strongly condemned and often harshly punished. The regime's policy for dealing with resurgent nationalism was rarely consistent, or able to remedy the serious problems that motivated ethnic conflict. Although a violent outburst of nationalism by Albanian nationalists and their sympathizers in Kosovo during 1968 was quashed, Tito, together with the weak Serbian communist leadership, permitted Albanian communist leaders in Kosovo to consolidate their hold on the province's political machine.

For Serbs, Tito's policy in Kosovo amounted to a process of officially sanctioned Albanianization that, they believed, threatened the influence and survival of the local Serbian community in the province. When the prominent Serbian writer and longtime Communist, Dobrica Ćosić, warned in 1968 of dangers connected with League Albanian nationalism, he was promptly expelled from the league. Outside public view, however, intellectual concern regarding Serbian rights in Kosovo intensified during the 1970s, along with popular dissatisfaction with the regime's policy toward Serbian interests generally. The republican leadership's political position was further weakened by crudely managed repression of neo-Marxist dissidents and other political nonconformist Serbs in the mid and late

1970s, and also by the Belgrade regime's failure to adequately address the republic's looming economic problems. Thus, in the first years following Tito's death in mid-1980, the Serbian leadership faced a groundswell of dissatisfaction within both the general population and the ranks of the Serbian intelligentsia.

Ivan Stambolić tended to regard creative constitutional engineering as the best strategy for deflecting anti-communist and anti-regime criticism in Serbia. Like Stambolić, many Serbs felt that the republic's major economic and ethnic difficulties were fundamentally related to flaws in the 1974 federal constitution, which had essentially fragmented Serbia by granting the republic's two autonomous provinces, Kosovo and Vojvodina, near republican-level status. The devolutionary and divisive trends stimulated by the 1974 constitution were viewed by many Serbs as having encouraged Albanian nationalism in Kosovo, and stimulated a growing drive for political autonomy by leaders in Vojvodina. In order to rectify matters, and also to reverse the regime's debilitated image, many Serbian leaders argued for a full-scale revision of the 1974 constitution.

The outbreak of the 1981 round of Albanian nationalist demonstrations in Kosovo once again brought the issue of provincial powers and ethnic relations within Serbia to the top of the political agenda. Thus, during the first part of the 1980s, Ivan Stambolić would have to spend much of his time trying to assuage an upsurge of Serbian dissatisfaction by dangling the promise of constitutional and economic reforms that would, he maintained, reassert Serbian paramountcy vis-à-vis its two provincial units, as well as improve the republic's alleged weakness within Yugoslavia. While such claims identified problems and raised expectations, promises of eventual constitutional change did not resolve immediate ethnic and economic discontent. Thus, political resentment against the constitution and regime grew, while gratification continued to be postponed.

Throughout this period, Stambolić attempted to calm the atmosphere in Serbia and reassure communist leaders in the other Yugoslav republics. Thus, while downplaying the dangerous political potential of assimilationist policies favored by extreme Serbian ultranationalists, he was not reluctant to speak out against the growing chorus of strident Serbian nationalism that had appeared both within and outside communist ranks. For example, in May 1985 at a meeting of the Serbian Central Committee dealing with ideology, Stambolić warned against any "reconciliation" between Partisan perspectives on nationalism and the officially discredited view of the anti-communist Chetniks. "Nationalist views and action," Stambolić insisted, "must be beaten everywhere and at all times. We have realistically grasped this danger and have tried to examine its roots and causes." Stambolić also cautioned that Serbian Communists must take a "permanent militant attitude to nationalistic poisoning of the young."[4]

During the entire period from roughly 1981 through early 1987, Slobodan Milošević appeared to adhere very closely to the Stambolić line. Indeed, statements by Milošević regarding political matters amounted to little more than ritualistic incantations of accepted Titoist orthodoxy, and uninspired variations of the latest views espoused by Stambolić. For example, at the May 1985 Serbian Central Committee Meeting on Ideology, Milošević, who was the first speaker on the roster, attacked efforts by the "old dogmatic opportunists" and new anti-communists to "question the fundamental values" of Yugoslav society, including the "reality of the concept of brotherhood and unity." Milošević's ostensible orthodoxy and loyalty to his sponsor were rewarded in early 1986 when Stambolić advanced Milošević's name as the sole candidate for the important post of President of the Central Committee of the Serbian League of Communists.

Stambolić hoped that Milošević could assist him in obtaining a moderate resolution of Serbia's internal problems, and also improving relations with the other republics. In April 1986, just one month before securing Milošević's promotion as leader of Serbia's Communists, Stambolić had visited two communities in Kosovo Polje, the heart of Kosovo's Serbian ethnic community. During his visit, Stambolić had urged that "paranoia and 'ghosts'" be placated, and he pleaded for "disinformation which introduces confusion to be prevented." Stambolić also commented on the serious threats to the security of Serbs in Kosovo, on the unfortunate emigration of Serbs and Montenegrins out of the province, and on the need to challenge "irredentists" and "separatists." But the Serbian leader also warned his listeners that they should not seek to resolve their local difficulties by a broader mobilization of Serbian nationalist solidarity, especially through rallies and demonstrations. "This is a great evil and is playing with fire," he warned.[5] One year later, the citizens of Kosovo Polje would receive another guest from the Belgrade communist leadership. However, the second visitor's response to Serbian concerns in Kosovo would depart significantly from the Stambolić line.

MILOŠEVIĆ'S METAMORPHOSIS: "POWER ABOVE IDEAS"

In late September 1986, the Belgrade newspaper, *Večernje Novosti*, published sections of a draft "Memorandum" that had been under preparation by members of the Serbian Academy of Arts and Sciences (SANU) since May 1985. Serbia's top political leaders were aware that the SANU document was being written, but had no idea of the controversial details that would soon engender a firestorm of critical comment throughout Yugoslavia. Among other things, the Memorandum asserted that since before World War II, when the Comintern directed the underground Communist Party of Yugoslavia, Yugoslav communist leaders had adopted policies contrary to Serbian interests; a longtime anti-Serb coalition had existed between Croatian and Slovenian Communists that was responsible for Serbia's growing difficulties; the anti-Serb coalition had deliberately weakened Serbia by strengthening the power of the republic's two provinces, and; except for the period of the Independent State of Croatia during World War II, the position of the Serbian minority communities in Croatia and Bosnia-Hercegovina had never been worse.[6]

The events set out in the Memorandum were also alleged to have contributed to the communist regime's repression of the Serbian cultural intelligentsia in Yugoslavia, as well as the dire situation reputedly faced by the Serbs of Kosovo. In essence, the Memorandum characterized the entire Titoist approach to the "national question" as an elaborate deceit and failure that had seriously harmed Serbia, and also had stimulated interethnic and inter-regional conflict throughout the country. Although the solutions recommended by the Memorandum's authors indicated their loyalty to Marxist political ideals, and to the potential reformability of socialist Yugoslavia, their attack sharply undercut the political and constitutional legitimacy of the Titoist regime.[7] As for Serbia itself, the Memorandum urged that after "four decades of Serbian passivity," it was time for the republic "to define and declare its own national interests." Only through "Social Democracy," and the assertion of Serbian equality in Yugoslavia, the Memorandum suggested, could Serbs overcome the legacy of an "historically worn-out ideology."[8]

The publication of the Memorandum naturally added grist to the mill of those political forces in Yugoslavia, and also in Serbia, who believed that the Serbian Communist leadership was committed to the goal of restoring Greater Serbian hegemony on both the republican and federal levels. Thus, Stambolić and his leadership group were immediately forced to respond to the controversial contents of the Memorandum, and also to adopt an attitude toward the Serbian Academy and Serbian intellectuals who had prepared the document. Interestingly, Milošević, who for years had passionately voiced his devotion to Titoist precepts regarding internationality relations, adopted an unusually cautious and ambiguous approach to the Memorandum. For example, his remarks about the Memorandum at a February 1987 meeting of the Belgrade City Committee of the League of Communists amounted to a lukewarm and rather hesitant condemnation of the SANU members who, he suggested, must change their views and exercise "responsibility toward their communist consciences."[9] Although Milošević took a somewhat harsher view of the Memorandum behind closed doors, he left public condemnation of the document's contents to Stambolić and other Serbian party leaders.

Polemics concerning the Memorandum continued to preoccupy Serbian politicians throughout the late fall of 1986. In early 1987, however, attention once again shifted to Kosovo as relations worsened between the province's Serbs and Albanians.[10] Near the end of April, Milošević was invited to make an official visit to Kosovo Polje—a journey Ivan Stambolić encouraged him to accept—where the Serbian community was politically mobilized and in a state of considerable agitation. On April 24, at 8:30 in the evening, Milošević and local Albanian communist leaders arrived at the hall of Kosovo Polje's cultural center *(Dom kulture)*, where an unexpectedly large crowd of approximately 15,000 Serbs and Montenegrins had gathered to meet the visiting communist officials. The crowd surged forward chanting slogans, and trying to break through the police cordon in order to speak directly to Milošević. When Milošević and his delegation finally entered the hall the crowd outside began shouting insults and throwing stones at the building and windows. Members of the crowd again tried to break through police lines and into the building, but they were brutally clubbed and beaten back by the police (composed mainly of Albanian officers). Informed of what was taking place outside, Milošević exited the building and approached the still highly volatile crowd. According to reports at the time, the Serbian leader was visibly upset and physically shaken. When a dialogue ensued between the demonstrators and Milošević, they complained to him about the rough police tactics. Milošević quickly responded with his soon-to-be legendary remarks: "No one will be allowed to beat you! No one will be allowed to beat you!"

Acting on a journalist's suggestion that he reenter the hall and speak to the crowd though a window, Milošević invited the demonstrators to send in a delegation to discuss their grievances. That meeting was to last twelve hours and would become a major benchmark in contemporary Serbian history. As the crowd outside dissipated, Milošević listened to a litany of complaints by local Serbs and Montenegrins. It was one of those rare occasions in Eastern Europe when a high communist official was forced to come face to face with the views of the working class, in this case, the aggrieved members of the shrinking Serbian and Montenegrin ethnic group in Kosovo. Before leaving Kosovo Polje, Milošević reassured the members of his audience that they were entitled to reside safely in Kosovo, and to struggle for their rights. "We must not let the misfortunes of people to be exploited by nationalists," Milošević told those who remained. "We must preserve brotherhood and unity as the apple of our eye." But, he added: "We cannot and we do not want to divide people into Serbs and Albanians *but we must draw the line that divides the honest and progressive people . . . from the counter-revolutionaries and nationalists on the other side*" (emphasis added). "This is your country," he told the audience, "your homes, your fields, your gardens, your memories are here. Surely you will not leave your land because it is difficult to live there and you are oppressed. . . . You should stay here because of your ancestors and because of your descendants. Otherwise you should disgrace your ancestors, and disappoint your descendants."[11] At the conclusion of his remarks, Milošević reassured the Serbs and Montenegrins that "Yugoslavia does not exist without Kosovo. Yugoslavia disintegrates without Kosovo, Yugoslavia and Serbia will not give Kosovo away."[12] It was a remarkable exchange between members of an angst-ridden ethnic community and a communist official who was still by no means the advocate of their ethnic interests. And it was a remarkable performance by a communist functionary whose previous speeches and style were hardly dramatic or exceptional among his peers.

The intensity of the views advanced by the demonstrators at Kosovo Polje in their dialogue with Milošević undoubtedly had a major impact on both his perception of the seriousness and depth of nationalist feeling in the province, and also his subsequent decision to derive political capital from politicized nationalism. Milošević certainly recognized, well before his arrival in Kosovo, the political benefits that might accrue from a skillful use of Serbian nationalist grievances. However, the particular dynamic of the episode at Kosovo Polje, and the results of his intuitive response to the demonstrators, constituted the elements for a major turning point in Milošević's, and ultimately Serbia's, political development.[13] Serbian analysts who have researched the events of April in Kosovo Polje claim that the episode had a profound affect on Milošević's behavior as a politician. When he arrived at Kosovo, he had been a cautious and reserved Titoist apparatchik offering the population words from a lexicon of well-honed and officially condoned platitudes. Leaving Kosovo, Milošević had acquired a far more intimate appreciation of nationalist sentiments in Serbia—feelings that the local Serbs regarded as legitimate defensive or reactive nationalism—and also the limitations of existing Serbian communist methods and policies to address those concerns. After Kosovo Polje, one observer noted that Milošević was "a different man."[14] He had still not determined, however, just how to exploit his revelation and opportunity.

As word of Milošević's Kosovo meeting spread among Serbs within and outside Serbia, his popularity rapidly grew. The Serbian leader's instinctive decision to protect the demonstrators against the police was interpreted as a sign of bravery and Serbian patriotism. The nature and setting of his encounter in Kosovo Polje—a nighttime meeting in an unimpressive hall located in a remote European province—hardly seemed the stuff of momentous historical change. But for the nationally downtrodden Serbian psyche, and for many members of the Serbian intelligentsia searching for an event to excite national consciousness in the general population, Milošević's visit to Kosovo Polje began to take on certain idealized and romantic overtones.

Prior to April 1987, Milošević had rarely commented officially on the situation in Kosovo. During the mid-1980s, like other Serbian leaders, Milošević had supported the idea of amending the 1974 constitution in order to reassert Serbian control over its provinces. In one meeting of the Serbian Central Committee held in November 1984, he had also made some interesting remarks about the need of Serbian Communists to liberate themselves from a sense of guilt about the historic nationalism of the Serbian bourgeoisie. On the contrary, he observed that Serbian Communists were untainted by "unitarism," had no reason to cover their heads in shame, and should say what they think.¹⁵ At the time, such remarks were not unusual or at odds with dominant Serbian communist thinking and the Stambolić line. After his April 1987 encounter in Kosovo Polje, however, the issue of Serbian-Albanian relations and Kosovo became frequently recurring themes in Milošević's speeches. The Kosovo experience had undoubtedly changed Milošević's outlook in many respects, but he still had not decided how or when to openly break with his fellow leaders regarding the matter of nationalism, and particularly its growing attraction to the Serbian intelligentsia. Milošević was on the verge of playing his own "national" card, but only after he had completely prepared the political ground. Meanwhile, he took the occasion of a closed meeting with Communists from the Federal Secretariat of Internal Affairs on June 4, 1987—just ten weeks after the episode in Kosovo Polje—to make an uncharacteristically impassioned attack on the infamous Memorandum.¹⁶ Considering his remarks in light of the policies he would later espouse, and the impact of those policies on the disintegration and aftermath of the Second Yugoslavia, Milošević appears to have been a master of political guile who was willing to both attack and forecast his own course of action. Only a short time after making this speech, Milošević would begin appropriating and encouraging viewpoints that he had earlier condemned as examples of the "darkest nationalism," and within a year would also coopt many of the Memorandum's authors and supporters as an intellectual brain trust.

During mid-1987, Ivan Stambolić's position within the Serbian elite and federal political leadership was significantly weakened by various factional struggles and intrigues within both the higher ranks of the League of Communists and the military establishment. It was at this juncture that Milošević decided to step completely out the shadow cast by his former mentor and friend. The pretext for Milošević's move was a controversial news conference held on September 11, 1987, by Dragiša Pavlović, the president of the city committee for the Belgrade League of Communists (who had held the job since 1986 when he had replaced Milošević).¹⁷ Most of Pavlović's comments—made to a political group composed of chief editors from the media and local party secretaries—offered a relatively moderate and sensible assessment of how the League could best manage growing nationalism in Serbia, and particularly the grievances of Kosovo Serbs regarding Albanian nationalism. Pavlović warned that a dangerous atmosphere had arisen in Serbia, and that any sober words uttered against ascendant Serbian nationalism were wrongly being construed as yielding to Albanian nationalism. In preserving their rights, Pavlović cautioned, the Serbian people "must not be led astray through wrongly chosen methods of struggle.... Inflammatory words result in nothing, but a conflagration."[18] Pavlović was clearly encouraging Serbian public leaders to exercise responsibility when dealing with the highly incendiary "national question." But his remarks were also undoubtedly a thinly veiled indictment of Milošević's intemperate response to the demonstrators at Kosovo Polje the previous spring, not to mention the media's sensational celebration of that incident during the following months. Still riding the wave of his experience in Kosovo, where he had established a special plebiscitarian-type bond with the province's aggrieved Serbs, Milošević was in no mood to accept such criticism from one of his junior colleagues in the Belgrade political establishment.

On September 18 and 19, 1987, at the Eighth Session of the Central Committee of the Serbian League of Communists, Milošević, together with a coalition of prominent Serbian political and military figures that he had been assembling over the past several months, launched a sharp assault on Dragiša Pavlović and his policies. Their major target was the leading moderate and antinationalist in the Serbian political leadership, Ivan Stambolić. At Kosovo Polje in April, Milošević had cannily identified the instrument necessary for his political advancement; now, less than six months later, he began to openly wield that political tool. Milošević had also undoubtedly determined that the substance and style of his future approach to Serbian-Albanian relations, and more broadly toward the assertion of Serbian interests within Yugoslavia, could be modelled on the emotional and populist dynamics of Kosovo Polje. Having committed himself to this new course of action, Milošević had also made the coldblooded decision to completely end his past alliance and mentor-follower relationship with Ivan Stambolić.

The Eighth Session turned into an intense and lengthy debate between Serbian party moderates and Milošević's adherents. Many members of the latter group had only recently migrated over to Milošević's side. Such repositioning derived from a variety of motives, including the issue of Serbian nationalism. Faced with a torrent of criticism and a proposal for his dismissal, Pavlović attempted to explain his earlier remarks, claiming that he may have "exaggerated something," and that at his news conference he did not have

Milošević or the Serbian party leadership in mind. Stambolić proved more pugnacious in standing up to the new Milošević line. Pavlović was being thrown out, Stambolić observed, because "in one of his [Pavlović's] sentences Slobodan Milošević or some others saw an allusion to themselves."[19] Stambolić chastised Milošević for always speaking about party "unity," but taking measures which actually encouraged dissent in the ranks of the league. He also urged his formerly junior colleague to "manifest a greater degree of ability" and to avoid conflict. After all, Stambolić lectured Milošević, "nobody is right about everything and nobody is wrong about everything."[20]

When Stambolić had completed his remarks Milošević took the floor, and denounced Stambolić's efforts to personally link him with the assault on Pavlović, claiming that such remarks were "insulting" to the Central Committee Presidium. As the session came to an end, Milošević remained unapologetic about his orientation to the issues under debate, and was especially enigmatic in his commentary about Serbian nationalism. Removing Pavlović was not a "purge" or "squaring of accounts," Milošević claimed. He further observed that it was

> politically unacceptable for the leaders of the Serbian League of Communists to be threatened with accusations of Serbian nationalism. Serbian nationalism today is not only intolerance and hatred of another nation or nations, but is itself a serpent deep in the bosom of the Serbian people. . . . Serbian nationalists would do the greatest harm to the Serbian people today by what they offer as being allegedly the best thing, namely isolating the Serbian people. . . . No one can label us Serbian nationalists because we want to, and really will, resolve the problem of Kosovo.[21]

Close observers of Serbian politics generally regard the Eighth Session as the moment Slobodan Milošević took control of Serbia. For his part, Milošević's former mentor, Ivan Stambolić, had signaled his political death in defending Dragiša Pavlović and personally attacking Milošević. Thus, at the conclusion of the Eighth Session, Pavlović was removed from his position on the Serbian Party Presidium (he had already resigned from the Belgrade Committee). Stambolić was replaced as president of Serbia's collective presidency in mid-December 1987. Not long afterward he left political life and resumed a career in the Serbian economy.[22]

For some observers, such as several Serbian opposition journalists from the Belgrade weekly, *Vreme*, the SANU Memorandum has been viewed as being the intellectual impetus and framework for the Eighth Session. Thus, it has been argued, the authors and supporters of the Memorandum constituted a kind of "nationalistic pseudo-opposition" ready "at the signal" to endorse Milošević.[23] According to this perspective, members of the intelligentsia who, only a few months earlier, Milošević had accused of endorsing "the darkest nationalism," actually engaged in a tacit or secret alliance with the Serbian leader in order to ensure his political victory. What seems more likely, however, is that Milošević, buoyed by his newfound popularity and seeking to expand his power through the immoderate style as a leader in mass interaction that he had experienced at Kosovo Polje, had decided to push aside Stambolić and other moderate Serbian communist leaders. While it is still not known exactly what contacts occurred between Milošević and the authors of the Memorandum during the summer of 1987, it does not appear that by the time of the Eighth Session in September, Milošević had fully consolidated his ties with the leading nationalist intellectuals; although he was undoubtedly counting on their tacit support, and was preparing to unabashedly appropriate various components of their nationalist platform. The Memorandum, as Stambolić would later observe, represented the "great divide" between two factions in the Serbian League of Communists: "the dogmatists (potentially nationalistic) and the reform currents."[24] Sensing the mood in Serbia, after his long night at Kosovo Polje, the ambitious Milošević deftly took advantage of the split in party ranks and enlisted the dogmatists and disgruntled nationalists in order to topple the principal reform figure who stood in his way.

EXPLAINING MILOŠEVIĆ'S APPEAL: PATRIOTISM AND POLITICAL CULTURE

Answering the question of why Milošević chose to play the nationalist card is easier than explaining the reasons why his ethnic constituency found his appeal so attractive, and also how he managed to retain popular support during the recent and extremely difficult stage of Serbian national development. As Gale Stokes has aptly pointed out, political leaders typically adopt nationalist programs in order to acquire and maintain power. What is more difficult to understand is why the message of such leaders so often proves successful.[25] Thus in one sense, Milošević's rise to power can be viewed as a classic case of unbridled political ambition and brilliant political opportunism. In that regard, Aleksa Djilas has correctly described Milošević's exploitation of nationalism as an inspired "act of political cannibalism" by a Communist seeking to develop a new legitimating formula for his politically bankrupt but still power-hungry party machine. Thus, Djilas observes: "The opponent [of the Communists], Serbian nationalism, was devoured and its spirit permeated the eater. Milošević reinvigorated the party by forcing it to embrace nationalism."[26]

But beyond the all too familiar drives and cynical methods of power-seeking politicians, Milošević also intuitively understood and could effectively express the nationalist yearning of large numbers of Serbs on both the elite and popular levels. Indeed, Milošević's presumptuous decision to become the "voice" of the Serbian people, his shifting political tactics toward apparent friends, close associates, and former opponents, and also the strident tone of his statements on behalf of Serbian interests, all represented the kind of pragmatic and plebiscitarian political style that has had a deep resonance in the Serbian and Balkan body politic.

COLLECTIVIST NATIONALISM AS A CULTURAL DIMENSION

Jettisoning the political constraints and exhausted platitudes of the Titoist apparatus, Milošević's political techniques and methods clearly exhibited many aspects of the "heroic," patriarchal, and aggressively patriotic characteristics associated with Serbian political culture. While many "national-anthropological" features of Serbian political tradition are often deprecated by educated and urban Serbs, those attitudes remain deeply engrained facets of Serbian political life. Milošević not only clearly perceived what was troubling the majority of his ethnic brethren, he also very shrewdly anticipated how they would respond to his rhetoric and problematic remedies. Thus, the hundreds of thousands of Serbs who attended rallies organized by the Milošević-controlled Serbian Communist Party machine during 1988 and 1989 did not feel they were exponents of radical, expansionist, or potentially violent nationalism, but rather supporters of a genuine and long overdue outpouring of democratic patriotism.

While aspects of political repression, electoral chicanery, and media manipulation would later emerge as prominent components of Milošević's management style, his political ascendancy and initial consolidation of power depended as much on factors having to do with the cultural underpinnings of the Serbian polity, as on its structural features. Granted, during his early ascent to power, Milošević patiently consolidated his hold on the machinery of Serbia's League of Communists, both in Belgrade and in the republic's smaller towns, and also on winning the votes of party officials for his move against Stambolić. But, he also shrewdly appreciated the way in which the cultural components of Serbian society could work in his favor. Thus during the second part of the 1980s, Milošević appealed to patriotic sentiments, which were deeply rooted in Serbian political culture, as a means to enhance his popularity within the Serbian working class, agricultural population, employees of the state apparatus, and segments of the intelligentsia. Milošević discerned that many urban and highly educated Serbs with liberal-democratic leanings might view his reliance on mass rallies and "street democracy" as expressions of authoritarian manipulation. However, he recognized that most Serbs would regard such populist tactics as an appropriate method with which to forge the traditional linkage between strong Serbian leaders and the Serbian people; a legitimating bond that had the added value of circumventing the established intermediacy of discredited communist bureaucrats and the largely powerless edifice of "self-managing" institutions.

In his early career as an enterprise manager and a bank president, Milošević exhibited signs of non-ideological pragmatism, which lead some observers to believe that he was a committed liberal technocrat and a modernizer. However, at the time, few appreciated his talent and appetite for power, and also his very unusual chameleonic character. Moreover, in view of the fact that he was politically socialized in the oppositionless and bureaucratic environment of the Tito regime's restricted pluralism and that in the early 1980s he became deeply enmeshed in the network of patron-client communist recruitment, it is hardly surprising that the ambitious Milošević ultimately utilized political techniques drawing upon the illiberal facets of Serbian political culture. An inventory of such historically shaped facets of that political culture would include: support for traditionally centralized modes of political control; a popular penchant for "heroic leaders" who can maintain political order and preserve the "unity" of the nation; a disinclination to accept the rules-of-the-game that would allow the fragmentation of the Serbian nation among different Balkan political units (or, in other words, would allow minority status for Serbs within a multi-national state dominated by other ethnic groups); and an exaggerated emphasis on sanguinity ("Serbian blood and origins"), territorial control, and national religious myths as defining features of collective identity.[27] Such features might be regarded as the dominant components of the traditional Serbian elite and mass political mindset, although—particularly in the modern history of urban Serbia—such perspectives are certainly not all-pervasive or unchallenged by important strands of liberal thought and outlook.

While it is analytically difficult, and even dangerous, to extrapolate from the presence of such dimensions in the historically conditioned Serbian political mindset directly to contemporary and current political dynamics, the importance of cultural factors in understanding Serbian politics should not be ignored. Indeed, many analysts of Balkan historical development have pointed to the important role of patriarchal patterns stemming from tribal society, and especially the *zadruga* form of landholding and family organization, as major elements shaping contemporary Serbian political culture.[28] Thus although important elements of "democratic" participation—for example, the right of members of the community to openly express their individual ambitions and views—can be identified as dimensions of tribal society and the *zadruga* system, the overall collectivist nature of the patriarchal legacy gives the Balkan notion of democracy a "somewhat different meaning than in the Western world."[29]

Under the strong influence of the patriarchal tradition, it has been argued, the meaning of democracy in Serbian and other Balkan contexts came to include strong imperatives for politicians and policies to reach unanimity, to overcome minority nonconformism, and to assert the "sole truth." The influence of patriarchal and aggressively patriotic components of Serbian political culture appear to be particularly strong among Serbs living in, or originating from, the Dinaric areas of the Balkan region, which include most of Bosnia-Hercegovina, southwestern Serbia, southeastern Croatia, and Montenegro.[30] Dinaric Serbs are characterized as extremely patriotic, and having a highly developed "consciousness of nationality." For example, according to the ethnographer, Jovan Cvijić, who provided a rich and detailed, if rather idealized, portrait of Dinaric Serbian characteristics: "Dinaric people feel themselves just as closely connected with their national heroes as with blood relatives."[31] According to Cvijić, Dinaric Serbs have a consuming and often violently expressed commitment to the "national mission." Moreover, he asserts: "They will stop at absolutely nothing. It does not matter in the least if they 'drown in blood' so long as they preserve the heroic traditions, their great name and their 'sacred freedom.'"[32]

Cultural explanations of Serbian politics cannot, of course, neglect the influence of western liberal values in Serbian society and intellectual circles, especially during the nineteenth and twentieth centuries. However, it is the illiberal facets in the Serbian political legacy reinforced by the long period of Ottoman rule, and subsequently by one-party communism,[33] that appear to be predominant and most enduring. Thus while enthusiasm for "instinctive democracy," "self-determination," and "democratic" participation are often noted as major components of the Serbian "national character," it has been frequently observed that Serbian political culture places even more emphasis on the value of strong leaders who can achieve their community's national mission and constrain tendencies toward "democratic chaos"[34] and "excessive individualism."[35]

If deeply engrained facets of Serbian political culture provided especially fertile soil for Milošević's patriotic populism and antiestablishment rhetoric, survey research during the late 1970s and early 1980s has also revealed that popular Serbian attitudes congruent with such cultural expectations and values remained highly salient dimensions of the prevailing political mood. Surveys conducted by the Belgrade Institute of Social Sciences, for example, pointed to an increasing disenchantment with, and abandonment of, regime-sponsored values connected with self-management socialism, and also a growing preference for a "traditional syndrome" of beliefs. Thus, survey results demonstrated an emerging or reemerging mentality in Serbian society that reflected a deep strain of authoritarianism. Such attitudes were highly supportive of social conformism, egalitarianism, and a immoderate devotion to preferred political leaders that bordered on "idolatry."[36] Aspects of what are characterized as an "authoritarian syndrome" were particularly apparent among the agricultural population in the rural and underdeveloped regions of Serbia, as well as among unskilled, semiskilled, and highly skilled industrial workers.

"PATRIARCHAL PATRIOTISM" IN THE INTELLIGENTSIA

Milošević's alliance with sections of the Serbian cultural intelligentsia during the second part of the 1980s also represented a fascinating case where reemergent "patriotic" political values converged with mutual political interests. For the savvy Milošević, the creative intelligentsia and particularly the SANU intellectuals, represented an established opposition bloc that needed, from his perspective, to be coopted and contained. They were also a group, Milošević calculated, that could provide an intellectual underpinning for his national-patriotic program. Meanwhile, many of the intellectuals who had broken with the communist regime, and who now espoused an eclectic blend of nationalist and communist views, saw Milošević as a unique opportunity to advance their own agenda. For many intellectuals, Milošević represented the first Serbian politician since Aleksandar Ranković (removed by Tito in 1966) who was willing to remain ideologically committed to socialism, but still take a strong stand on behalf of Serbian national interests. Thus by the summer of 1988, Milošević was closely collaborating with the authors of the Memorandum, or the same intellectuals he had conveniently criticized during 1986 and 1987.

Badly disappointed by the failures and repression of the communist regime, many of the SANU intellectuals, and their peers, reverted to a framework of beliefs that has usefully been characterized as "patriarchal patriotism." Among other things, such views prescribe a "morality of simple but inflexible duties towards one's nation."[37] Thus, many of the intellectuals embracing such patriotic attitudes found it profitable to idealize Milošević as the personification of the best Serbian political principles and traditional values. For example, Antonije Isaković, the president of the SANU commission that prepared the Memorandum, claimed that Milošević's mode of behavior and policies combined the positive features of the nineteenth-century Serbian politicians, Karadjordje (Djordje Petrović, known as Kara or Black Djordje) and Miloš Obrenović; the first political figure allegedly exhibiting the principles of a well-meaning revolutionary nationalist, and the second leader typifying aspects of an "evolutionary" but essentially pragmatic, conspiratorial, and sometimes ruthless (Obrenović eventually murdered Karadjordje) administrator and politician. While most Serbs, including his supporters, often characterize Milošević's aloofness and reclusiveness as rather "strange" behavior, Isaković's sycophantic and rather defensive description of the same traits illustrates how such idiosyncrasies may be perceived and recast as qualities that serve the interests of the nation.[38]

Viewing Milošević's alliance with the SANU intellectuals in retrospect, some Balkan and foreign analysts have incorrectly assumed that the Serbian leader sympathetically observed the preparation of the Memorandum during 1985 and 1986, and plotted from the very outset to exploit its general principles as part of his own pursuit of power.[39] It would also be wrong to assume that the blueprint for the entire course of events connected with the disintegration of Yugoslavia, the subsequent wars in Croatia and Bosnia, and various policies such as "ethnic cleansing," were all part of some master plan or conspiracy hatched by Milošević and a coterie of Serbian intellectuals during the 1987-88 period.

What can be concluded, however, is that after an initial political career (1982-87) in which he exhibited no traces of an aggressively nationalist orientation, Milošević decided—once having seen that Ivan Stambolić had turned his back on the politically rich opportunities deriving from Serbian ethnic grievances, and after having experienced the potential force of those grievances at Kosovo Polje—to utilize nationalism as a political weapon. Only after removing Stambolić, did Milošević establish a calculated alliance with the SANU academicians in order to give his views a patina of intellectual respectability and coherence. He thereby also obtained an important vehicle for disseminating and defending his policies in the Serbian media and Serbian cultural circles. In his drive to maintain and enlarge his power after 1987, Milošević selectively appropriated the views and energies of leading Serbian national ideologues. But it was Milošević's interests, instincts, and imperatives, not the Memorandum or its authors, that guided Serbian policy in the 1990s and ultimately provoked the violent disintegration of the Yugoslav communist federation. Thus as the political situation evolved in the decade after 1987, Milošević would frequently demonstrate his willingness to callously, and even ruthlessly sacrifice those Serbian nationalists who previously appeared to be his close friends and allies. Unlike most Balkan politicians in the 1990s for whom power was a means to achieve their nationalist goals, for Milošević nationalism was simply the paramount instrument to achieve and solidify political power. Astutely understanding his cultural milieu, he knew precisely how to package and convey such nationalist appeals, and also when to adopt a new style of political discourse.

Milošević's political pragmatism and nonideological style also contributed to his appeal among segments of the intelligentsia that had previously remained more or less committed to the communist regime. For example, Milošević was able to coopt a small subgroup of neo-Marxist dissidents who had conducted a protracted struggle with the political establishment throughout the 1970s and early 1980s. Thus, well-known and vocal Belgrade University professors such as Mihajlo Marković and Svetozar Stojanović—whose espousal of participatory forms of socialist democracy and ideological distance from the Tito regime had made them the darlings of the neo-Marxist community around the world—decided (like the SANU intellectuals who had broken completely with the League of Communists in the 1960s and 1970s) that Milošević's creatively mixed cocktail of skin-deep socialism and Serbian patriotism justified their return to the mainstream of what was still a one-party regime. Meanwhile, most members of the communist cultural intelligentsia in Serbia, who had worked loyally for the regime, simply continued their allegiance to Milošević as the new head of the political establishment.[40]

Milošević's appeal to the communist and neo-Marxist intelligentsia was clearly enhanced by the political role of his wife. Mirjana Marković's well-known communist family background,[41] and her orthodox Yugoslav communist views, provided a natural bridge to sections of the intelligentsia who had remained suspicious of Slobodan Milošević's break with Titoist policy on the national question, and uncomfortable with his unconventional populist tactics. Thus in 1988, Mirjana Marković would help coordinate a "hard Marxist-Leninist core" at Belgrade University where she worked as a sociology professor. In October 1989, she also became more directly involved in the Belgrade City League of Communists. Following the advent of multiparty politics in 1990, she emerged as a top leader and chief ideologist of the League of Communists—Movement for Yugoslavia, which served as an adjunct to Milošević's newly formed Socialist Party of Serbia (a reconfigured combination of the Serbian League of Communists and the Serbian Socialist Alliance) in maintaining links to conservative communist politicians, military officers, and pro-regime intellectuals. Like her husband, who brazenly and often reiterated his opposition to nationalism (despite the connection of his policies at various times with the most aggressive and egregious aspects of Serbian patriotism), Mirjana Marković has frequently maintained that she is repelled by the explosion of nationalist views in the 1980s and 1990s, not to mention extreme policies that contributed to "Serbian apartheid."[42] As with many other communist and neo-Marxist intellectuals, Milošević's wife—who has been his closest political confidante—undoubtedly has felt, or has needed to convey, that she has been participating in a patriotic (as opposed to a nationalistic) regime devoted to socialist principles.

Although Milošević was successful at coopting the bulk of the patriotic dissidents at SANU, as well as most neo-marxist and communist intellectuals, a sizable portion of the intelligentsia, and especially the anti-communist nationalists and the small group of liberal-democrats, remained steadfastly opposed to his regime. Personal and political divisions within the ranks of the anti-Milošević intelligentsia, however, made it difficult for them to mount a viable opposition during the late 1980s, or even after the advent of pluralist politics in the early 1990s. Moreover, once Milošević was ensconced at the summit of the socialist regime, and could claim to be the official representative of Serbian national interests, it became very difficult for his intellectual opponents to attract popular support on the basis of their own patriotic programs. Indeed, often unwilling to completely transcend or forego the emotional and illiberal components of their own appeals to Serbian nationalism, the self-styled "liberal opposition" often found it difficult to either steal Milošević's thunder, or claim they were offering citizens a genuine democratic alternative.[43] Meanwhile, in the climate of the 1980s and early 1990s,[44] those few Serbian intellectuals who did advance a truly non-nationalist and liberal democratic program were largely marginalized and ostracized.

Looking back at Milošević's political career during the last phase of the communist regime, one is most impressed by his proficiency in utilizing specifically Serbian notions of patriotism and democracy as a means of sustaining a diverse coalition of seemingly incompatible constituencies. As incisive journalists from the Belgrade magazine, *Vreme,* have observed: "He succeeded in tricking both the Communists and the nationalists; the Communists believed he was only pretending to be a nationalist, and the nationalists that he was only pretending to be Communist."[45] Caught up in their yearnings to overcome the perceived political subordination of the Serbs in Yugoslavia, few of Milošević's supporters during the second half of the 1980s fully considered where his still evolving and ostensibly patriotic program would eventually lead. Those that did speak out regarding the dangers of runaway Serbian nationalism, either within or outside the League of Communists, proved powerless to resist the culturally based infatuation with Milošević on the part of so many of his ethnic brethren. Thus, having successfully consolidated his hold on the communist regime from 1987 to 1989 using his wily admixture of socialist and nationalist rhetoric, Milošević would go on to successfully utilize the same factors—complemented by the perks and full technology of modern state power (he was elected the last communist President of Serbia in May 1989)—to win several competitive, albeit not fully democratic, elections in the 1990s.

It was only after 1992, when the citizens of Serbia began to experience for themselves the full consequences of the Second Yugoslavia's disintegration, and especially the negative effects of war-related difficulties and international sanctions, that Milošević could no longer depend upon Serbian nationalism as a tool for power maintenance and political mobilization. Perhaps it was the politically ill-fated Ivan Stambolić who has offered the best insight into the changing tactics of Slobodan Milošević:

> He came to power by advocating my policy, he broke with me and with his wife's policy when he adopted the policy of the Serbian nationalists, he thereby disintegrated Yugoslavia and ushered in a war. By accepting the policy of the international community he now [1995] wants peace! And if he does have a policy of his own, it's a policy of retaining power.[46]

Notes

1. This chapter is the initial report of a broader inquiry into Serbian politics and Milošević's career that will subsequently include a discussion of his political management of Serbia, the sources of his political support, opposition to his rule, and also the disturbing legacy of his policies and methods.

2. Milošević's mother and father, who were both of Montenegrin origin, separated after the war. His father left for Montenegro where he worked as a language teacher at a religious high school, while Slobodan and his brother (who regards himself as a Montenegrin) stayed with their mother. Both of his parents later committed suicide; his father in 1962, when Slobodan was on a student excursion in Russia, and his mother in 1973.

3. Stephen Engelberg, "Carving Out of Greater Serbia," *New York Times Magazine*, (1 September 1991), 23.

4. *BBC Summary of World Broadcasts*, EE/7939/B/1, May 1, 1985.

5. *BBC Summary of World Broadcasts*, EE/8229/B/6, April 10, 1986.

6. *Nacrt memoranduma Srpske Akademije Nauka u Beogradu* (Toronto: Srpske Narodne Odbrane, 1987).

7. Aleksandar Pavković, "The Serb National Idea: A Revival, 1986-1992," *Slavonic and East European Review*, 72, no. 3 (July 1994): 440-55.

8. *Nacrt memoranduma Srpske Akademije Nauka u Beogradu*, 41-42.

9. Slavoljub Djukić, *Kako se dogodio vodja: borba za vlast u Srbiji posle Josipa Broza* (Belgrade: Filip Višnjić, 1992), 189.

10. The following two paragraphs draw heavily on Djukić, ibid., 122-30.

11. *Foreign Broadcast Information Service, Daily Bulletin Eastern Europe* (hereafter *FBIS*) (April 27, 1987), 17.

12. Ibid., 18.

13. In September 1995, Milošević's wife told the BBC that prior to his going to Kosovo Polje she and her husband had discussed "how he should speak and what he should say. I felt that he should speak constructively, offering the Serbs the support that belongs to them." *"Vreme" News Digest Agency* (hereafter *VND*), November 13, 1995, no. 215. Ivan Stambolić claims that prior to the trip to Kosovo, he had warned Milošević "not to yield to emotions," but that Milošević "succumbed to the atmosphere. He even fueled the fire." *Put u bespuće* (Belgrade: Radio B-92, 1995), 167.

14. Djukić, *Kako se dogodio vodja*, 127.

15. Slobodan Milošević, *Godine raspleta* (Belgrade: Beogradski izdavačko-grafički zavod, 1989), 34.

16. Internal Bulletin of the League of Communists in the Federal Secretariat of Internal Affairs, "Naše aktuelnosti," (June 1987) cited in *VND*, no. 99 (August 16, 1993), 15.

17. Milošević had been unenthusiastic when Pavlović was brought into the political elite by Ivan Stambolić. Two years younger than Milošević, Pavlović had completed the faculties of both machine engineering and economics, and had a doctorate in political science. Djukić, *Kako se dogodio vodja*, 108-9.

18. *FBIS*, (October 8, 1987), 49-51.

19. *FBIS*, (October 16, 1987), 62.

20. Ibid. Stambolić would later admit that he had been "set-up" by Milošević. Stambolić also claims that he had reservations about Milošević when he advanced him for high office, and had received strong warnings about

Milošević's character from others. Stambolić recounts that he ignored such warnings, believing that he could control Milošević's "vices," or that they would "disappear." Stambolić, *Put u bespuće* (Belgrade: Radio B-92, 1995), 135-36, 138-39, 141.

21. *Nedeljne informativne novine* (hereafter *NIN*), no. 30, 1918 (October 4, 1987), 12-13.

22. His successor was retired General Petar Gracanin. Pavlović's views on the Eighth Session can be found in *Olako obecana brzina* (Zagreb: Globus, 1988).

23. Miloš Vasić, Roksanda Ninčić, and Tanja Topić, "A Tired Serbia," *VND*, no. 52 (September 21, 1992), 5.

24. Stambolić, *Put u bespuće* (Belgrade: Radio B-92, 1995), 131.

25. Gale Stokes, "Cognition, Consciousness, and Nationalism," *Ethnic Studies*, 10 (1993): 27-42.

26. Aleksa Djilas, "A Profile of Slobodan Milošević," *Foreign Affairs*, 72, no. 3 (summer 1993): 87.

27. For the impact of Serbian historical patterns on political culture, see Dunja Melcic, "Communication and National Identity: Croatian and Serbian Patterns," *Praxis International*, 13, no. 4 (1993): 360-63, and Paul Hehn, "Man and the State in Serbia, From the Fourteenth to the Mid-Nineteenth Century: A Study in Centralist and Anti-Centralist Conflict," *Balkan Studies*, 27, no. 1 (1986): 3-27.

28. For important studies of this aspect of Serbian political culture as it relates to democracy and the mobilization of nationalist sentiments, see Jovan Cvijić, *Iz društvenih nauka* (Belgrade: "Vuk Karadžić," 1965), 79-135; Vladimir Dvorniković, *Karakterologija Jugoslovena* (Belgrade: Kosmos, 1939), 193-250; Slobodan Jovanović, "Jedan prilog za proučavanje Srpskog nacionalnog karaktera," in *Sabrana dela Slobodana Jovanovića* (Belgrade: Beogradski izdavačko-grafički zavod, 1990), 12, 543-82; Vera St. Erlich, *Family in Transition: A Study of Three Hundred Yugoslav Villages* (Princeton, NJ: Princeton University Press, 1966), 373-93; Jozo Tomasevich, *Peasants, Politics and Economic Change in Yugoslavia* (Stanford, CA: Stanford University Press, 1955), 192-97 and 247-49; Olivera Buric, "The Zadruga and the Contemporary Family in Yugoslavia," in Robert F. Brynes, ed., *Communal Families in the Balkans: The Zadruga* (South Bend, IN: University of Notre Dame Press, 1976), 117-38; and Ivan Lučev, "Socijalni karaktera i politička kultura," *Sociologija*, no. 1 (1974): 23-41.

29. St. Erlich, *Family in Transition*, 393.
30. Milošević's Montenegrin family background and also his origins in Sumadija place his roots squarely in the "Dinaric Zone."
31. Jovan Cvijić, "Studies in Jugoslav Psychology (I)," *The Slavonic Review*, 9, no. 26 (1930-31) 381.
32. Ibid., 383. It is important to note that aspects of the syndrome of Dinaric characteristics described by Cvijić and other analysts are also exhibited by members of several Balkan ethnic groups, and particularly by Croats and Moslems living in the Dinaric zone.
33. Zagorka Golubović argues that the mentality and operation of Yugoslavia's communist state bureaucracy—including its monopoly over the agencies of political socialization—reinforced traditional habits and attitudes despite the self-management system. Zagorka Golubović, *Kriza identiteta savremenog Jugoslovenskog društva* (Belgrade: Filip Višnjić Vičnjić, 1988), 285-391.
34. Cvijić, "Studies in Jugoslav Psychology (I)," 383.
35. Nearly a half century ago, for example, such dual and seemingly contradictory features of Serbian political culture were noted by Cvijić in his incisive inventory of Serbian folkways. "The whole national tradition is democratic in trend. It is true that we have a long succession of famous emperors, heros, and martyrs: but the Serbs regard this in a way of their own . . . one does find individual persons or families who seem to have a natural instinct towards leadership: and for this reason people consider that we have undemocratic tendencies. These are individual cases however, and do not occur often." Jovan Cvijić, "Studies in Jugoslav Psychology (II)," *The Slavonic Review*, 9, no. 27 (1930-31): 676-78.
36. The discussion of survey results that follows is based on several studies by Dragomir Pantić (Belgrade: SSO Srbije, 1981); "Odnos mladih prema (inter)nacionalnom, zatvorenost-otvorenost prema svetu," in *Omladina '86: Sondaža javnog mnjenija* (Belgrade: Kultura, 1986), 136-59; *Klasična i svetovna religioznost* (Belgrade: Institut društvenih nauka, 1988), and *Promene vrednosnih orientacija mladih u Srbiji* (Belgrade: Institut društvenih nauka, 1990).
37. Aleksandar Pavkovic, "Intellectuals into Politicians: Serbia 1990-1992," *Meanjin*, 52, no. 1 (1993): 107-16. Pavkovic argues that the Serbian cultural intelligentsia is strongly attached to patriotic values expressed in traditional Serbian folk epics, nineteenth century Serbian literature, and

historiography. In his opinion, both patriotically oriented intellectuals, and those who were more attracted by the European liberal tradition, rejected communist rule.

38. *NIN*, no. 2158 (May 8, 1993), 18-21. As an example of the Miloš Obrenović style of behavior, Isaković gave the example of Milošević's willingness to support the interests of the Krajina Serbs in Croatia—in the name of "all Serbs living in one state"—and then (in 1992, after the cease-fire in Croatia and the arrival of UN peacekeeping troops) to pragmatically inform Krajina leaders that such a position was no longer tenable. The Belgrade journalist, Slavoljub Djukić, has described Milošević's distinctive patron-client relationship with intellectual subordinates in a rather less favorable light than Isaković: "Tito never had as much control and influence over his supporters as Milošević does . . . there is a tremendous division between the first man [of Serbia] and all others. While alongside Tito there arose many personalities of considerable capability, Milošević has gone in an entirely opposite direction. . . . Among [his] Socialists there doesn't exist a second and third personality as you found Kardelj, Ranković and Djilas next to Tito. . . . Between Milošević and his party comrades there exists an unbridgeable gap. . . . Between Milošević and his allies and enemies there is no hate, nor love or disappointment, and least of all any ideological burden. Only raw interest exists. People are [politically] secure, only if they are indebted. In general one does not deal with biographies." *NIN*, no. 2285 (October 14, 1994), 29.

39. It is true that since the late fall of 1984, Milošević had become associated with the view that Serbs should not feel guilty about expressing their patriotic feelings, or have a "complex" about the misdeeds of Serbs in the past. Moreover, there is also evidence that while Milošević played the role of a loyal member of the Stambolić team, his wife, Mirjana Marković, was ambitiously laying the groundwork in Belgrade's intellectual and political circles for her husband's political advancement. For example, she has observed that it was in November 1984 that her Belgrade circle of left-wing university intellectuals (and presumably her husband who spoke out in the same vein at the time) began their "just and fine struggle for the national affirmation of all the interests of the Serbian people in Yugoslavia." She also claims, however, that by 1989 various "primitive" nationalists perverted such legitimate cultural and national sentiments into "aggressive nationalism." *Odgovor* (Belgrade: BMG, 1993), 209; and *Noć i dan* (Belgrade: BMG, 1994), 163-64. I am indebted to Chip Gagnon for directing my attention to Marković's views on this issue.

Milošević's wife also had played a key role behind the scenes at the important Eighth Session of the Central Committee of the Serbian League of Communists (drafting his speeches, communicating with allies, and so on). However, Milošević appears not to have established a close working political relationship with the Memorandum authors until mid-1988, that is, a year after his visit to Kosovo Polje, and months after he played the nationalist card against Pavlović and Stambolić in the latter part of 1987.

40. Milošević could also count on the loyalty of conservative political and managerial elites on the local level throughout Serbia, who—particularly in the less-developed and rural areas—were more interested in job security than democratic reform or economic change. See Silvano Bolčić, "Nejednakosti i protivrečnosti u preobražavanju nedovoljno razvijenih područja u Srbiji," in Mihailo V. Popović, et al., eds., *Srbija krajem osamdesetih* (Belgrade: Institut za socioločka istraživanja, 1991), 193-240.

41. Milošević met his future wife, Mirjana Marković, at the beginning of secondary school. Her mother, Vera Miletić, was shot during the war when she was head of the Belgrade Communist Party organization. Mirjana's father was Moma Marković, an influential communist political leader for several decades, and her aunt was Davorjanka Paunović, who was Tito's secretary and mistress during the war.

42. *Washington Post*, (17 June, 1993), 5.

43. For interesting discussions of problems faced by the democratic opposition, see Srdja Trifkovic, "Illiberal Legacy in Former Yugoslavia as an Impediment to Market Reforms," *Serbian Studies*, 6, no. 4 (fall 1992): 5-20; Vladimir Gligorov, "The Discovery of Liberalism in Yugoslavia," *East European Politics and Societies*, 5, no. 1 (winter 1991): 5-21; and Srdja Popovic, "Political Opposition in Serbia," *New Politics*, 4, no. 4 (winter 1993): 91-97.

44. For the views of one of Serbia's leading non-nationalist intellectuals, see Vesna Pesić, "The Cruel Face of Nationalism," *Journal of Democracy*, 4, no. 4 (October 1993): 100-103.

45. Vasić, Ninčić, and Topić, "A Tired Serbia," 6.

46. Stambolić, *Put u bespuće* (Belgrade: Radio B-92, 1995), 151.

Conclusion

The Yugoslav Experience in Comparative Perspective

Valerie Bunce

The purpose of this volume has been to reassess the evolution of socialist Yugoslavia—from the victory of the Partisans during World War II to the recent and calamitous collapse of socialism and the state. This reassessment has brought together an impressive array of specialists from a broad range of disciplines. What we gain from their analyses are richly detailed interpretations of various aspects of political, social, economic, and cultural developments in Yugoslavia over the past 50 years. These interpretations, it must be noted, involve analysis of new as well as old data. They represent, as a consequence, a valuable contribution to our understanding of Yugoslavia, past and present.

Such informed judgments are particularly welcome at this time. There has been a pronounced tendency of late for analysts as well as policymakers to misread the history of Yugoslavia (while holding forth in confident fashion on its central themes), and to fall back in their explanations of the current war in that unhappy land on simplistic stereotypes—of Yugoslavia, the Balkans and, more generally, such complex concepts as ethnic identity and nationalism.[1] These overly simplified and misleading interpretations of Yugoslav developments are far from accidental. Yugoslavia is in the news and thus invites commentary from all who feel a need to have a voice in contemporary affairs. Moreover, it is far easier to cite "ancient ethnic hatreds" and the like as the cause of the war than to go through the laborious task of tracing its antecedents in detail. It is also face-saving—for western policymakers at least—to locate the causes of this war in the march and mess of Balkan history than to target blame on the actions taken (and not taken) by western governments and international institutions.

More generally, the richness of these chapters reminds us—the recent observations of transitologists to the contrary[2]—that one of the costs of the end of the state socialism has been a sharp decline in the quality of intellectual dialogue on Eastern Europe. The region as a whole has been transformed overnight into what is arguably the most popular destination for social scientists seeking data and social engineers seeking an outlet for their advice. The end result is that anyone and everyone now seems to feel qualified to put forward their own interpretation of political, economic, and social developments throughout the post-communist region.

If there are clear gains to be had from assembling experts from a number of disciplines to ponder the rise and fall of both socialism in Yugoslavia and Yugoslavia itself, there are also some unavoidable costs to such a convocation of specialists. The main cost is that it is easy to lose sight—in the mounds of data and in the specificity of the arguments—of the larger issues posed by the evolution of socialist Yugoslavia. What can be lost, in particular, is a comparative perspective that would allow us to rethink the socialist experience, to identify what is unique to Yugoslavia and what is not, and to provide answers to questions that have significance beyond the borders of what was once Yugoslavia.

The purpose of this chapter is to provide such a comparative perspective. I will begin by making some observations about what the chapters in this work have to say to some larger issues in the study of socialist systems. I will then add a comparative perspective to what could be termed *the* underlying issue of this volume; that is, the end of the Yugoslav state.

PLACING THE YUGOSLAV EXPERIENCE IN A LARGER SOCIALIST CONTEXT

When taken together, the chapters in this volume help us rethink some of the most cherished generalizations we have developed about socialist systems. One example is the question of popular support for the revolution. The common wisdom has been that communist regimes that came to power as a consequence of a popular revolution (as in Yugoslavia, the Soviet Union, and China) were more stable and their parties in a stronger position to carry through on their ideological agenda than communist regimes that came into existence as a consequence of Soviet geopolitical concerns after World War II (for instance, Romania, Poland, and the German Democratic Republic). The most obvious contrast in this regard is between Poland—where limited popular support for communism at the time of the "revolution" worked by all accounts to weaken the regime, exacerbate conflicts between the regime and the society, and dilute the revolutionary thrust of the party's policies—versus the example of Yugoslavia, where popular support for the revolution was understood by most analysts to have contributed to a stronger regime, more pacific relations between the regime and the society and, finally, a heightened capacity on the part of the party to carry out an innovative program of self-managing socialism at home and nonalignment abroad.

The logic of this argument seems unassailable. Popular support should translate into political capital and thus into a certain freedom of policy maneuvering for party leaders. However, what emerges from the work presented in this volume is quite a different conception of the costs and benefits of popular support. In particular, what we see is a ruling socialist party that is burdened by three factors, *all* of which arise, interestingly enough, from its empowerment through a popular revolution. The first was the fear of losing support.[3] The second constraint was the existence of an already mobilized public, willing and able to express their preferences. The third was the presence within the party of a number of leaders who were in a strong position to claim independent bases of political support.

When combined, these factors suggest that being popular was in fact a *problem* for the Yugoslav Communists. Popularity limited the policy agenda of the party; it led to significant gaps between decisions made and the actual implementation of those decisions; and it challenged at times (through intraparty conflict and through public protests of the everyday type as well as of the more spectacular type) the very stability of the system. Thus, the usual contrast when comparing socialist systems between the benefits of public support versus the costs of having little such support begins to muddy, once we look in greater detail at the Yugoslav experience.

Indeed, one could go even further. It might be the case that unpopular communist parties had certain advantages—at least in the early years. They had little to lose, and they operated within an environment wherein publics were demobilized and party leaders deprived of separable and powerful constituencies (especially after 1948, with the Sovietization of these ruling communist parties). These purportedly vulnerable communist parties were empowered, in short, by their political weakness. There is much in this interpretation, for example, which helps us make sense of developments in Romania and the German Democratic Republic.

Another common generalization that is challenged by the arguments in this book is that communist power was highly institutionalized, because these regimes featured so many institutions that through their numbers and their interdependent relations allowed for extraordinary penetration by the party of social, political, cultural, and economic life. Indeed, the institutional density of communist systems led many to go even further by assuming that organizational density led to regime durability, albeit with the proviso that this was joined with a factor working in the other direction; that is, negligible public support. Even the rapid and sudden collapse of state socialist systems has not altered this assumption. Rather than question the institutionalization of the system, analysts have tended to locate the causes of the end of communism to such factors as minimal and declining public support, the deterioration of the economy, and the destabilizing consequences of the Gorbachev reforms.

By contrast, what this work suggests (and what the collapse of communism reinforces) is that we should reconsider our equation of institutional density with institutional strength. First, what was striking in Yugoslavia over its final ten years of existence was the rapid decomposition—or at least territorial fragmentation—of party and state institutions. If these institutions were strong and rooted, this should not have happened. Moreover, while we might understand the rapid mobilization of publics into protest movements in Yugoslavia and elsewhere as indicative of institutional decay or the contradictions generated by state socialism,[4] we might also think of these processes as testimony to the incomplete institutionalization of state socialism. We can further buttress this interpretation by noting the following: If we map the introduction of new political and economic institutions in socialist Yugoslavia over time, we find that the creation of new institutions was less an indicator of institutional strength than a recognition of institutional weakness. It was also less a contribution to expansion of the party's penetrative capacity than an exercise in creating yet more institutional layers to the system. Thus, the repeated introduction of new institutions and the resulting proliferation of institutions over the course of socialist rule—a pattern that was echoed throughout Eastern Europe—cannot be so easily equated with either the notion of growing institutionalization or with the notion of growing institutional strength. In this case, quantity spoke to the absence of quality, and this was apparent long before publics mobilized, the economy deteriorated, and Gorbachev came to power.[5]

The essays found here also complicate some of the distinctions we have traditionally made in analyzing state socialism. One such distinction is between the party and the state. It was commonplace in the "old days" (that is, before the end of state socialism in Europe) to make a great deal of the fact that there was a dual party and state apparatus and to focus on such questions as conflicts between the party and the state. However, what seems to emerge from this volume is the defining importance of intraparty conflict, not party-state conflict and less the notion of the party and the state as separate and competitive institutions than the party-state as a conjoined network of relationships. In this sense, the fate of the party was also the fate of the state. This is why, for example, the end of Communist Party hegemony was followed in four of the nine cases in the region (the Soviet Union, Yugoslavia, Czechoslovakia, and the German Democratic Republic) with the rapid disappearance of the state, and why in the remaining post-communist cases the state is so weak.

More generally, the Yugoslav case (and the Soviet and Czechoslovak cases as well) carries two further lessons. It reminds us that it is better to think of "stateness" as being on a continuum (with Yugoslavia's losing its stateness from the 1970s onward and its republics gaining statehood during the same period), rather than to think in the familiar dichotomous terms of state versus non-state. It also reminds us that, for state socialism at least, the distinction between regime and state is a hard one to make. To a large extent, because of the fusion of politics and economics and the monopolistic role of the party in both arenas, the regime was nearly coterminous with the state. Again, this helps explain the issue of state collapse after state socialism. Post-communism, therefore, is not just a change in regime; it is also a change in the state.

This also brings home the point that post-communist transitions are quite different from other cases of democratization—as in, say, Latin America and southern Europe.[6] They are simultaneously exercises in democratization *and* state-building—a combination that, at least in historical comparative terms, renders post-communism far more like the post-colonial Third World experience than like contemporary Latin America and southern Europe. This is not to mention, moreover, the other peculiarities of the post-communist experience—in particular, the construction as well of capitalism and the reconfiguration of the state's relationship to the international system.

Finally, the chapters in this book alert us to some important methodological issues in the analysis of communist and post-communist states. One issue is the bias of knowing the end of the story. One is struck, for instance, by the fact that so many of the recent studies of the end of Communist Party rule seem to lead to a single conclusion; that is, that state socialism as a system was doomed from the beginning. This might be the case. However, one cannot help but be suspicious of arguments that claim inevitability, especially when the "inevitable" took so long to materialize (for example, more than 70 years in the Soviet case), and such conclusions are drawn only after, but not before the fact.[7]

Let us now take these observations to the Yugoslav case. Some analysts in this work have constructed their studies of developments in Yugoslavia over the past 50 years in order to account for the collapse of socialism and the state. This is understandable, if the purpose of the study is to explain the end of the regime and the state. However, this seems to be even the case in those studies where the purpose is to address quite different developments taking place long before the end of Yugoslavia and Yugoslav socialism. What I am suggesting is that there is some pressure to provide what might be termed a "linear" Yugoslav story. This is despite the fact that the end of Yugoslavia does not have to be understood as the culmination of a long-term process of decay. It could be explained, for example, as a function of some very bad decisions taken at crucial moments in the last years of its existence; as a reflection of the fact that what the system did well was less relevant in its later years than what the system did badly; as a consequence of the fact that the structure of the system was set up to maximize power, but not to defend power; or as the result of a series of actions that were external to the operation of the system, but that nonetheless had powerful systemic consequences—for example, interventions in Yugoslav affairs by the International Monetary Fund in the 1980s,[8] the introduction of the Gorbachev reforms, the collapse of communism in the Soviet bloc, western disarray in response to the mounting crisis in Yugoslavia and, finally, pressures by Germany on its allies to proceed with quick recognition of Croatia and Slovenia.[9] The point is that one can assume that Yugoslavia was a viable entity for much of its existence, just as one can assume that socialism was a viable system for much of its existence. Such assumptions, moreover, fit in well with long-term historical patterns of regime survival.[10] The fact is that socialism was, by comparative historical standards, a rather durable system.[11]

A second methodological issue introduced by this volume is that the very phrasing of the question we want to answer shapes the very explanations we develop and thus the variables we choose to emphasize or ignore. How we pose our questions, therefore, is critical. For example, should we ask why the Yugoslav economy performed so poorly, or should we ask the obvious question posed by taking a longer term perspective; that is, why the Yugoslav economy performed so well for so long? It is striking that answers to the first question often leave us at a loss when trying to answer the second question. To take another example: should we ask why Croatian nationalism kept rearing its head, or why (despite its purported importance and durability) it was in political evidence for so few years of postwar Yugoslav history? Finally, we would have very different arguments about the end of Yugoslavia if we merely asked the question of why the state collapsed than if we also asked what is an equally interesting and equally plausible question; that is, why did the Yugoslav state, despite its many problems, last so long? In the first case, the many burdens on socialist Yugoslavia would occupy the center stage and the adaptive mechanisms of the system would be minimized, whereas in the second case, the focus would be on the interaction between adaptive mechanisms and the many problems of the system. The result would be two very different pictures of the historical evolution of socialist Yugoslavia. One would be a kind of linear free fall, whereas the second would be a more variegated picture.

WHY DID THE YUGOSLAV, SOVIET, AND CZECHOSLOVAK STATES COLLAPSE?

This brings us to the second purpose of this commentary; that is, to use comparative reasoning in order to analyze state termination after the end of Communist Party hegemony. This is an ideal issue for the purpose of comparison, because Yugoslavia was not the only state in the region to exit after the collapse of Commmunist Party hegemony. This is also what happened in Czechoslovakia and the Soviet Union. What makes such a comparison even more apt is that it introduces variance as well as similarities. While all three states ended, it was only in Yugoslavia where there was (and is) a violent parting of ways between the center and the periphery. While Serbia (and Serbs in areas outside Serbia) has used violence in order to defend the territorial integrity of the Yugoslav state and then to refigure the boundaries of the new states in the region, the dominant republic in the other two cases—that is, Russia and the Czech Republic—did not. As a result, the division of Yugoslavia has been extraordinarily violent, whereas the division of the Soviet Union and Czechoslovakia was peaceful—at least at the time the state was formally ended.[12]

The first question posed by a comparison of Yugoslavia, Czechoslovakia, and the Soviet Union, then, is the following: Why did these states end? We can answer this question by referring to the interaction among three factors, two of which are common to all states in the region and the third that is distinctive to these three cases. First, the end of Communist Party hegemony weakened the state, and this is why every case of state termination in the region follows the particular sequence of the end of the communist regime first and the end of the state second. As already noted, the state was vulnerable, because of the close interdependence between the state and the party and, thus, the regime and the state. However, there is another factor of equal importance. The party-state system was composed of a dense network of atomized individuals who were connected in one-on-one fashion with other atomized individuals.[13] Thus, the commonly noted atomization of society in state socialism had its equivalent within the party-state—a factor that was ignored by many analysts. One consequence of this was that the party-state was externally strong, because of its monopoly, but internally quite weak. Another consequence was that it was poorly structured to defend itself when its authority was decisively challenged. This explains, for example, why communist parties did not in most cases put up a real fight when they lost political power. It also explains why the collapse of the party's monopoly also involved a considerable weakening of the state. Stripped of its party connections and reduced to its atomized linkages, the state was necessarily fragmented and vulnerable.

Second, the end of communism was also the end of the postwar international order. It was this order—primarily through the operation of bipolarity (though some would add nuclear weapons)—which enforced the maintenance of state boundaries throughout Europe from the end of World War II to the end of the 1980s. While many took this situation to be the norm, it was not. States have risen and fallen throughout history, sometimes peacefully and sometimes through a violent process. There is nothing immutable about states—especially, we must remember, in Europe.[14] Moreover, when international orders end, state boundaries tend to change—as witnessed, for example, in eastern Europe in particular after World Wars I and II. Thus, with the end of the Cold War international order, state boundaries were once again open to reconfiguration. The weakness of the post-communist state, moreover, facilitated this process as did the poor correspondence between national and state boundaries throughout eastern Europe, the stresses of post-communist transitions and the national legacies of state socialism. The final point is crucial. It is decidedly not that state socialism functioned to repress national identities and international tensions; rather, it was that it created in many cases and in many ways those identities and those tensions.[15] Thus, just as the states in the region were quite vulnerable to challenges to their authority "from below," so they began to lose the guarantee of their sovereignty "from above." Juridical stateness in a post-Cold War period could no longer be a cover for weak states.[16]

These two factors—the weakness of the state after communism and the disintegration of the Cold War international order—go a long way toward explaining the end of the state after state socialism. However, they do not explain why some communist states survived into the post-communist era while others did not. How can we distinguish, in particular, between Albania, Romania, Bulgaria, Hungary, and Poland, on the one hand, and Czechoslovakia, the Soviet Union, and Yugoslavia, on the other? It is here where the third factor becomes crucial; that is, the presence or absence of a federal system. It is not accidental that the three federal states in the region were also the only three socialist states that subdivided into multiple units. It is also not accidental that the boundaries of the new states that came into being were precisely the boundaries of the republics that once made up the Soviet, Yugoslav, and Czechoslovak federations.[17] What, then, is the relationship between federalism and state dismemberment?

What federalism did in the socialist context was to create proto-nations and proto-states. This occurred, because the political-administrative structure of these federalized states was based on units defined in ethnoterritorial terms.[18] This had a number of important consequences, including, first of all, the development of strong national identities within the ethnoterritorial republican units (especially in the titular nationality and where there was a history of national identity and stateness); second, the development of republic-level political, economic and cultural elites who were of the titular nationality and whose careers were closely tied to the republic; and third, the framing of conflict over power and money as matters of conflict between the center and periphery and, because of the overlap among territory, ethnicity, and administration, between the dominant ethnic group of the state (or the Russians, Serbs, and Czechs) versus the titular nationalities of the remaining republics. All of these factors worked together to create strains over time in federalized communist systems in the political and economic relationship between the center and the republics and between dominant and subordinate ethnic groups, as well as republics. One measure of this is what happened during periods of reform and crisis in federal communist systems. Each time we see greater expression of national identity, more pressures for republican autonomy, and growing tensions between the center and the republics within the federation. We also see the center responding to the crisis in ways that advertise the centrality of nationality in the socialist experience—for instance, the very creation of a federal state in Czechoslovakia following the Soviet invasion of 1968, the execution of Lavrenti Beria in the Soviet Union in response to his evocation of the national question during the struggle for Stalin's mantle, and the harsh crackdown in Croatia in the 1970s in response to growing nationalist fervor (which had to be followed—for balancing purposes—by a similar, albeit far less draconian crackdown in Serbia). Whether the purpose of federalism was to encourage national identity, to discourage it, to replace it with a socialist identity or to forge a new and synthetic identity, then, the fact remains that federalism in practice created nations and states-in-the-making in Yugoslavia, Czechoslovakia, and the Soviet Union.

However, there were certain specific developments prefacing the end of these three states that moved the question from one of jousting within a federal order to a series of constitutional wars between the center and the republics and, ultimately, to the question of actual secession.[19] These included the slowdown of elite mobility within the federation and, with that, an expansion of the capacity and incentives of republican leaders to build local economic and political fiefdoms; a decline in the economic performance of the regime and thus a reduction in the economic and political linkages between the center and the republics; and the introduction of major reforms that further undermined political and economic connections between the center and the republics and that pressured republican leaders—now made vulnerable and thrown to their own devices—to construct local political parties, local economies, and local bases of political support.

Thus, developments over the last ten to 15 years of state socialism worked throughout the region to weaken the party and the state. Federalism gave a particular cast to this process by redistributing power and resources from the center to the republics, by opening up the possibility that mobilization against the regime could be based on territory and ethnicity, by creating strong incentives for republic-level leaders to defend themselves through construction of nation-states on their territories, and by encouraging counter-elites to do the same in their struggles against regime elites at the center and in the republics. Thus, federalism tied ever more closely the future of the state itself to the future of Communist Party hegemony. Without federalism, there was no organized counterweight to the state, and the state, as a result, survived, albeit weakened. With federalism, such a counterweight existed in the republics. Federal states, as a result, were subdivided along republican lines.

PEACEFUL VERSUS VIOLENT STATE TERMINATION

This leaves us with the final question; that is, the variance among these three countries in the process of state collapse. Put more straightforwardly: why did Serbia defend the state, whereas the Russian and Czech republics did not?

At the very least, placing these three cases side by side allows us to reject certain common explanations of the violent dismemberment of Yugoslavia. For example, the presence of a large diaspora community—as, for example, with the Serbs outside of Serbia—has been used to explain the actions of Serbia, as well as Serbian minorities living in Croatia and Bosnia, in using violence in order to defend the Yugoslav state. However, there is also a very large Russian community outside the boundaries of Russia (some 25 million), yet this did not cause the Russian republic to use force to defend the Soviet state. This is despite the fact that the Russian government could no more assume fair and equitable treatment of Russian minorities outside of Russia than the Serbian government could for the treatment of the Serbian minorities in Croatia and Bosnia. Indeed, there are significant parallels between Estonian legal discrimination against Russians and Croatian legal discrimination against the Serbian minority. Moreover, this comparison allows us to question those arguments that explain the Yugoslav war in terms of such factors as Serbia's economically disadvantaged position within federal Yugoslavia (which created political resentment and political pressures to maintain and recentralize the larger Yugoslav market), and the special access of the Serbs to the federal military as a consequence of their dominance within the officer corps. Again, the Russian case presents a similar profile, yet the process of Soviet dismemberment was quite peaceful.

How, then, do we explain the violence in Yugoslavia? The obvious answer is to search for factors that are relevant to the question at hand and that do a good job as well of distinguishing Yugoslavia from the Soviet Union and Czechoslovakia. There are three. The first is the specific character of federalism during the last decade or so of Communist Party rule. Only for Yugoslavia it is accurate to characterize the state (and the party) at this time as a *con*federal, not a federal structure. By confederation I refer to the development in Yugoslavia of an ever-weakening economic and political center, on the one hand, and, on the other, republics that over time had accumulated the economic and political resources to act as nearly independent political and economic units. Confederation in Yugoslavia was the culmination of developments from the 1970s onward—for example, the implementation of the 1974 constitution, the creation during the same period of territorial defense forces that had the potential to become republican militaries, the death of Tito in 1980 and the rise in the party and the state of collective decisionmaking based on representation of the republics and the autonomous provinces (and, thus, national representation as well), the decisive defeat of reform politics and economics in Serbia by the 1980s and, finally, the rise of a constitutional war among the republics from the mid-1980s onward in response to the economic crisis, the growing pressures for economic and political centralization from the International Monetary Fund,[20] and the increasingly nationalist and centralist policies of the Serbian Communist Party leadership. What all this meant in practice was that the state *and* the party were already partitioned into republican units by the time Communist Party hegemony formally ended in Yugoslavia. Sovereignty was already parceled out, and the state was already in serious question. This is in contrast to Czechoslovakia and the Soviet Union, where such developments were telescoped into a few years and where the key to their unfolding was the end of Communist Party hegemony.

Thus, what we saw the last ten years of Yugoslavia was a center that was little more than the sum of its highly conflictual republican and provincial parts. It is not accidental, then, that the end of socialist Yugoslavia led so rapidly to the end of Yugoslavia itself, or that the Yugoslav state was the first of the federal communist states to exit from the political scene. All that had held the state together was the party, but the party, like the state, had long been confederalized. The "formal" end of the party as a single unit embracing the entire system meant, quite naturally, the "formal" end of a single Yugoslav state as well.

It is also no accident, given the operation of confederalism, that the process of dismemberment was violent. This was not a struggle of the center versus the republics—as was the case, for example, in the constitutional battles prefacing the end of the Czechoslovak and Soviet states. Rather, with a very weak center long in evidence and with constitutional battles between Serbia and Slovenia in particular long predating the actual collapse of Communist Party rule, the battle in Yugoslavia was defined very early on as a struggle of the republics against one another. Because of different domestic politics within each republic and because of the different economic bases and potential of the republics, moreover, the interests that informed each republic's position in this battle were very different as well. Thus there were heated exchanges on such questions as the advisability of economic and political liberalization and the merits of a centralized versus a decentralized state. These issues, of course, surfaced in Czechoslovakia and in the Soviet Union as well, and in both cases they led to a questioning of the very nature and then the very existence of the state. What was different in Yugoslavia, however, was that the state was in question from the beginning, the battlefield was solely interrepublican and the battle itself was older and more well-defined. With such high stakes, such irreconcilable positions and such a weak center, violence among republics as a method of conflict resolution became all the easier. Finally, confederalism contributed to violence by leading to a rapid disintegration of the Yugoslav state. This was important, because western governments and international institutions were caught by surprise when the Yugoslav state unraveled. This led them to react in ways that only contributed to the violent end of Yugoslavia—by, for example, supporting initially the continuation of the state, by providing military support to irredentist Croatia and Slovenia, by recognizing Croatia prior to constitutional guarantees of full rights for minorities, and by forcing Bosnia to choose between two terrible alternatives: staying in rump Yugoslavia or declaring independence.[21] It is ironic, of course, that part of what drove western policymaking in the Yugoslav crisis from 1990 onward was the fear that the Soviet state would follow the "Yugoslav model," yet the very fact that Yugoslavia disintegrated and disintegrated first meant that western policy toward the end of the Soviet state was far more informed and far more supportive of a peaceful process.

Confederalism in Yugoslavia was joined with a second factor that encouraged violent dismemberment; that is, the character of the Yugoslav People's Army (or JNA). Let us turn, first, to the structure of this military versus the structure of the Czechoslovak and Soviet militaries. One distinguishing aspect was that the confederal character of the Yugoslav party and the state had created a rather confused chain of military command. Authorization to deploy military force at home and abroad could come, variously, from the state and party collective presidencies (together or separately, as individuals or as voting collectivities), from the prime minister, from the minister of defense, and/or from representatives of the military in the highest structures of the party and the state. This is in contrast, for example, to the relatively clear line of control extending from the Communist Party of the Soviet Union to the Soviet military and, in the Czechoslovak case, from the Communist Party of the Soviet Union to the commanders of the Warsaw Pact forces to the Czechoslovak military. At the same time, only in Yugoslavia do we find the existence of territorially based militias that were under the control of the republics and that had unclear linkages—in terms of funding as well as command and control—to the central military or the central political structure. If we combine the existence in Yugoslavia of both a blurred chain of command and semi-independent militias tied to the republics, we can see considerable potential for the military in Yugoslavia to function as a major participant in times of political turmoil—as it did, for example, in the Croatian crisis of the 1970s and, then later, during the wars of secession, beginning in 1990.

What also enhanced the potential for praetorian politics in Yugoslavia was the domestic political role of the military in socialist Yugoslavia—which was very different than in the Soviet Union and Czechoslovakia. The contrast can be easily put. The military in Yugoslavia played a central role in domestic politics. This reflected a variety of factors—for instance, the historical role of the military in defending the society against fascism and in building support for socialism during World War II; the extent to which the legitimacy of the regime and of socialism varied with the legitimacy of the military (and vice versa); the political influence accorded the military as a consequence of its unique role as a representative of the center and of Yugoslavia as a whole and as a result of its centrality to a system burdened by the national question at home and threats emanating from both East and West abroad; direct representation of the military at the highest levels of the party and the state (particularly in the last decades of the regime and the state); and the use of the military, beginning in the 1970s, as a defense against internal, as well as external enemies of the state. By contrast, the Czechoslovak military was kept quite separate from civilian life in general and domestic politics in particular. In the Soviet case, the same conclusion could be drawn, though the Soviet military by 1989 had been to be sure politicized by the Gorbachev reforms. However, this had the effect of dividing the Soviet military, rather than rendering it a powerful instrument for the preservation of the state.[22]

This leads us to our third and final contrast: the struggle for political power during the process of reform and its impact on Russian, Czech, and Serbian behavior with respect to defense of the state. In the Soviet case, the struggle was between Gorbachev, who represented an increasingly bankrupt reform process, who had no electoral or territorial base of support, and who defended the center, versus Yeltsin, who came to represent "genuine" reform and whose political base in the Russian republic was evidenced by his election to the Russian republican presidency. Thus Yeltsin's struggle with Gorbachev became not just a struggle over approaches to reform, but also a struggle between different bases of political power—one all-union, but weak, and the other, the Russian republic and strong. It made sense, therefore, for Yeltsin to take on Gorbachev by supporting Russian defection from the union and thus the dismemberment of the Soviet state. What made this position even more rational (in the political sense of maximizing individual power) was that first, the Russian state was a viable political and economic unit (especially since it could take over the central organs of the Soviet state), and second, a campaign against the union would expand the size of Yeltsin's winning coalition by including crucial allies from those republics seeking autonomy from the center. The politics of reform in the Soviet Union, therefore, had left only very weak defenders of the Soviet state—portions of the military and Mikhail Gorbachev—and very strong proponents of state dismemberment—Yeltsin with his ties to the dominant Russian republic and his allies in the other irredentist republics.

The Czechoslovak case was different.[23] The confederation of Czecho-Slovakia after the fall of communism, the very different economic bases and ideological profiles of the political parties in the Czech versus the Slovak republics, the blockage of a referendum on ending the state, and the results of the elections that took place in the Czech lands and in Slovakia in 1992 had worked together to suggest the possibility of ending the Czechoslovak state, to exclude the center and the public from the process of deciding the future of the state and to leave the fate of Czechoslovakia in the hands of two elected politicians: Vladimir Meciar, who represented Slovakia, and Vaclav Klaus, who represented the Czech lands. Meciar had campaigned on a platform of representing the interests of the Slovak nation. This was both a symbolic issue and a practical one—the latter having to do with the desire to build more Slovak independence into the federation and to slow down an economic reform process that would be particularly costly in Slovakia. Klaus, by contrast, had campaigned for rapid transformation, especially on the economic front. This implied a single economic reform embracing all of Czecho-Slovakia, and it implied a strong state capable of directing the reform process. As a result, Meciar and Klaus were in serious disagreement about the structure of the state and about economic reform. However, they were in another way in substantial agreement. Both had goals that could only be realized through the division of Czecho-Slovakia into two states. Thus the economic and political interests of the two leaders, while opposed, were nonetheless symmetrical. This allowed for a peaceful partition of Czecho-Slovakia. It also allowed Czech leaders, like Russian leaders, to claim the central institutions of the former "empire" as the property of their new states. Moreover, the Czechs could argue, as the Russians had, that they had a viable state without the "empire." This was particularly the case, since the loss of Slovakia was a clear economic gain. It freed the Czech government to pursue what it saw as a winning strategy for economic reform, and it removed the economic "drag" of Slovakia.

The struggle for political power in Yugoslavia, by contrast, took a third form. Here, there was no center, and the battle was focussed on the actions of three players: Slobodan Milošević of Serbia, Franjo Tudjman of Croatia, and Milan Kučan of Slovenia. Milošević—the leader of the dominant republic, Serbia—opposed economic and political reform and supported recentralization of the Yugoslav state. This position both followed from developments long in the making in Serbian politics and was a function as well of the economic and political interests of Serbia and the interests of Milošević as a former communist building support within Serbia and among Serbs. By contrast, Tudjman and Kučan (for somewhat different reasons having to do with the contrasting interaction in Croatia versus Slovenia among nationalism, democratization, and the end of Communist Party hegemony) took an opposing stance; that is, support of rapid economic and political reform and further decentralization of the Yugoslav state.

Thus we find in Yugoslavia a very different game prefacing the end of the state. On the one hand, unlike Czechoslovakia, there was no symmetrical solution (though the bargaining in both cases was interrepublican and involved diametrically opposed positions). Moreover, it was in the interests of the Czechs—or at least Klaus—to oversee the end of the state, whereas this was not in the interests of the Serbs—or at least Milošević. On the other hand, unlike the Soviet Union, there were no economic and political incentives for the dominant republic and its leader to opt out of the federation.

The key differences in the state breakup in the Soviet Union, Yugoslavia, and Czechoslovakia, then, can be reduced to three aspects of partition politics: one, whether the conflict was one between republics (Yugoslavia and Czechoslovakia) or between the center and the republics (the Soviet Union); two, whether the republics were opposed to each other (Czechoslovakia and Yugoslavia) or on the same side (the Soviet Union); and, three, whether dismemberment as an outcome satisfied the republics (Czechoslovakia and the Soviet Union) or generated conflicts between them (Yugoslavia). It is the structure of the game of partition, then, plus confederalism and the military (its structure and domestic role) that explain why the decomposition of the Yugoslav state generated enormous conflict whereas the partition of the Soviet and Czechoslovak states did not.

CONCLUSIONS

The purpose of this commentary has been to add a comparative perspective to the analysis of Yugoslav evolution over the past 50 years. What we have discovered is that the Yugoslav case, when placed in a comparative context, helps us understand a number of important issues—from the role of the state and the party in socialism to the termination of states after socialism. This exercise should not be construed, however, as an argument for comparison and against area scholarship. As noted in the introduction, recent scholarship about the post-communist world could stand a great deal more grounding in area studies. Moreover the distinction between comparative study and area scholarship is a false one, since area scholarship is usually driven by theoretical concerns, since many of the most durable comparative theories are based on study of a single case, and since good comparisons are based necessarily on detailed knowledge of cases. Rather, the point here is that comparison can help us do three things. It can tell us what is unique and what is not unique about Yugoslavia, it can help us distinguish between central and extraneous factors when constructing explanations about Yugoslav developments, and it can force us to address questions of broad significance.

Notes

1. See, for example, Ivo Banac, "Interview with Ivo Banac," in Rabia Ali and Lawrence Lifschultz, eds., *Writings on the Balkan War: Why Bosnia?* (New York: The Pamphleteers Press, 1993), 134-64; Maria Todorova, "The Balkans: From Discovery to Invention." *Slavic Review,* 53 (summer 1994): 453-82.

2. They argue in particular that the fall of state socialism has allowed eastern European studies to be integrated at long last into the mainstream of social science and therein to partake of its theoretical and conceptual bounty. See, especially, Philippe C. Schmitter and Terry Lynn Karl, "The Conceptual Travels of Transitologists and Consolidologists: How Far East Should They Attempt to Go?" *Slavic Review,* 53 (spring 1994): 173-85.

For a response (which is, in effect, "not very far"), see Valerie Bunce, "Should Transitologists Be Grounded?" *Slavic Review,* 54, no. 1 (spring 1995): 111-28.

3. It is interesting to note in this connection that in game theoretic models of politics, it is this factor—losing what one has (as opposed to, say, trying to expand what one has)—that emerges as one of the most powerful influences on the calculation of individual interests and on the actions taken to maximize those interests.

4. See, for example, Valerie Bunce, "The Empire Strikes Back: The Transformation of the Eastern Bloc From a Soviet Asset to a Soviet Liability," *International Organization,* 39 (winter 1984/1985): 1-46.

5. This reflected as well a certain tension in the structure of state socialism. On the one hand, the fused character of the party-state, its overlapping jurisdictions and its mosaic of individual-to-individual connections made it easy for individuals at the top of the system to be very powerful. This was a structure, in short, which was very good at preventing the formation of durable coalitions. On the other hand, this structure generated considerable inefficiencies and pressures as well for leaders to repeatedly introduce institutional reforms in order to regularize their control and to efficiency. In this sense, the party-state was powerful in relation to society, but weak—and highly fragmented—in relationship to itself.

6. See, for example, Robert Fishman, "Rethinking State and Regime: Southern Europe's Transition to Democracy," *World Politics* 42 (April 1990): 422-40; Valerie Bunce, "Comparing East and South," *Journal of Democracy,* 6, no. 3 (July 1995): 87-100.

7. Analysts on the right end of the political continuum, of course, routinely predicted the end of socialism. However, this was more often an exercise in wish fulfillment than a matter of making a carefully constructed argument based on data. Moreover, the very same analysts quite often advocated policies that were premised on the inherent durability, as well as the inherent evil of communist systems.

8. Susan Woodward, *Balkan Tragedy: Chaos and Dissolution After the Cold War* (Washington, D.C: The Brookings Institution, 1995).

9. My thanks to Paul Shoup for outlining these competing interpretations.

10. Ted Robert Gurr, "Persistence and Change in Political Systems, 1800-971," *American Political Science Review,* 68 (December 1974): 1482-504.

11. One might also have drawn the conclusion in the 1930s (as some did) that democracy was not a viable system. This, plus the fact that ex-communists have maintained important political, as well as economic, positions throughout eastern Europe, should lead us to be more cautious in the conclusions we draw about the end of state socialism. We may not in fact be so sure that we know the end of the story.

12. This is not to argue, of course, that the dismantling of the Soviet Union did not produce violence in its wake. However, violence in the Soviet case has been a matter of struggles *within* the republics-now-states.

13. The single best empirically based analysis of state socialism is by Maria Csanadi. See Maria Csanadi *From Where to Where: The Party-State and the Transformation* (Budapest: T-Twins and Institute of Economics, Hungarian Academy of Sciences, 1995).

14. See, for example, Mark Beissinger, "Demise of an Empire-State: Identity, Legitimacy and the Deconstruction of Soviet Politics," in Crawford Young, ed., *The Rising Tide of Cultural Pluralism: The Nation-State at Bay?* (Madison, WI: University of Wisconsin Press, 1993): 93-115.

15. See, especially, Katherine Verdery, "Nationalism and National Sentiment in Post-Socialist Romania," *Slavic Review,* 52 (summer 1993): 179-204.

16. Robert Jackson and Carl Rosenberg, "Why Africa's Weak States Persist: The Empirical and Juridical in Statehood," *World Politics,* 35 (October 1982): 1-24.

17. These boundaries, of course, may very well be redrawn in the future as state-building progresses—witness, for example, the battle between the Russian state and Chechnia or the less violent battle now going on between the Croatian state and Istria. However, what is important for our discussion here is that the initial decision to disband the state used the republican boundaries to differentiate among the new state boundaries.

18. See, for example, Rogers Brubaker, "Nationhood and the National Question in the Soviet Union and Post-Soviet Eurasia: An Institutionalist Account," *Theory and Society,* 23 (February 1993):47-78; Philip Goldman, Gail Lapidus, and Victor Zaslavsky, "Introduction: Soviet Federalism—Its Origins, Evolution, and Demise." In Philip Goldman, Gail Lapidus, and Victor Zaslavsky, eds., *From Union to Commonwealth: Nationalism and Separatism in the Soviet Republics* (Cambridge: Cambridge University Press, 1992): 1-21; Philip Roeder, "Soviet Federalism and Ethnic Mobilization," *World Politics,* 43 (January 1991): 196-232; Yuri Slezkine,

"The USSR as a Communal Apartment, or How a Socialist State Promoted Ethnic Particularism," *Slavic Review*, 53 (summer 1994): 414-52; Steven L. Burg, *Conflict and Cohesion in Socialist Yugoslavia: Political Decision Making Since 1966* (Princeton, NJ: Princeton University Press, 1983); Sharon Wolchik, *Czechoslovakia in Transition: Politics, Economics and Society* (New York: St. Martin's, 1991).

19. For a theoretical analysis of secession, see Michael Hector, "The Dynamics of Secession," *Acta Sociologica*, 35 (1992): 267-83.

20. See Woodward, *Balkan Tragedy*.

21. Steven Burg, "The International Community and the Yugoslav Crisis," in Milton Esman and Shibley Telhami, eds., *International Organizations and Ethnic Conflict* (Ithaca, NY: Cornell University Press, 1995), 235-71; Michael Kelly, "Surrender and Blame," *The New Yorker* (19 Dec. 1994): 44-51.

22. See, in particular, Stephen Meyer, "How the Threat (and the Coup) Collapsed: The Politicization of the Soviet Military," *International Security*, 16 (winter 1991/1992): 5-38; Thomas M. Nichols, *The Sacred Cause: Civil-Military Conflict Over Soviet National Security, 1917-1992*. (Ithaca, NY: Cornell University Press, 1993).

23. See, for example, Sharon Wolchik, "The Politics of Ethnicity in Post-Communist Czechoslovakia," *East European Politics and Societies* 8 (winter 1994): 153-88.

Contributors

Jill Benderly is co-director of the STAR Project (Strategies, Training, and Advocacy for Reconciliation), a project providing organizational and financial support to women's NGO's in the Yugoslav successor states.

Melissa Bokovoy is an Assistant Professor of History at the University of New Mexico.

Valerie Bunce is Professor of Government at Cornell University.

Lenard Cohen is Professor of Political Science at Simon Fraser University.

Josef Figa is a sociologist and is teaching at Hamilton College.

Francine Friedman is Assistant Professor of Political Science and Director of the Office of European Studies at Ball State University.

James Gow is an analyst at the Centre for Defense Studies at Kings College, London.

Wolfgang Höpken is a historian at the Historisches Seminar at Universait Leipzig, Leipzig, Germany.

Jill Irvine is Assistant Professor of Political Science at the University of Oklahoma.

Carol Lilly is Assistant Professor of History at the University of Nebraska at Kearney.

Nick Miller is Assistant Professor of History at Boise State University.

Paul Mojzes is Professor of Religion at Rosemont College.

Robin Remington is Professor of Political Science at the University of Missouri—Columbia.

Stefan Troebst is a historian. He is presently the Director of the European Centre for Minority Issues in Flensburg, Germany.

Index

Academy of Arts and Sciences, Serbian (SANU), 176, 239, 240, 304, 306-309, 322-37; Slovene, 149
Adventists, 170
Aegean Macedonia, 246, 247
Agrarian council, 116, 121, 122
Albania and Albanians, 67, 257, 296-97, 300-305, 319, 326, 353
Alliance of Reform Forces, 69
Andonov, Metodi, 236-37, 248. *See also* ento
Andrić, Ivo, 64
Anthias, Floya, 197
Anti-Fascist Assembly of the National Liberation of Macedonia (ASNOM), 246, 248, 249, 252
Antifascist Council, 236
Antifascist Women's Front (AWF), 185, 203
Antiwar Campaign, 200
Apostolski, Mihailo, 249
Army, 27, 33, 35-36, 40-41, 50, 52, 84, 108, 127, 173, 175-77, 254. *See also* Military; Yugoslav People's Army
Australia, 254
Austria, 91
Austro-Hungarian Empire, 270, 274

Bajalica, Dimitrije, 126
Bajt, Alexander, 176
Bakarić, Vladimir, 45
Baptists, 214
The Basic Law on the Legal Position of Religious Communities, 218
Baucal, Dimitrije, 68
Belgrade, location of federal capital in, 50-51
"Belgrade Feminists 1992: Separation, Guilt and Identity Crisis," 203
Beloff, Nora, 49
Benderly, Jill, 112, 367
Benn, Gottfried, 93, 97
Beria, Lavrenti, 354
Bogomilism, 269-70
Bojnah, Ladislav, 121

Bokovoy, Melissa K., 10, 109, 367
Borba, 118-20
Bosnia and Bosnians, 40, 49-50, 200, 229, 291-93, 358; Bosnian Muslims, 267-85; Serbs living in, 355, 356. *See also* Bosnia-Hercegovina
Bosnia-Hercegovina, 42, 71, 126, 130, 294; creation of, 274; Muslim national sentiments in, 14; Muslims living in, 237-238, 267-85, 296; Serbs living in, 15, 296. *See also* Bosnia and Bosnians
Bosnian Church, 270
Bosnianism, 272
Brašnar(ov), Panko, 249, 257
"Bratstvo i jedinstvo." *See* "Brotherhood and Unity"
Brezhnev Doctrine, 64
Britain, Tito's standing with, 36
"Brotherhood and Unity," 32, 63, 82, 88-89, 246
Broz, Josip. *See* Tito
Bulat, General Rade, 65
Bulatović, Miodrag, 176
Bulgaria and Bulgarians, 91, 244-46, 254, 255-57, 258, 353
Bunce, Valerie, 13, 27-28, 367
Burg, Steven, L., 4

"The Call to Reason" (letter), 174
Carević, Miloš, 121
Castro, Fidel, 280
Catholicism, 113, 140, 176, 196, 213-14, 217-19, 225-28, 270, 307
Čento, 248-50, 255, 256, 257. *See also* Andonov, Metodi
Četković, Nadežda, 190, 201
Četniks, 92, 96, 321
Chernobyl, 169
Christian Democrats, Slovene, 196
Christian-Marxism, 220-22
Christianity, 268, 271, 281
Churchill, Winston, 46

Civil society, definition of, 163, 191-92, 211; role of religious communities in, 211-29; Slovene, 163-78
"Club of 41," 63
Cohen, Lenard, 236, 239-41, 367
Cold War, 44, 53, 353; Yugoslav's position during, 38
Collectivization, agricultural, 116-32; SRZ, 128, 129, 130
Comic strips, 154-55
Communist Party of Croatia (CPC), 118, 122
Communist Party of Macedonia (CPM), 237, 244, 246, 248, 250-53, 258
Communist Party of Macedonia Members (table), 251
Communist Party of Serbia (CPS), 18, 123
Communist Party of the Soviet Union, 215, 358
Communist Party of Yugoslavia (CPY), 4, 7, 9, 62, 107-110, 139-58, 215, 218-19, 224, 316, 322; civil society and, 116-32, 211-12; cultural policies of, 139-58; feminism and, 185; nation-building strategies of, 236-38; Partisans and, 62; Second Plenum, 123-26; Third Plenum, 131, 149; Vardar Macedonia and, 244-246, 248. *See also* League of Communists
Confederalism, 276-78, 356-58, 362
Conference for the Social Activity for Women (CSAW), 185, 189
Constitution of 1945, 216-18
Constitution of 1974, 11, 15, 40, 41, 73, 88, 197, 239, 276-78, 298, 302, 303, 320
Ćosić, Dobrica, 239, 298-302, 304, 306-309, 319
Crnković, Gordana, 188
Croatia and Croats, 18, 37, 63, 64, 69, 73, 126, 282-83, 354, 358, 359; Catholicism and, 226-27; crisis of 1970-71, 72; civil war in, 71, 199; declaration of independence, 70, 199; education and, 90, 92, 96-97; Muslims and, 219, 268-78; nationalism, 15, 48, 52; Serbs living in, 15, 291-95, 297, 307, 309, 355-56
Croatia, Independent State of (NDH), 51, 293, 307, 322
Croatian Democratic Union (CDU), 15, 18, 190, 196, 197
Croatian militia, 70, 200
Croatian Peasant Party, 273
Croatian Spring, 14, 16, 195, 297, 301, 302
Cuba, 280
Čubrilović, Vaso, 116, 122

Čučkov, Mane (Emanuil), 249
Cultural Club, 172
Culture. *See* Popular Culture
Cvijić, Jovan, 332
Czech Republic, 352
Czechoslovakia, 13, 54, 64, 349, 252-55, 357-61; collapse of, 13; Warsaw Pact invasion of, 46

Dahlerup, Drude, 187
Danas, 190
Dapčević-Kučar, Savka, 302
Day of Youth, 49, 173-75
Deak, Istvan, 31
Decentralization, 31, 33, 38-40, 238, 275, 296; of armed forces, 65
Dedijer, Vladimir, 44, 145, 307; *Tito Speaks*, 36
Delo, 190
Deutsch, Karl W., 253
Dimitrijević, Vojo, 145
DiPalma, Giuseppe, 6, 28, 33
Djilas, Aleksa, 330
Djilas, Milovan, 44-45, 47-49, 116, 149, 153, 156, 223, 224, 295
Djuretić, Veselin, 307
Dobnikar, Mojca, 194
Dragosavac, Dušan, 297
Drakulić, Slavenka, 188-89, 190, 195, 202
Drenovac, Bora, 156
Duga, 190
Dušan, Stefan, 269

East Germany, 164, 225, 348, 349
Eastern Orthodoxy, 113, 213
Ecclesiastic absolutism, 213-15, 222-24, 228
Economic council, 116, 119, 122
Education, 27, 31, 79-97, 254
Eisenhower, Dwight D., 46
Elias, Norbert, 93
Engels, Friedrich, 115
Environmentalism, 175
Estonia, 356
Ethiopia, 172
Ethnic cleansing, 228, 268, 284-85
Ethnic mobilization, 15-16, 18-19
Ethnonationalism, 73, 212; Croatian, 65; Slovene, 67
Ethnoreligious identity, 226-29
European Community, 71, 72

Fascism, 165-67, 173-74, 255, 359
Federalism, 9, 10-14, 37, 39, 40-41, 171, 296,

INDEX

353-55, 356
Feminism and feminists, 112-13, 183-205; definition of, 184
Figa, Jozef, 10-12, 111, 367
Fine, John V. A., 270
Fotev, Bogoja, 249
Friedman, Francine, 14, 236, 237-38, 367
"Friends of Yugoslavia," 49

Gantar, Pavle, 174
Gazimestan, 80
Geertz, Clifford, 79
German Democratic Republic. *See* East Germany
Germany, 64, 245, 293. *See also* East Germany
Gierek, Edward, 8
Gligorov, Kiro, 249
Golubović, Zagorka, 308
Gorbachev, Mikhail, 349, 359-60; reforms, 348, 350, 359
Gow, James, 8, 27, 29-30, 63, 73, 367
Great Transformation, 216, 223-24
Greece, 91, 246, 250, 255
Greek Cominformists, 257
Gross, Mirjana, 83

Habermas, Jürgen, 79
Havel, Vaclav, 164; "The Power of the Powerless," 10, 192
Hebrang, Andrija, 116, 119, 237
Hegel, Georg Wilhelm Friedrich, 61
Hercegovina, 269, 272, 279-85. *See also* Bosnia-Hercegovina
Historical memory, 31-32, 79
History, national, 254
Hodža, Mustafa, 120
Hollywood entertainment, 141, 145, 157
Homosexuals and lesbians, 186, 189, 192; congress of, 174, 194
Höpken, Wolfgang, 8, 27, 31-32, 367
Hren, Marko, 189
Hroch, Miroslav, 236, 244, 245, 247
Hungary, 11, 54, 269, 353
Huntington, Samuel P., 229

Identity, group or collective, 11, 12, 79-97, 241
Ilinden Uprising of 1903, 95, 244-46, 258
IMRO, 237, 256-57
International Monetary Fund, 42, 350, 356-57
Irvine, Jill, 367
Isaković, Antonije, 306, 334; *Tren 2*, 306
Islam, 113, 213, 219, 228, 268, 280-83

Italy, 245
Iveković, Rada, 188, 189, 202
Izetbegović, Alija, 238, 282; *The Islamic Declaration*, 282

Jalušić, Vlasta, 190
Janša, Janez, 67, 70, 177
Jasenovac controversy, 93
Jehovah Witnesses, 170
Jelavich, Charles, 80-81
Jež, 145
Judaism and Jews, 213, 214, 227, 228

Kadijević, Veljko, 71
Kangrga, Milan, 308
Karadjordje, 334
Karadžić, Radovan, 54-55
Kardelj, Edvard, 14, 45, 47, 116, 123-25, 127, 149, 239, 295, 306
Kareta, 194
Kesić, Vesna, 190, 202
Kidrič, Boris, 116, 122, 131
King, Robert R., *Yugoslav Communism and the Macedonian Question*, 247-48
Kiš, Janoš, 192
Kjellén, Rudolf, 243
Klaus, Vaclav, 360, 361
Kloss, Heinz, 253
Kocbek, Edvard, 152
Koliševski, Lazar, 236, 248, 249-51, 252, 255
Konrad, George, 192
Kornyjčuk, Okelsandr, 253
Kosmet. *See* Kosovo
Kosovar Albanians, 66, 73
Kosovo, 16, 80, 129, 218, 239, 240, 319-21, 324-29; as Autonomous Region, 292, 294, 296, 298, 300-301, 304-307, 320; Battle of, 309; and the military, 66, 69, 71, 73; Muslims and, 282-83
Kostić, Branko, 71
Krajina, 65
Krestić, Vasilije, 307
Krleča, Miroslav, 156
Krško nuclear power station, 169, 195
Krushchev, Nikita, 45, 64
Kučan, Milan, 361
Kuzmanović, Jasmina, 190

Language and languages, 6, 10, 89, 93, 301; Bulgarian, 251, 252; Croatian, 301; Macedonian, 236, 237, 249, 251-55, 258; Serbian, 176, 251, 252, 254, 302; Slovene, 173, 176-77; Turkish, 251

Lazić, Branka, 189
League of Communists of Bosnia and Hercegovina, 276
League of Communists of Serbia (LCS), 239, 240, 298, 301, 305, 309, 318, 321, 327, 328, 331, 336, 337
League of Communists of Slovenia, 112, 171
League of Communists of Yugoslavia (LCY), 8, 9, 40-41, 89, 111, 187, 191, 204, 236, 277, 279, 281, 284, 316; control of, 27-33; dissolution of, 5, 13; Tenth Congress, 66; Eleventh Congress, 48, 66; Twelfth Congress, 189; Fourteenth Extraordinary Party Congress, 67-68. See also Communist Party of Yugoslavia
League of Communists-Movement for Yugoslavia (LC-MY), 69
League of Socialist Youth of Slovenia (LSYS), 111, 164-67, 169-75, 178
Legitimation, sources of, 28; strategies for, 6-8, 27-33
Lilit, 194-95
Lilly, Carol S., 10, 142-44, 367
Lisinski, Alemka, 190
Litrižin, Vera, 202
Ljubljana, 71, 73, 166
Lokar, Sonja, 195
Lutheran Church, 164, 214
Lytle, Paula, 30

Macedonia, 14, 71, 90, 218, 236, 237, 243-59, 292, 293
Macedonian language, 236, 237, 249, 251-55, 258
Macedonian National Theater, 253
Maček, Vladko, 273
MacKinnon, Catharine, 201
Maclean, Sir Fitzroy, 46
Makavejev, Dušan, 44
Makedonski, Kiril, *Goce*, 253
Mamula, Branko, 67, 172
MANAPO, 256
Marjanović, Jovan, 301
Marković, Ante, 69, 70, 73
Marković, Mihailo, 300, 308, 336
Marković, Moma, 127
Markovski, Venko, 249
Martinović, Djordje, 305
Marxism, 28-30, 33, 61, 84, 212, 215, 228, 281, 300-301, 308, 317
Marxism-Leninism, 6, 144, 148, 149, 151, 215-18, 294
Mastnak, Tomaž, 191-92
Matić, Dušan, 152

Meciar, Vladimir, 360
"Memorandum of the Serbian Academy," 306-309, 322-39, 334-35
Memory, collective, 79
Mesić, Stipe, 70-72
Methodists, 214
Mežnarić, Silva, 190; "Theory and Reality: The Status of Employed Women in Yugoslavia," 187-88
Mihajlov, Ivan, 255, 257
Mihaljac, Donji, 128
Miličević, Milivoje, 129
Military, 8-9, 30-31, 35; role of in supporting state cohesion, 61-74. See also Army; Yugoslav People's Army
Miller, Nicholas, 16, 236, 238, 239, 367
Milojević, Sanja, 193
Milošević, Slobodan, 15-16, 18, 69, 70, 80, 176, 197, 239, 240, 315-38, 361; his "anti-bureaucratic revolution," 308-309; dissatisfaction with, 200; rise of, 52, 67, 96, 302
Misirkov, Krste P., 244
Mladina, 172-75, 190
Mladjenović, Lepa, 190, 202
Mobilization, 115-16, 236
Moćnik, Rastko, 174
Mojzes, Paul, 113; *Yugoslavian Inferno: Ethnoreligious Warfare in the Balkans*, 224, 367
Montenegro and Montenegrins, 42, 63-64, 72, 238, 294; "new Yugoslavia" created by, 50; Tito's image in, 49
Mosse, George L., 202
Muhi, Fuad, 283
Muslim and Muslims, 14, 40, 96, 129, 214, 217, 219, 237-38, 296-97, 301; Bosnian, 14, 267-85

Nagy, Imre, 45
Narodna Armija, 50
Naše Teme, 187, 189
Nasser, Abd'el, 276
Nation, definition of, 267-68
National Assembly of Macedonia, 250
National Liberation Front, 251
National Liberation Struggle (NOB), 82, 118, 124
Nazareans, 170
Nazis, 92, 167, 173
NDH. See Croatia, Independent State of
Nedeljković, Dušan, 152
Nedić, Milan, 293
Nehru, Jawaharlal, 276

Neue Slovenische Kunst, 167
New Collectivism (artist group), 173-74
New Social Movements (NSM), 111-12, 184, 186, 189, 191-93, 204; Slovene, 111, 164-65, 167-69, 173, 175, 183, 192. *See also indivudual NSMs*
Nikezić, Marko, 302
Nin, 173, 190
Non-Aligned Movement, 38, 46, 171, 237, 275, 276, 279, 347
Nova Makedonija, 254
Nova Revija, 176

Obradović, Vuk, 68
Obrenović, Miloš, 334
Omladina, 154
"Open Letter," 201
Orthodox church, 217, 228; Macedonian, 219, 227, 249, 251; Serbian, 40, 219, 226, 227
Otkup. *See* Collectivization, agricultural
Ottomans, 269, 270-71, 274, 333

Palmer, Stephen E., Jr., *Yugoslav Communism and the Macedonian Question*, 247-48
Papić, Žarana, 190, 199
Partisans and Partisan Movement, 7, 37, 44, 63, 115, 185, 236, 245-48, 252, 253, 274, 293, 294
"Partisans to Patriots: State-Society Relations in Yugoslavia, 1945-1992" (conference), vii
Party of Democratic Change, 18
Pavelić, Ante, 51
Pavlović, Dragiša, 240, 326-28
Peace movement, 112; Slovene, 170-73
Peasants and peasantry, 109, 115-32
People's Youth (PY), 150, 152, 154-55
Petrović, Djordje, 334
Petrušev, Kiril, 249
Pijade, Moša, 116, 123
Pirin Macedonia, 248
Piruze, Petre, 249
Pluralism, 4, 11, 50-51, 67-68, 112, 144, 175, 183, 190, 192, 196, 225, 331
Pluralistic liberty, 214-15, 223-24
Poland, 5, 8, 10, 11, 163, 164, 225, 347, 353
Politika, 190
Popović, Mica, 144, 305
Popular Culture, 139-58; Slovene, 163-78
Pornography, 158
Poster affair, 173
Postmodernism, 168
Pragmatism, Tito's, 44, 47, 54-55
Praxis Group, 306, 308

Privredna Banka of Zagreb, 41
Problemi, 173
Propaganda, 140-41
Protestantism, 140, 213, 225, 227, 228
Punk movement, 111; Bastards, 165; Laibach, 167; Slovene, 157, 163, 164-68, 170, 178

Račan, Ivica, 18
Ramet, Pedro, 4
Ranković, Aleksandar, 40, 47-48, 52, 276, 283, 295, 296-97
Reform movements, 52; Croatian, 39; Slovene, 39
Religious communities, 113, 211-29, 268
Religious toleration, 213-15, 222, 224, 228
Remington, Robin, 8-9, 27, 30, 367
Revija 2000, 176
Rexhepi, Hašhim, 174
Risteski, Stojan, 252
Roman Catholicism. *See* Catholicism
Romania, 67, 89, 348, 353
Russia, 352, 356, 360-61. *See also* Soviet Union

Sabalić, Ines, 190
Salecl, Renata, 198
Samardžić, Radovan, 220
Sandžak, 49
SANU. *See* Academy of Arts and Sciences, Serbian
Sarajevo, 51
Šatev, Pavel, 257
Scott, James, 116
Secularistic absolutism, 214-15, 222, 223-24
Self-management and self-managed socialism, 7-10, 32, 38-39, 82-84, 89, 165-66, 168, 171, 176, 177, 347; as a factor in legitimation, 38-39; feminism and, 112, 183, 186, 187, 188; purpose of, 44-45, 82, 275, 294; religion and, 217
Separation of church and state, 215-16, 218
Serbia and Serbs, 18, 42, 63-64, 95, 96, 249, 254, 268-70, 291-310, 315-38, 352, 356-57, 361; autonomous provinces of, 40; Bosnian Muslims and, 273-79, 282-83; in the League of Communists, 40; and the military, 69, 70, 72; nationalism in, 15-16, 67, 238, 240, 315-38, 337; "new Yugoslavia" created by, 50. peasants in, 126-27, 128, 129; Orthodox Church, 219, 226; Slovenia and, 175. *See also* Bosnia, Bosnia-Hercegovina, and Croatia, Serbs living in
Simić, Petar, 68
Sklevicky, Lydia, 185

Skopje, 248, 249
Slavonia, 129
Slovene Youth Movement, 49
Slovenia and Slovenes, 42, 63-64, 67, 69, 71-73, 96, 111-12, 163-78, 192-97, 227, 357-58; declaration of independence, 70-71, 73, 177, 199; nationalism in, 67
Smith, Anthony D., 258
Smole, Jože, 171
Sobranie, Narodno, 250
"Social Consciousness, Marxist theory and women's emancipation today," 189
Socialist Alliance, 41, 171, 172, 175
Socialist Party of Serbia (SPS), 69, 336
Socialist Realism, 142-46
Socialist Youth Organization (SYO), 193, 198
Sokolov, Lazar, 249
South Slav textbooks, the distribution of subjects in (table), 85
South Slav Union, 81
Soviet Union, 36-39, 45-47, 125-26, 349, 352-55, 357-60; collapse of, 13-14; 1948 split with Yugoslavia, 8, 38, 44, 45, 52, 63, 142, 148, 153, 217, 257, 258
Spaho, Dr. Mehmed, 273
Split, 222
SRZ. *See* Collectivization
Stalin, 38; death of, 48, 217. *See also* Soviet Union
Stambolić, Ivan, 240, 303, 307, 315, 317-21, 323, 326, 327-29, 335, 338
Stambolić, Petar, 317
Start, 158, 190
State, definition of, 61, 267
Stepinac, Alojzije Cardinal, 217
Stojanović, Svetozar, 336
Stokes, Gale, 329
Šumadija, 292, 299
Šuvar, Stipe, 14, 90, 189
Svijet, 190

Tadić, Ljubomir, 308
Taylor, Vertra, 186
Teleks, 173, 190
Territorial Defense Units (TDUs), 30, 65-66, 72-73, 74
Textbooks, 81-89
Tismaneanu, Vladimir, 192, 310
Tito, 4, 8, 9, 14, 27, 29-30, 33, 35-56, 65-66, 73, 259, 306, 319; Bosnian Muslims and, 276, 277-78, 281; as Croat, 50; death of, 29, 49, 54, 177, 221, 239, 283, 303, 356; education during the Tito era, 81-97;
foreign policy of, 280; nationalism and, 302; personality of, 43-47; Serbia and, 295, 297; wife Jovanka, 47-48; writers, his frustration with, 147
Tito Relays. *See* Day of Youth
Titoism, 36-47, 303, 304, 306, 322
Tomc, Gegor, 165
Tomšič, Vida, 185-86, 187
Totalitarianism, 224, 225
Trial of the Four, 176-77
Tribuna, 174
Tripalo, Miko, 302
Troebst, Stefan, 14, 236, 237, 367
Tudjman, Franjo, 18, 55, 96, 196, 200, 361
Turkey and Turks, 292, 305. *See also* Ottomans
Tvrtko, King, 269

UDB, UDBa, 256-58, 295
Union of Yugoslav Writers, 176
United Nations, 250
Ustaša, 51, 63, 92, 96, 129, 274, 293

Vardar Macedonia, 243-57
Večernje Novosti, 173
Veselinov, Jovan, 131
Vidmar, Josip, 176
Vlahov, Dimitar, 251
Vlahović, Veljko, 148
Vojvodina, 15, 71, 89, 120, 200, 292, 293, 294, 298, 300-301, 320
Vrcan, Srdjan, *From the Crisis of Religion to the Religion of Crisis,* 222
Vreme, 328, 337
Vukmanović-Tempo, Svetozar, 48, 236, 248

Warsaw Pact, 358
Weber, Max, 28, 80
"What Is the Alternative," 163
Women's movement, 112; South Slav, 185. *See also* Feminism and Feminists
World War I, 272
World War II, 36-37, 226, 293, 297; treatment of in textbooks, 88, 92, 96
Writers' Union of Macedonia, 253, 258

Yeltsin, Boris, 359-60
Youth League, 173
Yugoslav crisis, 94-97
Yugoslav Feminist Network, 194
Yugoslav Muslim Party, 273
Yugoslav People's Army (YPA), 8, 48, 62-74, 112, 171, 173, 175, 200, 358

Yugoslav Writer's Union, 156
Yugoslavism, 275
Yuval-Davis, Nira, 197

Zagreb, 73, 202
Žena, 187, 189
ŽEST, 196
Živojinović, Dragoljub, 307